THE FATE OF THE EARTH

and

THE ABOLITION

THE
FATE OF
THE EARTH

and

THE ABOLITION

Jonathan Schell

STANFORD UNIVERSITY PRESS
Stanford, California

Stanford University Press
Stanford, California

© 2000 by the Board of Trustees
of the Leland Stanford Junior University

ISBN 0-8047-3705-3 (cloth)
ISBN 0-8047-3702-9 (paperback)
Library of Congress Card Number: 99-67025

Printed in the United States of America

This book is printed on acid-free, archival quality paper.

The introduction is followed by the complete texts, notes,
and indexes of the original editions of *The Fate of the Earth*
and *The Abolition* (Knopf, 1982 and 1984).

NUCLEAR WEAPONS AND THE REAL TWENTIETH CENTURY

The Fate of the Earth and *The Abolition*, published here in one volume, first appeared in *The New Yorker* magazine in 1982 and 1984, respectively. They belong simultaneously to two eras. One of these periods, the age of the cold war, is over, and much in the books that has to do with that closed chapter is now chiefly of historical interest. The other, the nuclear age, continues, and much of what pertains to this period remains current. In this essay, however, I seek not so much to bring the nuclear issue up to date as to step back from both the cold war and the post–cold war periods to reflect upon the role of nuclear weapons in the larger historical context of this ending century.

A TALE OF THREE AUGUSTS

An age ended, we know, when the Berlin Wall fell, auguring, soon after, the dissolution of the Soviet Union. But which age was it? The cold war was over—that much was clear. Yet many felt and understood that some longer historical period, or perhaps several, had also come to a close. One clear candidate is the age of totalitarianism—a period coextensive with the life of the Soviet Union, which bracketed the rise and fall of Nazi Germany. (China's current government, which has evolved into a strange hybrid that some are calling "market communism," is the only one of the great totalitarian states of the twentieth century that has not actually been overthrown.) Another candidate is the age of world wars, which, as suggested by the war that remained cold, have been rendered unwinnable and therefore unlikely by the invention of nuclear weapons. And when the histories of the two world wars and the two great totalitarian regimes are considered together, they form a third candidate—an age that many historians are now calling the "short twentieth century." The calendar's divisions of the years, they've observed, match up inexactly with history's turning points. According to this way of reckoning, the nineteenth century began not in 1800 but in 1789, with the French Revolution, and came to its close not in 1900 but in 1914, when the First World War broke out, putting an end to the so-called long nineteenth century. The twentieth century, having begun in August of 1914, lasted only until the failed hard-line Communist coup in Moscow in 1991, which, in another pivotal August of the twentieth century, set in motion the Soviet collapse. Some years before, the Russian poet Akhmatova had expressed a similar idea:

> *Snowdrifts covered the Nevskii Prospéct . . .*
> *And along the legendary quay,*
> *There advanced, not the calendar,*
> *But the real Twentieth Century.*[1]

It is this real twentieth century—the twentieth century of the Somme, of the Gulag, of the Holocaust—that in 1991 startled the

---

1. Martin Malia, *Russia Under Western Eyes* (Cambridge: Harvard/Belknap, 1999), p. 233.

world, the historians are now saying, by turning out to be short. On either side of it were the calmer seas of a predominantly liberal civilization. A bolder assertion of this notion was Francis Fukuyama's renowned claim that the liberal restoration of 1991 marked the "end of history"—by which he meant not that the end of days had arrived but, only a little more modestly, that humanity's long search for the best form of government had reached its destination in a nearly global embrace of liberal democracy.

The distinction between the real twentieth century and the calendrical one is based on the convincing idea that the century's bouts of unprecedented violence, both within nations and between them, possess a definite historical coherence—that they constitute, to put it simply, a single story. The proposed periodization is clearly optimistic, suggesting that the tide of bloodshed has reached its high-water mark and is now receding. The failure of the cold war to become hot and the liquidation in 1991 of the world's last thoroughly totalitarian regime lend substance to the hope. I wish to suggest, however, that this appraisal remains starkly incomplete if it fails to take into account one more age that reached a turning point in 1991. I mean the nuclear age, which opened in another epochal August of the twentieth century, August 1945. (Somehow in this century August was the month in which history chose to produce a disproportionately large number of its most important events.) No narrative of the extraordinary violence of the twentieth century can possibly be told without taking into account the greatest means of violence ever created.

The Greeks used to say that no man should be called happy before he died. They meant not only that even the most contented life could be undone by misfortune at the last minute but also that the meaning of an entire life might depend on its ending. For a life's last chapter was not merely an event, with its freight of suffering or joy; it was a disclosure, in whose light the story's beginning and middle might need to be drastically rewritten. Or, to vary the metaphor, stories, including the stories of historical epochs, are like pictures of heavenly constellations drawn by connecting dots—in this case, historical facts. The addition of new dots may merely add detail to the picture that has already taken shape, but it may also alter the entire image. The swan will turn out to be a crab; what looked like a whale turns into a dragon. Such was the case, certainly, with the end of the Soviet Union and the cold war. The Soviet Union's infirmities, we now must suppose, were eating away at its power long before, one fine day in 1991, the empire evaporated. It is understandable that contemporaries are usually startled by events, but historians have no right to present surprise endings to the tales they tell. Their new job will be to retell the story of the Soviet Union in such a way that the sudden collapse at the end makes sense.

So it must eventually be with the nuclear age. The story of a cold war that was the scene of history's only nuclear arms race will be very different from the story of a cold war that turned out to be only the first of many interlocking nuclear arms races in many parts of the world. The nuclear dilemma, in sum, hangs like a giant question mark over our waning century. To 1914 and 1991 two dates therefore need to be added. The first is 1945 and the second is the as yet unknown future date on which the end of the nuclear age will be disclosed. Whether this conclusion will be the elimination of nuclear weapons (either before or after their further use) or, conceivably, the elimination of the species that built them is the deepest of the questions that need answering when we consider the still-open book of the real twentieth century.

In the United States, the historians' oversight is only one symptom of a wider inattention to the nuclear question. In the first years of the post–cold war period, the nuclear peril seemed to all but disappear from public awareness. Some of the reasons were understandable. As long as the cold war lasted, it had seemed almost indistinguishable from nuclear danger—the more so since both looked as if they were going to last indefinitely. One half of this assumption was of course negated by the Soviet collapse. For a while, the public seemed to imagine that nuclear danger, too, had unexpectedly proven ephemeral. The political antagonism that had produced the only nuclear terror Americans had ever known had, after all, really ended with the cold war. The prospect of a second Cuban Missile Crisis became remote. It was reasonable for a while to imagine that the end of the struggle in whose name nuclear weapons had been built would lead to their end. Perhaps it would happen quietly and smoothly. The Comprehensive Test Ban Treaty would be accepted and succeeded by arms reductions. START II would be ratified and followed by START III, START III by START IV (at some point the lesser nuclear powers would be drawn into the negotiations), and so on, until the last warhead was gone. American presidents encouraged the public complacency. "I saw the chance to rid our children's dreams of the nuclear nightmare, and I did," President George Bush said at the Republican convention in 1992; and in 1997, President Bill Clinton boasted that "our children are growing up free from the shadows of the cold war and the threat of nuclear holocaust."

The news media took their cue from this official fantasy. Nuclear weapons all but dropped out of the news and opinion pages. In the decade since the Berlin Wall was torn down, newspaper readers and television viewers were given little indication that some 31,000 nuclear weapons remained in the world, or that 7,000 of them were targeted at the United States. A whole generation came of age lacking even rudimentary information regarding nuclear arms and nuclear peril. On the tenth anniversary of the end of the wall, few commentators taking stock of the decade bothered to mention the persistence of nuclear danger or the full-scale breakdown of arms control.

A second nuclear age, in which old nuclear dangers declined to disappear and new ones were springing up, had begun, but fresh thinking and fresh initiatives to deal with it were missing. A frightening new landscape was coming into view. The presidents who said that they had ended nuclear danger had not acted that way. Clinton's repeated though little-reported "bottom up" reviews of defense policy left the strategy of nuclear deterrence—and the arsenals it justified—untouched. His spokesmen let it be known that nuclear weapons were to remain the foundation of American security for the indefinite future. Russia followed suit—abandoning a willingness expressed by Gorbachev to eliminate nuclear weapons and stalling on the ratification of the START II Treaty. And so the nuclear arsenals of the cold war, instead of withering away with the disappearance of that conflict, were delivered intact, like a package from a deceased sender, into the new age, though now lacking the benefit of new justification—or, for that matter, of new opposition.

Meanwhile, newcomers to the nuclear game, evidently taking their cue from the senior nuclear powers, moved to acquire the weapons. If nuclear powers such as Russia and the United States, which no longer had a quarrel, were entitled to maintain nuclear arsenals, why not countries that, like India and Pakistan, were chronically at war? To insist otherwise would, in the words of India's foreign minister Jaswant Singh, be to shut the Third World out of the "nuclear paradigm" established by the First and Second worlds, and so to accept "nuclear apartheid." In May of 1998, India and Pakistan, accordingly, fired off their rival salvos of nuclear tests. The antagonism between the Soviet Union and the United States had been "cold," but this conflict was hot. The three wars that the two countries had fought since the late 1940s were in short order followed by a fourth in the summer of 1999. The world's multiplying nuclear arsenals were meanwhile supplemented by a new prominence of their repellent siblings in the family of weapons of mass destruction—chemical and biological weapons, which may become the instrument of choice of nations or terrorist groups worried about the expense and difficulty of making nuclear weapons.

By the century's end, the web of arms-control agreements that had been painstakingly woven during the last half century of the cold war was tearing apart. The United States Senate voted down the Comprehensive Test Ban Treaty—an act that cut away the foundation of several decades of effort by the United States to halt the spread of nuclear weapons. The same Senate that rejected the CTBT persuaded the Clinton Administration to develop National Missile Defenses, which would violate the Antiballistic Missile

Treaty of 1972, thereby threatening to turn Russia's stalling on the START negotiations into outright opposition. The combined resolve of the senior powers to keep their arsenals and of other countries to obtain them likewise threatened the breakdown of the Nuclear Nonproliferation Treaty, under which 185 countries have agreed to forgo nuclear weapons in exchange for promises by the nuclear powers to abolish theirs.

From the very first moments of the nuclear age, scientists have warned the world that it is in the nature of nuclear technology—as of all technology—to become universally available and therefore that, in the absence of political will, the world would tend to become nuclear armed. In a world boiling with local (and not so local) hatreds, the retrogression of arms control raises the question of whether the cold war, instead of being the high point of danger in a waning nuclear age, will prove to have been a mere bipolar rehearsal for a multipolar second nuclear age.

A number of voices have challenged this status quo by calling for the abolition of nuclear weapons, but their views went largely unreported by the news media that had ignored the dangers of which they warned. Among them are leaders of the traditional anti-nuclear peace movement; the seven governments of the New Agenda coalition, composed of Brazil, Egypt, Ireland, Mexico, New Zealand, Sweden, and South Africa; and an impressive array of retired military officers and civilian leaders, including President Jimmy Carter, Senator Alan Cranston, former commander of the Strategic Air Command General George Lee Butler, and the commander of the allied air forces in the Gulf War, General Charles Horner. In a series of reports and statements, these people have argued that the end of the cold war has provided a historically unique but perishable opportunity to remove nuclear danger by eliminating nuclear arsenals everywhere. (Since only eight nations—the United States, Russia, England, France, China, India, Pakistan, and Israel— possess nuclear weapons, and of these only India, Pakistan, and Israel have not signed the Nonproliferation Treaty, abolition means persuading just three nations to live as would the other 185 signatories.) Notable among the new abolitionists were some of the most hawkish figures of the cold war, including Paul Nitze, drafter in 1950 of National Security Council Memorandum 68, regarded by many as the charter of American cold war policy. He argued that the United States' huge lead in the development of high-precision weaponry—a "military revolution" in its own right, according to many observers—created a new military context in which the United States simply did not need nuclear weapons. The Gulf War and the war against Serbia had, of course, placed this discriminating yet fearsome technology on display. Considering these advantages, Nitze could "think of no circumstances under which it would be wise for the United States to use nuclear weapons," and therefore recommended that the nation "unilaterally get rid" of them entirely. The emergence of this hawkish strain of abolitionism, in which precision, high-explosive conventional bombing would give the United States a usable military superiority that nuclear weapons could never confer, assured that, should the idea of abolition ever take hold, a debate within the ranks of the abolitionists themselves would be robust. But Nitze's dramatic and provocative proposal fell into the media silence that had swallowed up all other proposals for abolition.

PREFACE TO A CENTURY

It seems timely, then, to take a fresh look at the nuclear question in the context of the century that has just ended. The exercise, we can hope, will shed light on both the nuclear dilemma and the story of the century, short or otherwise, in which nuclear weapons have played, and unfortunately go on playing, so important a part. One place to begin is a work that, as it happens, was first published in *Blackwood's Edinburgh Magazine*, in London, at the turn of the last century, in 1899: Joseph Conrad's *Heart of Darkness*. Conrad wrote in the heyday of a liberal civilization that had seemed to spread steadily and grow stronger for most of the nineteenth century. Its articles of faith were that science and technology were the sources of a prosperity without limits; that the free market would spread the new bounty across the boundaries of both classes and nations; that liberty and democracy, already established in several of the most powerful and advanced nations, were gaining ground almost everywhere; and that all of these forces were contributing to an unstoppable tide of overall human progress. It is, of course, a revival of these beliefs—minus, notably, the idea of progress—that has inspired the belief that the twentieth century, or even history itself, ended in 1991. Conrad was not an acolyte of this faith. He was perhaps the most acute among a number of observers who, having witnessed firsthand what the "civilized" countries were doing in the "backward" parts of the world, where colonialism was at its zenith, discerned the shape of a radically different future. *Heart of Darkness* was many things. It was a tale of travel to an exotic place. It was a glimpse, through the eyes of the seaman Marlow, of the atrocities committed by King Leopold's International Association of the Congo. It was an investigation by literary means of the extremes of evil. And it was, as we today are in position to appreciate, a topographic map, clairvoyant in its specificity, of the moral landscape of the twentieth century.

"It was like a weary pilgrimage amongst hints for nightmares," Marlow says of his sea journey to the Congo along the African coast. The hinted nightmares turned out to be the waking experience of the century ahead. That century, Conrad apparently understood, was about to open up new possibilities for evil. In *Heart of Darkness*, he seems to thumb through them prospectively, as if through a deck of horrific tarot cards. The concentration camps are there. The black men "dying slowly," "in all the attitudes of pain, abandonment, and despair," whom Marlow witnesses in a grove of trees immediately upon arriving at an outer station, are unmistakable precursors of the millions of men and women who were to die in the concentration camps soon to be built in Europe. The monster Kurtz, the charismatic station chief who murders in the name of progress, and who, although "hollow at the core," was gifted with magnificent eloquence and "electrified large meetings," is a sort of prefiguration of Hitler.

Conrad even has a Belgian journalist comment that Kurtz would have made a "splendid leader of an extreme party." Which one? "Any party," is the answer. For, the journalist stammers, "he was an— an—extremist." But Kurtz is not to be understood as a fringe character. "All Europe contributed to the making of Kurtz," Marlow says, in a rare moment of editorializing.

Consider, by way of inexplicably refined forecasting, the likeness of some of Marlow's comments about Kurtz to some comments Hitler makes about himself in 1936. The power of Hitler's voice, carried to the German public over the radio, was a basic element of his power. Conrad notes something similar in Kurtz. Marlow:

> Kurtz's discoursed. A voice! a voice! It rang deep to the very last.

Yet beneath the rich and resonant voice lay an emptiness:

> The voice was gone. What else had been there?

And, for comparison, Hitler speaking at a rally in 1936 about his appeal to the German people:

> At this hour do we not again feel the miracle that has brought us together! Long ago you heard the voice of a man, and it struck to your hearts, it awakened you, and you followed this voice. You followed it for years, without so much as having seen him whose voice it was; you heard only a voice, and you followed.[2]

To give just one more example, anyone who witnessed the monotonous, ceaseless American artillery fire into "free-fire zones" in Vietnam will experience a shock of recognition in the following description of a French naval vessel firing into the African jungle:

> In the empty immensity of earth, sky, and water, there she was, incomprehensible, firing into a continent. Pop, would go one of the six-inch guns; a small flame would dart and vanish, a little white smoke would disappear, a tiny projectile would

---

2. Joachim Fest, *Hitler* (New York: Harvest, 1973), p. 515.

give a feeble screech—and nothing happened. Nothing could happen. There was a touch of insanity in the proceeding, a sense of lugubrious drollery in the sight.

Nor did Conrad fail to take note of those indispensable props of the gigantic, insane, state-sponsored crimes of our time: the obedient functionaries. The "banality" of their evil, famously described after the fact by Hannah Arendt in *Eichmann in Jerusalem*, is foreshadowed in Conrad's description of a minor bureaucrat in the ivory-gathering operation at the Central Station. This man, mistaking Marlow for an influential figure, curries favor with him, prompting Marlow to observe, "I let him run on, this papier-maché Mephistopheles." He adds, "It seemed to me that if I tried I could poke my forefinger through him, and would find nothing inside but a little loose dirt, maybe." Conrad described well the humiliation that so many decent people were to experience in having to take ridiculous personages seriously solely because of the immense suffering they were causing. Face to face with Kurtz in the jungle at night, Marlow comments, "I resented bitterly the absurd danger of our situation, as if to be at the mercy of that atrocious phantom had been a dishonoring necessity." The inspired anti-Nazi diarist Friedrich Reck-Malleczewen, who was executed by the Nazis in 1944, experienced a similar feeling of humiliation when he thought back to an accidental encounter he had once had with another atrocious phantom—Hitler. "If I had had an inkling of the role this piece of filth was to play, and of the years of suffering he was to make us endure," he wrote, "I would have done it [shot him] without a second thought. But I took him for a character out of a comic strip, and did not shoot."[3]

The most remarkable and telling augury of *Heart of Darkness*, however, was the glimpse that Conrad, vaulting ahead in prophecy to 1945, provided of the destination toward which all these preposterous and terrifying tendencies somehow were heading; namely, the

---

3. Friedrich Reck-Malleszewen, *Diary of a Man in Despair* (New York: Collier, 1970), p. 28.

threat that, with the help of the Kurtzes of this world, the human species might one day get ready to wipe itself off the face of the earth. After his climactic meeting with Kurtz in the jungle, Marlow further comments, "There was nothing either above or below him, and I knew it. He had kicked himself loose of the earth. Confound the man! he had kicked the very earth to pieces." This foreboding of annihilation was no incidental feature of the work; it returns several times, always at critical moments in the story. The most renowned passage in which this occurs is the legendary addendum "Exterminate all the brutes" that Kurtz pinned to the bottom of the dithyramb to nineteenth-century progress that he left as his legacy. The foreboding recurs even more explicitly when, after Kurtz has died and Marlow is on his way to inform Kurtz's betrothed of the fact, he reports, "I had a vision of him on the stretcher, opening his mouth voraciously, as if to devour all the earth with all its mankind." The technical means for destroying the species lay far in the future, but the psychological and moral preparations, it appears, were well under way in 1899.

THE FIRST AUGUST: THE BEGINNING OF THE REAL TWENTIETH CENTURY

As the scholar Jessica Reifer has pointed out, Conrad's intimations in a single text of virtually all the unprecedented evils, including the threat of self-extinction, that Western humanity was about to visit upon itself and the world in the twentieth century are evidence before the fact of their common roots and essential unity. These "hints for nightmares," however, were not actualized in Europe as real historical events until, during the first of the century's fateful Augusts, the First World War broke out. Then the nightmares followed, one after another, in a chain whose unusually clear linkage points to the underlying continuity.

The judgment that the outbreak of the First World War was the starting point in the twentieth century's plunge into horror did not originate with the inventors of the idea of the short twentieth century; it has been the belief of a remarkably wide consensus of historians. George Kennan spoke for this consensus in his diplomatic history *The Decline of Bismarck's European Order*:

> With the phenomenon of the Second World War before me, it was borne in upon me to what overwhelming extent the determining phenomena of the interwar period, Russian Communism and German Nazism and indeed then the Second World War itself, were the products of that first great holocaust of 1914–18. . . . And thus I came to see the First World War . . . as the great seminal catastrophe of the century. . . .

As Kennan suggests, the stories of the two world wars on the one hand and of the two great totalitarian regimes on the other were as tightly intertwined at every crucial juncture as the proteins on the strands of a double helix. Total war and totalitarianism were kin in more than name. From 1914 onward, each fed the other in a vicious spiral of violence.

To begin with, the shock of the First World War is widely understood to have created the social conditions essential to the success of the Bolshevik revolution in Russia. In the words of the historian Martin Malia, "This war disorganized Russia's still immature political structures to the point where the Bolshevik Party, a throwback to the violent and conspiratorial politics of the 1870s, was able to seize power. . . ." Many understood even at the time that the brutality of the war had been carried over to the system of rule that followed. As the contemporary socialist Victor Chernov put it, "The moral nature of the Bolshevik revolution was inherited from the war in which it was born."

That the Nazis' rise to power in Germany was made possible by the war is also accepted widely. It will be enough here—without trying to recount the story of the embitterment and destabilization of German politics and society by her defeat and the harsh terms of the peace settlement—to recall two comments made by Hitler. The first is his remark that "if at the beginning of the war twelve or fifteen thousand of these Hebrew corrupters of the people had been held under poison gas, as happened to hundreds of thousands of our very best German workers in the field, the sacrifice of millions at the front would not have been in vain." The idea of killing Jews by gas was not one that Hitler, who had been a victim of an English gas attack, was to forget. The second comment is his description of his reaction to the declaration of the First World War. "Even today," he wrote in *Mein Kampf*, "I am not ashamed to say that, overpowered by stormy enthusiasm, I fell down on my knees and thanked Heaven from an overflowing heart."

If in the century's Teens and Twenties total war prepared the way for totalitarianism, in the Thirties, when Hitler carried out the series of aggressions that pushed the world into the Second World War, the process worked the other way around. Hitler's biographers tell us that while at the front in the First World War he felt so much at home in the trenches and so ill at ease in civilian society that he canceled all his leaves. For him, it seems, not war but peace was hell, and there is a sense in which the interwar period was just one more leave that was canceled by a peace-weary Hitler.

The plainest of these links, finally, is that between the war against Hitler and the decision by the United States and England to build atomic weapons. In October of 1939 (more than two years before the United States went to war with Germany and Japan), when the businessman Alexander Sachs visited President Franklin Roosevelt to recommend an atomic-weapons program, Roosevelt commented, "Alex, what you are after is to see that the Nazis don't blow us up." Sachs replied, "Precisely." Throughout the war, the scientists at Los Alamos—many of them refugees from Europe—held before their eyes the prospect that Hitler would succeed in building the bomb first.

Evil, even when opposed, has a way of preparing the ground for more evil, and Hitler by this route became a progenitor of the bomb. His extraordinary malevolence induced his adversaries to embrace an evil that otherwise they conceivably might have forgone. Through this indirect paternity were reborn key aspects of the policies that he, more than anyone else, had pioneered. As in a magic trick— appropriately accompanied by a gigantic world-blinding flash and (mushroom-shaped) puff of smoke—the politics of mass annihilation, even as they were going down to defeat in Hitler's bunker, were in 1945 transferred to the care of Washington.

EXTERMINATION

What was the nature of the new possibilities for evil that Conrad had discerned in the Congo and that the series of calamities inaugurated by the war in 1914 brought, as if through the action of a pendulum swinging in an ever-widening arc, to fuller and fuller realization, until the human species created weapons whereby it could destroy itself? Violence on a previously unimaginable scale was the obvious common denominator. This violence was the basis for the increasing use of that lingua franca of twentieth-century politics, terror—terror as an instrument of rule, which is to say totalitarian rule; terror as a strategy of war, and especially of "strategic" bombing, aimed at breaking the morale of civilian populations; and, finally, nuclear terror, rather optimistically referred to as a "balance of terror." (Terror in nuclear strategy, let us note, is terror in not only its most extensive but also its purest form, inasmuch as its practitioners sometimes imagine that it can be projected forever without actual use of the instruments that produce it.) But something more than a colossal increase in violence and terror was involved. In Kurtz's phrase "Exterminate all the brutes," Conrad gives us the concept we need: extermination. The capacity and will to destroy not just large numbers of people but entire classes of people was the new invention. Policies of extermination, of course, require slaughter on a mass scale, but they aim at more than slaughter. By seeking to eradicate defined human collectivities, extermination aims not only at these groups but at their progeny, who are shut out of existence when the policy succeeds. The distinction is basic. Mass slaughter is a crime against the living; extermination is, in addition, a crime against the future. When Hitler launched the Final Solution, his target was not just the living Jews but all future Jews together with the culture they had created and, if they were permitted to live, would go on creating. (Jewish life, he once said, would remain on earth only as a memory, in a museum of Jewry he planned to build in Frankfurt am Main. The museum would have been a libel upon a murdered race.) Murder is a crime that, by destroying individual lives, violates the legal and moral order of a community; extermination is a crime that, by destroying an entire community, is a crime against the family of communities that makes up humankind—a crime, as international law has come to recognize, "against humanity."

Genocide—the destruction of a people, whether defined as a race or a tribe or a nation—is the quintessential act of extermination, but it is not the only one. Another is the extermination of social classes, practiced by Stalin and Mao Zedong and Pol Pot, among others. In the Bolsheviks' very first year in power, they discovered a category of crime that they called "objective." A crime was "subjective" when you had done something wrong; it was "objective" when, through no deed of your own, you belonged to a social class that the government wanted to liquidate. As early as 1918, Latvian Latsis, one of the chiefs of the Cheka, the precursor of the KGB, announced the goal in plain language: "We are engaged in annihilating the bourgeoisie as a class." Thus there was no need, Latsis explained, to "prove that this or that man acted against the interests of Soviet power." It was enough to ask, "To what class does he belong, where does he come from, what kind of education did he have, what is his occupation?" The answers to these questions "decide the fate of the accused." "That," he said, "is the quintessence of the Red Terror"— terror that was to cost the Soviet people an estimated 50 or 60 million lives in the coming half-century.

A third target of policies of extermination was cities and their populations. Let us consider two examples. The first is the bombing of Hamburg by the British air force in 1943. As early as July 1940, Churchill, while commanding the Battle of Britain, had called for "exterminating" air attacks on Germany. From then until 1942, the Bomber Command, afflicted by high loss rates and fearful of losing out in interservice rivalry with the navy and the army, drifted away from "precision" bombing, which had to be carried out in daylight, into "area bombing," which could be carried out at night. The aim was to destroy the morale of the German people by killing German civilians and destroying their homes. By the end of 1942, giant raids on Lübeck and Cologne had made it clear that the annihilation of entire cities in one or a few raids was feasible. Accordingly, Most Secret Operation Order No. 173, of May 27, 1943, stated, under the heading "Intention," that the aim of the raid was "to destroy HAMBURG." The order estimated that 10,000 tons of bombs would have to be dropped to "complete the process of elimination." And thus it was done, producing a firestorm in the city and killing some 45,000 people in a single night.

The second example is Hitler's plan, formed even before his attack on Russia, in June of 1941, for the annihilation of Moscow and Leningrad. Moscow was to be razed because it was "the center of [Bolshevik] doctrine"—for Hitler's larger goal was an "ethnic catastrophe" that would "deprive not only Bolshevism of its centers, but wipe out the Muscovites." He intended to dig a resevoir where Moscow had once been. At first, he planned to spare Leningrad, because it was "incomparably more beautiful" than Moscow; but soon he put Leningrad, too, on the list of cities to be destroyed. His explanation sheds light on the mentality of those who are preparing to exterminate entire human communities:

> I suppose that some people are clutching their heads with both hands to find an answer to the question, "How can the Führer destroy a city like St. Petersburg?". . . I would prefer not to see anyone suffer, not to do harm to anyone. But when I realize the species is in danger, then in my case sentiment gives way to the coldest reason.

The Nazi General Franz Halder concurred with this supposedly cold reasoning: annihilating the two cities, he wrote, would be a "national catastrophe which would deprive not only Bolshevism but also Muscovite nationalism of their centers."

A plan was drawn up. Leningrad would be sealed off, to weaken it "by terror and growing starvation"; then the Germans would "remove the survivors in captivity in the interior of Russia, level Leningrad to the ground with high explosives, and leave the area to the north of the Neva to the Finns."

Of course, we know that the two cities survived, owing not to any thaw in Hitler's cold reasoning but to the almost superhuman resistance mounted by the Russian people.

EXTERMINATION AS A SYSTEMIC EVIL

Just as the twentieth century's policies of extermination—whether of peoples, classes, or cities—enveloped entire human communities, so also they were carried out by entire communities—or, at any rate, by the state authorities that putatively represented those communities. Extermination, a species of crime requiring extensive social resources, is—can only be—a systemic evil. To the extent that popular support was present, the policies amounted to attempted murders of one society by another. Although there can be debate over just how extensive popular support was for Stalin's and Hitler's policies of extermination, there can be no doubt that, through the states that ruled over these peoples, the resources of entire societies were placed at the disposal of those carrying out the policies.

Those resources were not just the obvious ones—the secret police, the transportation systems, the concentration-camp administrations, the armies, the bomber forces. They had to include mass cooperation of the kind that control of the state alone provides. When the state becomes an exterminator, and the law, instead of enjoining evil, supports and enforces it—as does the whole tremendous weight of custom, habit, bureaucratic inertia, and social pressure—the individual who might seek to oppose the policies is left in an extremity of moral solitude. Even the voice of conscience, in these circumstances, can become an enlistee in the ranks of the evildoers. People find themselves in the dilemma defined by Mark Twain when he presented Huck Finn's inner deliberations whether to turn in his friend the runaway black slave, Jim. Huck's "conscience," he believes, is telling him that it is wrong not to turn Jim in. Nevertheless, Huck decides to do what is "wrong" and hides Jim. Adolph Eichmann, too, heard the voice of an inverted conscience, but he, unlike Huck, obeyed it. At the end of the war, with the defeat of Germany in sight, he had an opportunity to slow down or even halt the transports of the Jews to the killing centers, but instead he redoubled his efforts. "The sad and very uncomfortable truth," Arendt writes, "probably was that it was not his fanaticism but his very conscience that prompted Eichmann to adopt his uncompromising attitude during the last year of the war. . . ." For "he remembered perfectly well that he would have had a bad conscience only if he had not done what he had been ordered to do—to ship millions of men, women, and children to their death with great zeal and the most meticulous care."

EXTERMINATION AS PSEUDOSCIENCE

As if to leave individual judgment in even greater perplexity, science—or, to be precise, pseudoscience (otherwise known as ideology)—was summoned to lend its pseudoauthority to the policies of extermination. In the late nineteenth century, in a wholesale resort to the persuasive power of sheer metaphor, social Darwinists had taught that nations in history, like species in evolution, were subject to the law of survival of the fittest. As early as 1848, Friedrich Engels had distinguished between "historical nations" (they included Germany, England, and France), which were destined to flourish, and "ahistorical nations" (they included most of the Balkan peoples), which, in his view, were destined for history's scrap heap. His interest in these ideas is one illustration of the intellectual roots that the Marxist theory of classes shared with racial theories of evolution. In Stalin's Russia, classes—some doomed, some destined to rule—played the role that races played in Hitler's Germany.

Hitler's Final Solution of the Jewish "problem" was in his mind only one part of a vast scheme of ethnic expulsion, resettlement, extermination, and racial engineering, in which he planned to eradicate Poland and Ukraine, among other nations. For example,

INTRODUCTION

"of forty-five million inhabitants in Western Russia," according to a memo prepared by the Ministry for Occupied Eastern Territories, thirty-one million were "to be expatriated or killed." "Drop a few bombs on their cities, and the job will be done," Hitler suggested.[4]

The extent to which Hitler, caught up in the grandiose theories of racial pseudoscience, had transcended mere nationalism is shown by his often-stated readiness to sacrifice even the German people if they showed themselves cowardly or weak. No nationalist could have said, as Hitler did in 1941, when still at the height of his power, that if the Germans were "no longer so strong and ready for sacrifice that they will stake their own blood on their existence, they deserve to be annihilated by another, stronger power." In that event, he added, "I would not shed a tear for the German people." He made good his promise when, facing defeat in 1945, he ordered the destruction of the entire infrastructure of German society, including its industry, buildings, and food stocks. But then had he not warned the world, as if in fulfillment of Conrad's vision of Kurtz devouring all the earth with all its mankind, that "we may perish, perhaps. But we shall take the world with us. Muspili, universal conflagration"? Hitler's willingness to accept—and even to carry out—the destruction of Germany (and the whole world into the bargain) was an early warning of the ease, later illustrated on a much greater scale in the nuclear policy of "mutual assured destruction" during the cold war, with which those who adopt policies of annihilation can overshoot the mark and wind up involving themselves in suicidal plans. Unfortunately, once the scruples that inhibit the extermination of millions of "others" have been discarded, there are very few left with which to protect "ourselves."

EXTERMINATION AS A RADICAL EVIL

The new policies—of which the extermination of human populations was the objective, states or whole societies were the authors, the

---

4. Fest, *Hitler*, p. 685.

instruments of modern science were the means, and for which the concepts of pseudoscience were the rationalization—prompted new thinking about the nature of evil. They precipitated what might be called a crisis in the meaning of evil, by which I mean a crisis in all of the human capacities whereby, once evils have occurred, the world tries, as best it can, to respond to them—to incorporate them into memory and the historical record, to understand them, to take appropriate action against their recurrence. The crimes of the twentieth century seemed to make a mockery of these powers. In *The Origins of Totalitarianism*, Arendt, making use of a phrase of Immanuel Kant's, named the new phenomenon "radical evil." According to Kant, ordinary evil occurred when the will, driven by some fear or lured by some temptation away from obedience to the principals of equity and justice, committed a selfish act. Radical evil occurred when the will, even when unafraid or unswayed by temptation, somehow inspired itself to commit evil. Whereas ordinary evil, being dependent on the happenstance of external threats or temptations, was by its nature occasional, radical evil, being ever-present in the will, might infect any or all of a person's actions. If we extend this idea from the individual to the state, we arrive at the distinction between a state that commits a crime in violation of its own good laws and a state whose laws ordain and enforce evil. Obviously, the latter is more dangerous, for it has corrupted one of the main defenses we sometimes have against evil—the state and its laws. This nullification of the human power of response brings a new feeling of bafflement and helplessness. For outbreaks of radical evil, Arendt explained, do not only destroy their victims, often in stupefying numbers, but "dispossess *us* of all power" (italics mine), for they "transcend the realm of human affairs," and "we can neither punish nor forgive such offenses."

The problem for the most elementary of responses, memory—a problem deliberately created by totalitarian regimes, which have sought to erase their crimes from the historical record—was simply to rescue the facts from their intended oblivion. Against these efforts were eventually pitted heroic acts of witness—by an Alexandr

Solzhenitsyn, a Nadezhda Mandelstam, a Primo Levi. The problem for feeling was the exhaustion that empathy must encounter in the face of suffering on such a scale. And the problem for thought was *nothingness*—the sheer absence created by the extinction of communities. The problem for law, in addition to the corruption of the perpetrators' own laws, was the likely destruction of the victims' legal system, if one ever existed. What remained were third parties who might seek to judge the wrongdoers by newly created laws, as was done in the Nuremberg trials. (This problem was solved after the fact for the Jews by the foundation of the state of Israel, which put Eichmann on trial.)

The twentieth century's policies of extermination were radical in one more sense. "Radical" evil, as the Latin origins of the word suggest, is evil that goes to the root. The root, though, of what? The answer must be: that which extermination afflicts and destroys; namely, life. The root of life, the spring from which life arises—as distinct from life itself—is birth, which is the power that enables communities composed of mortal beings to regenerate and preserve themselves in history. And it is this power, precisely, that acts of extermination annul.

After witnessing the trial of Eichmann, a "papier-maché Mephistopheles" if there ever was one, Arendt backed away from the phrase "radical evil." "Only the good has depth and can be radical," she wrote in a letter to her friend Gershom Scholem. Evil, she now believed, "is never 'radical,' only extreme." It was this very shallowness, she concluded, that produced the frustration of the mind faced with the new crimes. "It is 'thought-defying,'" she explained, "because thought tries to reach some depth, to go to the roots, and the moment it concerns itself with evil, it is frustrated because there is nothing." (This relationship between evil and nothingness, though it has been most clearly manifested in history only in this century, was signposted in Christian theology, in which, as St. Augustine maintains, being, taken as a whole, is good, and its absence is called evil.)

In truth, though, "there is nothing" in two senses where radical evil is concerned. First, there is nothing (perhaps just "a little loose dirt") in the souls of bureaucrats such as Eichmann, for when the state of which they are a part goes berserk, they can, merely by thoughtlessly doing their jobs (*quitting* would take some imagination), participate in gargantuan evils. Second, as Arendt had pointed out earlier, the erasure of a community from the face of the earth leaves a kind of "nothing" behind; namely, the "hole of oblivion" in the human order where that community had once existed. Perhaps banal evildoers, as Conrad knew, are capable of committing evil that is radical (or "extreme," if you prefer), as if the emptiness of their minds and souls prefigures the emptiness in the world that they and the policies they serve leave behind. What is "thought-defying" after the fact is, appropriately, done thoughtlessly to begin with.

THE SECOND AUGUST:
NUCLEAR EXTERMINATION

In her reflections on radical evil, Arendt was addressing policies of extermination that had been adopted before the advent of nuclear weapons, but it is plain that what she had to say applies in almost every particular to nuclear policies and nuclear danger. In other words, although Hiroshima came as a great surprise and shock to the world, it did not arrive without a historical context and historical precedents. On the contrary, it was the supreme expression of forces that had been developing ever since Conrad had Kurtz write, "Exterminate all the brutes." Behind Hiroshima stood not only the obvious precedent of strategic bombing but all of the twentieth century's policies of extermination. These amounted, by the end of the Second World War, to what might be called a legacy of extermination, and in August of 1945 the United States fell heir to it. The hallmarks of the legacy were all present. The nuclear threat was a threat of extermination—extermination, this time, not only of nations and peoples but of the human species. The root of life that now would be severed would be the root of all human life, birth itself, and would shut all future human beings out of existence. The evil was a systemic evil: The system posing the threat, once the "balance of terror" was established, went beyond any single state to incorporate the greatest powers of the world, which, in the system of mutual assured destruction, became jointly complicit in the project. The threat was supported by pseudoscience, spun this time from game theory and other forms of futurology manufactured in think tanks and academic institutions that subserved power. Nuclear "strategy"—regarded by many as a contradiction in terms—became the very epicenter of banality. Nuclear arms increased the capacity of human beings to destroy one another to its absolute limit, beyond which any further improvements would merely be "overkill." The arsenals threatened radical evil, in the fullest and most exact sense of that term: they brought radical evil to perfection. The powers of human response to evil would be utterly overwhelmed by the evil deed itself. Policies of extermination again spilled over into suicidal policies. The "coldest reason" again was invoked to rationalize genocide. The conscience of the individual was again thrown into crisis by the policies of the state. The deeds in question again were, as Arendt had said, "thought-defying." The "nothingness" that now awaited was absolute, the crisis of meaning full-blown. The atomic bomb that burst over Hiroshima burned for a moment as bright as the sun, but at its heart was a darkness that was eternal. The twentieth century had, so to speak, arrived at the heart of the heart of darkness.

The advent of the nuclear age, however, brought with it another major change in the development of the century's policies of extermination. At a stroke, it removed them from their totalitarian residence and planted them at the core of liberal civilization, which is to say at the core of the national security policy of the powerful democratic nation about to assume leadership of the non-Communist world—the United States. The new location brought with it a new moral and practical riddle of the first order. Instruments of the most radical evil imaginable—the extinction of the human species—had appeared, but they were first placed in the hands of a liberal republic. The fact that, more or less by an accident of history, the bomb was born in New Mexico, U.S.A., in 1945, rather than, say, Heidelberg, Germany, in 1944 (no sheer impossibility of science or history rules out our imagining the latter possibility), lent it a triple warrant of virtue that it otherwise would have lacked.

In the first place, the bomb gained luster from its new residence. Without becoming jingoistic about the United States or overlooking the dark passages in its history, including slavery and the near extinction of Native Americans, it must be said that the United States was no Nazi Germany or Stalinist Russia. History had in a sense played a trick on the world, as it so often does. If history had been logical, it would have given the bomb to Hitler, whose policies (including his suicidal inclinations) so clearly pointed in the direction of extermination on the new scale. It's easy to imagine what civilized people would have said if Hitler had been the first to use nuclear weapons—perhaps against Moscow or London. They very likely would have said that nuclear war was a natural culmination of *Vernichtungskrieg* and an ideology that sanctioned the extermination of peoples, and that with nuclear weapons Hitler was enabled to do quickly and efficiently what he had already been doing slowly and clumsily with gas chambers. The United States, on the other hand, had shown no recent inclination for policies of extermination, as was demonstrated shortly by its mild, liberal, extremely successful occupation policies in Germany and Japan. In the second place, the bomb arrived just in time to hurry along the end of the most destructive war in history. It made its appearance as a war-ending, war-winning device. The totalitarian and the liberal regimes had arrived at their policies of extermination along very different historical paths. Whereas Hitler and Stalin destroyed peoples, classes, and cities for reasons that even today defy rational explanation, the United States destroyed Hiroshima and Nagasaki for the perfectly clear and comprehensible purposes of ending the war quickly and getting the upper hand over the Soviet Union in the embryonic cold war. (To point this is out is not to justify these acts; it is only to observe that the goals of policy were conventional and rational.) In the third place, the almost immediate outbreak of the cold war with the totalitarian Soviet Union created a justification for continuing to build nuclear arsenals, lending the bomb still another warrant of virtue. It assumed the role of guardian of the free world.

To this triple validation of policies of nuclear extermination, accorded by the accident of timing and place, a fourth, of later origin, must be added. Although it was true that with the growth of the arsenals the depth and range of terror were soon increased to their earthly maximum (single bombs of the largest size contained several times the explosive power of all the weapons used in the Second World War), it also happened that none was ever used after Nagasaki. Instead, they were held suspended, like the sword of Damocles cited by President John Kennedy, over a completely jeopardized yet undevastated world. It was as if, in the nuclear arsenals of the cold war, the destruction and mass killing of the entire first half of the twentieth century had been distilled into a poison of fantastic potency but then this poison, instead of being administered to a doomed world, had been held in reserve, being employed only to produce terror. To the question whether Western Civilization had put behind it the legacy of extermination that it had been developing for half a century, the nuclear policymakers of the cold war in effect gave an equivocal answer. Their answer was, "No, for we have plans for extermination that beggar Hitler's and Stalin's, but our sincere wish is never to be provoked into actually committing the deed." Certainly, the legacy of extermination had not been renounced. Rather, it had been hugely developed and assigned a more important role in world affairs than ever before. Now the world's greatest power as well as its adversary relied upon it for basic security. On the other hand, the very fearsomeness of the new threat was invoked to prevent its being carried out. According to this reasoning, embodied in the doctrine of nuclear deterrence, the purpose of possessing nuclear arsenals was not to use them but to not use them. And not only did the bomb prevent its own nuclear war, the theorists said; it prevented the worst of the conventional wars: no conventional third world war broke out. In the meantime, however, an estimated 40 million people, most of them civilians, were killed in local wars—a fact suggesting that major war was as much displaced as deterred.

Whether a third world war was headed off because of nuclear deterrence or for some other reason is a question not easily resolved. It is a historical fact, however, that in the minds of most policy-makers as well as millions of citizens nuclear deterrence worked. The bomb, already seen as a war-winner and a freedom defender, now was granted the additional title of peacemaker. (The MX missile was given this very name, and the Strategic Air Command adopted the motto "Peace Is Our Profession.") In the telling of officialdom, it became almost a pacifist device. All of the highest benefits of civilization, it now seemed, were in the gift of the bomb. Here was a bargain with the devil to make Faust green with envy. Victory, freedom, peace: was there anything else for which the world might petition an openhanded Lucifer?

And yet none of these benefits altered in the slightest particular the irreducible facts of what nuclear weapons were, what they could do, and what they were meant to do "if deterrence failed." One bomb of the appropriate megatonnage would still obliterate any city; ten bombs, ten cities. Hitler had killed an estimated 6 million Jews; Stalin had sent an estimated 20 million of his fellow Soviet citizens to their deaths. A few dozen well-placed nuclear bombs could outdo these totals by an order of magnitude. But at the height of the cold war, there were not a few dozen nuclear bombs; there were almost 70,000, with thousands poised on hair-trigger alert. A policy of extermination did not cease being that because the goals it supported were laudable. Described soberly and without the slightest hyperbole, it was a policy of retaliatory genocide.

For most people most of the time, these perils remained all but unimaginable. But every now and then the reality of the policy was borne in on someone. That happened, for instance, to Robert McNamara shortly after he became secretary of defense in 1961, when he received a briefing on the Single Integrated Operational Plan at the headquarters of the Strategic Air Command. In the event of a Soviet conventional attack on Europe—or merely the plausible likelihood of such an attack—the United States' Plan 1-A, which was its only true option for major nuclear war, McNamara learned, was to annihilate every Communist country from Poland to China. There was no operational means, he further learned, by which, if the president desired, he could spare one or more of these countries. Albania, then engaged in bitter polemics with Moscow, was to be obliterated merely because a Soviet radar facility was stationed on its soil. The plan was for obligatory multiple acts of genocide. In *The Wizards of Armageddon*, Fred Kaplan reports that "McNamara was horrified." He set about trying to create other options. Today McNamara favors the abolition of nuclear weapons because, in his carefully chosen words, they threaten "the destruction of nations."

Hiroshima, in sum, had created a gulf between ends and means. Never had evil been more radical; never had the good that was hoped from it been greater. The means were an evil that exceeded the capacity of the human being to imagine them; the ends were all the splendors of liberal civilization and peace.

Thus, through the invention, production, and deployment of nuclear arsenals, was the tradition of extermination, glimpsed in prospect by Conrad in colonized Africa, pioneered and developed under totalitarian government and in total war, conjoined to the liberal tradition that had been knocked off course at the beginning of the real twentieth century by the First World War. In a political as well as a moral sense, however, the union was tentative. During the cold war years, the Western nuclear powers (the United States, England, and France) did indeed learn the art of *Living with Nuclear Weapons*, in the title of the Harvard-sponsored book of 1983, but they had not taken the marriage vows. Reliance on nuclear arms was widely considered an extraordinary, provisional response to an extraordinary, provisional emergency: the threat, as many people in the West believed, to the freedom of the entire world by the Soviet Union, which, of course, soon developed nuclear arsenals of its own.

The Soviet threat shaped the West's embrace of nuclear terror in two fundamental ways. First, it was placed in the moral scales opposite the nuclear threat, rendering the latter acceptable. The mere physical existence of humankind, many people believed, was worth risking for the sake of its moral and spiritual existence, represented by the survival of freedom. Second, most people were persuaded that the secretive nature of the Soviet regime ruled out effective inspection of radical nuclear-arms-control agreements, thus making full nuclear disarmament impossible. In 1946, when the United States put forward the Baruch Plan, which proposed universal abolition of nuclear arms, the Soviet Union, now working at full tilt to develop its own bomb, turned it down. Historians still argue whether it was reasonable for the United States, already in possession of the secret of the bomb, to expect the Soviet Union, which did not yet possess the secret, to close down its nuclear program as part of a global agreement to abolish nuclear weapons. However that may be, there is no doubt that the Soviet rejection of the Baruch Plan played an important role in the United States' understanding of its own moral and historical responsibility for the nuclear arms race that followed. The United States, Americans believed from 1946 on, had proved itself ready to eliminate nuclear weapons, but the Soviet Union stood in the way. The Soviet threat, in American eyes, thus both justified nuclear arms and placed an insuperable practical obstacle in the way of their abolition. As long as this appeared to be the case, the United States could regard itself as a reluctant threatener of nuclear destruction, merely forced into this unwelcome role by the character of the regimes it felt obliged to oppose.

THE FUTURE OF EXTERMINATION:
THE THIRD AND THE FOURTH AUGUSTS

The third of our Augusts, in which the failed coup in Moscow brought on the collapse of the Soviet Union, dissolved this equation. The age of totalitarianism, which had opened in October of 1917, was over. The balancing factor in the moral equation that for almost fifty years had justified nuclear arsenals had fallen away. Would total war survive the loss of its linguistic and historical brother? Could the one exist without the good of the other? Should nuclear weapons survive the end of the "short twentieth century," not to speak of the "end of history"? And if they did, had the century (the "real" one) or history really "ended"? This question, which has hung over the decade between the end of the proposed short twentieth century and its calendrical end, has acquired even greater urgency as we move into the next century and millennium.

At the beginning of this essay, I recalled the old Greek idea that because the end of a story can force us to rewrite its earlier chapters, we cannot know what the story is until it is over. No single narrative can or should attempt to encompass the history of an epoch, which contains a limitless variety of entwined tales; yet, as the concept of a real twentieth century suggests, the very choice of the dates that mark off one era from another means that certain stories lay special claim to our attention. It's already clear that it will be impossible to write the political history of the twentieth century without reference to the many-chaptered story of the century's policies of extermination, some of whose main chapter headings will surely be the three Augusts we have mentioned. The final shape of that story, however, will not be known until the arrival of that future date— some future August day, perhaps—on which the ultimate fortunes of the arms that were born in 1945 are decided. Interpretations of the real twentieth century now require not so much smarter interpreters as the world's decision whether, in the wake of the cold war, it will reject nuclear weapons or once again embrace them.

Let us, then, perform a thought experiment in which we try to imagine how the twentieth century will appear in retrospect, in light of two possible next chapters of the nuclear story. In the first, we will imagine that the next chapter is the last—that the world decides to eliminate nuclear weapons. In the second, we will imagine that the cold war legacy of nuclear arms has been accepted and has led to their proliferation. Our glance, in the two cases, is not chiefly forward, to the world that lies ahead, but backward upon the century that has just ended.

In the event that abolition is embraced, we will find, I suggest, that what the American government said and the American public believed from 1946, when the Soviet Union rejected the Baruch Plan, until 1991, when the Soviet Union collapsed, was essentially true: that the policymakers were as dismayed by nuclear danger as ordinary people were; that in their minds the reason for enduring the risk of human extinction really had been the threat to freedom around the world posed by the Soviet Union; that the government would indeed have preferred to abolish nuclear weapons in 1946 but had been prevented by the Soviet Union; and that was truly why, when the Soviet Union collapsed, the United States seized the opportunity to lead the world to nuclear abolition. We will, further, take seriously the often-repeated argument that "arms-control" was an invaluable temporary holding action for reducing nuclear danger until political conditions were ripe for full nuclear disarmament. We will take even more seriously the arguments of those who held that it was not nuclear arms that fueled the political differences of the cold war but the political differences of the cold war that fueled the nuclear-arms race, and who therefore argued against arms control. And then we will show how, precisely because the anti-Communism of the time had been authentic, Communism's end naturally opened the way to abolition of the arms that had protected us against Communism. We will be unsurprised to record that many of the cold war's fiercest hawks had become abolitionists. And we will note with satisfaction how the example of these former hawks was emulated by hawks in other nations, including India, Pakistan, and Israel, who therefore agreed to relinquish their countries' nuclear weapons as part of the general settlement.

Even the evolution of high nuclear strategy, historians may go on to relate, will then seem to have been a slow education in the realities of the nuclear age, especially after the shock of the Cuban Missile Crisis in 1962, which left such a deep impression of the horror of nuclear war in the minds of later abolitionists, such as Robert McNamara. It will be the gratifying task of analysts to record how, even on the political right, the most militant believers in armed force slowly came around to an understanding that, in the words of Ronald Reagan, the most conservative president of the era, "nuclear war can never be won and must never be fought," and they will trace the path from that understanding to his discussion of nuclear abolition at the Reykjavik summit meeting of 1986 with the Soviet leader Mikhail Gorbachev.

Paralleling this slow evolution in thought, we would see, was the equally slow development in practice of the so-called tradition of nonuse, which gradually taught statesmen that even when they possessed a nuclear monopoly they could extract no military or political benefit from it and so did not use nuclear weapons after Nagasaki. In this story, acts of nuclear restraint—by the United States in Vietnam, by the Soviet Union in Afghanistan, by China in its border war with Vietnam in 1979—will have the place that battles have in bloodier narratives. The cold war thus will be partially redeemed in our eyes as a vast laboratory in which, at the price of a few hair-raising close calls, the world learned through patient reflection and oblique experience that nuclear weapons were as futile as they were abhorrent and that they could and should be eliminated.

The lessons would go deeper still. When the last nuclear plutonium pit had been liquidated (or, more likely, adulterated and buried away in some deep cavern), we would see that the ground for nuclear disarmament had been prepared by, on the one hand, the peace movement in the United States, and, on the other, by the movement against Soviet power by dissidents in the Soviet empire (two movements that at the time failed, on the whole, to grasp the common drift of their activity). The astounding success of the resistance movement in the East would emerge as the first stage in a global movement against not only Soviet terror but all terror— against not only totalitarianism but its close relative, total war— whose last stage would be the elimination of nuclear arms, thereby truly ending the spiral of violence that began in 1914.

The rise and fall of totalitarianism from start to finish would wear an altered aspect. It would turn out to have been a ghastly, protracted detour from the progress (the word itself might even gain new credit) and enlightenment offered by liberal civilization, which, although capsized in 1914 by the First World War, will have righted itself in 1991, bringing on an era of prosperity and peace. Then liberal civilization itself, freed of its complicity in the policies of extermination it adopted in 1945, will rest at last on a sure foundation. The political history of the twentieth century will thus be the story not only of the rise of policies of extermination in all their variety but also of the human recoil against them, leading, first, to the renewed rejection of totalitarianism and embrace of democracy in the 1990s and then, in the years following, to the abolition of nuclear weapons along with other weapons of mass destruction.

In the second thought experiment—in which we suppose that the nuclear powers have renewed their embrace of their nuclear arsenals in the post–cold war period, setting the example for several other powers, and so installing nuclear weapons as a deep- and many-rooted structural feature of life in the twenty-first century— the political and military history of the twentieth century will have to be written very differently. To begin with, we will not be able to take so seriously the West's stated justifications for building nuclear arsenals. How will we continue to believe that the democratic nations endured the risk of human annihilation for the sake of human freedom when, with the threat to freedom gone, the threat of annihilation is preserved? How will we continue to say that the totalitarianism of the Soviet Union was the great obstacle to full disarmament when, with the Soviet Union collapsed and Russia inviting full inspection and proposing (under Gorbachev) full disarmament, the United States refused? Having discovered that the end of Communism left our will to possess nuclear arms intact, the old claim that in the cold war we chose to risk being "dead" rather than going "Red" will ring hollow. The entire fifty-year confrontation between totalitarianism and democracy will shrink in importance as an explanatory factor. Our attention will be drawn instead to the ease with which the United States shifted its nuclear planning in

1945 from Germany to Japan, and then from Japan to the Soviet Union, and we will see this flexibility as a precedent for the much more drastic and shocking shift of targeting at the end of the cold war from the Soviet Union to . . . well, what? A few feeble "rogue" states, the mere possibility that Russia will again become an enemy of the United States?

We'll hardly be surprised to see that several nations outside the original nuclear "club" have followed the "nuclear paradigm." As for arms control, it will be understood as just one of the means by which public anxiety about the nuclear danger was put to sleep. Our policy of nonproliferation will seem to have been half-hearted, since it will have been shown that we preferred to permit the whole world to acquire nuclear arms than to give up our own.

The process of education that occurred during the cold war will seem to be the opposite of what it would have seemed had we abolished nuclear weapons: one not of deepening understanding of the horror and futility of the arsenals but of simply getting used to them, in preparation for accepting them fully and without reservation as a normal instrument of national policy, of learning to "stop worrying and love the bomb," in the words of the subtitle to the movie *Dr. Strangelove*, which will have lost their ironic connotations.

A graver suspicion will be confirmed: that the United States and its nuclear allies did not build nuclear weapons chiefly in order to face extraordinary danger, whether from Germany, Japan, or the Soviet Union, but for more deep-seated, unarticulated reasons growing out of its own, freely chosen conceptions of national security. Nuclear arsenals will seem to have been less a response to any particular external threat, totalitarian or otherwise, than an intrinsic element of the dominant liberal civilization itelf—an evil that first grew and still grows from within that civilization rather than being imposed from without. And then we will have to remember that the seminal event of the real twentieth century, the First World War, sprang in all its pointless slaughter and destructive fury from the midst of that same liberal civilization, and we will have to ask what it is in the makeup of liberalism that pushes it again and again, even at the moment of its greatest triumphs, into an abyss of its own making.

Our understanding of the historical place of totalitarianism will likewise change. Instead of seeming a protracted bloody hiatus between the eclipse of liberal civilization of 1914 and its restoration in 1991, totalitarianism will appear to have been a harsh and effective tutor to liberalism, which was its apt pupil. The degree of moral separation from the tradition of extermination that was maintained during the cold war will have disappeared. If we look at nuclear arms as a lethal virus that spreads by contagion around the world, then totalitarianism in this picture of events becomes a sort of filthy syringe with which the dominant liberal civilization managed to inject the illness into its bloodstream, where it remained even after, in 1991, the syringe was thrown away. Liberalism will itself have unequivocally embraced extermination.

At stake is the very character of the victorious civilization that in the twentieth century buried its two greatest totalitarian antagonists and now bids to set the tone and direction of international life in the century ahead. Will it shake off the twentieth century's legacy of terror or, by embracing nuclear weapons even in the absence of totalitarian threat, incorporate that legacy into itself? Will we find that protecting civilization is unimaginable without threatening extermination? If so, a critical watershed will have been crossed, and we will have passed, by default, from a period in which an extraordinary justification, such as the Soviet threat, seemed needed to justify the extraordinary peril of nuclear arms to a period in which the quotidian fears, jealousies, ambitions, and hatreds that are always with us are found to be justification enough. At that moment, a nuclear arsenal will cease to be felt as Conrad's "dishonoring necessity" and become a fully legitimized voluntary component of the state: a permanent subbasement, or catacomb, on which the fairer upper floors of civilization—the freedom, the democracy, the prosperity—rest. But if this happens, can liberalism itself survive, or will it in the long run find itself sucked, as in 1914, into a vortex of destruction that it cannot stop?

Nuclear arsenals do not exist in isolation from the rest of politics, and no single one policy, whether regarding these arms or anything else, can decide the character of the century that is about to begin. Nor will a decision to abolish nuclear weapons even put an end to the legacy of extermination that disfigured the century now ending. The deeds of Pol Pot in Cambodia and of the former Hutu government in Rwanda have made it clear that genocide remains attractive and achievable for many governments in many parts of the world. No nuclear weapons or other weapons of mass destruction are needed to bring it off; Kalashnikovs, or even machetes or hoes, will do. What seems clear, however, is that if the triumphantly restored liberal order of the 1990s cannot renounce the threat of extermination of peoples as a condition for its own survival, then it will forfeit any chance that it can successfully oppose a resurgence of barbarism anywhere else in the twenty-first century. We will be unable to say that any year—whether 1991 or 2000 or 2050—has undone 1914 until we have also undone 1945. More than any other decision before us, this one will decide who we are, who we are to be, and who, when the last line of the story of the real twentieth century is truly written, we will have been.

THE
FATE OF
THE EARTH

*I dedicate this book
with love to my sister, Suzy.*

CONTENTS

I.
A REPUBLIC OF INSECTS AND GRASS

S INCE JULY 16, 1945, when the first atomic bomb was detonated, at the Trinity test site, near Alamogordo, New Mexico, mankind has lived with nuclear weapons in its midst. Each year, the number of bombs has grown, until now there are some fifty thousand warheads in the world, possessing the explosive yield of roughly twenty billion tons of TNT, or one million six hundred thousand times the yield of the bomb that was dropped by the United States on the city of Hiroshima, in Japan, less than a month after the Trinity explosion. These bombs were built as "weapons" for "war," but their significance greatly transcends war and all its causes and outcomes. They grew out of history, yet they threaten to end history. They were made by men, yet they threaten to annihilate man. They are a pit into which the whole world can fall—a nemesis of all human intentions, actions, and hopes. Only life itself, which they threaten to swallow up, can give the measure of their significance. Yet in spite of the immeasurable importance of nuclear weapons, the world has declined, on the whole, to think about them very much. We have thus far failed to fashion, or to discover within ourselves, an emotional or intellectual or political response to them. This peculiar failure of response, in which hundreds of millions of people acknowledge the presence of an immediate, unremitting threat to their existence and to the existence of the world they live in but do nothing about it—a failure in which both self-interest and fellow-feeling seem to have died—has itself been such a striking phenomenon that it has to be regarded as an extremely important part of the nuclear predicament as this has existed so far. Only very recently have there been signs, in Europe and in the United States, that public opinion has been stirring awake, and that ordinary people may be beginning to ask themselves how they should respond to the nuclear peril.

In what follows, I shall offer some thoughts on the origin and the significance of this predicament, on why we have so long resisted attempts to think about it (we even call a nuclear holocaust "unthinkable") or deal with it, and on the shape and magnitude of the choice that it forces upon us. But first I wish to describe the consequences for the world, insofar as these can be known, of a full-scale nuclear holocaust at the current level of global armament. We have lived in the shadow of nuclear arms for more than thirty-six years, so it does not seem too soon for us to familiarize ourselves with them—to acquaint ourselves with such matters as the "thermal pulse," the "blast wave," and the "three stages of radiation sickness." A description of a full-scale holocaust seems to be made necessary by the simple but basic rule that in order to discuss something one should first know what it is. A considerable number of excellent studies concentrating on various aspects of the damage that can be done by nuclear arms do exist, many of them written only in the last few years. These include a report entitled "The Effects of Nuclear War," which was published in 1979 by the Congressional Office of Technology Assessment, and which deals chiefly with the consequences of a holocaust for the societies of the United States and the Soviet Union; the latest (1977) edition of the indispensable

4

classic textbook "The Effects of Nuclear Weapons," which is edited
by Samuel Glasstone and Philip J. Dolan (hereafter I shall refer to
it as "Glasstone") and was published jointly by the Department of
Defense and the Energy Research and Development Administration,
and which makes use of the government's findings from the bombing of Hiroshima and Nagasaki and from the American nuclear-test
program to describe the characteristics and the destructive effects
of nuclear explosions of all kinds; "Hiroshima and Nagasaki," a
comprehensive study, carried out by a group of distinguished Japanese scientists and published here in 1981, of the consequences of
the bombing of those two cities; "Long-Term Worldwide Effects of
Multiple Nuclear-Weapons Detonations," a report on the global
ecological consequences of a nuclear holocaust which was published
in 1975 by the National Academy of Sciences (hereafter referred to
as the N.A.S. report); a report of research conducted in 1974 and
1975 for the Department of Transportation's Climatic Impact Assessment Program on the consequences of man-made perturbances
—including the explosion of nuclear weapons—of the earth's atmosphere; and "Survival of Food Crops and Livestock in the Event of
Nuclear War," proceedings of a 1970 symposium held at Brookhaven National Laboratory, on Long Island, and sponsored by the
Office of Civil Defense, the Atomic Energy Commission, and the
Department of Agriculture, at which the effects of radiation from
fallout on both domesticated and natural ecosystems were discussed. Drawing on these and other printed sources, and also on
interviews that I conducted recently with a number of scientists, I
have attempted to piece together an account of the principal consequences of a full-scale holocaust. Such an account, which in its
nature must be both technical and gruesome, cannot be other than
hateful to dwell on, yet it may be only by descending into this hell
in imagination now that we can hope to escape descending into
it in reality at some later time. The knowledge we thus gain cannot
in itself protect us from nuclear annihilation, but without it we cannot begin to take the measures that can actually protect us—or, for
that matter, even begin to think in an appropriate way about our
plight.

5

The widespread belief that a nuclear holocaust would in some sense bring about the end of the world has been reflected in the pronouncements of both American and Soviet leaders in the years since the invention of nuclear weapons. For example, President Dwight Eisenhower wrote in a letter in 1956 that one day both sides would have to "meet at the conference table with the understanding that the era of armaments has ended, and the human race must conform its actions to this truth or die." More recently—at a press conference in 1974—Secretary of State Henry Kissinger said that "the accumulation of nuclear arms has to be constrained if mankind is not to destroy itself." And President Jimmy Carter said in his farewell address a year ago that after a nuclear holocaust "the survivors, if any, would live in despair amid the poisoned ruins of a civilization that had committed suicide." Soviet leaders have been no less categorical in their remarks. In late 1981, for example, the Soviet government printed a booklet in which it stated, "The Soviet Union holds that nuclear war would be a universal disaster, and that it would most probably mean the end of civilization. It may lead to the destruction of all mankind." In these and other statements, examples of which could be multiplied indefinitely, Soviet and American leaders have acknowledged the supreme importance of the nuclear peril. However, they have not been precise about what level of catastrophe they were speaking of, and a variety of different outcomes, including the annihilation of the belligerent nations, the destruction of "human civilization," the extinction of mankind, and the extinction of life on earth, have been mentioned, in loose rhetorical fashion, more or less interchangeably. No doubt, the leaders have been vague in part because of the difficulty of making reliable predictions about an event that has no precedent. Yet it seems important to arrive, on the basis of available information, at some judgment concerning the likelihood of these outcomes, for they are not the same. Nor, presumably, would the appropriate political response to all of them be the same. The annihilation of the belligerent nations would be a catastrophe beyond anything in history, but it would not be the end of the world. The destruction of human civilization, even without the biological destruction of

6

the human species, may perhaps rightly be called the end of the world, since it would be the end of that sum of cultural achievements and human relationships which constitutes what many people mean when they speak of "the world." The biological destruction of mankind would, of course, be the end of the world in a stricter sense. As for the destruction of all life on the planet, it would be not merely a human but a planetary end—the death of the earth. And although the annihilation of other forms of life could hardly be of concern to human beings once they themselves had been annihilated, this more comprehensive, planetary termination is nevertheless full of sorrowful meaning for us as we reflect on the possibility now, while we still exist. We not only live on the earth but also are of the earth, and the thought of its death, or even of its mutilation, touches a deep chord in our nature. Finally, it must be noted that a number of observers have, especially in recent years, denied that a holocaust would obliterate even the societies directly attacked. If this were so, then nuclear weapons, while remaining fearsome, would be qualitatively no different from other weapons of war, and the greater part of the nuclear predicament would melt away. (In the discussions of some analysts, nuclear attacks are made to sound almost beneficial. For example, one official of the Office of Civil Defense wrote a few years back that although it might be "verging on the macabre" to say so, "a nuclear war could alleviate some of the factors leading to today's ecological disturbances that are due to current high-population concentrations and heavy industrial production." According to a different, less sanguine view of things, this observation and other cheerful asides of the kind which crop up from time to time in the literature go well over the verge of the macabre.)

Anyone who inquires into the effects of a nuclear holocaust is bound to be assailed by powerful and conflicting emotions. Preëminent among these, almost certainly, will be an overwhelming revulsion at the tremendous scene of devastation, suffering, and death which is opened to view. And accompanying the revulsion there may be a sense of helplessness and defeat, brought about by an awareness of the incapacity of the human soul to take in so much

7

horror. A nuclear holocaust, widely regarded as "unthinkable" but never as undoable, appears to confront us with an action that we can perform but cannot quite conceive. Following upon these first responses, there may come a recoil, and a decision, whether conscious or unconscious, not to think any longer about the possibility of a nuclear holocaust. (Since a holocaust is a wholly prospective rather than a present calamity, the act of thinking about it is voluntary, and the choice of not thinking about it is always available.) When one tries to face the nuclear predicament, one feels sick, whereas when one pushes it out of mind, as apparently one must do most of the time in order to carry on with life, one feels well again. But this feeling of well-being is based on a denial of the most important reality of our time, and therefore is itself a kind of sickness. A society that systematically shuts its eyes to an urgent peril to its physical survival and fails to take any steps to save itself cannot be called psychologically well. In effect, whether we think about nuclear weapons or avoid thinking about them, their presence among us makes us sick, and there seems to be little of a purely mental or emotional nature that we can do about it.

A part of our quandary may lie in the fact that even a denial of the reality stems from what is, in a sense, a refusal to accept nuclear annihilation; that is, a refusal to accept even in imagination what Dr. Robert Jay Lifton, the author of pioneering studies of the psychology of the nuclear predicament, has appropriately called an "immersion in death." As such, the denial may have intermixed in it something that is valuable and worthy of respect. Like active revulsion and protest against nuclear weapons, a denial of their reality may spring—in part, at least—from a love of life, and since a love of life may ultimately be all that we have to pit against our doom, we cannot afford thoughtlessly to tear aside any of its manifestations. Because denial is a form of self-protection, if only against anguishing thoughts and feelings, and because it contains something useful, and perhaps even, in its way, necessary to life, anyone who invites people to draw aside the veil and look at the peril face to face is at risk of trespassing on inhibitions that are a part of our humanity. I

8

hope in these reflections to proceed with the utmost possible respect for all forms of refusal to accept the unnatural and horrifying prospect of a nuclear holocaust.

When men split the nucleus of the atom, they unleashed into terrestrial nature a basic energy of the cosmos—the energy latent in mass—which had never before been active in any major way on earth. Until then, this energy had been kept largely within the nucleus by a force known to physicists as the strong force, which is the glue that holds the nucleus of an atom together, and is by far the strongest of the four basic forces that determine the behavior of all matter in the universe. The strong force and what is called the weak force are chiefly responsible for the static properties of nuclei. The two others, which, being outside the nucleus, had until the explosion of nuclear weapons been responsible for virtually all life and motion on earth since the earth's formation, four and a half billion years ago, are the electromagnetic force, which is responsible for, among other things, all chemical bonds, and the gravitational force, which is a force of attraction between masses. It is largely because strong-force reactions, in which the energy in mass is released, were almost entirely excluded from terrestrial affairs (one of the few exceptions is a spontaneous nuclear chain reaction that once broke out in a West African uranium deposit) and because weak-force reactions (manifested in the decay of radioactive materials) were inconspicuous enough to go mostly unnoticed that the two great conservation laws of nineteenth-century physics —the law of the conservation of energy and the law of the conservation of mass—appeared to physicists of that time to hold true. Nineteenth-century science believed that mass and energy constituted separate, closed systems, in which the amount of each remained forever constant, no matter what transformations each might undergo. It was not until twentieth-century physicists, pursuing their investigations into the realms of the irreducibly small and the unexceedably large, examined the properties of energy, mass, time, and space in the subatomic realm and the cosmic realm that mass and energy were discovered to be interchangeable entities. The new relationship was governed by Albert Einstein's laws of relativity and by quantum theory, and these—not to go deeply into theoretical matters—can be described as general physical laws of the universe, of which the Newtonian laws proved to be limiting cases. (It is because the limits included almost all the middle-sized phenomena readily available to human inspection that the need for more encompassing laws was not felt until our century.)

Broadly speaking, Newtonian physics emerged as a human-scale or earthly-scale physics, valid for velocities and sizes commonly encountered by human senses, while relativity together with quantum theory was recognized as a universal physics, valid for all phenomena. (Something of the uncanny quality of modern physics' violation of common sense—by, for instance, the concept of "curved space"—inheres in the seemingly ungraspable, and therefore "unreal," power of nuclear weapons, whose construction is based on the new principles.) Likewise, the laws of conservation of mass and energy held, to a high degree of approximation, for most then observable earthly energies, masses, and velocities but broke down for the energies, masses, and velocities in the subatomic realm. Einstein noted, "It turned out that the inertia of a system necessarily depends on its energy content, and this led straight to the notion that inert mass is simply latent energy. The principle of the conservation of mass lost its independence and became fused with that of the conservation of energy." Of mass in its slow-moving, relatively unenergetic terrestrial state, Einstein remarked, "It is as though a man who is fabulously rich [i.e., mass] should never spend or give away a cent [i.e., of its energy]; no one could tell how rich he was," and on that ground Einstein excused his nineteenth-century predecessors for failing to notice what he called the "tremendous energy" in mass. By comparison with the forms of energy active on earth during its first four and a half billion years, the amount of energy latent in mass was indeed tremendous. The rate of conversion of mass into energy is given by Einstein's formula $E = mc^2$, or energy equals mass times the speed of light squared—a formula that has won what is, considering the fateful importance it has assumed for the survival of human life, a well-justified place in popular folklore. Since the speed of light is over a hundred and eighty-six thousand miles per second—the greatest velocity attainable by anything in the universe—the value in energy obtained from the transformation of even small quantities of mass is extremely high. For example, the amount of mass expended in the destruction of Hiroshima was about a gram—or one-thirtieth of an ounce. (The bomb itself, a complex machine, weighed four tons.) It would have required twelve thousand five hundred tons of TNT to release the same amount of energy. You might say that the energy yielded by application of the universal physics of the twentieth century exceeds the energy yielded by that of the terrestrial, or planetary, physics of the nineteenth century as the cosmos exceeds the earth. Yet it was within the earth's comparatively tiny, frail ecosphere that mankind released the newly tapped cosmic energy. In view of this scientific background, President Harry Truman was speaking to the point when, in his announcement that the United States had dropped an atomic bomb on Hiroshima, he told the world that "the basic power of the universe" had been harnessed for war by the United States, and added that "the force from which the sun draws its powers has been loosed against those who brought war to the Far East." The huge—the monstrous—disproportion between "the basic power of the universe" and the merely terrestrial creatures by which and against which it was aimed in anger defined the dread predicament that the world has tried, and failed, to come to terms with ever since.

It was fortunate for earthly life that it grew up sheltered from strong-force reactions and from the nuclear energies that they release; in fact, it is doubtful whether life could have developed at all on earth if it had somehow been conditioned by continuous strong-force reactions. These release enormous bursts of energy themselves, but they also set the stage for the protracted release of energy by the other nuclear force—the weak force—in the form of nuclear radiation. When an atomic nucleus is split, releasing energy, various unstable isotopes are produced, and these new nuclei, acting under the influence of the weak force, decay, emitting radioactivity into the environment. Most of the radioactivity that occurs naturally on earth is emitted by radioactive isotopes created in strong-force reactions that occurred before the formation of the earth—in early supernovae or at the beginning of the universe, when atoms were taking shape—and by new unstable isotopes that are the products of this radioactivity. (A smaller amount of radioactivity is being continually created by the bombardment of the earth with cosmic rays.) The original radioactive isotopes are like clocks that were wound up once and have been running down ever since. Their numbers have been decreasing as their nuclei have decayed and become stable, with each species dwindling at a precise and different rate. Left to itself, the planet's supply of radioactivity would, over billions of years, have gradually declined. But when man began to split the nuclei of atoms, in bombs and in nuclear reactors, he began to create fresh batches of radioactive materials and these, like new clocks set ticking, emitted new radiation as they also began to dwindle away toward stability. (Testing in the atmosphere was banned by treaty in 1963—France and China did not concur and have since held atmospheric tests—but before that it increased the background radiation of the earth. As a result, the present annual per-capita radiation dose in the United States is four and a half per cent above the natural background level for this country.) In general magnitude, the energy of radioactive emissions greatly overmatches the strength of the chemical bonds that hold living things together. The vulnerability to radioactivity of genetic material, in particular, is well known. It is perhaps not surprising that when cosmic energies are turned loose on a small planet overwhelming destruction is the result. Einstein was only one among many far-seeing people to express an understanding of this fundamental mismatch of strengths when he stated, in 1950, as he contemplated the likely detonation of a hydrogen—or thermonuclear—bomb (the first one was actually exploded, by the United States, in the fall of 1952), that "radioactive poisoning of the atmosphere and hence

annihilation of any life on earth has been brought within the range
of technical possibilities."

The path of scientific discovery from Einstein's formulation, in 1905,
for the conversion of mass into energy to the actual release by man
of nuclear energy—a path in which the principles of quantum mechanics had to be developed and the basic structure of matter had
to be unfolded—took several decades to travel. As late as the early
nineteen-thirties, many of the best-qualified scientists had no notion
that the nucleus of the atom could be fissioned. But in 1938 two
Austrian physicists, Lise Meitner and Otto Frisch, correctly inter-
preting the results of some earlier experiments, announced that if
uranium atoms were bombarded with neutrons they would split—
or fission—into nearly equal parts, forming new elements and releasing some of their mass as energy, the amount being calculable
by Einstein's renowned equation. The next step in obtaining usable
energy from matter would be to bring about a chain reaction of
fissioning uranium atoms, and this was undertaken in 1939 by the
United States government, first under the auspices of an Advisory
Committee on Uranium and later by the secret, multi-billion-dollar
program known as the Manhattan Project, whose aim was to build
an atomic bomb for use by the Allies in the Second World War.
When a uranium nucleus is split, it releases several neutrons at
high velocity. In a chain reaction, the neutrons released split other
nuclei, which, in turn, release other neutrons, and these neutrons
split still further nuclei, and so on—in a series that ends only when
the available material is used up or dispersed. In some substances,
such as uranium-235 or plutonium-239, a spontaneous chain reaction will start when enough of the material—a quantity known as a
critical mass—is assembled in one place. But a chain reaction does
not necessarily make a bomb. For an explosion to occur, the reaction has to go on long enough for explosive energies to build up
before the immensely rapid expansion of the fissionable material
brought about by the energy released in the chain reaction terminates the reaction. The required prolongation can be produced by

sudden compression of the fissionable material to a very high density. Then the neutrons, flying about among the more tightly packed atoms, will spawn a larger number of "generations" of fissioned nuclei before the chain reaction is halted by dispersion. Since the number of fissions increases exponentially with each new generation, a huge amount of energy is created very rapidly in the late generations of the reaction. According to Glasstone, the release of energy equivalent to one hundred thousand tons of TNT would require the creation of fifty-eight generations before the reaction ended, and ninety-nine and nine-tenths per cent of the energy would be released in the last seven generations. Since each generation would require no more than a hundred-millionth of a second, this energy would be released in less than a tenth of a millionth of a second. ("Clearly," Glasstone remarks, "most of the fission energy is released in an extremely short period.")

In a fission reaction, energy is released in an expenditure of mass. Each atom contains a balance of forces and energies. Within the nucleus, the "tremendous energy" latent in mass is kept out of general circulation by the binding action of the strong force, holding the particles of the nucleus—its protons and neutrons—together. The strong force, however, is opposed by positive electrical charges that are carried by the protons in the nucleus and tend to drive the protons apart. The nuclei of the heaviest atoms, such as uranium and plutonium, are the least tightly bound together, because they contain the largest numbers of protons and so the electrical repulsion is greatest in them. (In fact, the presence of the disintegrative pressure of the electrical force within nuclei, which increases with the number of protons, forms an upper limit to the size of nuclei; there is a point beyond which they cannot cohere for any length of time.) Because of the relative weakness of the binding force in the heaviest nuclei, they are the best for fissioning. When the nucleus of an atom of uranium-235 is struck by a neutron, the binding grip of the strong force is loosed, electrical repulsion takes over, the nucleus divides, and its fragments are driven apart with an energy of motion which, in obedience to Einstein's equation, is equal to the amount of the mass lost times the speed of light squared.

Energy can also be released by fusion, which is the basis for the hydrogen bomb. To cause fusion, nuclei must be driven against one another with such velocity that the electrical repulsion between their respective protons is overcome and the strong force can act to bind them together into new nuclei. The best nuclei for fusion are the lightest—those of hydrogen and its isotopes and the elements nearest them in mass, because, having the fewest protons, they have the smallest amount of electrical repulsion to overcome. Dr. Henry Kendall, who teaches physics at the Massachusetts Institute of Technology and guides research in particle physics there, and who, as chairman of the Union of Concerned Scientists, has for many years devoted much of his time and attention to the nuclear question in all its aspects, recently described to me what happens in a fusion reaction. "Let a small rounded depression—or 'well,' to use the proper physical term—in a level board stand for a nucleus, and let a much smaller steel ball stand for a particle," he said. "If you roll the ball along the board at the well, it will travel down one side of the well, up the other, and out again. On the other hand, if you start the ball rolling at a point partway down one side of the well, it will rise to an equal height on the other side, then return to its starting point, and, barring other influences, continue to oscillate like that forever. This is a good representation of the bound state of the particle in the nucleus. The problem of fusion is to introduce the steel ball into the well from the outside and have it remain there in the bound state instead of shooting out the other side. It can do this only by somehow *giving up* energy. In fusion, we give the name 'binding energy' to the amount that must be given up for the outside particle to become bound in the well. A good example of this loss of energy occurs in the fusion of deuterium and tritium, two isotopes of hydrogen. The tritium nucleus contains one proton and two neutrons, and the deuterium nucleus contains one proton and one neutron, for a total of five particles. In the fusion of these isotopes, four of the particles—two neutrons and two protons—hang together very tightly, and are able to swat out the remaining neutron with incredible violence, thus getting rid of the necessary amount of energy. And this is the energy that a fusion reaction releases.

Once the four other particles have done that, they can run around in their hole undisturbed. But in order for this or any fusion reaction to take place the nuclei have to be driven very close together. Only then can the strong force reach out its stubby but powerful arms in the giant handshake that fuses the nuclei together and unleashes the explosive energy of the hydrogen bomb."

Fission and fusion can occur in a great many forms, but in all of them mass is lost, the grip of the strong force is tightened on the products of the reaction, and energy is released. A typical hydrogen bomb is a four-stage device. In the first stage, a conventional explosion is set off; in the second stage, the conventional explosion initiates a fission reaction, which is, in fact, an atomic bomb; in the third stage, the heat from the atomic bomb initiates a fusion reaction; and in the fourth stage neutrons from the fusion reaction initiate additional fission, on a scale vastly greater than the first, in a surrounding blanket of fissionable material. In my conversation with Dr. Kendall, he described the explosion of an average hydrogen bomb to me in somewhat more detail. "The trigger," he said, "consists of a carefully fashioned, subcritical, spherical piece of plutonium, with a neutron-initiator device in its interior and a high-explosive jacket surrounding it. Things begin when detonators all over the sphere of the high-explosive jacket go off—as nearly simultaneously as the design permits. Now the high-explosive jacket explodes and sends a shock wave travelling inward in a shrinking concentric sphere, and gaining in force and temperature as it proceeds. When its leading edge reaches the plutonium core, there is an abrupt jump in pressure, which squeezes the plutonium in on all sides with great precision. The pressure makes the plutonium go from subcritical to supercritical. At this point, the neutron initiator fires, and the chain reaction begins. The trick is to compress the plutonium as much as possible as quickly as possible because then more generations of nuclei will be fissioned, and more energy will be released, before the explosion, in effect, blows itself out. When that happens, all the energy from the plutonium trigger will have been released, and particles whose atomic identity has been lost will be boiling and surging in an expanded sphere whose temperature exceeds stellar

16

levels. In all the universe, temperatures of equal heat are to be found only in such transient phenomena as exploding supernovae. Now the fusion—otherwise known as the thermonuclear reaction, because of the extreme heat needed to initiate it—can begin. The fusion fuels—lithium and isotopes of hydrogen—fly around with such velocity that they can simply coast right into one another, spitting out nuclear particles as they fuse. This is not a chain reaction, but again the explosion is stopped by the expansion caused by its own heat. By the time that happens, however, the last stage—the fissioning, by neutrons released both by the fission trigger and by the fusion reaction, of the surrounding blanket of material, which might be uranium-238—is under way. There is basically no limit to the size or yield of a thermonuclear weapon. The only limits on a bomb's destructive effect are the earth's capacity to absorb the blast."

Whereas most conventional bombs produce only one destructive effect—the shock wave—nuclear weapons produce many destructive effects. At the moment of the explosion, when the temperature of the weapon material, instantly gasified, is at the superstellar level, the pressure is millions of times the normal atmospheric pressure. Immediately, radiation, consisting mainly of gamma rays, which are a very high-energy form of electromagnetic radiation, begins to stream outward into the environment. This is called the "initial nuclear radiation," and is the first of the destructive effects of a nuclear explosion. In an air burst of a one-megaton bomb—a bomb with the explosive yield of a million tons of TNT, which is a medium-sized weapon in present-day nuclear arsenals—the initial nuclear radiation can kill unprotected human beings in an area of some six square miles. Virtually simultaneously with the initial nuclear radiation, in a second destructive effect of the explosion, an electromagnetic pulse is generated by the intense gamma radiation acting on the air. In a high-altitude detonation, the pulse can knock out electrical equipment over a wide area by inducing a powerful surge of voltage through various conductors, such as antennas, overhead power lines, pipes, and railroad tracks. The Defense Department's Civil Preparedness Agency reported in 1977 that a single multi-kiloton nuclear weapon detonated one hundred and twenty-five miles over Omaha, Nebraska, could generate an electromagnetic pulse strong enough to damage solid-state electrical circuits throughout the entire continental United States and in parts of Canada and Mexico, and thus threaten to bring the economies of these countries to a halt. When the fusion and fission reactions have blown themselves out, a fireball takes shape. As it expands, energy is absorbed in the form of X rays by the surrounding air, and then the air re-radiates a portion of that energy into the environment in the form of the thermal pulse—a wave of blinding light and intense heat—which is the third of the destructive effects of a nuclear explosion. (If the burst is low enough, the fireball touches the ground, vaporizing or incinerating almost everything within it.) The thermal pulse of a one-megaton bomb lasts for about ten seconds and can cause second-degree burns in exposed human beings at a distance of nine and a half miles, or in an area of more than two hundred and eighty square miles, and that of a twenty-megaton bomb (a large weapon by modern standards) lasts for about twenty seconds and can produce the same consequences at a distance of twenty-eight miles, or in an area of two thousand four hundred and sixty square miles. As the fireball expands, it also sends out a blast wave in all directions, and this is the fourth destructive effect of the explosion. The blast wave of an air-burst one-megaton bomb can flatten or severely damage all but the strongest buildings within a radius of four and a half miles, and that of a twenty-megaton bomb can do the same within a radius of twelve miles. As the fireball burns, it rises, condensing water from the surrounding atmosphere to form the characteristic mushroom cloud. If the bomb has been set off on the ground or close enough to it so that the fireball touches the surface, in a so-called ground burst, a crater will be formed, and tons of dust and debris will be fused with the intensely radioactive fission products and sucked up into the mushroom cloud. This mixture will return to earth as radioactive fallout, most of it in the form of fine ash, in the fifth destructive effect of the explosion. Depending upon the composition of the surface, from forty to seventy per cent of this fallout—often called the "early" or "local" fallout—descends to earth within about a day of the explosion, in the vicinity of the blast and downwind from it, exposing human beings to radiation disease, an illness that is fatal when exposure is intense. Air bursts may also produce local fallout, but in much smaller quantities. The lethal range of the local fallout depends on a number of circumstances, including the weather, but under average conditions a one-megaton ground burst would, according to the report by the Office of Technology Assessment, lethally contaminate over a thousand square miles. (A lethal dose, by convention, is considered to be the amount of radiation that, if delivered over a short period of time, would kill half the able-bodied young adult population.)

The initial nuclear radiation, the electromagnetic pulse, the thermal pulse, the blast wave, and the local fallout may be described as the local primary effects of nuclear weapons. Naturally, when many bombs are exploded the scope of these effects is increased accordingly. But in addition these primary effects produce innumerable secondary effects on societies and natural environments, some of which may be even more harmful than the primary ones. To give just one example, nuclear weapons, by flattening and setting fire to huge, heavily built-up areas, generate mass fires, and in some cases these may kill more people than the original thermal pulses and blast waves. Moreover, there are—quite distinct from both the local primary effects of individual bombs and their secondary effects—global primary effects, which do not become significant unless thousands of bombs are detonated all around the earth. And these global primary effects produce innumerable secondary effects of their own throughout the ecosystem of the earth as a whole. For a full-scale holocaust is more than the sum of its local parts; it is also a powerful direct blow to the ecosphere. In that sense, a holocaust is to the earth what a single bomb is to a city. Three grave direct global effects have been discovered so far. The first is the "delayed," or "worldwide," fallout. In detonations greater than one hundred kilotons, part of the fallout does not fall to the ground in the vicinity of the explosion but rises high into the troposphere and into the stratosphere, circulates around the earth, and then, over months or years, descends, contaminating the whole surface of the globe—although with doses of radiation far weaker than those delivered by the local fallout. Nuclear-fission products comprise some three hundred radioactive isotopes, and though some of them decay to relatively harmless levels of radioactivity within a few hours, minutes, or even seconds, others persist to emit radiation for up to millions of years. The short-lived isotopes are the ones most responsible for the lethal effects of the local fallout, and the long-lived ones are responsible for the contamination of the earth by stratospheric fallout. The energy released by all fallout from a thermonuclear explosion is about five per cent of the total. By convention, this energy is not calculated in the stated yield of a weapon, yet in a ten-thousand-megaton attack the equivalent of five hundred megatons of explosive energy, or forty thousand times the yield of the Hiroshima bomb, would be released in the form of radioactivity. This release may be considered a protracted afterburst, which is dispersed into the land, air, and sea, and into the tissues, bones, roots, stems, and leaves of living things, and goes on detonating there almost indefinitely after the explosion. The second of the global effects that have been discovered so far is the lofting, from ground bursts, of millions of tons of dust into the stratosphere; this is likely to produce general cooling of the earth's surface. The third of the global effects is a predicted partial destruction of the layer of ozone that surrounds the entire earth in the stratosphere. A nuclear fireball, by burning nitrogen in the air, produces large quantities of oxides of nitrogen. These are carried by the heat of the blast into the stratosphere, where, through a series of chemical reactions, they bring about a depletion of the ozone layer. Such a depletion may persist for years. The 1975 N.A.S. report has estimated that in a holocaust in which ten thousand megatons were detonated in the Northern Hemisphere the reduction of ozone in this hemisphere could be as high as seventy per cent and in the Southern Hemisphere as high as forty per cent, and that it could take as long as thirty years for the ozone level to return to normal. The ozone layer is crucial to life on earth, because it shields the surface of the earth from lethal levels of ultraviolet radiation, which is present in sunlight. Glasstone remarks simply, "If it were not for the absorption of much of the solar ultraviolet radiation by the ozone, life as currently known could not exist except possibly in the ocean." Without the ozone shield, sunlight, the life-giver, would become a life-extinguisher. In judging the global effects of a holocaust, therefore, the primary question is not how many people would be irradiated, burned, or crushed to death by the immediate effects of the bombs but how well the ecosphere, regarded as a single living entity, on which all forms of life depend for their continued existence, would hold up. The issue is the habitability of the earth, and it is in this context, not in the context of the direct slaughter of hundreds of millions of people by the local effects, that the question of human survival arises.

Usually, people wait for things to occur before trying to describe them. (Futurology has never been a very respectable field of inquiry.) But since we cannot afford under any circumstances to let a holocaust occur, we are forced in this one case to become the historians of the future—to chronicle and commit to memory an event that we have never experienced and must never experience. This unique endeavor, in which foresight is asked to perform a task usually reserved for hindsight, raises a host of special difficulties. There is a categorical difference, often overlooked, between trying to describe an event that has already happened (whether it is Napoleon's invasion of Russia or the pollution of the environment by acid rain) and trying to describe one that has yet to happen— and one, in addition, for which there is no precedent, or even near-precedent, in history. Lacking experience to guide our thoughts and impress itself on our feelings, we resort to speculation. But speculation, however brilliantly it may be carried out, is at best only a poor substitute for experience. Experience gives us facts, whereas in pure speculation we are thrown back on theory, which has never been a very reliable guide to future events. Moreover, experience engraves its lessons in our hearts through suffering and the other consequences that it has for our lives; but speculation leaves our lives untouched, and so gives us leeway to reject its conclusions, no matter how well argued they may be. (In the world of strategic theory, in particular, where strategists labor to simulate actual situations on the far side of the nuclear abyss, so that generals and statesmen can prepare to make their decisions in case the worst happens, there is sometimes an unfortunate tendency to mistake pure ratiocination for reality, and to pretend to a knowledge of the future that it is not given to human beings to have.) Our knowledge of the local primary effects of the bombs, which is based both on the physical principles that made their construction possible and on experience gathered from the bombings of Hiroshima and Nagasaki and from testing, is quite solid. And our knowledge of the extent of the local primary effects of many weapons used together, which is obtained simply by using the multiplication table, is also solid: knowing that the thermal pulse of a twenty-megaton bomb can give people at least second-degree burns in an area of two thousand four hundred and sixty square miles, we can easily figure out that the pulses of a hundred twenty-megaton bombs can give people at least second-degree burns in an area of two hundred and forty-six thousand square miles. Nevertheless, it may be that our knowledge even of the primary effects is still incomplete, for during our test program new ones kept being discovered. One example is the electromagnetic pulse, whose importance was not recognized until around 1960, when, after more than a decade of tests, scientists realized that this effect accounted for unexpected electrical failures that had been occurring all along in equipment around the test sites. And it is only in recent years that the Defense Department has been trying to take account strategically of this startling capacity of just one bomb to put the technical equipment of a whole continent out of action.

When we proceed from the local effects of single explosions to the effects of thousands of them on societies and environments, the picture clouds considerably, because then we go beyond both the certainties of physics and our slender base of experience, and speculatively encounter the full complexity of human affairs and of the biosphere. Looked at in its entirety, a nuclear holocaust can be said to assail human life at three levels: the level of individual life, the level of human society, and the level of the natural environment— including the environment of the earth as a whole. At none of these levels can the destructiveness of nuclear weapons be measured in terms of firepower alone. At each level, life has both considerable recuperative powers, which might restore it even after devastating injury, and points of exceptional vulnerability, which leave it open to sudden, wholesale, and permanent collapse, even when comparatively little violence has been applied. Just as a machine may break down if one small part is removed, and a person may die if a single artery or vein is blocked, a modern technological society may come to a standstill if its fuel supply is cut off, and an ecosystem may collapse if its ozone shield is depleted. Nuclear weapons thus do not only kill directly, with their tremendous violence, but also kill indirectly, by breaking down the man-made and the natural systems on which individual lives collectively depend. Human beings require constant provision and care, supplied both by their societies and by the natural environment, and if these are suddenly removed people will die just as surely as if they had been struck by a bullet. Nuclear weapons are unique in that they attack the support systems of life at every level. And these systems, of course, are not isolated from each other but are parts of a single whole: ecological collapse, if it goes far enough, will bring about social collapse, and social collapse will bring about individual deaths. Furthermore, the destructive consequences of a nuclear attack are immeasurably compounded by the likelihood that all or most of the bombs will be detonated within the space of a few hours, in a single huge concussion. Normally, a locality devastated by a catastrophe, whether natural or man-made, will sooner or later receive help from untouched outside areas, as Hiroshima and Nagasaki did after they were bombed; but a nuclear holocaust would devastate the "outside" areas as well, leaving the victims to fend for themselves in a shattered society and natural environment. And what is true for each city is also true for the earth as a whole: a devastated earth can hardly expect "outside" help. The earth is the largest of the support systems for life, and the impairment of the earth is the largest of the perils posed by nuclear weapons.

The incredible complexity of all these effects, acting, interacting, and interacting again, precludes confident detailed representation of the events in a holocaust. We deal inevitably with approximations, probabilities, even guesses. However, it is important to point out that our uncertainty pertains not to *whether* the effects will interact, multiplying their destructive power as they do so, but only to *how*. It follows that our almost built-in bias, determined by the limitations of the human mind in judging future events, is to underestimate the harm. To fear interactive consequences that we cannot predict, or even imagine, may not be impossible, but it is very difficult. Let us consider, for example, some of the possible ways in which a person in a targeted country might die. He might be incinerated by the fireball or the thermal pulse. He might be lethally irradiated by the initial nuclear radiation. He might be crushed to death or hurled to his death by the blast wave or its debris. He might be lethally irradiated by the local fallout. He might be burned to death in a firestorm. He might be injured by one or another of these effects and then die of his wounds before he was able to make his way out of the devastated zone in which he found himself. He might die of starvation, because the economy had collapsed and no food was being grown or delivered, or because existing local crops had been killed by radiation, or because the local ecosystem had been ruined, or because the ecosphere of the earth as a whole was collapsing. He might die of cold, for lack of heat and clothing, or of exposure, for lack of shelter. He might be killed by people seeking food or shelter that he had obtained. He might die of an illness spread in an epidemic. He might be killed by exposure to the sun if he stayed outside too long following serious ozone depletion. Or he might be killed by any combination of these perils. But while there is almost no end to the ways to die in and after a holocaust, each person has only one life to lose: someone who has been killed by the thermal pulse can't be killed again in an epidemic. Therefore, anyone who wishes to describe a holocaust is always at risk of depicting scenes of devastation that in reality would never take place, because the people in them would already have been killed off in some earlier scene of devastation. The task is made all the more confusing by the fact that causes of death and destruction do not exist side by side in the world but often encompass one another, in widening rings. Thus, if it turned out that a holocaust rendered the earth uninhabitable by human beings, then all the more immediate forms of death would be nothing more than redundant preliminaries, leading up to the extinction of the whole species by a hostile environment. Or if a continental ecosystem was so thoroughly destroyed by a direct attack that it could no longer sustain a significant human population, the more immediate causes of death would again decline in importance. In much the same way, if an airplane is hit by gunfire, and thereby caused to crash, dooming all the passengers, it makes little difference whether the shots also killed a few of the passengers in advance of the crash. On the other hand, if the larger consequences, which are less predictable than the local ones, failed to occur, then the local ones would have their full importance again.

Faced with uncertainties of this kind, some analysts of nuclear destruction have resorted to fiction, assigning to the imagination the work that investigation is unable to do. But then the results are just what one would expect: fiction. An approach more appropriate to our intellectual circumstances would be to acknowledge a high degree of uncertainty as an intrinsic and extremely important part of dealing with a possible holocaust. A nuclear holocaust is an event that is obscure because it is future, and uncertainty, while it has to be recognized in all calculations of future events, has a special place in calculations of a nuclear holocaust, because a holocaust is something that we aspire to keep in the future forever, and never to permit into the present. You might say that uncertainty, like the thermal pulses or the blast waves, is one of the features of a holocaust. Our procedure, then, should be not to insist on a precision that is beyond our grasp but to inquire into the rough probabilities of various results insofar as we can judge them, and then to ask ourselves what our political responsibilities are in the light of these probabilities. This embrace of investigative modesty—this acceptance of our limited ability to predict the consequences of a holocaust—would itself be a token of our reluctance to extinguish ourselves.

There are two further aspects of a holocaust which, though

25

they do not further obscure the factual picture, nevertheless vex our understanding of this event. The first is that although in imagination we can try to survey the whole prospective scene of destruction, inquiring into how many would live and how many would die and how far the collapse of the environment would go under attacks of different sizes, and piling up statistics on how many square miles would be lethally contaminated, or what percentage of the population would receive first-, second-, or third-degree burns, or be trapped in the rubble of its burning houses, or be irradiated to death, no one actually experiencing a holocaust would have any such overview. The news of other parts necessary to put together that picture would be one of the things that were immediately lost, and each surviving person, his vision drastically foreshortened by the collapse of his world, and his impressions clouded by his pain, shock, bewilderment, and grief, would see only as far as whatever scene of chaos and agony happened to lie at hand. For it would not be only such abstractions as "industry" and "society" and "the environment" that would be destroyed in a nuclear holocaust; it would also be, over and over again, the small collections of cherished things, known landscapes, and beloved people that made up the immediate contents of individual lives.

The other obstacle to our understanding is that when we strain to picture what the scene would be like after a holocaust we tend to forget that for most people, and perhaps for all, it wouldn't be *like* anything, because they would be dead. To depict the scene as it would appear to the living is to that extent a falsification, and the greater the number killed, the greater the falsification. The right vantage point from which to view a holocaust is that of a corpse, but from that vantage point, of course, there is nothing to report.

The specific train of events that might lead up to an attack is, obviously, among the unpredictables, but a few general possibilities can be outlined. One would be a wholly accidental attack, triggered by human error or mechanical failure. On three occasions in the last couple of years, American nuclear forces were placed on the early stages of alert: twice because of the malfunctioning of a computer chip in the North American Air Defense Command's warning system, and once when a test tape depicting a missile attack was inadvertently inserted in the system. The greatest danger in computer-generated misinformation and other mechanical errors may be that one error might start a chain reaction of escalating responses between command centers, leading, eventually, to an attack. If in the midst of a crisis Country A was misled by its computers into thinking that Country B was getting ready to attack, and went on alert, Country B might notice this and go on alert in response. Then Country A, observing the now indubitably real alert of Country B, might conclude that its computers had been right after all, and increase its alert. This move would then be noticed by Country B, which would, in turn, increase its alert, and so on, until either the mistake was straightened out or an attack was launched. A holocaust might also be touched off by conventional or nuclear hostilities between smaller powers, which could draw in the superpowers. Another possibility would be a deliberate, unprovoked preëmptive strike by one side against the other. Most observers regard an attack of this kind as exceedingly unlikely in either direction, but the logic of present nuclear strategy drives both sides to prepare to respond to one, for the central tenet of nuclear strategy is that each side will refrain from launching an all-out first strike against the other only if it knows that even after it has done so the other side will retain forces sufficient to launch an utterly devastating counterblow. What is more likely, in the opinion of many, is a preëmptive strike launched in the midst of an international crisis. Neither quite planned (in the sense of being a cold-blooded, premeditated strike, out of the blue) nor quite accidental (in the sense of being caused by technical failure), such an attack would be precipitated by a combination on one side or both sides of belligerency, reckless actions, miscalculation, and fear of a first strike by the other side. Each side's possible fear of a first strike by the other side has become an element of increasing danger in recent years. Modern weapons, such as the Soviet SS-18 and SS-19 and the improved American Minuteman III missile and planned MX missile, have a greatly increased ability to destroy enemy missiles in their silos, thus adding to the incentive on both sides to strike first. The peril is that in a crisis either side, fearful of losing the preëmptive advantage, would go ahead and order a first strike.

It was during an international crisis—the Cuban missile crisis, in 1962—that the world apparently came as close as it has yet come to a nuclear holocaust. On that occasion, and perhaps on that occasion alone, a dread of nuclear doom became palpable not only in the councils of power but among ordinary people around the world. At the height of the crisis, it is reported, President John Kennedy believed that the odds on the occurrence of a holocaust were between one out of three and even. In the memoir "Thirteen Days," Robert Kennedy, the President's brother, who was Attorney General at the time, and who advised the President in the crisis, offered a recollection of the moments of greatest peril. President Kennedy had ordered a blockade of all shipping to Cuba, where, American intelligence had found, the Soviet Union was emplacing missiles capable of carrying nuclear warheads. Missile crews in the United States had been placed on maximum alert. Now, at a few minutes after ten o'clock on the morning of October 24th, two Russian ships, accompanied by a Russian submarine, had approached to within a few miles of the blockade. Robert Kennedy wrote in his memoir:

I think these few minutes were the time of gravest concern for the President. Was the world on the brink of a holocaust? Was it our error? A mistake? Was there something further that should have been done? Or not done? His hand went up to his face and covered his mouth. He opened and closed his fist. His face seemed drawn, his eyes pained, almost gray. We stared at each other across the table. For a few fleeting seconds, it was almost as though no one else was there and he was no longer the President.

Inexplicably, I thought of when he was ill and almost died; when he lost his child; when we learned that our oldest brother had been killed; of personal times of strain and

hurt. . . . We had come to the time of final decision. . . .
I felt we were on the edge of a precipice with no way off.
This time, the moment was now—not next week—not tomorrow, "so we can have another meeting and decide";
not in eight hours, "so we can send another message to
Khrushchev and perhaps he will finally understand." No,
none of that was possible. One thousand miles away in the
vast expanse of the Atlantic Ocean the final decisions were
going to be made in the next few minutes. President Kennedy had initiated the course of events, but he no longer
had control over them.

Any number of future crises that would lead to an attack can be
pictured, but I would like to mention one possible category that
seems particularly dangerous. In the theory of nuclear deterrence,
each side would ideally deter attacks at every level of violence
with a deterrent force at the same level. Thus, conventional attacks
would be deterred with conventional forces, tactical attacks would
be deterred with tactical forces, and strategic attacks would be
deterred with strategic forces. The theoretical advantage of match-
ing forces in this fashion would be that the opening moves in hypothetical hostilities would not automatically lead to escalation—for
example, by leading the side weaker in conventional forces to respond to a conventional attack with nuclear weapons. However,
the facts of geography make such ideal deterrent symmetry impracticable. The Soviet Union's proximity both to Western Europe and
to the Middle East gives it a heavy conventional preponderance in
those parts of the world. Therefore, throughout the postwar period
it has been American policy to deter a Soviet conventional attack
in Europe with tactical nuclear arms. And in January of 1980 President Carter, in effect, extended the policy to include protection of
the nations around the Persian Gulf. In his State of the Union
address for 1980, Carter said, "An attempt by any outside force to
gain control of the Persian Gulf region will be regarded as an assault
on the vital interests of the United States of America. And such an
assault will be repelled by any means necessary, including military

force." Since the United States clearly lacked the conventional power to repel a Soviet attack in a region near the borders of the Soviet Union, "any means" could refer to nothing but nuclear arms. The threat was spelled out explicitly shortly after the speech, in a story in the New York *Times*—thought to be a leak from the Administration—about a 1979 Defense Department "study," which, according to the *Times,* said that American conventional forces could not stop a Soviet thrust into northern Iran, and that "to prevail in an Iranian scenario, we might have to threaten or make use of tactical nuclear weapons." The words of this study put the world on notice that the use of nuclear arms not only was contemplated in past crises but will continue to be contemplated in future ones.

It is possible to picture a nuclear attack of any shape or size. An attack might use all the weapons at the attacker's disposal or any portion of them. It might be aimed at military targets, at industry, at the population, or at all or some combination of these. The attack might be mainly air-burst, and would increase the range of severe damage from the blast waves, or it might be mainly ground-burst, to destroy hard targets such as land-based nuclear missiles or command-and-control centers, or to deliver the largest possible amount of fallout, or it might combine air bursts and ground bursts in any proportion. It could be launched in the daytime or at night, in summer or in winter, with warning or without warning. The sequence of events once hostilities had begun also lies open. For example, it seems quite possible that the leaders of a nation that had just suffered a nuclear attack would be sparing in their response, tailoring it to political objectives rather than to the vengeful aim of wiping out the society whose leaders had launched the attack. On the other hand, they might retaliate with all the forces at their disposal, as they say they will do. Then again, the two sides might expend their forces gradually, in a series of ad-hoc "exchanges," launched in an atmosphere of misinformation and intellectual and moral disorientation. The state of mind of the decision-makers might be one of calm rationality, of hatred, of shock, of hysteria, or even of outright insanity. They might follow coldly reasoned scenarios of destruction to the letter, and exterminate one another in that way. Or, for all we are able to know now, having at first hardened their "resolve" to follow the scenarios through to the end, they might suddenly reverse themselves, and proceed to the negotiating table after only incompletely destroying one another. Lacking any experience of what decisions human beings make under full-scale nuclear attack, we simply do not know what they would do.

Not surprisingly, predictions of the course of an attack are subject to intellectual fashion (there being nothing in the way of experience to guide them). In the nineteen-sixties, for example, it was widely believed that the most important attack to deter was an all-out one, but in the last few years the idea that a "limited nuclear war" might be fought has come into vogue. (The concept of limited nuclear war also had an earlier vogue, in the late nineteen-fifties, when some strategists were seeking an alternative to Secretary of State John Foster Dulles's strategy of "massive retaliation.") The premise of the limited-war theory is that nuclear hostilities can be halted at some new equilibrium in the balance of forces, before all-out attacks have been launched. In particular, it has been argued recently by nuclear theorists that the Soviet Union is now able to launch a devastating first strike at American bombers and land-based missiles, leaving the United States in the unfavorable position of having to choose between using its less accurate submarine-based missiles to directly attack Soviet society—and thus risk a direct attack on its own society in return—and doing nothing. Rather than initiate the annihilation of both societies, it is argued, American leaders might acquiesce in the Soviet first strike. But there is something dreamlike and fantastic in this concept of a wholly one-way nuclear strike, which, while leaving intact the power of the assaulted country to devastate the society of the aggressor, would somehow allow the aggressor to dictate terms. What seems to have been forgotten is that, unless one assumes that the adversary has gone insane (in which case not even the most foolproof scenarios can save us), military actions are taken with some aim in mind— for example, the aim of conquering a particular territory. This imagined first strike would in itself achieve nothing, and the moment the Soviet Union might try to achieve some actual advantage—for example, by marching into the Middle East to seize its· oil fields—two or three nuclear weapons from among the thousands remaining in American arsenals would suffice to put a quick end to the undertaking. Or if the United States retaliated with only ten bombs on Soviet cities, holding back the rest, the Soviet Union would suffer unprecedented losses while gaining nothing. In other words, in this scenario—and, indeed, in any number of other scenarios for "limited nuclear war" which could be mentioned—strategic theory seems to have taken on a weird life of its own, in which the weapons are pictured as having their own quarrel to settle, irrespective of mere human purposes. In general, in the theoretically sophisticated but often humanly deficient world of nuclear strategic theory it is likely to be overlooked that the outbreak of nuclear hostilities in itself assumes the collapse of every usual restraint of reason and humanity. Once the mass killing of a nuclear holocaust had begun, the scruples, and even the reckonings of self-interest, that normally keep the actions of nations within certain bounds would by definition have been trampled down, and would probably offer little further protection for anybody. In the unimaginable mental and spiritual climate of the world at that point it is hard to imagine what force could be counted on to hold the world back from all-out destruction.

However, it would be misleading to suggest that once one nuclear weapon had been used it would be inevitable for all of them to be used. Rather, the point is that once a catastrophe that we now find "unthinkable" actually commenced, people would act in ways that are unforeseeable by theorists—or, for that matter, by the future actors themselves. Predictions about the size and form of a nuclear holocaust are really predictions about human decisions, and these are notoriously incalculable in advance—especially when the decisions in question are going to be made in the midst of unimaginable mayhem. Secretary of Defense Robert McNamara probably said the last word on this subject when he remarked before the House Armed Services Committee in 1963, in regard to a possible defense of Europe, that once the first tactical nuclear weapon had been used the world would have been launched into "a vast unknown." Therefore, in picturing a Soviet attack on the United States I shall not venture any predictions concerning the shape and size of the attack, since to do so, it seems to me, would be to pretend to a kind of knowledge that we are incapable of. Instead, I shall simply choose two basic assumptions—using the word to mean not predictions but postulates. The first assumption is that most of the Soviet strategic forces are used in the attack, and the second is that the attack is aimed at military facilities, industry, and the population centers of the United States. I have chosen these assumptions not because I "predict" an attack of this kind, which is the most damaging of the attacks that appear to have a likely chance of occurring, but because, in the absence of any basis for confident prediction, and, in particular, of any reliable assurance that an attack would remain "limited," they are the only assumptions that represent the full measure of our peril. At the very least, they are not farfetched. The first assumption is supported by many statements by leaders on both sides. The Soviet government, which, of course, is one of the actors concerned, has frequently stated the view that nuclear hostilities cannot be limited, and Secretary of Defense Harold Brown also said, in 1977, that a nuclear conflict probably could not be limited. Concerning the second assumption, the significant point is that the fundamental logic of the strategy of both sides is, in McNamara's words, to hold not just the military forces of the other side hostage but also its "society as a whole." Just how the strategists on both sides achieve this is unknown, but it seems unwarranted to suppose that there will be much relief for either population in the merciful sentiments of targeters.

A further set of assumptions that influence one's judgment of the consequences of a holocaust concerns the possibility of civil defense. These assumptions also depend in part on certain circumstances that are unknowable in advance, such as whether the attack occurs in the daytime or at night, but they also depend on circumstances that are more or less built into the situation, and can therefore be predicted. The two main components of a conceivable civil defense against nuclear attack are evacuation and sheltering. In a protracted crisis, a country might seek to protect its population by evacuating its cities and towns before any attack had actually been launched; but, for a variety of reasons, such a strategy seems impracticable or useless. To begin with, an enemy that was bent on attacking one's population might retarget its missiles against people in the places to which they had fled. Also, during the days of evacuation people would be more vulnerable to attack than they were even in their cities. (Probably the worst assumption regarding evacuation would be that the attack came while evacuation was under way.) A further disadvantage of a policy of evacuation is that it would offer the foe a means of utterly disrupting the society by threats alone, since an evacuated society would be one that had stopped functioning for any other purpose. Shelters appear to be no more promising than evacuation. The Soviet missiles closest to the United States, which are stationed on submarines several hundred miles from our shores, can deliver their warheads on coastal targets about ten minutes after they are fired, and on inland targets a few minutes later. The intercontinental ballistic missiles, which are all launched from within the Soviet Union, would arrive fifteen or twenty minutes after that. The bombers would arrive in several hours. But, according to the Arms Control and Disarmament Agency, it requires fifteen minutes after missiles have been launched for the earliest warnings to be given to the population. Even assuming—very optimistically, I think—that it would take only another fifteen minutes or so for any significant number of people to become aware of the warnings and go to shelters, a surprise attack would indeed catch the great majority of people by surprise.

For most people, however, the lack of any opportunity to proceed to shelters would be without importance in any case, since shelters, even if they existed, would be of no use. It is now commonly acknowledged that economically feasible shelters cannot provide protection against the blast, heat, intense radiation, and mass fires that would probably occur in densely populated regions of the country—that such shelters could save lives only in places that were subjected to nothing worse than modest amounts of fallout. Furthermore, there is a very serious question whether many people would survive in the long run even if they did manage to save themselves in the short run by sealing themselves up in shelters for several weeks or months. Finally, it seems worth mentioning that, whatever the potential value of shelters might be, most existing ones either are situated in places where they are useless (in large cities, for example) or lack some or all of the following necessary equipment for an effective shelter: adequate shielding from radiation; air filters that would screen out radioactive particles; food and water to last as long as several months; an independent heating system, in places where winters are severe; medical supplies for the injured, sick, and dying, who might be in the majority in the shelters; radiation counters to measure levels of radiation outdoors, so that people could know when it was safe to leave the shelter and could determine whether food and drink were contaminated; and a burial system wholly contained within the shelter, in which to bury those who died of their injuries or illness during the shelter period.

Systems setting up evacuation procedures and shelters are often presented as humanitarian measures that would save lives in the event of a nuclear attack. In the last analysis, however, the civil-defense issue is a strategic, not a humanitarian, question. It is fundamental to the nuclear strategy of both the Soviet Union and the United States that each preserve the capacity to devastate the population of the other after itself absorbing the largest first strike that is within the other's capacity. Therefore, any serious attempt by either side to make its population safe from nuclear attack—assuming for the moment that this could be done—would be extremely likely to call forth a strategic countermove by the other side, probably taking the form of increased armament. Since the extraordinary power of modern weapons makes such compensation quite easy, it is safe to assume that for the foreseeable future the population of each side is going to remain exactly as vulnerable as the other side wants it to be.

The yardsticks by which one can measure the destruction that will be caused by weapons of different sizes are provided by the bombings of Hiroshima and Nagasaki and American nuclear tests in which the effects of hydrogen bombs with up to sixteen hundred times the explosive yield of the Hiroshima bomb were determined. The data gathered from these experiences make it a straightforward matter to work out the distances from the explosion at which different intensities of the various effects of a bomb are likely to occur. In the back of the Glasstone book, the reader will find a small dial computer that places all this information at his fingertips. Thus, if one would like to know how deep a crater a twenty-megaton ground burst will leave in wet soil one has only to set a pointer at twenty megatons and look in a small window showing crater size to find that the depth would be six hundred feet—a hole deep enough to bury a fair-sized skyscraper. Yet this small circular computer, on which the downfall of every city on earth is distilled into a few lines and figures, can, of course, tell us nothing of the human reality of nuclear destruction. Part of the horror of thinking about a holocaust lies in the fact that it leads us to supplant the human world with a statistical world; we seek a human truth and come up with a handful of figures. The only source that gives us a glimpse of that human truth is the testimony of the survivors of the Hiroshima and Nagasaki bombings. Because the bombing of Hiroshima has been more thoroughly investigated than the bombing of Nagasaki, and therefore more information about it is available, I shall restrict myself to a brief description of that catastrophe.

On August 6, 1945, at 8:16 A.M., a fission bomb with a yield of twelve and a half kilotons was detonated about nineteen hundred feet above the central section of Hiroshima. By present-day standards, the bomb was a small one, and in today's arsenals it would be classed among the merely tactical weapons. Nevertheless, it was

A Republic of Insects and Grass

large enough to transform a city of some three hundred and forty thousand people into hell in the space of a few seconds. "It is no exaggeration," the authors of "Hiroshima and Nagasaki" tell us, "to say that the whole city was ruined instantaneously." In that instant, tens of thousands of people were burned, blasted, and crushed to death. Other tens of thousands suffered injuries of every description or were doomed to die of radiation sickness. The center of the city was flattened, and every part of the city was damaged. The trunks of bamboo trees as far away as five miles from ground zero— the point on the ground directly under the center of the explosion— were charred. Almost half the trees within a mile and a quarter were knocked down. Windows nearly seventeen miles away were broken. Half an hour after the blast, fires set by the thermal pulse and by the collapse of the buildings began to coalesce into a firestorm, which lasted for six hours. Starting about 9 A.M. and lasting until late afternoon, a "black rain" generated by the bomb (otherwise, the day was fair) fell on the western portions of the city, carrying radioactive fallout from the blast to the ground. For four hours at midday, a violent whirlwind, born of the strange meteorological conditions produced by the explosion, further devastated the city. The number of people who were killed outright or who died of their injuries over the next three months is estimated to be a hundred and thirty thousand. Sixty-eight per cent of the buildings in the city were either completely destroyed or damaged beyond repair, and the center of the city was turned into a flat, rubble-strewn plain dotted with the ruins of a few of the sturdier buildings.

In the minutes after the detonation, the day grew dark, as heavy clouds of dust and smoke filled the air. A whole city had fallen in a moment, and in and under its ruins were its people. Among those still living, most were injured, and of these most were burned or had in some way been battered or had suffered both kinds of injury. Those within a mile and a quarter of ground zero had also been subjected to intense nuclear radiation, often in lethal doses. When people revived enough from their unconsciousness or shock to see what was happening around them, they found that where a second before there had been a city getting ready to go

37

about its daily business on a peaceful, warm August morning, now there was a heap of debris and corpses and a stunned mass of injured humanity. But at first, as they awakened and tried to find their bearings in the gathering darkness, many felt cut off and alone. In a recent volume of recollections by survivors called "Unforgettable Fire," in which the effects of the bombing are rendered in drawings as well as in words, Mrs. Haruko Ogasawara, a young girl on that August morning, recalls that she was at first knocked unconscious. She goes on to write:

> How many seconds or minutes had passed I could not tell, but, regaining consciousness, I found myself lying on the ground covered with pieces of wood. When I stood up in a frantic effort to look around, there was darkness. Terribly frightened, I thought I was alone in a world of death, and groped for any light. My fear was so great I did not think anyone would truly understand. When I came to my senses, I found my clothes in shreds, and I was without my wooden sandals.

Soon cries of pain and cries for help from the wounded filled the air. Survivors heard the voices of their families and their friends calling out in the gloom. Mrs. Ogasawara writes:

> Suddenly, I wondered what had happened to my mother and sister. My mother was then forty-five, and my sister five years old. When the darkness began to fade, I found that there was nothing around me. My house, the next door neighbor's house, and the next had all vanished. I was standing amid the ruins of my house. No one was around. It was quiet, very quiet—an eerie moment. I discovered my mother in a water tank. She had fainted. Crying out, "Mama, Mama," I shook her to bring her back to her senses. After coming to, my mother began to shout madly for my sister: "Eiko! Eiko!"
>
> I wondered how much time had passed when there were cries of searchers. Children were calling their parents' names, and parents were calling the names of their chil-

dren. We were calling desperately for my sister and listening for her voice and looking to see her. Suddenly, Mother cried "Oh Eiko!" Four or five meters away, my sister's head was sticking out and was calling my mother. . . . Mother and I worked desperately to remove the plaster and pillars and pulled her out with great effort. Her body had turned purple from the bruises, and her arm was so badly wounded that we could have placed two fingers in the wound.

Others were less fortunate in their searches and rescue attempts. In "Unforgettable Fire," a housewife describes a scene she saw:

A mother, driven half-mad while looking for her child, was calling his name. At last she found him. His head looked like a boiled octopus. His eyes were half-closed, and his mouth was white, pursed, and swollen.

Throughout the city, parents were discovering their wounded or dead children, and children were discovering their wounded or dead parents. Kikuno Segawa recalls seeing a little girl with her dead mother:

A woman who looked like an expectant mother was dead. At her side, a girl of about three years of age brought some water in an empty can she had found. She was trying to let her mother drink from it.

The sight of people in extremities of suffering was ubiquitous. Kinzo Nishida recalls:

While taking my severely wounded wife out to the riverbank by the side of the hill of Nakahiro-machi, I was horrified, indeed, at the sight of a stark naked man standing in the rain with his eyeball in his palm. He looked to be in great pain, but there was nothing that I could do for him.

Many people were astonished by the sheer sudden absence of the known world. The writer Yoko Ota later wrote:

I just could not understand why our surroundings had changed so greatly in one instant. . . . I thought it might have been something which had nothing to do with the war—the collapse of the earth, which it was said would take place at the end of the world, and which I had read about as a child.

And a history professor who looked back at the city after the explosion remarked later, "I saw that Hiroshima had disappeared."

As the fires sprang up in the ruins, many people, having found injured family members and friends, were now forced to abandon them to the flames or to lose their own lives in the firestorm. Those who left children, husbands, wives, friends, and strangers to burn often found these experiences the most awful of the entire ordeal. Mikio Inoue describes how one man, a professor, came to abandon his wife:

It was when I crossed Miyuki Bridge that I saw Professor Takenaka, standing at the foot of the bridge. He was almost naked, wearing nothing but shorts, and he had a ball of rice in his right hand. Beyond the streetcar line, the northern area was covered by red fire burning against the sky. Far away from the line, Ote-machi was also a sea of fire.

That day, Professor Takenaka had not gone to Hiroshima University, and the A-bomb exploded when he was at home. He tried to rescue his wife, who was trapped under a roofbeam, but all his efforts were in vain. The fire was threatening him also. His wife pleaded, "Run away, dear!" He was forced to desert his wife and escape from the fire. He was now at the foot of Miyuki Bridge.

But I wonder how he came to hold that ball of rice in his hand. His naked figure, standing there before the flames with that ball of rice, looked to me as a symbol of the modest hopes of human beings.

In "Hiroshima," John Hersey describes the flight of a group of German priests and their Japanese colleagues through a burning section of the city:

> The street was cluttered with parts of houses that had slid into it, and with fallen telephone poles and wires. From every second or third house came the voices of people buried and abandoned, who invariably screamed, with formal politeness, "*Tasukete kure!* Help, if you please!" The priests recognized several ruins from which these cries came as the homes of friends, but because of the fire it was too late to help.

And thus it happened that throughout Hiroshima all the ties of affection and respect that join human beings to one another were being pulled and rent by the spreading firestorm. Soon processions of the injured—processions of a kind that had never been seen before in history—began to file away from the center of the city toward its outskirts. Most of the people suffered from burns, which had often blackened their skin or caused it to sag off them. A grocer who joined one of these processions has described them in an interview with Robert Jay Lifton which appears in his book "Death in Life":

> They held their arms bent [forward] . . . and their skin—not only on their hands but on their faces and bodies, too—hung down. . . . If there had been only one or two such people . . . perhaps I would not have had such a strong impression. But wherever I walked, I met these people. . . . Many of them died along the road. I can still picture them in my mind—like walking ghosts. They didn't look like people of this world.

The grocer also recalls that because of people's injuries "you couldn't tell whether you were looking at them from in front or in back." People found it impossible to recognize one another. A woman who at the time was a girl of thirteen, and suffered disfiguring burns on her face, has recalled, "My face was so distorted and changed that people couldn't tell who I was. After a while I could call others' names but they couldn't recognize me." In addition to being injured, many people were vomiting—an early symptom of radiation sickness. For many, horrifying and unreal events occurred in a chaotic jumble. In "Unforgettable Fire," Torako Hironaka enumerates some of the things that she remembers:

1. Some burned work-clothes.
2. People crying for help with their heads, shoulders, or the soles of their feet injured by fragments of broken window glass. Glass fragments were scattered everywhere.
3. [A woman] crying, saying "Aigo! Aigo!" (a Korean expression of sorrow).
4. A burning pine tree.
5. A naked woman.
6. Naked girls crying, "Stupid America!"
7. I was crouching in a puddle, for fear of being shot by a machine gun. My breasts were torn.
8. Burned down electric power lines.
9. A telephone pole had burned and fallen down.
10. A field of watermelons.
11. A dead horse.
12. What with dead cats, pigs, and people, it was just a hell on earth.

Physical collapse brought emotional and spiritual collapse with it. The survivors were, on the whole, listless and stupefied. After the escapes, and the failures to escape, from the firestorm, a silence fell over the city and its remaining population. People suffered and died without speaking or otherwise making a sound. The processions of the injured, too, were soundless. Dr. Michihiko Hachiya has written in his book "Hiroshima Diary":

> Those who were able walked silently toward the sub-urbs in the distant hills, their spirits broken, their initiative gone. When asked whence they had come, they pointed to the city and said, "That way," and when asked where they were going, pointed away from the city and said, "This

way." They were so broken and confused that they moved and behaved like automatons.

Their reactions had astonished outsiders, who reported with amazement the spectacle of long files of people holding stolidly to a narrow, rough path when close by was a smooth, easy road going in the same direction. The outsiders could not grasp the fact that they were witnessing the exodus of a people who walked in the realm of dreams.

Those who were still capable of action often acted in an absurd or an insane way. Some of them energetically pursued tasks that had made sense in the intact Hiroshima of a few minutes before but were now utterly inappropriate. Hersey relates that the German priests were bent on bringing to safety a suitcase, containing diocesan accounts and a sum of money, that they had rescued from the fire and were carrying around with them through the burning city. And Dr. Lifton describes a young soldier's punctilious efforts to find and preserve the ashes of a burned military code book while people around him were screaming for help. Other people simply lost their minds. For example, when the German priests were escaping from the firestorm, one of them, Father Wilhelm Kleinsorge, carried on his back a Mr. Fukai, who kept saying that he wanted to remain where he was. When Father Kleinsorge finally put Mr. Fukai down, he started running. Hersey writes:

> Father Kleinsorge shouted to a dozen soldiers, who were standing by the bridge, to stop him. As Father Kleinsorge started back to get Mr. Fukai, Father LaSalle called out, "Hurry! Don't waste time!" So Father Kleinsorge just requested the soldiers to take care of Mr. Fukai. They said they would, but the little, broken man got away from them, and the last the priests could see of him, he was running back toward the fire.

In the weeks after the bombing, many survivors began to notice the appearance of petechiae—small spots caused by hemorrhages—on their skin. These usually signalled the onset of the critical stage of radiation sickness. In the first stage, the victims characteristically vomited repeatedly, ran a fever, and developed an abnormal thirst. (The cry "Water! Water!" was one of the few sounds often heard in Hiroshima on the day of the bombing.) Then, after a few hours or days, there was a deceptively hopeful period of remission of symptoms, called the latency period, which lasted from about a week to about four weeks. Radiation attacks the reproductive function of cells, and those that reproduce most frequently are therefore the most vulnerable. Among these are the bone-marrow cells, which are responsible for the production of blood cells. During the latency period, the count of white blood cells, which are instrumental in fighting infections, and the count of platelets, which are instrumental in clotting, drop precipitously, so the body is poorly defended against infection and is liable to hemorrhaging. In the third, and final, stage, which may last for several weeks, the victim's hair may fall out and he may suffer from diarrhea and may bleed from the intestines, the mouth, or other parts of the body, and in the end he will either recover or die. Because the fireball of the Hiroshima bomb did not touch the ground, very little ground material was mixed with the fission products of the bomb, and therefore very little local fallout was generated. (What fallout there was descended in the black rain.) Therefore, the fatalities from radiation sickness were probably all caused by the initial nuclear radiation, and since this affected only people within a radius of a mile and a quarter of ground zero, most of the people who received lethal doses were killed more quickly by the thermal pulse and the blast wave. Thus, Hiroshima did not experience the mass radiation sickness that can be expected if a weapon is ground-burst. Since the Nagasaki bomb was also burst in the air, the effect of widespread lethal fallout on large areas, causing the death by radiation sickness of whole populations in the hours, days, and weeks after the blast, is a form of nuclear horror that the world has not experienced.

In the months and years following the bombing of Hiroshima, after radiation sickness had run its course and most of the injured had either died of their wounds or recovered from them, the inhabitants of the city began to learn that the exposure to radiation they had experienced would bring about a wide variety of illnesses, many of them lethal, throughout the lifetimes of those who had been exposed. An early sign that the harm from radiation was not restricted to radiation sickness came in the months immediately following the bombing, when people found that their reproductive organs had been temporarily harmed, with men experiencing sterility and women experiencing abnormalities in their menstrual cycles. Then, over the years, other illnesses, including cataracts of the eye and leukemia and other forms of cancer, began to appear in larger than normally expected numbers among the exposed population. In all these illnesses, correlations have been found between nearness to the explosion and incidence of the disease. Also, fetuses exposed to the bomb's radiation in utero exhibited abnormalities and developmental retardation. Those exposed within the mile-and-a-quarter radius were seven times as likely as unexposed fetuses to die in utero, and were also seven times as likely to die at birth or in infancy. Surviving children who were exposed in utero tended to be shorter and lighter than other children, and were more often mentally retarded. One of the most serious abnormalities caused by exposure to the bomb's radiation was microcephaly—abnormal smallness of the head, which is often accompanied by mental retardation. In one study, thirty-three cases of microcephaly were found among a hundred and sixty-nine children exposed in utero.

What happened at Hiroshima was less than a millionth part of a holocaust at present levels of world nuclear armament. The more than millionfold difference amounts to more than a difference in magnitude; it is also a difference in kind. The authors of "Hiroshima and Nagasaki" observe that "an atomic bomb's massive destruction and indiscriminate slaughter involves the sweeping breakdown of all order and existence—in a word, the collapse of society itself," and that therefore "the essence of atomic destruction lies in the totality of its impact on man and society." This is true also of a holocaust, of course, except that the totalities in question are now not single cities but nations, ecosystems, and the earth's ecosphere.

Yet with the exception of fallout, which was relatively light at
Hiroshima and Nagasaki (because both the bombs were air-burst),
the immediate devastation caused by today's bombs would be of a
sort similar to the devastation in those cities. The immediate effects
of a twenty-megaton bomb are not different in kind from those of a
twelve-and-a-half-kiloton bomb; they are only more extensive. (The
proportions of the effects do change greatly with yield, however. In
small bombs, the effects of the initial nuclear radiation are important, because it strikes areas in which people might otherwise have
remained alive, but in larger bombs—ones in the megaton range—
the consequences of the initial nuclear radiation, whose range does
not increase very much with yield, are negligible, because it strikes
areas in which everyone will have already been burned or blasted
to death.) In bursts of both weapons, for instance, there is a radius
within which the thermal pulse can ignite newspapers: for the
twelve-and-a-half-kiloton weapon, it is a little over two miles; for
the twenty-megaton weapon, it is twenty-five miles. (Since there is
no inherent limit on the size of a nuclear weapon, these figures can
be increased indefinitely, subject only to the limitations imposed by
the technical capacities of the bomb builder—and of the earth's
capacity to absorb the blast. The Soviet Union, which has shown a
liking for sheer size in so many of its undertakings, once detonated a
sixty-megaton bomb.) Therefore, while the total effect of a holocaust is qualitatively different from the total effect of a single bomb,
the experience of individual people in a holocaust would be, in the
short term (and again excepting the presence of lethal fallout wherever the bombs were ground-burst), very much like the experience
of individual people in Hiroshima. The Hiroshima people's experience, accordingly, is of much more than historical interest. It is a
picture of what our whole world is always poised to become—a
backdrop of scarcely imaginable horror lying just behind the surface of our normal life, and capable of breaking through into that
normal life at any second. Whether we choose to think about it or
not, it is an omnipresent, inescapable truth about our lives today
that at every single moment each one of us may suddenly become
the deranged mother looking for her burned child; the professor

with the ball of rice in his hand whose wife has just told him "Run away, dear!" and died in the fires; Mr. Fukai running back into the firestorm; the naked man standing on the blasted plain that was his city, holding his eyeball in his hand; or, more likely, one of millions of corpses. For whatever our "modest hopes" as human beings may be, every one of them can be nullified by a nuclear holocaust.

One way to begin to grasp the destructive power of present-day nuclear weapons is to describe the consequences of the detonation of a one-megaton bomb, which possesses eighty times the explosive power of the Hiroshima bomb, on a large city, such as New York. Burst some eighty-five hundred feet above the Empire State Building, a one-megaton bomb would gut or flatten almost every building between Battery Park and 125th Street, or within a radius of four and four-tenths miles, or in an area of sixty-one square miles, and would heavily damage buildings between the northern tip of Staten Island and the George Washington Bridge, or within a radius of about eight miles, or in an area of about two hundred square miles. A conventional explosive delivers a swift shock, like a slap, to whatever it hits, but the blast wave of a sizable nuclear weapon endures for several seconds and "can surround and destroy whole buildings" (Glasstone). People, of course, would be picked up and hurled away from the blast along with the rest of the debris. Within the sixty-one square miles, the walls, roofs, and floors of any buildings that had not been flattened would be collapsed, and the people and furniture inside would be swept down onto the street. (Technically, this zone would be hit by various overpressures of at least five pounds per square inch. Overpressure is defined as the pressure in excess of normal atmospheric pressure.) As far away as ten miles from ground zero, pieces of glass and other sharp objects would be hurled about by the blast wave at lethal velocities. In Hiroshima, where buildings were low and, outside the center of the city, were often constructed of light materials, injuries from falling buildings were often minor. But in New York, where the buildings are tall and are constructed of heavy materials, the physical collapse of the city would certainly kill millions of people. The streets of New York are narrow ravines running be-

47

tween the high walls of the city's buildings. In a nuclear attack, the walls would fall and the ravines would fill up. The people in the buildings would fall to the street with the debris of the buildings, and the people in the street would be crushed by this avalanche of people and buildings. At a distance of two miles or so from ground zero, winds would reach four hundred miles an hour, and another two miles away they would reach a hundred and eighty miles an hour. Meanwhile, the fireball would be growing, until it was more than a mile wide, and rocketing upward, to a height of over six miles. For ten seconds, it would broil the city below. Anyone caught in the open within nine miles of ground zero would receive third-degree burns and would probably be killed; closer to the explosion, people would be charred and killed instantly. From Greenwich Village up to Central Park, the heat would be great enough to melt metal and glass. Readily inflammable materials, such as newspapers and dry leaves, would ignite in all five boroughs (though in only a small part of Staten Island) and west to the Passaic River, in New Jersey, within a radius of about nine and a half miles from ground zero, thereby creating an area of more than two hundred and eighty square miles in which mass fires were likely to break out.

If it were possible (as it would not be) for someone to stand at Fifth Avenue and Seventy-second Street (about two miles from ground zero) without being instantly killed, he would see the following sequence of events. A dazzling white light from the fireball would illumine the scene, continuing for perhaps thirty seconds. Simultaneously, searing heat would ignite everything flammable and start to melt windows, cars, buses, lampposts, and everything else made of metal or glass. People in the street would immediately catch fire, and would shortly be reduced to heavily charred corpses. About five seconds after the light appeared, the blast wave would strike, laden with the debris of a now nonexistent midtown. Some buildings might be crushed, as though a giant fist had squeezed them on all sides, and others might be picked up off their foundations and whirled uptown with the other debris. On the far side of Central Park, the West Side skyline would fall from south to north. The four-hundred-mile-an-hour wind would blow from south to north, die down after a few seconds, and then blow in the reverse direction with diminished intensity. While these things were happening, the fireball would be burning in the sky for the ten seconds of the thermal pulse. Soon huge, thick clouds of dust and smoke would envelop the scene, and as the mushroom cloud rushed overhead (it would have a diameter of about twelve miles) the light from the sun would be blotted out, and day would turn to night. Within minutes, fires, ignited both by the thermal pulse and by broken gas mains, tanks of gas and oil, and the like, would begin to spread in the darkness, and a strong, steady wind would begin to blow in the direction of the blast. As at Hiroshima, a whirlwind might be produced, which would sweep through the ruins, and radioactive rain, generated under the meteorological conditions created by the blast, might fall. Before long, the individual fires would coalesce into a mass fire, which, depending largely on the winds, would become either a conflagration or a firestorm. In a conflagration, prevailing winds spread a wall of fire as far as there is any combustible material to sustain it; in a firestorm, a vertical updraft caused by the fire itself sucks the surrounding air in toward a central point, and the fires therefore converge in a single fire of extreme heat. A mass fire of either kind renders shelters useless by burning up all the oxygen in the air and creating toxic gases, so that anyone inside the shelters is asphyxiated, and also by heating the ground to such high temperatures that the shelters turn, in effect, into ovens, cremating the people inside them. In Dresden, several days after the firestorm raised there by Allied conventional bombing, the interiors of some bomb shelters were still so hot that when they were opened the inrushing air caused the contents to burst into flame. Only those who had fled their shelters when the bombing started had any chance of surviving. (It is difficult to predict in a particular situation which form the fires will take. In actual experience, Hiroshima suffered a firestorm and Nagasaki suffered a conflagration.)

In this vast theatre of physical effects, all the scenes of agony and death that took place at Hiroshima would again take place, but now involving millions of people rather than hundreds of thousands.

Like the people of Hiroshima, the people of New York would be burned, battered, crushed, and irradiated in every conceivable way. The city and its people would be mingled in a smoldering heap. And then, as the fires started, the survivors (most of whom would be on the periphery of the explosion) would be driven to abandon to the flames those family members and other people who were unable to flee, or else to die with them. Before long, while the ruins burned, the processions of injured, mute people would begin their slow progress out of the outskirts of the devastated zone. However, this time a much smaller proportion of the population than at Hiroshima would have a chance of escaping. In general, as the size of the area of devastation increases, the possibilities for escape decrease. When the devastated area is relatively small, as it was at Hiroshima, people who are not incapacitated will have a good chance of escaping to safety before the fires coalesce into a mass fire. But when the devastated area is great, as it would be after the detonation of a megaton bomb, and fires are springing up at a distance of nine and a half miles from ground zero, and when what used to be the streets are piled high with burning rubble, and the day (if the attack occurs in the daytime) has grown impenetrably dark, there is little chance that anyone who is not on the very edge of the devastated area will be able to make his way to safety. In New York, most people would die wherever the blast found them, or not very far from there.

If instead of being burst in the air the bomb were burst on or near the ground in the vicinity of the Empire State Building, the overpressure would be very much greater near the center of the blast area but the range hit by a minimum of five pounds per square inch of overpressure would be less. The range of the thermal pulse would be about the same as that of the air burst. The fireball would be almost two miles across, and would engulf midtown Manhattan from Greenwich Village nearly to Central Park. Very little is known about what would happen to a city that was inside a fireball, but one would expect a good deal of what was there to be first pulverized and then melted or vaporized. Any human beings in the area would be reduced to smoke and ashes; they would simply disappear. A crater roughly three blocks in diameter and two hundred feet deep would open up. In addition, heavy radioactive fallout would be created as dust and debris from the city rose with the mushroom cloud and then fell back to the ground. Fallout would begin to drop almost immediately, contaminating the ground beneath the cloud with levels of radiation many times lethal doses, and quickly killing anyone who might have survived the blast wave and the thermal pulse and might now be attempting an escape; it is difficult to believe that there would be appreciable survival of the people of the city after a megaton ground burst. And for the next twenty-four hours or so more fallout would descend downwind from the blast, in a plume whose direction and length would depend on the speed and the direction of the wind that happened to be blowing at the time of the attack. If the wind was blowing at fifteen miles an hour, fallout of lethal intensity would descend in a plume about a hundred and fifty miles long and as much as fifteen miles wide. Fallout that was sublethal but could still cause serious illness would extend another hundred and fifty miles downwind. Exposure to radioactivity in human beings is measured in units called rems—an acronym for "roentgen equivalent in man." The roentgen is a standard measurement of gamma- and X-ray radiation, and the expression "equivalent in man" indicates that an adjustment has been made to take into account the differences in the degree of biological damage that is caused by radiation of different types. Many of the kinds of harm done to human beings by radiation—for example, the incidence of cancer and of genetic damage—depend on the dose accumulated over many years; but radiation sickness, capable of causing death, results from an "acute" dose, received in a period of anything from a few seconds to several days. Because almost ninety per cent of the so-called "infinite-time dose" of radiation from fallout—that is, the dose from a given quantity of fallout that one would receive if one lived for many thousands of years—is emitted in the first week, the one-week accumulated dose is often used as a convenient measure for calculating the immediate harm from fallout. Doses in the thousands of rems, which could be expected throughout the city, would attack the central nervous system and

51

would bring about death within a few hours. Doses of around a thousand rems, which would be delivered some tens of miles downwind from the blast, would kill within two weeks everyone who was exposed to them. Doses of around five hundred rems, which would be delivered as far as a hundred and fifty miles downwind (given a wind speed of fifteen miles per hour), would kill half of all exposed able-bodied young adults. At this level of exposure, radiation sickness proceeds in the three stages observed at Hiroshima. The plume of lethal fallout could descend, depending on the direction of the wind, on other parts of New York State and parts of New Jersey, Pennsylvania, Delaware, Maryland, Connecticut, Massachusetts, Rhode Island, Vermont, and New Hampshire, killing additional millions of people. The circumstances in heavily contaminated areas, in which millions of people were all declining together, over a period of weeks, toward painful deaths, are ones that, like so many of the consequences of nuclear explosions, have never been experienced.

A description of the effects of a one-megaton bomb on New York City gives some notion of the meaning in human terms of a megaton of nuclear explosive power, but a weapon that is more likely to be used against New York is the twenty-megaton bomb, which has one thousand six hundred times the yield of the Hiroshima bomb. The Soviet Union is estimated to have at least a hundred and thirteen twenty-megaton bombs in its nuclear arsenal, carried by Bear intercontinental bombers. In addition, some of the Soviet SS-18 missiles are capable of carrying bombs of this size, although the actual yields are not known. Since the explosive power of the twenty-megaton bombs greatly exceeds the amount necessary to destroy most military targets, it is reasonable to suppose that they are meant for use against large cities. If a twenty-megaton bomb were air-burst over the Empire State Building at an altitude of thirty thousand feet, the zone gutted or flattened by the blast wave would have a radius of twelve miles and an area of more than four hundred and fifty square miles, reaching from the middle of Staten Island to the northern edge of the Bronx, the eastern edge of Queens, and well into New Jersey, and the zone of heavy damage from the blast wave (the zone hit by a minimum of two pounds of overpressure per square inch) would have a radius of twenty-one and a half miles, or an area of one thousand four hundred and fifty square miles, reaching to the southernmost tip of Staten Island, north as far as southern Rockland County, east into Nassau County, and west to Morris County, New Jersey. The fireball would be about four and a half miles in diameter and would radiate the thermal pulse for some twenty seconds. People caught in the open twenty-three miles away from ground zero, in Long Island, New Jersey, and southern New York State, would be burned to death. People hundreds of miles away who looked at the burst would be temporarily blinded and would risk permanent eye injury. (After the test of a fifteen-megaton bomb on Bikini Atoll, in the South Pacific, in March of 1954, small animals were found to have suffered retinal burns at a distance of three hundred and forty-five miles.) The mushroom cloud would be seventy miles in diameter. New York City and its suburbs would be transformed into a lifeless, flat, scorched desert in a few seconds.

If a twenty-megaton bomb were ground-burst on the Empire State Building, the range of severe blast damage would, as with the one-megaton ground blast, be reduced, but the fireball, which would be almost six miles in diameter, would cover Manhattan from Wall Street to northern Central Park and also parts of New Jersey, Brooklyn, and Queens, and everyone within it would be instantly killed, with most of them physically disappearing. Fallout would again be generated, this time covering thousands of square miles with lethal intensities of radiation. A fair portion of New York City and its incinerated population, now radioactive dust, would have risen into the mushroom cloud and would now be descending on the surrounding territory. On one of the few occasions when local fallout was generated by a test explosion in the multi-megaton range, the fifteen-megaton bomb tested on Bikini Atoll, which was exploded seven feet above the surface of a coral reef, "caused substantial contamination over an area of more than seven thousand square miles," according to Glasstone. If, as seems likely, a twenty-megaton bomb ground-burst on New York would produce at least a comparable amount of fallout, and if the wind carried the fallout onto populated areas, then this one bomb would probably doom upward of twenty million people, or almost ten per cent of the population of the United States.

The "strategic" forces of the Soviet Union—those that can deliver nuclear warheads to the United States—are so far capable of carrying seven thousand warheads with an estimated maximum yield of more than seventeen thousand megatons of explosive power, and, barring unexpected developments in arms-control talks, the number of warheads is expected to rise in the coming years. The actual megatonnage of the Soviet strategic forces is not known, and, for a number of reasons, including the fact that smaller warheads can be delivered more accurately, it is very likely that the actual megatonnage is lower than the maximum possible; however, it is reasonable to suppose that the actual megatonnage is as much as two-thirds of the maximum, which would be about eleven and a half thousand megatons. If we assume that in a first strike the Soviets held back about a thousand megatons (itself an immense force), then the attack would amount to about ten thousand megatons, or the equivalent of eight hundred thousand Hiroshima bombs. American strategic forces comprise about nine thousand warheads with a yield of some three thousand five hundred megatons. The total yield of these American forces was made comparatively low for strategic reasons. American planners discovered that smaller warheads can be delivered more accurately than larger ones, and are therefore more useful for attacking strategic forces on the other side. And, in fact, American missiles are substantially more accurate than Soviet ones. However, in the last year or so, in spite of this advantage in numbers of warheads and in accuracy, American leaders have come to believe that the American forces are inadequate, and, again barring unexpected developments in arms-control talks, both the yield of the American arsenal and the number of warheads in it are likely to rise dramatically. (Neither the United States nor the Soviet Union reveals the total explosive yield of its own forces. The public is left to turn to private organizations, which, by making use of hundreds of pieces of information that *have* been released by the two governments, piece together an over-all picture. The figures I have used to estimate the maximum capacities of the two sides are taken for the most part from tables provided in the latest edition of "The Military Balance," a standard yearly reference work on the strength of military forces around the world, which is published by a research institute in London called the International Institute for Strategic Studies.) The territory of the United States, including Alaska and Hawaii, is three million six hundred and fifteen thousand one hundred and twenty-two square miles. It contains approximately two hundred and twenty-five million people, of whom sixty per cent, or about a hundred and thirty-five million, live in various urban centers with a total area of only eighteen thousand square miles. I asked Dr. Kendall, who has done considerable research on the consequences of nuclear attacks, to sketch out in rough terms what the actual distribution of bombs might be in a ten-thousand-megaton Soviet attack in the early nineteen-eighties on all targets in the United States, military and civilian.

"Without serious distortion," he said, "we can begin by imagining that we would be dealing with ten thousand weapons of one megaton each, although in fact the yields would, of course, vary considerably. Let us also make the assumption, based on common knowledge of weapons design, that on average the yield would be one-half fission and one-half fusion. This proportion is important, because it is the fission products—a virtual museum of about three hundred radioactive isotopes, decaying at different rates—that give off radioactivity in fallout. Fusion can add to the total in ground bursts by radioactivation of ground material by neutrons, but the quantity added is comparatively small. Targets can be divided into two categories—hard and soft. Hard targets, of which there are about a thousand in the United States, are mostly missile silos. The majority of them can be destroyed only by huge, blunt overpressures, ranging anywhere from many hundreds to a few thousand pounds per square inch, and we can expect that two weapons might be devoted to each one to assure destruction. That would use up two thousand megatons. Because other strategic military targets—such as Strategic Air Command bases—are near centers of population, an attack on them as well, perhaps using another couple of hundred megatons, could cause a total of more than twenty million casualties, according to studies by the Arms Control and Disarmament Agency. If the nearly eight thousand weapons remaining were then devoted to the cities and towns of the United States in order of population, every community down to the level of fifteen hundred inhabitants would be hit with a megaton bomb—which is, of course, many, many times what would be necessary to annihilate a town that size. For obvious reasons, industry is highly correlated with population density, so an attack on the one necessarily hits the other, especially when an attack of this magnitude is considered. Ten thousand targets would include everything worth hitting in the country and much more; it would simply *be* the United States. The targeters would run out of targets and victims long before they ran out of bombs. If you imagine that the bombs were distributed according to population, then, allowing for the fact that the attack on the military installations would have already killed about twenty million people, you would have about forty megatons to devote to each remaining million people in the country. For the seven and a half million people in New York City, that would come to three hundred megatons. Bearing in mind what one megaton can do, you can see that this would be preposterous overkill. In practice, one might expect the New York metropolitan area to be hit with some dozens of one-megaton weapons."

In the first moments of a ten-thousand-megaton attack on the United States, I learned from Dr. Kendall and from other sources, flashes of white light would suddenly illumine large areas of the country as thousands of suns, each one brighter than the sun itself, blossomed over cities, suburbs, and towns. In those same moments, when the first wave of missiles arrived, the vast majority of the people in the regions first targeted would be irradiated, crushed, or burned to death. The thermal pulses could subject more than six hundred thousand square miles, or one-sixth of the total land mass

56

of the nation, to a minimum level of forty calories per centimetre squared—a level of heat that chars human beings. (At Hiroshima, charred remains in the rough shape of human beings were a common sight.) Tens of millions of people would go up in smoke. As the attack proceeded, as much as three-quarters of the country could be subjected to incendiary levels of heat, and so, wherever there was inflammable material, could be set ablaze. In the ten seconds or so after each bomb hit, as blast waves swept outward from thousands of ground zeros, the physical plant of the United States would be swept away like leaves in a gust of wind. The six hundred thousand square miles already scorched by the forty or more calories of heat per centimetre squared would now be hit by blast waves of a minimum of five pounds per square inch, and virtually all the habitations, places of work, and other man-made things there—substantially the whole human construct in the United States—would be vaporized, blasted, or otherwise pulverized out of existence. Then, as clouds of dust rose from the earth, and mushroom clouds spread overhead, often linking to form vast canopies, day would turn to night. (These clouds could blanket as much as a third of the nation.) Shortly, fires would spring up in the debris of the cities and in every forest dry enough to burn. These fires would simply burn down the United States. When one pictures a full-scale attack on the United States, or on any other country, therefore, the picture of a single city being flattened by a single bomb—an image firmly engraved in the public imagination, probably because of the bombings of Hiroshima and Nagasaki—must give way to a picture of substantial sections of the country being turned by a sort of nuclear carpet-bombing into immense infernal regions, literally tens of thousands of square miles in area, from which escape is impossible. In Hiroshima and Nagasaki, those who had not been killed or injured so severely that they could not move were able to flee to the undevastated world around them, where they found help, but in any city where three or four bombs had been used—not to mention fifty, or a hundred—flight from one blast would only be flight toward another, and no one could escape alive. Within these regions, each of three of the immediate effects of nuclear weapons—initial radia-

57

tion, thermal pulse, and blast wave—would alone be enough to kill most people: the initial nuclear radiation would subject tens of thousands of square miles to lethal doses; the blast waves, coming from all sides, would nowhere fall below the overpressure necessary to destroy almost all buildings; and the thermal pulses, also coming from all sides, would always be great enough to kill exposed people and, in addition, to set on fire everything that would burn. The ease with which virtually the whole population of the country could be trapped in these zones of universal death is suggested by the fact that the sixty per cent of the population that lives in an area of eighteen thousand square miles could be annihilated with only three hundred one-megaton bombs—the number necessary to cover the area with a minimum of five pounds per square inch of overpressure and forty calories per centimetre squared of heat. That would leave nine thousand seven hundred megatons, or ninety-seven per cent of the megatonnage in the attacking force, available for other targets. (It is hard to imagine what a targeter would do with all his bombs in these circumstances. Above several thousand megatons, it would almost become a matter of trying to hunt down individual people with nuclear warheads.)

The statistics on the initial nuclear radiation, the thermal pulses, and the blast waves in a nuclear holocaust can be presented in any number of ways, but all of them would be only variations on a simple theme—the annihilation of the United States and its people. Yet while the immediate nuclear effects are great enough in a ten-thousand-megaton attack to destroy the country many times over, they are not the most powerfully lethal of the local effects of nuclear weapons. The killing power of the local fallout is far greater. Therefore, if the Soviet Union was bent on producing the maximum over-kill—if, that is, its surviving leaders, whether out of calculation, rage, or madness, decided to eliminate the United States not merely as a political and social entity but as a biological one—they would burst their bombs on the ground rather than in the air. Although the scope of severe blast damage would then be reduced, the blast waves, fireballs, and thermal pulses would still be far more than enough to destroy the country, and, in addition, provided only that the bombs were dispersed widely enough, lethal fallout would spread throughout the nation. The amount of radiation delivered by the fallout from a ground burst of a given size is still uncertain—not least because, as Glasstone notes, there has never been a "true land surface burst" of a bomb with a yield of over one kiloton. (The Bikini burst was in part over the ocean.) Many factors make for uncertainty. To mention just a few: the relative amounts of the fallout that rises into the stratosphere and the fallout that descends to the ground near the blast are dependent on, among other things, the yield of the weapon, and, in any case, can be only guessed at; the composition of the fallout will vary with the composition of the material on the ground that is sucked up into the mushroom cloud; prediction of the distribution of fallout by winds of various speeds at various altitudes depends on a choice of several "models"; and the calculation of the arrival time of the fallout—an important calculation, since fallout cannot harm living things until it lands near them—is subject to similar speculative doubts. However, calculations on the basis of figures for a one-megaton ground burst which are given in the Office of Technology Assessment's report show that ten thousand megatons would yield one-week doses around the country averaging more than ten thousand rems. In actuality, of course, the bombs would almost certainly not be evenly spaced around the country but, rather, would be concentrated in populated areas and in missile fields; and the likelihood is that in most places where people lived or worked the doses would be many times the average, commonly reaching several tens of thousands of rems for the first week, while in remote areas they would be less, or, conceivably, even nonexistent. (The United States contains large tracts of empty desert, and to target them would be virtually meaningless from any point of view.)

These figures provide a context for judging the question of civil defense. With overwhelming immediate local effects striking the vast majority of the population, and with one-week doses of radiation then rising into the tens of thousands of rems, evacuation and shelters are a vain hope. Needless to say, in these circumstances evacuation before an attack would be an exercise in transporting people from one death to another. In some depictions of a holocaust, various rescue operations are described, with unafflicted survivors bringing food, clothes, and medical care to the afflicted, and the afflicted making their way to thriving, untouched communities, where churches, school auditoriums, and the like would have been set up for their care—as often happens after a bad snowstorm, say. Obviously, none of this could come about. In the first place, in a full-scale attack there would in all likelihood *be* no surviving communities, and, in the second place, everyone who failed to seal himself off from the outside environment for as long as several months would soon die of radiation sickness. Hence, in the months after a holocaust there would be no activity of any sort, as, in a reversal of the normal state of things, the dead would lie on the surface and the living, if there were any, would be buried underground.

To this description of radiation levels around the country, an addition remains to be made. This is the fact that attacks on the seventy-six nuclear power plants in the United States would produce fallout whose radiation had much greater longevity than that of the weapons alone. The physicist Dr. Kosta Tsipis, of M.I.T., and one of his students, Steven Fetter, recently published an article in *Scientific American* called "Catastrophic Releases of Radioactivity," in which they calculate the damage from a one-megaton thermonuclear ground burst on a one-gigawatt nuclear power plant. In such a ground burst, the facility's radioactive contents would be vaporized along with everything nearby, and the remains would be carried up into the mushroom cloud, from which they would descend to the earth with the rest of the fallout. But whereas the fission products of the weapon were newly made, and contained many isotopes that would decay to insignificant levels very swiftly, the fission products in a reactor would be a collection of longer-lived isotopes (and this applies even more strongly to the spent fuel in the reactor's holding pond), since the short-lived ones would, for the most part, have had enough time to reduce themselves to harmless levels. The intense but comparatively short-lived radiation from the weapon would kill people in the first few weeks and months, but the long-lived radiation that was produced both by the weapon and by the power plant could prevent anyone from living on a vast area of land for decades after it fell. For example, after a year an area of some seventeen hundred square miles downwind of a power plant on which a one-megaton bomb had been ground-burst (again assuming a fifteen-mile-an-hour wind) would still be delivering more than fifty rems per year to anyone who tried to live there, and that is two hundred and fifty times the "safe" dose established by the E.P.A. The bomb by itself would produce this effect over an area of only twenty-six square miles. (In addition to offering an enemy a way of redoubling the effectiveness of his attacks in a full-scale holocaust, reactors provide targets of unparalleled danger in possible terrorist nuclear attacks. In an earlier paper, Tsipis and Fetter observe that "the destruction of a reactor with a nuclear weapon, even of relatively small yield, such as a crude terrorist nuclear device, would represent a national catastrophe of lasting consequences." It can be put down as one further alarming oddity of life in a nuclear world that in building nuclear power plants nations have opened themselves to catastrophic devastation and long-term contamination of their territories by enemies who manage to get hold of only a few nuclear weapons.)

If, in a nuclear holocaust, anyone hid himself deep enough under the earth and stayed there long enough to survive, he would emerge into a dying natural environment. The vulnerability of the environment is the last word in the argument against the usefulness of shelters: there is no hole big enough to hide all of nature in. Radioactivity penetrates the environment in many ways. The two most important components of radiation from fallout are gamma rays, which are electromagnetic radiation of the highest intensity, and beta particles, which are electrons fired at high speed from decaying nuclei. Gamma rays subject organisms to penetrating whole-body doses, and are responsible for most of the ill effects of radiation from fallout. Beta particles, which are less penetrating than gamma rays, act at short range, doing harm when they collect on the skin, or on the surface of a leaf. They are harmful to plants on whose foliage the fallout descends—producing "beta burn"—

and to grazing animals, which can suffer burns as well as gastrointestinal damage from eating the foliage. Two of the most harmful radioactive isotopes present in fallout are strontium-90 (with a half-life of twenty-eight years) and cesium-137 (with a half-life of thirty years). They are taken up into the food chain through the roots of plants or through direct ingestion by animals, and contaminate the environment from within. Strontium-90 happens to resemble calcium in its chemical composition, and therefore finds its way into the human diet through dairy products and is eventually deposited by the body in the bones, where it is thought to cause bone cancer. (Every person in the world now has in his bones a measurable deposit of strontium-90 traceable to the fallout from atmospheric nuclear testing.)

Over the years, agencies and departments of the government have sponsored numerous research projects in which a large variety of plants and animals were irradiated in order to ascertain the lethal or sterilizing dose for each. These findings permit the prediction of many gross ecological consequences of a nuclear attack. According to "Survival of Food Crops and Livestock in the Event of Nuclear War," the proceedings of the 1970 symposium at Brookhaven National Laboratory, the lethal doses for most mammals lie between a few hundred rads and a thousand rads of gamma radiation; a rad—for "roentgen absorbed dose"—is a roentgen of radiation that has been absorbed by an organism, and is roughly equal to a rem. For example, the lethal doses of gamma radiation for animals in pasture, where fallout would be descending on them directly and they would be eating fallout that had fallen on the grass, and would thus suffer from doses of beta radiation as well, would be one hundred and eighty rads for cattle; two hundred and forty rads for sheep; five hundred and fifty rads for swine; three hundred and fifty rads for horses; and eight hundred rads for poultry. In a ten-thousand-megaton attack, which would create levels of radiation around the country averaging more than ten thousand rads, most of the mammals of the United States would be killed off. The lethal doses for birds are in roughly the same range as those for mammals, and birds, too, would be killed off. Fish are killed at doses of between one thousand one hundred rads and about five thousand six hundred rads, but their fate is less predictable. On the one hand, water is a shield from radiation, and would afford some protection; on the other hand, fallout might concentrate in bodies of water as it ran off from the land. (Because radiation causes no pain, animals, wandering at will through the environment, would not avoid it.) The one class of animals containing a number of species quite likely to survive, at least in the short run, is the insect class, for which in most known cases the lethal doses lie between about two thousand rads and about a hundred thousand rads. Insects, therefore, would be destroyed selectively. Unfortunately for the rest of the environment, many of the phytophagous species—insects that feed directly on vegetation—which "include some of the most ravaging species on earth" (according to Dr. Vernon M. Stern, an entomologist at the University of California at Riverside, writing in "Survival of Food Crops"), have very high tolerances, and so could be expected to survive disproportionately, and then to multiply greatly in the aftermath of an attack. The demise of their natural predators the birds would enhance their success.

Plants in general have a higher tolerance to radioactivity than animals do. Nevertheless, according to Dr. George M. Woodwell, who supervised the irradiation with gamma rays, over several years, of a small forest at Brookhaven Laboratory, a gamma-ray dose of ten thousand rads "would devastate most vegetation" in the United States, and, as in the case of the pastured animals, when one figures in the beta radiation that would also be delivered by fallout the estimates for the lethal doses of gamma rays must be reduced—in this case, cut in half. As a general rule, Dr. Woodwell and his colleagues at Brookhaven discovered, large plants are more vulnerable to radiation than small ones. Trees are among the first to die, grasses among the last. The most sensitive trees are pines and the other conifers, for which lethal doses are in roughly the same range as those for mammals. Any survivors coming out of their shelters a few months after the attack would find that all the pine trees that were still standing were already dead. The lethal doses for most deciduous trees range from about two thousand rads of gamma-ray radiation to about ten thousand rads, with the lethal doses for eighty per cent of deciduous species falling between two thousand and eight thousand rads. Since the addition of the beta-ray burden could lower these lethal doses for gamma rays by as much as fifty per cent, the actual lethal doses in gamma rays for these trees during an attack could be from one thousand to four thousand rads, and in a full-scale attack they would die. Then, after the trees had died, forest fires would break out around the United States. (Because as much as three-quarters of the country could be subjected to incendiary levels of the thermal pulses, the sheer scorching of the land could have killed off a substantial part of the plant life in the country in the first few seconds after the detonations, before radioactive poisoning set in.) Lethal doses for grasses on which tests have been done range between six thousand and thirty-three thousand rads, and a good deal of grass would therefore survive, except where the attacks had been heaviest. Most crops, on the other hand, are killed by doses below five thousands rads, and would be eliminated. (The lethal dose for spring barley seedlings, for example, is one thousand nine hundred and ninety rads, and that for spring wheat seedlings is three thousand and ninety rads.)

When vegetation is killed off, the land on which it grew is degraded. And as the land eroded after an attack life in lakes, rivers, and estuaries, already hard hit by radiation directly, would be further damaged by minerals flowing into the watercourses, causing eutrophication—a process in which an oversupply of nutrients in the water encourages the growth of algae and microscopic organisms, which, in turn, deplete the oxygen content of the water. When the soil loses its nutrients, it loses its ability to "sustain a mature community" (in Dr. Woodwell's words), and "gross simplification" of the environment occurs, in which "hardy species," such as moss and grass, replace vulnerable ones, such as trees; and "succession"—the process by which ecosystems recover lost diversity—is then "delayed or even arrested." In sum, a full-scale nuclear attack on the United States would devastate the natural environment on a scale unknown since early geological times, when, in response to natural catastrophes whose nature has not been determined, sudden mass extinctions of species and whole ecosystems occurred all over the earth. How far this "gross simplification" of the environment would go once virtually all animal life and the greater part of plant life had been destroyed and what patterns the surviving remnants of life would arrange themselves into over the long run are imponderables; but it appears that at the outset the United States would be a republic of insects and grass.

It has sometimes been claimed that the United States could survive a nuclear attack by the Soviet Union, but the bare figures on the extent of the blast waves, the thermal pulses, and the accumulated local fallout dash this hope irrevocably. They spell the doom of the United States. And if one imagines the reverse attack on the Soviet Union, its doom is spelled out in similar figures. (The greater land mass of the Soviet Union and the lower megatonnage of the American forces might reduce the factor of overkill somewhat.) Likewise, any country subjected to an attack of more than a few hundred megatons would be doomed. Japan, China, and the countries of Europe, where population densities are high, are especially vulnerable to damage, even at "low" levels of attack. There is no country in Europe in which survival of the population would be appreciable after the detonation of several hundred megatons; most European countries would be annihilated by tens of megatons. And these conclusions emerge even before one takes into account the global ecological consequences of a holocaust, which would be superimposed on the local consequences. As human life and the structure of human existence are seen in the light of each person's daily life and experience, they look impressively extensive and solid, but when human things are seen in the light of the universal power unleashed onto the earth by nuclear weapons they prove to be limited and fragile, as though they were nothing more than a mold or a lichen that appears in certain crevices of the landscape and can be burned off with relative ease by nuclear fire.

Many discussions of nuclear attacks on the United States devote considerable attention to their effect on the nation's economy,

THE FATE OF THE EARTH

but if the population has been largely killed off and the natural environment is in a state of collapse "the economy" becomes a meaningless concept; for example, it makes no difference what percentage of "the automobile industry" has survived if all the producers and drivers of automobiles have died. Estimates of economic survival after a full-scale holocaust are, in fact, doubly unreal, because, as a number of government reports have shown, the nation's economy is so much more vulnerable to attack than the population that even at most levels of "limited" attack a greater proportion of the economy than of the population would be destroyed. An intact economic plant that goes to waste because there aren't enough people left to run it is one absurdity that a nuclear holocaust does not present us with. At relatively low levels of attack, however, the more or less complete destruction of the economy, accompanied by the survival of as much as twenty or thirty per cent of the population, is conceivable. Since the notion of "limited nuclear war" has recently become attractive to the American leadership, it may not be digressive to discuss what the consequences of smaller attacks would be. Our knowledge of nuclear effects is too imprecise to permit us to know at exactly what level of attack a given percentage of the population would survive, but the fact that sixty per cent of the population lives in eighteen thousand square miles and could be eliminated by the thermal pulses, blast waves, and mass fires produced by about three hundred one-megaton bombs suggests some rough magnitudes. The fallout that would be produced by the bombs if they were ground-burst would very likely kill ten or fifteen per cent of the remaining population (it could lethally contaminate some three hundred thousand square miles), and if several hundred additional megatons were used the percentage of the entire population killed in the short term might rise to something like eighty-five. Or, to put it differently, if the level of attack on civilian targets did not rise above the low hundreds of megatons tens of millions of people might survive in the short term. But that same level of attack would destroy so much of the physical plant of the economy, and, of course, so many of the laborers and managers who make it work, that in effect the economy would be nearly one hundred per cent destroyed. (There is a tendency when one is analyzing nuclear attacks to begin to accustom oneself to such expressions as "a thousand megatons," and therefore to begin to regard lower amounts as inconsequential. Yet even one megaton, which contains the explosive yield of eighty Hiroshimas, would, if it should be dropped in the United States in the form of a number of small bombs, be an unimaginable catastrophe. Ten megatons—eight hundred Hiroshimas—would leave any nation on earth devastated beyond anything in our historical experience. A hundred megatons—eight thousand Hiroshimas—is already outside comprehension.)

As soon as one assumes that many tens of millions of people might survive the early stages of an attack, what are often called the long-term effects of a holocaust come into view; in fact, it is only when the imagined attack is reduced to this level that it begins to make sense to talk about many of the long-term effects, because only then will there be people left living to suffer them. The most obvious of these is injury. In an attack that killed from fifty to seventy per cent of the population outright, the great majority of the survivors would be injured. In a limited attack, some people might try to make their way to shelters to escape the fallout, which would be less intense than in the larger attack but still lethal in most populated areas. (If we again assume ground bursts, and also assume that two thousand megatons have been used on military targets, then average levels of radiation around the country would be in the low thousands of rems. But in this case averages would have little or no meaning; actual levels would be very high in some places and very low or nonexistent in others, depending on targeting and weather patterns.) People who reached shelters and sealed themselves in in time might have a chance of survival in some areas, but a large number of people would have received lethal doses of radiation without knowing it (since exposure to radiation is painless) and would enter the shelters and die there, making life in the shelters unbearable for the others. With many people seeking to get into the shelters, attempts to decide who was to be allowed to enter and who was to be kept out would begin in bitterness and end in chaos. (In the nineteen-fifties, when Americans gave greater thought to the matter of shelters than they do now, some communities began to prepare to defend their shelters against intruders by arming themselves.) Also, the withdrawal into shelters of the uninjured or lightly injured portion of the population would be more consequential for the survivors as a body, because in a limited attack there might be a considerable number of people on the surface who would have had a chance of surviving if they had not been abandoned. The widespread use of shelters would therefore mean additional deaths; the injured or sick people would die unattended on the surface while the uninjured and healthy people hid underground.

The injuries from the attack would very likely be compounded by epidemics. Dr. H. Jack Geiger, who teaches community medicine at the School of Biomedical Education of the City College of New York, recently described to me the likely medical conditions after a limited attack. "The landscape would be strewn with millions of corpses of human beings and animals," he pointed out. "This alone is a situation without precedent in history. There would be an immense source of pollution of water and food. If you read the literature concerning natural disasters such as floods and typhoons, you find that there is always an associated danger of cholera or typhoid. The corpses would also feed a fast-growing population of insects, and insects happen to be a prime vector of disease. Naturally, medical measures to fight disease would not be taken, since the blasts would have destroyed virtually all medical facilities. Nor, of course, would there be such elementary sanitary facilities as running water and garbage collection. Finally, the population's resistance to infection would have been weakened, since many would be suffering from sublethal radiation sickness and wounds. It would be impossible to devise circumstances more favorable to the spread of epidemics."

Strategists of nuclear conflict often speak of a period of "recovery" after a limited attack, but a likelier prospect is a long-term radical deterioration in the conditions of life. For a while, some supplies of food and clothing would be found in the rubble, but then these would give out. For a people, the economy—any kind of

A Republic of Insects and Grass

economy, whether primitive or modern—is the means of survival
from day to day. So if you ruin the economy—if you suspend its
functioning, even for a few months—you take away the means of
survival. Eventually, if enough people do live, the economy will
revive in one form or another, but in the meantime people will die:
they will starve, because the supply of food has been cut off; they
will freeze, because they have no fuel or shelter; they will perish of
illness, because they have no medical care. If the economy in question is a modern technological one, the consequences will be particularly severe, for then the obstacles to restoring it will be greatest.
Because a modern economy, like an ecosystem, is a single, interdependent whole, in which each part requires many other parts to
keep functioning, its wholesale breakdown will leave people unable to perform the simplest, most essential tasks. Even agriculture
—the immediate means of subsistence—is caught up in the operations of the interdependent machine, and breaks down when it
breaks down. Modern agriculture depends on fertilizers to make
crops grow, on machines to cultivate the crops, on transportation to
carry the produce thousands of miles to the consumers, on fuel to
run the means of transportation and the agricultural machinery,
and on pesticides and drugs to increase production. If fertilizers,
machines, transportation, fuel, pesticides, and drugs are taken away,
agriculture will come to a halt, and people will starve. Also, because
of the interdependence of the system, no sector of the economy can
be repaired unless many of the other sectors are in good order.

But in a nuclear attack, of course, all sectors of the economy
would be devastated at once. The task facing the survivors, therefore, would be not to restore the old economy but to invent a new
one, on a far more primitive level. But the invention of a primitive
economy would not be a simple matter. Even economies we think
of as primitive depend on considerable knowledge accumulated
through long experience, and in modern times this knowledge has
been largely lost. The economy of the Middle Ages, for example,
was far less productive than our own, but it was exceedingly complex, and it would not be within the capacity of people in our time
suddenly to establish a medieval economic system in the ruins of

their twentieth-century one. After a limited nuclear attack, the typical predicament of a survivor would be that of, say, a bus driver in a city who was used to shopping at a supermarket and found himself facing the question of how to grow his own food, or of a bookkeeper in a suburb who found that he must make his own clothing, not to mention the cloth for the clothing. Innumerable things that we now take for granted would abruptly be lacking. In addition to food and clothing, they would include: heating, electric lights, running water, telephones, mail, transportation of all kinds, all household appliances powered by electricity or gas, information other than by word of mouth, medical facilities, sanitary facilities, and basic social services, such as fire departments and police. To restore these essentials of life takes time; but there would be no time. Hunger, illness, and possibly cold would press in on the dazed, bewildered, disorganized, injured remnant of the population on the very day of the attack. They would have to start foraging immediately for their next meal. Sitting among the debris of the Space Age, they would find that the pieces of a shattered modern economy around them— here an automobile, there a washing machine—were mismatched to their elemental needs. Nor would life be made easier for them by the fact that their first need, once they left any shelters they might have found, would be to flee the heavily irradiated, burned-out territories where they used to live, and to start over in less irradiated, unburned territories, which would probably be in the wilderness. Facing these urgent requirements, they would not be worrying about rebuilding the automobile industry or the electronics industry; they would be worrying about how to find nonradioactive berries in the woods, or how to tell which trees had edible bark.

Lastly, over the decades not only would the survivors of a limited attack face a contaminated and degraded environment but they themselves—their flesh, bones, and genetic endowment—would be contaminated: the generations that would be trying to rebuild a human life would be sick and possibly deformed generations. The actual doses received by particular survivors would, of course, depend on their circumstances, but some notion of the extent of the contamination can perhaps be gathered from the fact that if people came out of shelters after three months into an area in which the fallout would in the long run deliver a dose of ten thousand rems they would still receive about three per cent of the total, or three hundred rems, over their lifetimes, with two hundred of those rems being received in the first year. I spoke to Dr. Edward Radford, who is a professor of environmental epidemiology at the University of Pittsburgh, and who was chairman from 1977 to 1980 of the National Academy of Sciences' Committee on the Biological Effects of Ionizing Radiations, about the medical consequences of such exposure. "The present incidence of cancer, exclusive of skin cancer, in the United States population is thirty per cent, and roughly seventeen per cent die of the disease," he told me. "Since the dose of radiation that doubles the cancer rate is about one hundred and fifty rems, we could expect that a dose of three hundred rems would cause just about everybody to get cancer of one kind or another, and perhaps half of them would die from it. In addition, the dose that is estimated to cause a doubling of the spontaneous-mutation rate—which now affects ten percent of all births—is also one hundred and fifty rems, and therefore we could also expect genetic abnormalities to increase dramatically." Whether a human community could survive bearing this burden of illness and mutation is at best questionable.

In considering the global consequences of a holocaust, the first question to be asked is how widespread the hostilities would be. It is often assumed that a holocaust, even if it were full-scale, would be restricted to the Northern Hemisphere, destroying the United States, the Soviet Union, Europe, China, and Japan, but in fact there is no assurance that hostilities would not spread to other parts of the world. Both Soviet and American leaders believe that the rivalry between their countries has worldwide ideological significance, and in the name of their causes they might well extend their attacks almost anywhere. Furthermore, it takes very little imagination to see that once the superpowers had absorbed several thousand megatons of nuclear explosives each they would no longer *be* super-

71

powers; indeed, they would no longer exist as nations at all. At that point, any sizable nation that had been spared attack—for example, Vietnam, Mexico, Nigeria, Australia, or South Africa—might, in the minds of the leaders of the ex-superpowers, become tempting as a target. It might suddenly occur to them that on a devastated earth mere survival would be the stuff of global might, and either or both of the ex-superpowers might then set about destroying those surviving middle-ranking powers that seemed closest to sharing the ideology of the enemy. Again, it is impossible to know what thoughts would go through the minds of men in caves, or perhaps in airborne command posts, who had just carried out the slaughter of hundreds of millions of people and whose nations had been annihilated in a similar slaughter (and it should always be borne in mind that sheer insanity is one of the possibilities), but it could be that in some confused attempt to shape the political future of the post-holocaust world (if there is one) they would carry their struggle into the would-be-neutral world. It could be that even now the United States has a few dozen megatons reserved in one contingency plan or another for, say, Cuba, Vietnam, and North Korea, while the Soviet Union may have a similar fate in mind for, among others, Israel, South Africa, and Australia. We also have to ask ourselves what the Chinese, the French, and the British, who all possess nuclear arms, and the Israelis, the South Africans, and the Indians, who are all suspected of possessing them, would attempt once the mayhem began. And this list of nuclear-armed and possibly nuclear-armed countries shows every sign of being a growing one.

Although it may seem inappropriate to mention "civilization" in the same breath as the death of hundreds of millions of people, it should at least be pointed out that a full-scale holocaust would, if it extended throughout the Northern Hemisphere, eliminate the civilizations of Europe, China, Japan, Russia, and the United States from the earth.

As I have already mentioned, there are uncertainties inherent in any attempt to predict the consequences of a nuclear holocaust; but when we try to estimate those consequences for the targeted countries it turns out that the readily calculable local primary effects of the bombs are so overwhelming that we never arrive at the uncertainties. Obviously, there can be no tangled interplay of destructive influences in society if there is no society; and the local primary effects are more than enough to remove society from the picture. This is why those observers who speak of "recovery" after a holocaust or of "winning" a nuclear "war" are dreaming. They are living in a past that has been swept away forever by nuclear arms. However, when it comes to inquiring into the global ecological consequences of a holocaust and, with them, the risk of human extinction, the uncertainties, and the political questions they raise, move to the fore. To begin with, this inquiry requires us to concentrate our attention on the earth. The earth is a compound mystery, for it presents us with the mystery of life in its entirety, the mystery of every individual form of life, and the mystery of ourselves, and all our thoughts and works. (Since we are earth-made, investigation of the earth eventually becomes introspection.) The reason for our ignorance is not that our knowledge of the earth is slight—on the contrary, it is extensive, and has grown in this century more than in all other centuries put together—but that the amount to be known is demonstrably so much greater. There is a sense, of course, in which knowledge can increase ignorance. By leading to fresh discoveries, knowledge may open up new wonders to our view but not yet to our understanding. Our century's discoveries in the earth sciences have increased our ignorance in just this sense: they have given us a glimpse of how much there is still to find out. Dr. Lewis Thomas, the noted biologist and essayist, has defined this ignorance in categorical terms, saying, "We are ignorant about how we work, about where we fit in, and most of all about the enormous, imponderable system of life in which we are embedded as working parts. We do not really understand nature, at all." Of all the things to be said in a discussion of the global effects of a nuclear holocaust, this is by far the most important: that because of the extent of what we know that we don't know, we are simply debarred from making confident judgments.

73

THE FATE OF THE EARTH

Since an awareness of the boundaries of present knowledge is a necessary part of science's effort to achieve precision and clarity, it is not surprising that the literature on global nuclear effects is littered with reminders of the fallibility and, above all, of the incompleteness of our present understanding. This appropriately modest, tentative spirit has perhaps been best summed up in the opening comments of the Office of Technology Assessment report, which states that the most important thing to know about a holocaust is not anything that "is known" but "what is not known." A similar acknowledgment of the importance of the unknown is implicit in a remark in a 1977 "interim" report by the National Academy of Sciences on the peril to the stratosphere from man-made disturbances in general. "It is unfortunately true," the report says, "that, accompanying very substantial over-all progress, the recent development of our understanding of stratospheric chemistry has been dominated by major upheavals caused by the recognition of the importance of processes whose role either had not been properly appreciated . . . or whose rate coefficient had been grossly misjudged. . . . To say how many more major upheavals we should expect in the future is rather like trying to foresee the unforeseeable." The report goes on to note that as knowledge of the chemistry of the stratosphere has improved, it has turned out that "even with the largest computers it is not possible to represent the detailed three-dimensional motions in the atmosphere while including the detailed chemical reactions." Before the "upheavals," scientists seemed to "know" a good deal; afterward, they knew that they knew less.

Our ignorance pertains to the possibility of altogether unknown major effects of nuclear explosions as well as to the magnitude of the known ones and their infinite interactions. Like so much else in science, the discovery of what is known so far about the effects of nuclear explosions is a story of surprises, starting with the surprise that the nucleus could be fissioned at all. Perhaps the second big surprise was the extent of harmful fallout; this came to light in the fifteen-megaton test at Bikini in 1954, when, to the amazement of the designers of the test, fallout began to descend on Marshall

74

Islanders and on American servicemen manning weather stations on atolls at supposedly safe distances from the explosion. It was not until this test that the world was alerted to the real magnitude—or, at any rate, to the magnitude as it is understood so far—of the peril from nuclear fallout. The next surprise was the extent of the effects of the electromagnetic pulse. Probably the most recent surprise has been the discovery, in the nineteen-seventies, of the peril to the ozone layer. Around 1970, a number of scientists became worried that the use of supersonic transports, which fly in the stratosphere and emit oxides of nitrogen, would deplete the ozone layer, and it occurred to two Columbia physicists—Henry M. Foley and Malvin A. Ruderman—that since nuclear weapons were known to produce nitric oxide in the stratosphere, the capacity of this compound for depleting the ozone might be tested by trying to find out whether ozone levels had dropped as a result of the atmospheric testing of nuclear weapons. The investigation was inconclusive, but it led the two men to worry about the fate of the ozone in the event of a nuclear holocaust. Their concern awakened the concern of other scientists, and in 1975 the National Academy of Sciences produced its report "Long-Term Worldwide Effects of Multiple Nuclear-Weapons Detonations," which attempted, among other things, to measure this peril. The sequence of events leading to our present awareness of this peril is illuminating, because it shows how a broad new development in scientific thought—in this case, the growing awareness in the nineteen-seventies of the vulnerability of the ecosphere to human intervention—brought to light an immense effect of nuclear weapons which had previously gone unnoticed. It is always difficult to become aware of one's ignorance, but as we try to give due weight to our present ignorance it can help us to recall that little more than a decade ago possibly the gravest global consequence of a holocaust which we now know of was totally unsuspected. Given the incomplete state of our knowledge of the earth, it seems unjustified at this point to assume that further developments in science will not bring forth further surprises.

The embryonic state of the earth sciences is one reason for our uncertainty concerning the outcome of a nuclear holocaust, but there is a moral and political reason that may be even more fundamental. Epistemologically, the earth is a special object. Scientific inquiry into the effects of a holocaust, like every other form of inquiry into this subject, is restricted by our lack of experience with large-scale nuclear destruction. But the lack of experience is not the result of neglect or accident, or even of our reluctance to face the horror of our predicament. In scientific work, experience means experiments, and scientific knowledge is not considered to be knowledge until it has been confirmed by experiment—or, at least, by observation. Until then, no matter how plausible a theory sounds, and no matter how dazzling it may appear intellectually, it is relegated to the limbo of hypothesis. But when it comes to judging the consequences of a nuclear holocaust there can be no experimentation, and thus no empirical verification. We cannot run experiments with the earth, because we have only one earth, on which we depend for our survival; we are not in possession of any spare earths that we might blow up in some universal laboratory in order to discover their tolerance of nuclear holocausts. Hence, our knowledge of the resiliency of the earth in the face of nuclear attack is limited by our fear of bringing about just the event—human extinction—whose likelihood we are chiefly interested in finding out about. The famous uncertainty principle, formulated by the German physicist Werner Heisenberg, has shown that our knowledge of atomic phenomena is limited because the experimental procedures with which we must carry out our observations inevitably interfere with the phenomena that we wish to measure. The question of extinction by nuclear arms—or by any other means, for that matter—presents us with an opposite but related uncertainty principle: our knowledge of extinction is limited because the experiments with which we would carry out our observations interfere with us, the observers, and, in fact, might put an end to us. This uncertainty principle complements the first. Both principles recognize that a limit to our knowledge is fixed by the fact that we are incarnate beings, not disembodied spirits, and that observation, like other human activities, is a physical process and so can interfere both with what is under observation and with the observer. Therefore, it is ultimately extinction itself that fixes the boundary to what we can know about extinction. No human being will ever be able to say with confidence, "*Now* I see how many megatons it takes for us to exterminate ourselves." To the extent that this check stands in the way of investigation, our uncertainty is forced on us not so much by the limitations of our intellectual ability as by the irreducible fact that we have no platform for observation except our mortal frames. In these circumstances, which are rudiments of the human condition, toleration of uncertainty is the path of life, and the demand for certainty is the path toward death.

We have had some experience of moral and political restraints on research in the field of medicine, in which, in all civilized countries, there are restrictions on experimenting with human beings; when the results might be injurious, laboratory animals are used instead. However, in investigating the properties of the earth we lack even any recourse that would be analogous to the use of these animals, for if we have no extra, dispensable earths to experiment with, neither are we in possession of any planets bearing life of some different sort. (As far as we now know, among the planets in the solar system the earth stands alone as a bearer of life.) And while it is true that we can run experiments in various corners of the earth and try to extrapolate the results to the earth as a whole, what is always missing from the results is the totality of the ecosphere, with its endless pathways of cause and effect, linking the biochemistry of the humblest alga and global chemical and dynamic balances into an indivisible whole. This whole is a mechanism in itself; indeed, it may be regarded as a single living being. Dr. Thomas, for one, has likened the earth to a cell. The analogy is compelling, but in one noteworthy respect, at least, there is a difference between the earth and a cell: whereas each cell is one among billions struck from the same genetic mold, the earth, as the mother of all life, has no living parent. If the behavior of cells is often predictable, it is because they exist en masse, and what a billion of them, programmed by their genetic material, have done a billion times the billion and first is likely to do again. But the earth is a member of no class as yet open to our observation which would permit the drawing of such inferences by generalization. When it comes to trying to predict its tolerance to perturbances, we are in the position of someone asked to deduce the whole of medicine by observing one human being. With respect to its individuality, then, the earth is not so much like a cell as like an individual person. Like a person, the earth is unique; like a person, it is sacred; and, like a person, it is unpredictable by the generalizing laws of science.

If we had no knowledge at all of the likely consequences of a holocaust for the earth, there would, of course, be no basis whatever for judgment. However, given the extent of what there is to know about the earth, it is no contradiction to say that while our ignorance is vast and, in a certain sense, irremediable (although, at the same time, the amount that we can and certainly will find out is also probably measureless), our knowledge is also vast, and that what we know is extremely alarming. Since in a global holocaust even the so-called local effects of the explosions may cover the whole land mass of the Northern Hemisphere, they may have secondary consequences that are truly global. The destruction of estuarine life throughout the Northern Hemisphere and the radioactive poisoning of the local waters could cause general harm to life in the oceans. Ecological collapse on the land in large parts of the Northern Hemisphere could have large consequences for the climate of the earth as a whole. Loss of vegetation, for example, increases the surface reflectivity of the earth, and this has a cooling effect on the atmosphere. In heavily irradiated zones, the mutation of plant pathogens might create virulent strains that could, in the words of the 1975 N.A.S. report, "produce disease epidemics that would spread globally." The irradiated northern half of the earth would in general become a huge radioecological laboratory, in which many species would be driven to extinction, others would flourish and possibly invade unharmed parts of the earth, and still others would evolve into new and unpredictable forms.

But more important by far, in all probability, than the global aftereffects of the local destruction would be the direct global effects, the most important of which is ozone loss. The concentration of ozone in the earth's atmosphere is very small—not more than ten parts by weight per million parts of air. Yet the ozone layer has a critical importance to life on earth, because it protects the earth's surface from the harmful ultraviolet radiation in sunlight, which would otherwise be "lethal to unprotected organisms as we now know them," to quote Dr. Martyn M. Caldwell, a leading authority on the biological effects of ultraviolet radiation, in a recent article of his in *BioScience* titled "Plant Life and Ultraviolet Radiation: Some Perspective in the History of the Earth's UV Climate." I have already mentioned Glasstone's remark that without the absorption of solar ultraviolet radiation by the ozone "life as currently known could not exist except possibly in the ocean." The 1975 N.A.S. report states, "As biologists, geologists, and other students of evolution recognize, the development of an oxygen-rich atmosphere, with its *ozone layer, was a precondition to the development of multicelled plants and animals, and all life forms on land have evolved under this shield*" (italics in the original). B. W. Boville, of the Canadian Atmospheric Environment Service, has written that the ozone layer is "a crucial element to climate and to the existence of all life on earth." Dr. Fred Iklé, who served as the director of the Arms Control and Disarmament Agency under Presidents Nixon and Ford, and now serves as Under Secretary of Defense for Policy under President Reagan, has stated that severe reduction of the ozone layer through nuclear explosions could "shatter the ecological structure that permits man to remain alive on this planet." And a paper delivered at a United Nations-sponsored scientific conference in March, 1977, states, "The whole biological world, so dependent on micro-organisms, may, if doses [of ultraviolet radiation] increase, be in serious trouble."

As the passage from the N.A.S. report states, the beginnings of multicelled life are associated with the formation of an ozone layer. In the earliest stages of evolution, when there was little or no oxygen in the atmosphere, and no ozone layer—ozone (O_3) is formed when sunlight strikes oxygen (O_2) in the upper atmosphere—ultraviolet radiation, which would then have reached the surface of the earth relatively unimpeded, may have been one of the most important sources of the energy that built up the first biological macromolecules, about three and a half billion years ago. But about two billion years ago, when those molecules had formed into single-celled organisms, the organisms freed themselves from dependence on ultraviolet light as a source of energy by coming to rely instead on photosynthesis—a method of extracting energy from sunlight by making use of carbon dioxide and water, which were available everywhere in the environment, as they are today. Photosynthesis was "probably the largest single step on the evolutionary path leading to the growth of higher life forms" (according to Dr. Michael McElroy, a physicist at Harvard's Center for Earth and Planetary Physics, who has done important new work in the study of the earth's atmosphere), and set the stage for terrestrial life as it exists today. For that life to develop, however, the genetic material, DNA, had also to develop, and ultraviolet light, as it happens, is particularly destructive of DNA, causing it to lose "biological activity," as Dr. Caldwell notes. Furthermore, ultraviolet light inhibits photosynthesis, and thus on the earth of two billion years ago it placed another barrier in the way of what turned out to be the next step in evolution. And there was still another barrier to evolution in the fact that oxygen, a by-product of photosynthesis, was poisonous to existing organisms. At first, it is suggested, organisms solved their oxygen problem by fixing oxygen to ferrous iron—a procedure that would explain the existence of banded iron formations found in sedimentary rock that is some two billion years old. But it was life's second solution to its oxygen problem—the development of enzymes capable of returning oxygen harmlessly to the environment—that proved to be the more successful one. It lifted the barriers to evolution just mentioned: by detoxifying oxygen it liberated life from its dependence on iron, leaving life "free to proliferate in the ocean, with rapid growth in oxygen" (McElroy); and by enriching the atmosphere with oxygen it assured the gradual creation of an ozone layer, which blocked out much of the ultraviolet radiation. Once this was done, the way was cleared, in the opinion of some scientists, for the "eruptive proliferation of species" (Caldwell) that geologists find in the fossil record of the Cambrian period, nearly six hundred million years ago. A hundred and eighty million years later, in the Silurian, life made a second leap ahead when, after more than three billion years in the ocean, it made its "dramatic appearance" (Caldwell) on land, and this leap, too, can be associated with the growth of the ozone shield, which, it is thought, around that time reached a density that would permit organisms to survive on land, without the partial protection from ultraviolet radiation which water affords.

If the formation of the ozone layer was one of the necessary preconditions for the "dramatic appearance" of life on land, then the question naturally arises whether heavy depletion of the ozone, by nuclear explosions or any other cause, might not bring about a dramatic disappearance of life, including human life, from the land. (Spray cans, incongruously, are one possible cause of harm to the ozone, because they put chlorocarbons into the atmosphere, and these are broken down by sunlight, releasing chlorine, which depletes ozone.) But that question, having been raised, is one of those which cannot be answered with confidence, given the present state of our knowledge of the workings of the earth. Even the estimates of ozone loss that would be brought about by holocausts of different sizes are highly uncertain (in calculating some of these figures, the National Academy of Sciences found the largest computers insufficient)—as is made clear in the 1975 N.A.S. report, which found that the explosion of ten thousand megatons of nuclear weapons would increase the amount of nitric oxide in the stratosphere to something between five and fifty times the normal amount (a tenfold uncertainty is characteristic of calculations in this field), that it would (as has been mentioned) reduce the ozone layer in the Northern Hemisphere, where the report assumes that the explosions would occur, by anything from thirty to seventy per cent, and that it would reduce it in the Southern Hemisphere by anything from twenty to forty per cent. I recently asked Dr. McElroy what the current estimation of danger to the ozone layer from man-made oxides of nitrogen in general was. "In the years after the N.A.S. report of 1975, the estimates of harm were lowered, but since about 1977 they

81

have risen again," he told me. He went on to discuss a possible increase in nitrous oxide in the atmosphere brought about by, say, agricultural fertilizers. "At present, it is estimated that a doubling of the nitrous oxide in the troposphere, which becomes nitric oxide —one of the compounds that deplete ozone—after it reaches the stratosphere, would bring about a fifteen-per-cent reduction in the ozone. That is a higher estimate for the nitrous-oxide effect than the one made in 1975. However, a nuclear holocaust would inject nitric oxide directly into the stratosphere, and in amounts much greater than would be produced, indirectly, by the twofold increase in nitrous oxide, and no one has done any study of the consequences for the ozone of these larger amounts in the light of the knowledge acquired since 1975. But my guess is that the figures would not have changed radically, and that the estimates for ozone reduction by a nuclear holocaust given in 1975 would not be far off." In mid-1981, the first measurement of an actual reduction of the ozone layer was made. The National Aeronautics and Space Administration reported "preliminary" findings indicating that ozone in a region of the stratosphere some twenty-five miles up—in the higher part of the ozone layer—had decreased at the rate of approximately half a per cent a year over the past decade. While this chilling discovery does not bear directly on the consequences of a holocaust for the ozone, it does tend to confirm the more general hypothesis that the ozone is vulnerable to human intervention.

The extent of the biological damage that would be done by various increases in ultraviolet radiation is, if anything, even less well known than what the increases caused by nuclear detonations might be, but the available information suggests that the damage to the whole ecosphere would be severe. One reason is that certain wavelengths of ultraviolet that are known to be particularly harmful biologically would be disproportionately increased by ozone reduction. Moreover, the cause of the biological damage—increased ultraviolet radiation—would be similar everywhere, but the effects would be different for each of the earth's species and ecosystems. And the effects of those effects, spreading outward indefinitely through the interconnected web of life, are not within the realm of the calculable. However, it is known with certainty that ultraviolet radiation is harmful or fatal to living things. In fact, precisely because of its abiotic qualities ultraviolet light has long been in use as a sterilizing agent in medical and other scientific work. The most comprehensive study of ultraviolet's effects which has been done so far is the Department of Transportation's Climatic Impact Assessment Program report "Impacts of Climatic Change on the Biosphere." It states that "excessive UV-B radiation"—the part of the ultraviolet spectrum which would be significantly increased by ozone depletion—"is a decidedly detrimental factor for most organisms, including man," and continues, "Even current levels of solar UV-B irradiance can be linked with phenomena such as increased mutation rates, delay of cell division, depression of photosynthesis in phytoplankton, skin cancer in humans, cancer eye in certain cattle, and lethality of many lower organisms, such as aquatic invertebrates and bacteria."

Research concerning the effects of UV-B irradiance on specific organisms—and especially on organisms in their natural habitats—has been slight, and in a recent conversation Dr. Caldwell, who was chairman of the scientific panel that produced the Climatic Impact Assessment Program report, told me that not enough experiments have been done for anyone to generalize with confidence about the ultimate fate of living things subjected to increased ultraviolet radiation. From the experiments that have been done, however, it is known that, among mammals, human beings are especially vulnerable, because of their lack of body hair. Since some ultraviolet light reaches the earth in normal circumstances, human beings (and other creatures) have developed adaptations to deal with it. The main adaptation in man is tanning, which helps to prevent sunburn. The susceptibility of fair-skinned people to these ailments and also to skin cancer is traceable to their relative inability to tan, and one consequence of reduced ozone could be higher rates of skin cancer among human beings. Of much greater seriousness, though, would be the temporary loss of sight through photophthalmia, or snow blindness, which can be contracted by exposure to heightened ultraviolet radiation and may last for several days after each exposure.

Photophthalmia is, in the words of the 1975 N.A.S. report, "disabling and painful"; also, "there are no immune groups," and "there is no adaptation." One can avoid photophthalmia by wearing goggles whenever one goes outside, but so far the world has made no provision for each person on earth to have a pair of goggles in case the ozone is depleted. However, if the higher estimates of depletion turn out to be correct, people will not be able to stay outdoors very long anyway. At these levels, "incapacitating" sunburn would occur in several minutes; if the reduction of the ozone reached the seventy per cent maximum that the report assigns to the Northern Hemisphere, the time could be ten minutes. Moreover, the report states that in the months immediately following the attack ozone depletion could be even higher than seventy per cent. "We have no simple way," the report observes, "to estimate the magnitude of short-term depletion." The ten-minute rule is not one that the strategists of "recovery" after a nuclear attack usually figure into their calculations. If high levels of ultraviolet radiation occur, then anyone who crawls out of his shelter after radiation from fallout has declined to tolerable levels will have to crawl back in immediately. In the meantime, though, people would not have been able to go out to produce food, and they would starve. A further possible harmful consequence—in itself a potential human and ecological catastrophe of global proportions—is that increased ultraviolet light would raise the amounts of Vitamin D in the skin of mammals and birds to toxic levels. But the experimentation necessary to determine whether or not this sweeping catastrophe would occur has not been done. The 1975 N.A.S. report observes, alarmingly but inconclusively, "We do not know whether man and other vertebrate animals could tolerate an increased Vitamin D synthesis that might result from a large and rapid increase in [ultraviolet] exposure." The report "urgently" recommends further study of the question.

The skin of many mammals would be protected by fur or other covering, but their eyes would remain exposed. In a recent lecture, Dr. Tsipis said that ozone reduction might bring about the blinding of the world's animals, and that this effect alone would have the makings of a global ecological catastrophe. I discussed the subject with Dr. Frederick Urbach, who teaches medicine at Temple University and is the editor of a volume titled "The Biologic Effects of Ultraviolet Radiation with Emphasis on the Skin," and who has conducted extensive research on the effect of ultraviolet radiation on animals. He confirmed that the peril to the eyes of animals is vast and real. "If you go much above fifty per cent reduction of the ozone, the increase in ultraviolet radiation begins to do injury to the cornea," he told me. "You get a bad sunburn of the eye. People don't usually get it, because at normal levels the anatomy of the face gives protection. But when there is snow on the ground the ultraviolet radiation is reflected back up into the eye. The problem is easily remedied by wearing glasses, but animals will hardly be able to do that. There is a story—probably apocryphal—that when Hannibal crossed the Alps, where ultraviolet is more intense, some of his elephants went blind. When animals can't see, they can't protect themselves. A blind animal does not survive well in nature. Repeated injury causes scarring of the cornea, and this would eventually make the animals permanently blind. We see this happening to the mice that we irradiate with ultraviolet wavelengths in the laboratory; after a while, they develop opaque corneas. In the event of ozone depletion, the same thing would happen not only to mammals but to insects and birds."

Sight and smell permit animals to find their way in the environment and to fulfill the roles mapped out for them by nature, and the loss of sight would throw the environment into disarray as billions of blinded beasts, insects, and birds began to stumble through the world. The disorientation of insects would be fateful not only for them but for plant life, much of which depends on insects for pollination and other processes essential to survival. Ultraviolet light is, in fact, known to play a role in many activities of insects, including phototaxis, celestial navigation, and sex identification, and an increase in ultraviolet light would no doubt impair these capacities. But plant life would in any case be under direct assault from increased ultraviolet radiation. While confident generalization about the fate of plants has to be ruled out, experiments that have been performed with crops show that while some are quite resistant, others, including tomatoes, beans, peas, and onions, would be killed or "severely scalded," according to the N.A.S. report. Because ultraviolet radiation breaks down DNA, which regulates reproduction, and because it also represses photosynthesis, which is the chief metabolic process of plants, the direct effect of increased ultraviolet radiation on plant life is likely to be widespread and serious. And because many species, the N.A.S. report states, "survive at an upper limit of tolerance," any increase in ultraviolet radiation is "a threat to the survival of certain species and accordingly to entire ecosystems." The global damage to plants and the global damage to the insects are synergistic: the damage to the insects damages the plants, which in turn, damage the insects again, in a chain of effects whose outcome is unforeseeable. On the question of the harm to the insects that would be caused by the harm to the rest of the ecosphere, Ting H. Hsiao, a professor of entomology at Utah State University, has written in the Climatic Impact Assessment Program report, "Since insects are important in the world's ecosystems, any changes in other components of the ecosystem could have an impact on insect populations. Ultraviolet radiation is a physical factor that directly influences all biotic components of the ecosystem. . . . A change in abiotic factors, such as temperature, rainfall, or wind, associated with elevated ultraviolet radiation could profoundly affect behavior, biology, population structure, dispersal, and migration of insects." Dr. Hsiao's observations about insects and the ecosphere can, in fact, be generalized to include all global effects of a holocaust, for there are few that do not have potentially large consequences for the character and severity of all the others.

The web of life in the oceans, perhaps more than any other part of the environment, is vulnerable to damage from increased ultraviolet radiation. John Calkins, of the Department of Radiation Medicine of the University of Kentucky, and D. Stuart Nachtwey, a professor of radiation biology at Oregon State University, remark in the Climatic Impact Assessment Program report that the experimentation that has been done so far, though it is inadequate, suggests that "many aquatic micro-organisms and invertebrates have

little reserve capacity to cope with surface levels of solar UV-B."
The organisms at greatest risk are the unicellular organisms that lie
at the base of the marine food chain, and thus ultimately sustain
the higher creatures in the oceans. Since the removal of an organism from the food chain can eliminate all the organisms above it
in the chain, the loss of even part of the chain's base could have
huge consequences. Once again, quantitative judgments are not
possible, but such experiments as have been carried out make the
danger clear. In the early nineteen-seventies, researchers discovered
that even normal levels of UV-B radiation are harmful or fatal to
many aquatic organisms if they are not permitted to descend deeper
into the water or otherwise shield themselves from exposure. The
finding is important, because it means that the question to be asked
about increased UV-B radiation is not whether it would be biologically harmful but whether the intensity would be great enough to
overpower the mechanisms of defense that organisms have built up
over billions of years of evolution to deal with normal levels of ultraviolet radiation. The defense mechanisms include the screening of
the DNA molecules with less critical molecules; enzymatic mechanisms by which damage done in the daytime is repaired at night;
and delay of cell divisions (when cells can be most sensitive to ultraviolet radiation) until the nighttime. But fleeing, which can save
some organisms from the ultraviolet peril, may get them into other
kinds of trouble. In general, organisms find the niche in the environment that is best suited to them, and if they are suddenly forced to
leave it they may die. Or, if they survive, they may destroy the ecological niche that permits some other species to survive. If a change
in the environment occurs slowly, an organism may prove able to
adapt, but a holocaust would bring a sudden change, and the usefulness of adaptation would be greatly reduced. A glimpse of a few
of the complexities involved in ultraviolet stress is offered by some
experiments that were done by Dr. Nachtwey and several colleagues on the unicellular alga called *Chlamydomonas reinhardi*.
If the alga is resting near the surface of the ocean on a cloudy day,
and the sun suddenly appears, it will dive for safety, and if ultraviolet radiation is at normal levels it will get deep enough fast

enough to survive. But if the ozone has been decreased by as little as sixteen per cent, the alga will be killed in mid-dive by the more intense ultraviolet rays. The crucial factor for *C. reinhardi* turns out to be its swimming speed.

Because experimentation has been so slight, and because the complexities are so immense, both the Climatic Impact Assessment Program report and the N.A.S. report hold back from sweeping judgments about the fate of oceanic life as a whole in the event of severe ozone reduction, but at one point the N.A.S. report does state that "under extreme circumstances, certain habitats could become devoid of living organisms," and at another point, speaking of the global effects in their entirety, it states, "Large-scale detonations will create conditions sufficient to modify the oceanic environment, on a global basis, with a resultant modification of the marine biota. In areas of major perturbations this influence will be in the form of local or extensive extinctions or reduction in susceptible species, with a subsequent disruption of the normal food web."

A second global consequence of ozone reduction would be climatic change. The earth's climate, like the ecosphere as a whole, the 1975 N.A.S. report reminds us, is "holocoenotic"; in other words, it is a whole in which "any action influencing a single part of the system can be expected to have an effect on all other parts of the system." As is hardly surprising, the totality of those effects is unknown even for a single major climatic disturbance, and the N.A.S. report notes that "no adequate climatic models exist that would permit prediction of the nature and degree of climatic changes that might result from a large-scale nuclear event." Of the three large components of the earth's surface—land, sea, and air—the air is probably the most changeable. The parts of this delicately balanced whole include, among many others, the chemical composition of both the troposphere and the stratosphere; the temperature levels of the atmosphere and the degree of moisture at all altitudes; the temperature and reflectivity of the earth's surface; the circulatory patterns of the air; the circulatory patterns of the ocean currents; and the degree of retention of the earth's reflected warmth by the atmosphere, in the so-called greenhouse effect. Each of these parts could be disturbed by a holocaust, and the disturbance of any one could disturb many or all of the others. According to present thinking, a depletion of the ozone layer would simultaneously act to warm the surface of the earth, by permitting more solar radiation to reach it, and act to cool it, by reducing the layer's capacity to radiate back to earth the heat reflected from the earth's surface. But, according to the N.A.S. report, the cooling at the surface of the earth, which might last for several years, is expected to exceed the warming by, at most, an amount estimated (very tentatively, considering that "no adequate climatic models exist") at approximately one degree Fahrenheit. Temperature change at the surface, however, may be less important than temperature change elsewhere in the atmosphere. For example, cooling of the upper troposphere and of the lower stratosphere "is likely to be much larger" than cooling at the surface, and may cause alterations in the cloud cover, which would, in turn, influence the climate. This whole subject, however, is one of the many subjects that remain relatively unexplored. It is estimated that dust and smoke lofted by the explosions would add to the cooling by another degree Fahrenheit. Temperatures on earth can fluctuate tens of degrees in a single day, yet the net reduction of a couple of degrees in the temperature of the entire surface of the earth after a holocaust would be of great consequence. For example, it could cut the biological productivity of deciduous forests by as much as twenty per cent, shift the monsoons in Asia in a way that could be ruinous for both agriculture and ecosystems, and eliminate all wheat-growing in Canada. The N.A.S. report also mentions that climatic change identified as "dramatic" and "major," but not otherwise specified, "cannot be ruled out," and adds that although the change is likely to last only a few years, the possibility exists that it "may not be reversible." Greater reductions would, of course, have larger consequences. Another global consequence of the injection of oxides of nitrogen into the stratosphere by nuclear explosions would be pollution of the environment as these gases fell back into the troposphere. Nitrogen dioxide, for example, is one of the most harmful components of the smog that afflicts many modern cities, such as Los Angeles. It reacts with hydrocarbons present in the air above these cities, actually causing in the process some ozone formation. While ozone in the stratosphere is beneficial to human beings, ozone near ground level is not. It has been found not only to increase respiratory problems among human beings but to be harmful to some plant life. The formation of nitrogen dioxide, accordingly, is still another global effect of a holocaust whose consequences are not calculable. In addition, nitrogen dioxide is responsible in polluted cities for turning the sky brown, and after a holocaust it might happen that the sky of the whole earth would turn from blue to brown for as long as the pollution lasted (perhaps several years).

The known consequences of global contamination by stratospheric fallout (as distinct from the tropospheric fallout on the targeted countries) would seem great in comparison with anything except other nuclear effects, but against this backdrop they seem moderate—although, as usual, the state of knowledge precludes confident prediction. The stratospheric portion of the fallout is much less intense than the tropospheric portion, because it can remain in the atmosphere for several years, and by the time it descends to earth its radioactivity has declined to very low levels. The N.A.S. report estimates that a ten-thousand-megaton holocaust would deliver over the following twenty to thirty years a dose of four rems to every person in the Northern Hemisphere and a third of that to every person in the Southern Hemisphere, and would cause a two-per-cent rise in the death rate from cancer. The same doses would cause serious genetic disease to increase around the world by up to about two per cent, with a noticeable but decreasing number of mutations appearing in the next thirty generations. There would, however, be "hot spots" in some parts of the world, where, because of certain patterns of weather, the doses of radiation would be many times as great. Also, the world would be contaminated with particles of plutonium, which would cause an as yet unestimated rise in the incidence of lung cancer. (All these effects, which were calculated by the N.A.S. in 1975 for a ten-thousand-megaton holocaust, would presumably be greater in a twenty-thousand-megaton holocaust.)

In recent years, scientists in many fields have accumulated enough knowledge to begin to look on the earth as a single, concrete mechanism, and to at least begin to ask how it works. One of their discoveries has been that life and life's inanimate terrestrial surroundings have a strong reciprocal influence on each other. For life, the land, oceans, and air have been the environment, but, equally, for the land, oceans, and air life has been the environment—the conditioning force. The injection of oxygen into the atmosphere by living things, which led to the formation of an ozone layer, which, in turn, shut out lethal ultraviolet rays from the sun and permitted the rise of multicellular organisms, was only one of life's large-scale interventions. The more closely scientists look at life and its evolution, the less they find it possible to draw a sharp distinction between "life," on the one hand, and an inanimate "environment" in which it exists, on the other. Rather, "the environment" of the present day appears to be a house of unimaginable intricacy which life has to a very great extent built and furnished for its own use. It seems that life even regulates and maintains the chemical environment of the earth in a way that turns out to suit its own needs. In a far-reaching speculative article entitled "Chemical Processes in the Solar System: A Kinetic Perspective," Dr. McElroy has described the terrestrial cycles by which the most important elements of the atmosphere—oxygen, carbon, and nitrogen—are kept in proportions that are favorable to life. He finds that in each case life itself—its birth, metabolism, and decay—is chiefly responsible for maintaining the balance. For example, he calculates that if for some reason respiration and decay were suddenly cut off, photosynthesis would devour all the inorganic carbon on the surface of the ocean and in the atmosphere within forty years. Thereafter, carbon welling up from the deep ocean would fuel photosynthesis in the oceans for another thousand years, but then "life as we know it would terminate." Dr. McElroy also observes that the amount of ozone in the stratosphere is influenced by the amount of organic decay, and thus by the amount of life, on earth. Nitrous oxide is a product of organic decay, and because it produces nitric oxide—one of the compounds responsible for ozone depletion—it plays the role of regulator. In the absence of human intervention, living things are largely responsible for introducing nitrous oxide into the atmosphere. When life is exceptionally abundant, it releases more nitrous oxide into the atmosphere, and may thus act to cut back on the ozone, and that cutback lets in more ultraviolet rays. On the other hand, when life is sparse and depleted, nitrous-oxide production is reduced, the ozone layer builds up, and ultraviolet rays are cut back. These speculative glimpses of what might be called the metabolism of the earth give substance to the growing conviction among scientists that the earth, like a single cell or a single organism, is a systemic whole, and in a general way they tend to confirm the fear that any large man-made perturbation of terrestrial nature could lead to a catastrophic systemic breakdown. Nuclear explosions are far from being the only perturbations in question; a heating of the global atmosphere through an increased greenhouse effect, which could be caused by the injection of vast amounts of carbon dioxide into the air (for instance, from the increased burning of coal), is another notable peril of this kind. But a nuclear holocaust would be unique in its suddenness, which would permit no observation of slowly building environmental damage before the full—and, for man, perhaps the final—catastrophe occurred. The geological record does not sustain the fear that sudden perturbations can extinguish all life on earth (if it did, we would not be here to reflect on the subject), but it does suggest that sudden, drastic ecological collapse is possible. It suggests that life as a whole, if it is given hundreds of millions of years in which to recuperate and send out new evolutionary lines, has an astounding resilience, and an ability to bring forth new and ever more impressive life forms, but it also suggests that abrupt interventions can radically disrupt any particular evolutionary configuration and dispatch hundreds of thousands of species into extinction.

The view of the earth as a single system, or organism, has only recently proceeded from poetic metaphor to actual scientific investigation, and on the whole Dr. Thomas's observation that "we do not really understand nature, at all" still holds. It is as much on the basis of this ignorance, whose scope we are only now in a position to grasp, as on the basis of the particular items of knowledge in our possession that I believe that the following judgment can be made: Bearing in mind that the possible consequences of the detonations of thousands of megatons of nuclear explosives include the blinding of insects, birds, and beasts all over the world; the extinction of many ocean species, among them some at the base of the food chain; the temporary or permanent alteration of the climate of the globe, with the outside chance of "dramatic" and "major" alterations in the structure of the atmosphere; the pollution of the whole ecosphere with oxides of nitrogen; the incapacitation in ten minutes of unprotected people who go out into the sunlight; the blinding of people who go out into the sunlight; a significant decrease in photosynthesis in plants around the world; the scalding and killing of many crops; the increase in rates of cancer and mutation around the world, but especially in the targeted zones, and the attendant risk of global epidemics; the possible poisoning of all vertebrates by sharply increased levels of Vitamin D in their skin as a result of increased ultraviolet light; and the outright slaughter on all targeted continents of most human beings and other living things by the initial nuclear radiation, the fireballs, the thermal pulses, the blast waves, the mass fires, and the fallout from the explosions; and, considering that these consequences will all interact with one another in unguessable ways and, furthermore, are in all likelihood an incomplete list, which will be added to as our knowledge of the earth increases, one must conclude that a full-scale nuclear holocaust could lead to the extinction of mankind.

To say that human extinction is a certainty would, of course, be a misrepresentation—just as it would be a misrepresentation to

THE FATE OF THE EARTH

say that extinction can be ruled out. To begin with, we know that a holocaust may not occur at all. If one does occur, the adversaries may not use all their weapons. If they do use all their weapons, the global effects, in the ozone and elsewhere, may be moderate. And if the effects are not moderate but extreme, the ecosphere may prove resilient enough to withstand them without breaking down catastrophically. These are all substantial reasons for supposing that mankind will not be extinguished in a nuclear holocaust, or even that extinction in a holocaust is unlikely, and they tend to calm our fear and to reduce our sense of urgency. Yet at the same time we are compelled to admit that there *may* be a holocaust, that the adversaries *may* use all their weapons, that the global effects, including effects of which we are as yet unaware, *may* be severe, that the ecosphere *may* suffer catastrophic breakdown, and that our species *may* be extinguished. We are left with uncertainty, and are forced to make our decisions in a state of uncertainty. If we wish to act to save our species, we have to muster our resolve in spite of our awareness that the life of the species may not now in fact be jeopardized. On the other hand, if we wish to ignore the peril, we have to admit that we do so in the knowledge that the species may be in danger of imminent self-destruction. When the existence of nuclear weapons was made known, thoughtful people everywhere in the world realized that if the great powers entered into a nuclear-arms race the human species would sooner or later face the possibility of extinction. They also realized that in the absence of international agreements preventing it an arms race would probably occur. They knew that the path of nuclear armament was a dead end for mankind. The discovery of the energy in mass—of "the basic power of the universe"—and of a means by which man could release that energy altered the relationship between man and the source of his life, the earth. In the shadow of this power, the earth became small and the life of the human species doubtful. In that sense, the question of human extinction has been on the political agenda of the world ever since the first nuclear weapon was detonated, and there was no need for the world to build up its present tremendous arsenals before starting to worry about it. At just what point the species crossed, or will have crossed, the boundary between merely having the technical knowledge to destroy itself and actually having the arsenals at hand, ready to be used at any second, is not precisely knowable. But it is clear that at present, with some twenty thousand megatons of nuclear explosive power in existence, and with more being added every day, we have entered into the zone of uncertainty, which is to say the zone of risk of extinction. But the mere risk of extinction has a significance that is categorically different from, and immeasurably greater than, that of any other risk, and as we make our decisions we have to take that significance into account. Up to now, every risk has been contained within the frame of life; extinction would shatter the frame. It represents not the defeat of some purpose but an abyss in which all human purposes would be drowned for all time. We have no right to place the possibility of this limitless, eternal defeat on the same footing as risks that we run in the ordinary conduct of our affairs in our particular transient moment of human history. To employ a mathematical analogy, we can say that although the risk of extinction may be fractional, the stake is, humanly speaking, infinite, and a fraction of infinity is still infinity. In other words, once we learn that a holocaust *might* lead to extinction we have no right to gamble, because if we lose, the game will be over, and neither we nor anyone else will ever get another chance. Therefore, although, scientifically speaking, there is all the difference in the world between the mere possibility that a holocaust will bring about extinction and the certainty of it, morally they are the same, and we have no choice but to address the issue of nuclear weapons as though we knew for a certainty that their use would put an end to our species. In weighing the fate of the earth and, with it, our own fate, we stand before a mystery, and in tampering with the earth we tamper with a mystery. We are in deep ignorance. Our ignorance should dispose us to wonder, our wonder should make us humble, our humility should inspire us to reverence and caution, and our reverence and caution should lead us to act without delay to withdraw the threat we now pose to the earth and to ourselves.

In trying to describe possible consequences of a nuclear holocaust, I have mentioned the limitless complexity of its effects on human society and on the ecosphere—a complexity that sometimes seems to be as great as that of life itself. But if these effects should lead to human extinction, then all the complexity will give way to the utmost simplicity—the simplicity of nothingness. We—the human race—shall cease to be.

II.
THE SECOND DEATH

I F A COUNCIL WERE TO BE EMPOWERED by the people of the earth to do whatever was necessary to save humanity from extinction by nuclear arms, it might well decide that a good first step would be to order the destruction of all the nuclear weapons in the world. When the order had been carried out, however, warlike or warring nations might still rebuild their nuclear arsenals—perhaps in a matter of months. A logical second step, accordingly, would be to order the destruction of the factories that make the weapons. But, just as the weapons might be rebuilt, so might the factories, and the world's margin of safety would not have been increased by very much. A third step, then, would be to order the destruction of the factories that make the factories that make the weapons—a measure that might require the destruction of a considerable part of the world's economy. But even then lasting safety would not have been reached, because in some number of years—at most, a few decades—everything could be rebuilt, including the nuclear arsenals, and mankind would again be ready to extinguish itself. A determined council might next decide to try to arrest the world economy in a pre-nuclear state by throwing the blueprints and technical manuals for reconstruction on the bonfires that had by then consumed every-thing else, but that recourse, too, would ultimately fail, because the blueprints and manuals could easily be redrawn and rewritten. As long as the world remained acquainted with the basic physical laws that underlie the construction of nuclear weapons—and these laws include the better part of physics as physics is understood in our century—mankind would have failed to put many years between itself and its doom. For the fundamental origin of the peril of human extinction by nuclear arms lies not in any particular social or politi-cal circumstances of our time but in the attainment by mankind as a whole, after millennia of scientific progress, of a certain level of knowledge of the physical universe. As long as that knowledge is in our possession, the atoms themselves, each one stocked with its prodigious supply of energy, are, in a manner of speaking, in a perilously advanced state of mobilization for nuclear hostilities, and any conflict anywhere in the world can become a nuclear one. To return to safety through technical measures alone, we would have to disarm matter itself, converting it back into its relatively safe, inert, nonexplosive nineteenth-century Newtonian state—something that not even the physics of our time can teach us how to do. (I mention these farfetched, wholly imaginary programs of demolition and suppression in part because the final destruction of all mankind is so much more farfetched, and therefore seems to give us license to at least consider extreme alternatives, but mainly because their obvious inadequacy serves to demonstrate how deeply the nuclear peril is ingrained in our world.)

It is fundamental to the shape and character of the nuclear predicament that its origins lie in scientific knowledge rather than in social circumstances. Revolutions born in the laboratory are to be sharply distinguished from revolutions born in society. Social revolutions are usually born in the minds of millions, and are led up to by what the Declaration of Independence calls "a long train of abuses," visible to all; indeed, they usually cannot occur unless they are widely understood by and supported by the public. By contrast, scientific revolutions usually take shape quietly in the minds of a few men, under cover of the impenetrability to most laymen of scientific theory, and thus catch the world by surprise. In the case of nuclear weapons, of course, the surprise was greatly increased by the governmental secrecy that surrounded the construction of the first bombs. When the world learned of their existence, Mr. Fukai had already run back into the flames of Hiroshima, and tens of thousands of people in that city had already been killed. Even long after scientific discoveries have been made and their applications have transformed our world, most people are likely to remain ignorant of the underlying principles at work, and this has been particularly true of nuclear weapons, which, decades after their invention, are still surrounded by an aura of mystery, as though they had descended from another planet. (To most people, Einstein's famous formula $E = mc^2$, which defines the energy released in nuclear explosions, stands as a kind of symbol of everything that is esoteric and incomprehensible.)

But more important by far than the world's unpreparedness for scientific revolutions are their universality and their permanence once they have occurred. Social revolutions are restricted to a particular time and place; they arise out of particular circumstances, last for a while, and then pass into history. Scientific revolutions, on the other hand, belong to all places and all times. In the words of Alfred North Whitehead, "Modern science was born in Europe, but its home is the whole world." In fact, of all the products of human hands and minds, scientific knowledge has proved to be the most durable. The physical structures of human life—furniture, buildings, paintings, cities, and so on—are subject to inevitable natural decay, and human institutions have likewise proved to be transient. Hegel, whose philosophy of history was framed in large measure in an attempt to redeem the apparent futility of the efforts of men to found something enduring in their midst, once wrote, "When we see the evil, the vice, the ruin that has befallen the most flourishing kingdoms which the mind of man ever created, we can scarce avoid being filled with sorrow at this universal taint of corruption; and, since this decay is not the work of mere Nature, but of Human Will —a moral embitterment—a revolt of the Good Spirit (if it have a place within us) may well be the result of our reflections." Works of thought and many works of art have a better chance of surviving, since new copies of a book or a symphony can be transcribed from old ones, and so can be preserved indefinitely; yet these works, too, can and do go out of existence, for if every copy is lost, then the work is also lost. The subject matter of these works is man, and they seem to be touched with his mortality. The results of scientific work, on the other hand, are largely immune to decay and disappearance. Even when they are lost, they are likely to be rediscovered, as is shown by the fact that several scientists often make the same discovery independently. (There is no record of several poets' having independently written the same poem, or of several composers' having independently written the same symphony.) For both the subject matter and the method of science are available to all capable minds in a way that the subject matter and the method of the arts are not. The human experiences that art deals with are, once over, lost forever, like the people who undergo them, whereas matter, energy, space, and time, alike everywhere and in all ages, are always available for fresh inspection. The subject matter of science is the physical world, and its findings seem to share in the immortality of the physical world. And artistic vision grows out of the unrepeatable individuality of each artist, whereas the reasoning power of the mind—its ability to add two and two and get four—is the same in all competent persons. The rigorous exactitude of scientific methods does not mean that creativity is any less individual, intuitive, or mysterious in great scientists than in great artists, but it does mean that scientific findings, once arrived at, can be tested and confirmed by shared canons of logic and experimentation. The agreement among scientists thus achieved permits science to be a collective enterprise, in which each generation, building on the accepted findings of the generations before, makes amendments and additions, which in their turn become the starting point for the next generation. (Philosophers, by contrast, are constantly tearing down the work of their predecessors, and circling back to re-ask questions that have been asked and answered countless times before. Kant once wrote in despair, "It seems ridiculous that while every science moves forward ceaselessly, this [metaphysics], claiming to be wisdom itself, whose oracular pronouncements everyone consults, is continually revolving in one spot, without advancing one step.") Scientists, as they erect the steadily growing structure of scientific knowledge, resemble nothing so much as a swarm of bees working harmoniously together to construct a single, many-chambered hive, which grows more elaborate and splendid with every year that passes. Looking at what they have made over the centuries, scientists need feel no "sorrow" or "moral embitterment" at any "taint of corruption" that supposedly undoes all human achievements. When God, alarmed that the builders of the Tower of Babel would reach Heaven with their construction, and so become as God, put an end to their undertaking by making them all speak different languages, He apparently overlooked the scientists, for they, speaking what is often called the "universal language" of their disciplines from country to country and generation to generation, went on to build a new tower—the edifice of scientific knowledge. Their phenomenal success, beginning not with Einstein but with Euclid and Archimedes, has provided the unshakable structure that supports the world's nuclear peril. So durable is the scientific edifice that if we did not know that human beings had constructed it we might suppose that the findings on which our whole technological civilization rests were the pillars and crossbeams of an invulnerable, inhuman order obtruding into our changeable and perishable human realm. It is the crowning irony of this lopsided development of human abilities that the only means in sight for getting rid of the knowledge of how to destroy ourselves would be to do just that—in effect, to remove the knowledge by removing the knower.

Although it is unquestionably the scientists who have led us to the edge of the nuclear abyss, we would be mistaken if we either held them chiefly responsible for our plight or looked to them, particularly, for a solution. Here, again, the difference between scientific revolutions and social revolutions shows itself, for the notion that scientists bear primary responsibility springs from a tendency to confuse scientists with political actors. Political actors, who, of course, include ordinary citizens as well as government officials, act with definite social ends in view, such as the preservation of peace, the establishment of a just society, or, if they are corrupt, their own aggrandizement; and they are accordingly held responsible for the consequences of their actions, even when these are unintended ones, as they so often are. Scientists, on the other hand (and here I refer to the so-called pure scientists, who search for the laws of nature for the sake of knowledge itself, and not to the applied scientists, who make use of already discovered natural laws to solve practical problems), do not aim at social ends, and, in fact, usually do not know what the social results of their findings will be; for that matter, they cannot know what the findings themselves will be, because science is a process of discovery, and it is in the nature of discovery that one cannot know beforehand what one will find. This element of the unexpected is present when a researcher sets out to unravel some small, carefully defined mystery—say, the chemistry of a certain enzyme—but it is most conspicuous in the synthesis of the great laws of science and in the development of science as a whole, which, over decades and centuries, moves toward destinations that no one can predict. Thus, only a few decades ago it might have seemed that physics, which had just placed nuclear energy at man's disposal, was the dangerous branch of science, while biology, which underlay improvements in medicine and also helped us to understand our dependence on the natural environment, was the beneficial branch; but now that biologists have begun to fathom the secrets of genetics, and to tamper with the genetic substance of life directly, we cannot be so sure. The most striking illustration of the utter disparity that may occur between the wishes of the scientist as a social being and the social results of his scientific findings is certainly the career of Einstein. By nature, he was, according to all accounts, the gentlest of men, and by conviction he was a pacifist, yet he made intellectual discoveries that led the way to the invention of weapons with which the species could exterminate itself. Inspired wholly by a love of knowledge for its own sake, and by an awe at the creation which bordered on the religious, he made possible an instrument of destruction with which the terrestrial creation could be disfigured.

A disturbing corollary of the scientists' inability even to foresee the path of science, to say nothing of determining it, is that while science is without doubt the most powerful revolutionary force in our world, no one directs that force. For science is a process of submission, in which the mind does not dictate to nature but seeks out and then bows to nature's laws, letting its conclusions be guided by that which *is*, independent of our will. From the political point of view, therefore, scientific findings, some lending themselves to evil, some to good, and some to both, simply pour forth from the laboratory in senseless profusion, offering the world now a neutron bomb, now bacteria that devour oil, now a vaccine to prevent polio, now a cloned frog. It is not until the pure scientists, seekers of knowledge for its own sake, turn their findings over to the applied scientists that social intentions begin to guide the results. The applied scientists do indeed set out to make a better vaccine or a bigger bomb, but even they, perhaps, deserve less credit or blame than we are sometimes inclined to give them. For as soon as our intentions enter the picture we are in the realm of politics in the broadest sense, and in politics it is ultimately not technicians but governments and citizens who are in charge. The scientists in the Manhattan Project could not decide to make the first atomic bomb; only President Roosevelt, elected to office by the American people, could do that.

If scientists are unable to predict their discoveries, neither can they cancel them once they have been made. In this respect, they are like the rest of us, who are asked not whether we would like to live in a world in which we can convert matter into energy but only what we want to do about it once we have been told that we do live in such a world. Science is a tide that can only rise. The individual human mind is capable of forgetting things, and mankind has collectively forgotten many things, but we do not know how, as a species, to *deliberately* set out to forget something. A basic scientific finding, therefore, has the character of destiny for the world. Scientific discovery is in this regard like any other form of discovery; once Columbus had discovered America, and had told the world about it, America could not be hidden again.

Scientific progress (which can and certainly will occur) offers little more hope than scientific regression (which probably cannot occur) of giving us relief from the nuclear peril. It does not seem likely that science will bring forth some new invention—some anti-ballistic missile or laser beam—that will render nuclear weapons harmless (although the unpredictability of science prevents any categorical judgment on this point). In the centuries of the modern scientific revolution, scientific knowledge has steadily increased the destructiveness of warfare, for it is in the very nature of knowledge, apparently, to increase our might rather than to diminish it. One of the most common forms of the hope for deliverance from the nuclear peril by technical advances is the notion that the species will be spared extinction by fleeing in spaceships. The thought seems to be that while the people on earth are destroying themselves communities in space will be able to survive and carry on. This thought does an injustice to our birthplace and habitat, the earth. It assumes that if only we could escape the earth we would find safety—as though it were the earth and its plants and animals that threatened us, rather than the other way around. But the fact is that wherever human beings went there also would go the knowledge of how to build nuclear weapons, and, with it, the peril of extinction. Scientific progress may yet deliver us from many evils, but there are at least two evils that it cannot deliver us from: its own findings and our own destructive and self-destructive bent. This is a combination that we will have to learn to deal with by some other means.

We live, then, in a universe whose fundamental substance contains a supply of energy with which we can extinguish ourselves. We shall never live in any other. We now know that we live in such a universe, and we shall never stop knowing it. Over the millennia, this truth lay in waiting for us, and now we have found it out, irrevocably. If we suppose that it is an integral part of human existence to be curious about the physical world we are born into, then, to speak in the broadest terms, the origin of the nuclear peril lies, on the one hand, in our nature as rational and inquisitive beings and, on the other, in the nature of matter. Because the energy that nuclear weapons release is so great, the whole species is threatened by them, and because the spread of scientific knowledge is unstoppable, the whole species poses the threat: in the last analysis, it is all of mankind that threatens all of mankind. (I do not mean to overlook the fact that at present it is only two nations—the United States and the Soviet Union—that possess nuclear weapons in numbers great enough to possibly destroy the species, and that they thus now bear the chief responsibility for the peril. I only wish to point out that, regarded in its full dimensions, the nuclear peril transcends the rivalry between the present superpowers.)

The fact that the roots of the nuclear peril lie in basic scientific knowledge has broad political implications that cannot be ignored if the world's solution to the predicament is to be built on a solid foundation, and if futile efforts are to be avoided. One such effort would be to rely on secrecy to contain the peril—that is, to "classify" the "secret" of the bomb. The first person to try to suppress knowledge of how nuclear weapons can be made was the physicist Leo Szilard, who in 1939, when he first heard that a nuclear chain reaction was possible, and realized that a nuclear bomb might be possible, called on a number of his colleagues to keep the discovery secret from the Germans. Many of the key scientists refused. His failure foreshadowed a succession of failures, by whole governments, to restrict the knowledge of how the weapons are made. The first, and most notable, such failure was the United States' inability to monopolize nuclear weapons, and prevent the Soviet Union from building them. And we have subsequently witnessed the failure of the entire world to prevent nuclear weapons from spreading. Given the nature of scientific thought and the very poor record of past attempts to suppress it, these failures should not have surprised anyone. (The Catholic Church succeeded in making Galileo recant his view that the earth revolves around the sun, but we do not now believe that the sun revolves around the earth.) Another, closely related futile effort—the one made by our hypothetical council—

would be to try to resolve the nuclear predicament through disarmament alone, without accompanying political measures. Like the hope that the knowledge can be classified, this hope loses sight of the fact that the nuclear predicament consists not in the possession of nuclear weapons at a particular moment by certain nations but in the circumstance that mankind as a whole has now gained possession once and for all of the knowledge of how to make them, and that all nations—and even some groups of people which are not nations, including terrorist groups—can potentially build them. Because the nuclear peril, like the scientific knowledge that gave rise to it, is probably global and everlasting, our solution must at least aim at being global and everlasting. And the only kind of solution that holds out this promise is a global political one. In defining the task so broadly, however, I do not mean to argue against short-term palliatives, such as the Strategic Arms Limitation Talks between the United States and the Soviet Union, or nuclear-nonproliferation agreements, on the ground that they are short-term. If a patient's life is in danger, as mankind's now is, no good cause is served by an argument between the nurse who wants to give him an aspirin to bring down his fever and the doctor who wants to perform the surgery that can save his life; there is need for an argument only if the nurse is claiming that the aspirin is all that is necessary. If, given the world's discouraging record of political achievement, a lasting political solution seems almost beyond human powers, it may give us confidence to remember that what challenges us is simply our extraordinary success in another field of activity—the scientific. We have only to learn to live politically in the world in which we already live scientifically.

Since 1947, the *Bulletin of the Atomic Scientists* has included a "doomsday clock" in each issue. The editors place the hands farther away from or closer to midnight as they judge the world to be farther away from or closer to a nuclear holocaust. A companion clock can be imagined whose hands, instead of metaphorically representing a judgment about the likelihood of a holocaust, would represent an estimate of the amount of time that, given the world's technical and political arrangements, the people of the earth can be

108

sure they have left before they are destroyed in a holocaust. At present, the hands would stand at, or a fraction of a second before, midnight, because none of us can be sure that at any second we will not be killed in a nuclear attack. If, by treaty, all nuclear warheads were removed from their launchers and stored somewhere else, and therefore could no longer descend on us at any moment without warning, the clock would show the amount of time that it would take to put them back on. If all the nuclear weapons in the world were destroyed, the clock would show the time that it would take to manufacture them again. If in addition confidence-inspiring political arrangements to prevent rearmament were put in place, the clock would show some estimate of the time that it might take for the arrangements to break down. And if these arrangements were to last for hundreds or thousands of years (as they must if mankind is to survive this long), then some generation far in the future might feel justified in setting the clock at decades, or even centuries, before midnight. But no generation would ever be justified in retiring the clock from use altogether, because, as far as we can tell, there will never again be a time when self-extinction is beyond the reach of our species. An observation that Plutarch made about politics holds true also for the task of survival, which has now become the principal obligation of politics: "They are wrong who think that politics is like an ocean voyage or a military campaign, something to be done with some end in view, something which levels off as soon as that end is reached. It is not a public chore, to be got over with; it is a way of life."

The scientific principles and techniques that make possible the construction of nuclear weapons are, of course, only one small portion of mankind's huge reservoir of scientific knowledge, and, as I have mentioned, it has always been known that scientific findings can be made use of for evil as well as for good, according to the intentions of the user. What is new to our time is the realization that, acting quite independently of any good or evil intentions of ours, the human enterprise as a whole has begun to strain and erode the natural terrestrial world on which human and other life depends. Taken in its entirety, the increase in mankind's strength has brought about a decisive, many-sided shift in the balance of strength between man and the earth. Nature, once a harsh and feared master, now lies in subjection, and needs protection against man's powers. Yet because man, no matter what intellectual and technical heights he may scale, remains embedded in nature, the balance has shifted against him, too, and the threat that he poses to the earth is a threat to him as well. The peril to nature was difficult to see at first, in part because its symptoms made their appearance as unintended "side effects" of our intended goals, on which we had fixed most of our attention. In economic production, the side effects are the peril of gradual pollution of the natural environment—by, for example, global heating through an increased "greenhouse effect." In the military field, the side effects, or prospective side effects —sometimes referred to by the strategists as the "collateral effects" —include the possible extinction of the species through sudden, severe harm to the ecosphere, caused by global radioactive contamination, ozone depletion, climatic change, and the other known and unknown possible consequences of a nuclear holocaust. Though from the point of view of the human actor there might be a clear difference between the "constructive" economic applications of technology and the "destructive" military ones, nature makes no such distinction: both are beachheads of human mastery in a defenseless natural world. (For example, the ozone doesn't care whether oxides of nitrogen are injected into it by the use of supersonic transports or by nuclear weapons; it simply reacts according to the appropriate chemical laws.) It was not until recently that it became clear that often the side effects of both the destructive and the constructive applications were really the main effects. And now the task ahead of us can be defined as one of giving the "side effects," including, above all, the peril of self-extinction, the weight they deserve in our judgments and decisions. To use a homely metaphor, if a man discovers that improvements he is making to his house threaten to destroy its foundation he is well advised to rethink them.

A nuclear holocaust, because of its unique combination of immensity and suddenness, is a threat without parallel; yet at the same time it is only one of countless threats that the human enterprise, grown mighty through knowledge, poses to the natural world. Our species is caught in the same tightening net of technical success that has already strangled so many other species. (At present, it has been estimated, the earth loses species at the rate of about three per day.) The peril of human extinction, which exists not because every single person in the world would be killed by the immediate explosive and radioactive effects of a holocaust—something that is exceedingly unlikely, even at present levels of armament—but because a holocaust might render the biosphere unfit for human survival, is, in a word, an *ecological* peril. The nuclear peril is usually seen in isolation from the threats to other forms of life and their ecosystems, but in fact it should be seen as the very center of the ecological crisis—as the cloud-covered Everest of which the more immediate, visible kinds of harm to the environment are the mere foothills. Both the effort to preserve the environment and the effort to save the species from extinction by nuclear arms would be enriched and strengthened by this recognition. The nuclear question, which now stands in eerie seclusion from the rest of life, would gain a context, and the ecological movement, which, in its concern for plants and animals, at times assumes an almost misanthropic posture, as though man were an unwanted intruder in an otherwise unblemished natural world, would gain the humanistic intent that should stand at the heart of its concern.

Seen as a planetary event, the rising tide of human mastery over nature has brought about a categorical increase in the power of death on earth. An organism's ability to renew itself during its lifetime and to reproduce itself depends on the integrity of what biologists call "information" stored in its genes. What endures—what lives—in an organism is not any particular group of cells but a configuration of cells which is dictated by the genetic information. What survives in a species, correspondingly, is a larger configuration, which takes in all the individuals in the species. An ecosystem is a still larger configuration, in which a whole constellation of species forms a balanced, self-reproducing, slowly changing whole. The ecosphere of the earth—Dr. Lewis Thomas's "cell"—is, finally, the largest of the living configurations, and is a carefully regulated and balanced, self-perpetuating system in its own right. At each of these levels, life is coherence, and the loss of coherence—the sudden slide toward disorder—is death. Seen in this light, life is information, and death is the loss of information, returning the substance of the creature to randomness. However, the death of a species or an ecosystem has a role in the natural order that is very different from that of the death of an organism. Whereas an individual organism, once born, begins to proceed inevitably toward death, a species is a source of new life that has no fixed term. An organism is a configuration whose demise is built into its plan, and within the life of a species the death of individual members normally has a fixed, limited, and necessary place, so that as death moves through the ranks of the living its pace is roughly matched by the pace of birth, and populations are kept in a rough balance that enables them to coexist and endure in their particular ecosystem. A species, on the other hand, can survive as long as environmental circumstances happen to permit. An ecosystem, likewise, is indefinitely self-renewing. But when the pace of death is too much increased, either by human intervention in the environment or by some other event, death becomes an extinguishing power, and species and ecosystems are lost. Then not only are individual creatures destroyed but the sources of all future creatures of those kinds are closed down, and a portion of the diversity and strength of terrestrial life in its entirety vanishes forever. And when man gained the ability to intervene directly in the workings of the global "cell" as a whole, and thus to extinguish species wholesale, his power to encroach on life increased by still another order of magnitude, and came to threaten the balance of the entire planetary system of life.

Hence, there are two competing forces at work in the terrestrial environment—one natural, which acts over periods of millions of years to strengthen and multiply the forms of life, and the other man-made and man-operated, which, if it is left unregulated and unguided, tends in general to deplete life's array of forms. Indeed, it is a striking fact that both of these great engines of change on earth depend on stores of information that are passed down from generation to generation. There is, in truth, no closer analogy to scientific progress, in which a steadily growing pool of information makes possible the creation of an ever more impressive array of artifacts, than evolution, in which another steadily growing pool of information makes possible the development of ever more complex and astonishing creatures—culminating in human beings, who now threaten to raze both the human and the natural structures to their inanimate foundations. One is tempted to say that only the organic site of the evolutionary information has changed—from genes to brains. However, because of the extreme rapidity of technological change relative to natural evolution, evolution is unable to refill the vacated niches of the environment with new species, and, as a result, the genetic pool of life as a whole is imperilled. Death, having been augmented by human strength, has lost its appointed place in the natural order and become a counterevolutionary force, capable of destroying in a few years, or even in a few hours, what evolution has built up over billions of years. In doing so, death threatens even itself, since death, after all, is a part of life: stones may be lifeless but they do not die. The question now before the human species, therefore, is whether life or death will prevail on the earth. This is not metaphorical language but a literal description of the present state of affairs.

One might say that after billions of years nature, by creating a species equipped with reason and will, turned its fate, which had previously been decided by the slow, unconscious movements of natural evolution, over to the conscious decisions of just one of its species. When this occurred, human activity, which until then had been confined to the historical realm—which, in turn, had been supported by the broader biological current—spilled out of its old boundaries and came to menace both history and biology. Thought and will became mightier than the earth that had given birth to them. Now human beings became actors in the geological time span, and the laws that had governed the development and the survival of life began to be superseded by processes in the mind of man. Here, however, there were no laws; there was only choice, and the thinking and feeling that guide choice. The reassuring, stable, self-sustaining prehistoric world of nature dropped away, and in its place mankind's own judgments, moods, and decisions loomed up with an unlooked-for, terrifying importance.

Regarded objectively, as an episode in the development of life on earth, a nuclear holocaust that brought about the extinction of mankind and other species by mutilating the ecosphere would constitute an evolutionary setback of possibly limited extent—the first to result from a deliberate action taken by the creature extinguished but perhaps no greater than any of several evolutionary setbacks, such as the extinction of the dinosaurs, of which the geological record offers evidence. (It is, of course, impossible to judge what course evolution would take after human extinction, but the past record strongly suggests that the reappearance of man is not one of the possibilities. Evolution has brought forth an amazing variety of creatures, but there is no evidence that any species, once extinguished, has ever evolved again. Whether or not nature, obeying some law of evolutionary progress, would bring forth another creature equipped with reason and will, and capable of building, and perhaps then destroying, a world, is one more unanswerable question, but it is barely conceivable that some gifted new animal will pore over the traces of our self-destruction, trying to figure out what went wrong and to learn from our mistakes. If this should be possible, then it might justify the remark once made by Kafka: "There is infinite hope, but not for us." If, on the other hand, as the record of life so far suggests, terrestrial evolution is able to produce only once the miracle of the qualities that we now associate with human beings, then all hope rides with human beings.) However, regarded subjectively, from within human life, where we are all actually situated, and as something that would happen to us, human extinction assumes awesome, inapprehensible proportions. It is of the essence of the human condition

114

that we are born, live for a while, and then die. Through mishaps of all kinds, we may also suffer untimely death, and in extinction by nuclear arms the number of untimely deaths would reach the limit for any one catastrophe: everyone in the world would die. But although the untimely death of everyone in the world would in itself constitute an unimaginably huge loss, it would bring with it a separate, distinct loss that would be in a sense even huger—the cancellation of all future generations of human beings. According to the Bible, when Adam and Eve ate the fruit of the tree of knowledge God punished them by withdrawing from them the privilege of immortality and dooming them and their kind to die. Now our species has eaten more deeply of the fruit of the tree of knowledge, and has brought itself face to face with a second death —the death of mankind. In doing so, we have caused a basic change in the circumstances in which life was given to us, which is to say that we have altered the human condition. The distinctness of this second death from the deaths of all the people on earth can be illustrated by picturing two different global catastrophes. In the first, let us suppose that most of the people on earth were killed in a nuclear holocaust but that a few million survived and the earth happened to remain habitable by human beings. In this catastrophe, billions of people would perish, but the species would survive, and perhaps one day would even repopulate the earth in its former numbers. But now let us suppose that a substance was released into the environment which had the effect of sterilizing all the people in the world but otherwise leaving them unharmed. Then, as the existing population died off, the world would empty of people, until no one was left. Not one life would have been short-ened by a single day, but the species would die. In extinction by nuclear arms, the death of the species and the death of all the people in the world would happen together, but it is important to make a clear distinction between the two losses; otherwise, the mind, overwhelmed by the thought of the deaths of the billions of living people, might stagger back without realizing that behind this already ungraspable loss there lies the separate loss of the future generations.

The possibility that the living can stop the future generations from entering into life compels us to ask basic new questions about our existence, the most sweeping of which is what these unborn ones, most of whom we will never meet even if they are born, mean to us. No one has ever thought to ask this question before our time, because no generation before ours has ever held the life and death of the species in its hands. But if we hardly know how to comprehend the possible deaths in a holocaust of the billions of people who are already in life how are we to comprehend the life or death of the infinite number of possible people who do not yet exist at all? How are we, who are a part of human life, to step back from life and see it whole, in order to assess the meaning of its disappearance? To kill a human being is murder, and there are those who believe that to abort a fetus is also murder, but what crime is it to cancel the numberless multitude of unconceived people? In what court is such a crime to be judged? Against whom is it committed? And what law does it violate? If we find the nuclear peril to be somehow abstract, and tend to consign this whole elemental issue to "defense experts" and other dubiously qualified people, part of the reason, certainly, is that the future generations really are abstract—that is to say, without the tangible existence and the unique particularities that help to make the living real to us. And if we find the subject strangely "impersonal" it may be in part because the unborn, who are the ones directly imperilled by extinction, are not yet persons. What are they, then? They lack the individuality that we often associate with the sacredness of life, and may at first thought seem to have only a shadowy, mass existence. *Where* are they? Are they to be pictured lined up in a sort of fore-life, waiting to get into life? Or should we regard them as nothing more than a pinch of chemicals in our reproductive organs, toward which we need feel no special obligations? What standing should they have among us? How much should their needs count in competition with ours? How far should the living go in trying to secure their advantage, their happiness, their existence?

The individual person, faced with the metaphysical-seeming

116

perplexities involved in pondering the possible cancellation of
people who do not yet exist—an apparently extreme effort of the
imagination, which seems to require one first to summon before the
mind's eye the countless possible people of the future generations
and then to consign these incorporeal multitudes to a more profound nothingness—might well wonder why, when he already has
his own death to worry about, he should occupy himself with this
other death. Since our own individual death promises to inflict a
loss that is total and final, we may find the idea of a second death
merely redundant. After all, can everything be taken away from
us twice? Moreover, a person might reason that even if mankind
did perish he wouldn't have to know anything about it, since in
that event he himself would perish. There might actually be something consoling in the idea of having so much company in death. In
the midst of universal death, it somehow seems out of order to
want to go on living oneself. As Randall Jarrell wrote in his poem
"Losses," thinking back to his experience in the Second World War,
"it was not dying: everybody died."

However, the individual would misconceive the nuclear peril
if he tried to understand it primarily in terms of personal danger,
or even in terms of danger to the people immediately known to
him, for the nuclear peril threatens life, above all, not at the level
of individuals, who already live under the sway of death, but at the
level of everything that individuals hold in common. Death cuts
off life; extinction cuts off birth. Death dispatches into the nothingness after life each person who has been born; extinction in one
stroke locks up in the nothingness before life all the people who
have not yet been born. For we are finite beings at both ends of
our existence—natal as well as mortal—and it is the natality of our
kind that extinction threatens. We have always been able to send
people to their death, but only now has it become possible to
prevent all birth and so doom all future human beings to un-
creation. The threat of the loss of birth—a beginning that is over
and done with for every living person—cannot be a source of immediate, selfish concern; rather, this threat assails everything that
people hold in common, for it is the ability of our species to produce

new generations which assures the continuation of the world in which all our common enterprises occur and have their meaning. Each death belongs inalienably to the individual who must suffer it, but birth is our common possession. And the meaning of extinction is therefore to be sought first not in what each person's own life means to him but in what the world and the people in it mean to him.

In its nature, the human world is, in Hannah Arendt's words, a "common world," which she distinguishes from the "private realm" that belongs to each person individually. (Somewhat surprisingly, Arendt, who devoted so much of her attention to the unprecedented evils that have appeared in our century, never addressed the issue of nuclear arms; yet I have discovered her thinking to be an indispensable foundation for reflection on this question.) The private realm, she writes in "The Human Condition," a book published in 1958, is made up of "the passions of the heart, the thoughts of the mind, the delights of the senses," and terminates with each person's death, which is the most solitary of all human experiences. The common world, on the other hand, is made up of all institutions, all cities, nations, and other communities, and all works of fabrication, art, thought, and science, and it survives the death of every individual. It is basic to the common world that it encompasses not only the present but all past and future generations. "The common world is what we enter when we are born and what we leave behind when we die," Arendt writes. "It transcends our life-span into past and future alike; it was there before we came and will outlast our brief sojourn in it. It is what we have in common not only with those who live with us, but also with those who were here before and with those who will come after us." And she adds, "Without this transcendence into a potential earthly immortality, no politics, strictly speaking, no common world, and no public realm is possible." The creation of a common world is the use that we human beings, and we alone among the earth's creatures, have made of the biological circumstance that while each of us is mortal, our species is biologically immortal. If mankind had not established a common world, the species would

118

still outlast its individual members and be immortal, but this immortality would be unknown to us and would go for nothing, as it
does in the animal kingdom, and the generations, unaware of one
another's existence, would come and go like waves on the beach,
leaving everything just as it was before. In fact, it is only because
humanity has built up a common world that we can fear our destruction as a species. It may even be that man, who has been
described as the sole creature that knows that it must die, can
know this only because he lives in a common world, which permits
him to imagine a future beyond his own life. This common world,
which is unharmed by individual death but depends on the survival
of the species, has now been placed in jeopardy by nuclear arms.
Death and extinction are thus complementary, dividing between
them the work of undoing, or threatening to undo, everything that
human beings are or can ever become, with death terminating the
life of each individual and extinction imperilling the common world
shared by all. In one sense, extinction is less terrible than death,
since extinction can be avoided, while death is inevitable; but in
another sense extinction is more terrible—is the more radical nothingness—because extinction ends death just as surely as it ends
birth and life. Death is only death; extinction is the death of death.

The world is made a common one by what Arendt calls "publicity," which insures that "everything that appears in public can
be seen and heard by everybody." She writes, "A common world
can survive the coming and going of the generations only to the
extent that it appears in public. It is the publicity of the public
realm which can absorb and make shine through the centuries
whatever men may want to save from the natural ruin of time."
But this publicity does not only shine on human works; it also
brings to light the natural foundations of life, enabling us to perceive what our origins are. It thereby permits us not only to endow
things of our own making with a degree of immortality but to see
and appreciate the preëxisting, biological immortality of our species
and of life on the planet, which forms the basis for any earthly
immortality whatever. The chief medium of the publicity of the
common world is, of course, language, whose possession by man

119

is believed by many to be what separates him from the other animals; but there are also the other "languages" of the arts and sciences. And standing behind language is that of which language is expressive—our reason, our psyche, our will, and our spirit. Through these, we are capable of entering into the lives of others, and of becoming aware that we belong to a community of others that is as wide as our species. The foundation of a common world is an exclusively human achievement, and to live in a common world— to speak and listen to one another, to read, to write, to know about the past and look ahead to the future, to receive the achievements of past generations, and to pass them on, together with achievements of our own, to future generations, and otherwise to participate in human enterprises that outlast any individual life—is part of what it means to be human, and by threatening all this nuclear weapons threaten a part of our humanity. The common world is not something that can be separated from the life we now live; it is intrinsic to our existence—something as close to us as the words we speak and the thoughts we think using those words. Descartes's famous axiom "I think, therefore I am" has perhaps been more extensively rebutted than any other single philosophical proposition. The rebuttal by Lewis Mumford happens to amount to a description of each person's indebtedness to the common world and to the common biological inheritance that the common world has brought to light. "Descartes forgot that before he uttered these words 'I think' . . . he needed the coöperation of countless fellow-beings, extending back to his own knowledge as far as the thousands of years that Biblical history recorded," Mumford writes in "The Pentagon of Power," a book published in 1970. "Beyond that, we know now he needed the aid of an even remoter past that mankind too long remained ignorant of: the millions of years required to transform his dumb animal ancestors into conscious human beings." In our long and arduous ascent out of biological darkness, it seems, we forgot our indebtedness to the natural world of our origins, and now, in consequence, threaten to plunge ourselves into an even deeper darkness. The nuclear predicament is thus in every sense a crisis of life in the common world. Only because there is a common world, in which knowledge of the physical world accumulates over the generations, can there be a threat to the common world and to its natural foundations. Only because there is a common world, which permits us knowledge of other generations and of the terrestrial nature of which human life is a part, can we worry about, or even know of, that threat. And only because there is a common world can we hope, by concerting our actions, to save ourselves and the earth.

The common world has been the work of every generation that has lived in it, back to the remotest ages. Much as poets begin by using language as they find it but, usually as an unself-conscious consequence of their work, leave usage slightly altered behind them, people in general pursue their various ends in the yielding medium of the world and shape its character by their actions. But although the world receives the imprint of the lives of those who pass through it, it has never been given to any single generation to dictate the character of the world. Not even the most thoroughgoing totalitarian regimes have succeeded in wholly shaping the lives of their peoples. One has only to think of Alexander Solzhenitsyn growing up in the Soviet Union but drawing so much of his spiritual sustenance from earlier centuries of Russian life, or to think of China, where so many of the customs and qualities of the people have outlasted what was probably the longest and most concentrated assault in history by a government on the national tradition of its own country, to realize how deeply a people's past is woven into its present.

The links binding the living, the dead, and the unborn were described by Edmund Burke, the great eighteenth-century English conservative, as a "partnership" of the generations. He wrote, "Society is indeed a contract. . . . It is a partnership in all science; a partnership in all art; a partnership in every virtue, and in all perfection. As the ends of such a partnership cannot be obtained except in many generations, it becomes a partnership not only between those who are living, but between those who are living, those who are dead, and those who are to be born." Pericles offered a similar, though not identical, vision of the common life of the generations

in his funeral oration, in which he said that all Athens was a "sepul-
chre" for the remembrance of the soldiers who had died fighting
for their city. Thus, whereas Burke spoke of common tasks that
needed many generations for their achievement, Pericles spoke of
the immortality that the living confer on the dead by remembering
their sacrifices. In the United States, Abraham Lincoln seemed to
combine these two thoughts when he said in his Gettysburg address
that the sacrifices of the soldiers who had died at Gettysburg laid
an obligation on the living to devote themselves to the cause for
which the battle had been fought. And, indeed, every political observer or political actor of vision has recognized that if life is to
be fully human it must take cognizance of the dead and the unborn.

But now our responsibilities as citizens in the common world
have been immeasurably enlarged. In the pre-nuclear common
world, we were partners in the protection of the arts, the institutions, the customs, and all "perfection" of life; now we are also
partners in the protection of life itself. Burke described as a common inheritance the achievements that one generation passed along
to the next. "By a constitutional policy, working after the pattern
of nature, we receive, we hold, we transmit our government and
our privileges, in the same manner in which we enjoy and transmit
our property and our lives," he wrote. "The institutions of policy,
the goods of fortune, the gifts of Providence, are handed down, to
us and from us, in the same course and order." These words appear
in Burke's "Reflections on the Revolution in France"—the revolution
being an event that filled him with horror, for in it he believed he
saw a single generation violently destroying in a few years the
national legacy of hundreds of years. But, whether or not he was
right in thinking that the inheritance of France was being squandered by its recipients, the inheriting generations and their successors were at least biologically intact. In our time, however,
among the items in the endangered inheritance the inheritors find
themselves. Each generation of mankind still receives, holds, and
transmits the inheritance from the past, but, being now a part of
that inheritance, each generation *is received, is held, and is transmitted,* so that receiver and received, holder and held, transmitter

and transmitted are one. Yet our jeopardy is only a part of the jeopardy of all life, and the largest item in the inheritance that we receive, hold, and must transmit is the entire ecosphere. So deep is the change in the structure of human life brought about by this new peril that in retrospect the Burkean concern about the "perfection" of life, indispensable as this concern is to the quality of our existence, seems like only the barest hint or suggestion of the incomparably more commanding obligation that is laid on us by the nuclear predicament. It strikes modern ears as prophetic that when Burke sought to describe the permanence in human affairs which he so valued he often resorted to metaphors drawn from the natural world—speaking, for example, of a "pattern of nature" that human society should imitate—as though he had had a premonition that an almost habitually revolutionary mankind would one day proceed from tearing society apart to tearing the natural world apart. Speaking of the society into which each of us is born, Burke angrily asked whether it could be right to "hack that aged parent in pieces." His words have acquired a deeper meaning than he could ever have foretold for them now that the parent in question is not merely human society but the earth itself.

Since all human aims, personal or political, presuppose human existence, it might seem that the task of protecting that existence should command all the energy at our disposal. However, the claims that the conduct of life lays upon us, including our desire for individual survival, have not suspended themselves in deference to the peril to life as a whole. As long as we keep from extinguishing ourselves, history continues at full flood, and the needs, desires, fears, interests, and ideals that have always moved people assert themselves with their usual vigor, even though extinction threatens them all with termination forever. For example, although people may want the species to survive, they may also want to be free, to be prosperous, to be treated justly, and so on. We are thus required to weigh the value of these goals of human life against the value of human life in its entirety. But while we are used to weighing

123

the various goals of human life against one another, this new task finds us unprepared. For with what measuring rods should we gauge our worth as a species, and how should we rate ourselves against things whose own worth derives from our existence? These questions are by no means academic. Every government and every citizen in the world—but especially the governments and the citizens of the United States and the Soviet Union—face the decision of how much weight to give to the survival of the world compared with the exigencies of business in the world. Ordinarily, when we look out upon each other and upon the world we measure the worth of what we find by making use of standards. For measuring the products of our labor, we may employ a standard of usefulness; for political activity, a standard of justice; for artistic and intellectual work, standards of beauty and truth; for human behavior in general, a standard of goodness. And when the things we value in life are in conflict we weigh them against one another by the perhaps indefinable but nevertheless comprehensible and useful standard of the common good. But none of these standards, including that of the common good, are suitable for gauging the worth of mankind as a whole, for none of them have any meaning or application unless one first assumes the existence of the very thing whose loss they are supposed to measure; namely, mankind. Anyone who prizes the usefulness of things assumes the existence of human beings to whom things can be useful; anyone who loves justice assumes the existence of a society whose parts can be brought into relationships that are just; anyone who loves beauty and truth assumes the existence of minds to which the beautiful and the true can manifest themselves; anyone who loves goodness assumes the existence of creatures who are capable of exhibiting it and being nourished by it; and anyone who wishes to promote the common good assumes the existence of a community whose divergent aims it can harmonize. These standards of worth, and any others that one might think of, are useful only in relating things that are in life to one another, and are inadequate as measures of life itself. We cannot, for example, say in any simple or unqualified sense that the end of the world is bad and its continuation good, because mankind is not in itself good or evil but is the source of both, providing the theatre in which good and evil actions appear as well as the actors by whom they are all enacted. (No stone, tree, or lion ever did anything either good or evil.) Neither can we say that mankind is useful. For to whom are we of any use? Human life is not needed by someone somewhere; rather, it is the seat of need, and need is one of the modes of our being.

The question of the worth of each individual human life, like the question of the worth of mankind, also poses the question of what life might be "for"—if, indeed, it is right to say that life is "for" anything—but with the crucial difference that while the individual can sacrifice his own life "for" others, mankind cannot do the same, since it includes all possible others within itself. Some philosophers, faced with the perplexing fact that although we can try to judge the worth of everything in creation by asking how well it serves as a means to some end of mankind's, mankind itself does not seem to be a means to anything, and therefore, by this estimation, is, strictly speaking, worthless, have attempted to solve the problem (as Kant, for example, did) by saying that man is "an end in himself" or a "final end," by which they meant that service to human beings was the highest good, and that human life was not to be treated as a means for achieving some other, supposedly higher good. However, this description is open to the criticism that by placing mankind at the final stage of a series of means and ends it seems to suggest that man creates himself—since the process of reaching ends through means is a purely human one—whereas in fact he was created by powers over which he had no influence whatever. It would be more appropriate, perhaps, to say that man is a beginning, for all chains of means and ends, no matter what their ultimate goals may be, start up out of man, whose existence they presuppose, and only then circle back into him, and so are wholly enclosed within human life. In that sense, man does not serve as a "final end" so much as stand prior to all means and ends, shaping and defining them according to his nature and his will. But this "beginning," whose existence is a fait accompli as far as we are concerned, is hard for us to see, because as soon as we start thinking something, intending something, enjoying something, or doing something, we have already taken it—"it" being our very selves and our fellow human beings—for granted. The forms that the life of the species can assume appear in innumerable clearly defined, often visible shapes, but mankind itself—the bare structure of human life, which underlies all these permutations—never appears as such, and remains, in a way, invisible.

One reason that standards fail us in our attempt to grasp the worth of our species is that they are meant to provide a common frame of reference against which the individuals in a given class of things can be measured, whereas mankind is a member of no class that we have as yet discovered. It is theoretically possible, of course, that other creatures endowed with the mental, psychological, and spiritual faculties that now distinguish human beings from all other forms of life will be discovered in outer space, and that we will then be able to rate ourselves in relation to them according to some suitable standard that will suggest itself once the creatures are in view. Even now, we are free to imagine that some extraterrestrial creature or god might take the measure of our loss by regarding it as a gap of a certain character and size in the order of a universal living creation of whose existence we are as yet unaware. But these lofty proceedings, in which we exchange our human perspective for a purely speculative superhuman one, are an evasion, for they lift us clean out of the human predicament that it is our obligation to face. By setting up an intelligence that itself escapes extinction and looks down upon the event, and by endowing that intelligence with suspiciously human characteristics, we in effect deny or evade the reality of extinction, for we have covertly manufactured a survivor. (Could it be that the vogue for science fiction and other types of pure fantasy stems in part from the reassurance we get from believing that there are other forms of life in the universe besides ours? The extra worlds offered by science fiction may provide us with an escape in imagination from the tight trap that our species is caught in in reality.) Seen in religious terms, such an assumption of a godlike perspective would be an attempted usurpation by man of God's omniscience, and, as such, a form of blasphemy. A second reason that standards fail us, then, is that employment of the only ones we actually have in our possession or have any real title to apply—the human ones—is terminated by our extinction, and we are left with the impossibility of a judgment without a judge to pass it.

A closely related, and more serious, perversion of religion is the suggestion, made by some Christian fundamentalists, that the nuclear holocaust we threaten to unleash is the Armageddon threatened by God in the Bible. This identification arrogates to ourselves not only God's knowledge but also His will. However, it is not God, picking and choosing among the things of His creation, who threatens us but we ourselves. And extinction by nuclear arms would not be the Day of Judgment, in which God destroys the world but raises the dead and then metes out perfect justice to everyone who has ever lived; it would be the utterly meaningless and completely unjust destruction of mankind by men. To imagine that God is guiding our hand in this action would quite literally be the ultimate evasion of our responsibility as human beings—a responsibility that is ours because (to stay with religious interpretation for a moment) we possess a free will that was implanted in us by God.

Human beings have a worth—a worth that is sacred. But it is *for* human beings that they have that sacred worth, and for them that the other things in the creation have their worth (although it is a reminder of our indissoluble connection with the rest of life that many of our needs and desires are also felt by animals). Hence, while our standards of worth have reference to the various possible worthy things in life, they all also point back to the life of the needy, or suffering, or rejoicing, or despairing, or admiring, or spiritually thirsting person in whose existence the things are found to be worthy or lacking in worth. To borrow elementary philosophical language, as objects the members of the species are among many things in existence that have worth in human eyes, but as the sum of all possible human subjects the species comprises all those "eyes," and in that sense is the sole originator of all worth as it is given to us to be aware of it. The death of an individual person is a loss of one subject, and of all its needs, longings, sufferings, and enthusiasms—of its being. But the extinction of the species goes farther, and removes from the known universe the human *kind* of being, which is different from any other kind that we as yet know of. It is, above all, the death of mankind as this immortal source of all human subjects, not the death of mankind as an object, that makes extinction radically unique and "unthinkable." In extinction, a darkness falls over the world not because the lights have gone out but because the eyes that behold the light have been closed. To assert this, however, is not to assert that only that which the human eye beholds is real. There is nothing in a holocaust that calls into doubt the existence of the physical world, which we can be confident will go on existing whether we destroy ourselves or not. We are even free to suppose that in a certain sense the worth of things will still reside in them in our absence, waiting for creatures who can appreciate it to reappear. But, without entering into the debate over whether beauty is in the eye of the beholder or in "the thing itself," we can at least say that without the beholder the beauty goes to waste. The universe would still exist, but the universe as it is imprinted on the human soul would be gone. Of many of the qualities of worth in things, we can say that they give us a private audience, and that insofar as they act upon the physical world they do so only by virtue of the response that they stir in us. For example, any works of art that survived our extinction would stare off into a void without finding a responding eye, and thus become shut up in a kind of isolation. (The physical qualities of things, on the other hand, will go on interacting among themselves without us.) Or, to put it differently, the qualities of worth find in us their sole home in an otherwise neutral and inhospitable universe. I believe that Rilke was saying something of this kind when, in the "Duino Elegies," he wrote the lines:

> Earth, isn't this what you want: an invisible
> re-arising in us? Is it not your dream
> to be one day invisible? Earth! invisible!
> What is your urgent command, if not transformation?

Earth, you darling, I will! Oh, believe me, you need
your Springs no longer to win me: a single one,
just one, is already more than my blood can endure.

Because we are the ones who hold everything that is of worth
to be so, the attempt to assign a worth to our species leads us in an
intellectual circle. We find ourselves trying to gauge the usefulness
of usefulness, the goodness of goodness, the worth of worth, and
these are questions that have no resolution. Mankind is to be
thought of not as something that possesses a certain worth (although in the eyes of one another we have that, too)—as something
with a certain measurable degree of usefulness, beauty, or goodness
(for just as often as we are useful, beautiful, or good we are destructive, ugly, or evil)—but as the inexhaustible source of all the
possible forms of worth, which has no existence or meaning without
human life. Mankind is not, in the ancient phrase, the measure of
all things; he is the measurer, and is himself measureless.

For the generations that now have to decide whether or not to
risk the future of the species, the implication of our species' unique
place in the order of things is that while things in the life of mankind have worth, we must never raise that worth above the life of
mankind and above our respect for that life's existence. To do this
would be to make of our highest ideals so many swords with which
to destroy ourselves. To sum up the worth of our species by reference to some particular standard, goal, or ideology, no matter how
elevated or noble it might be, would be to prepare the way for
extinction by closing down in thought and feeling the open-ended
possibilities for human development which extinction would close
down in fact. There is only one circumstance in which it might be
possible to sum up the life and achievement of the species, and that
circumstance would be that it had already died; but then, of course,
there would be no one left to do the summing up. Only a generation
that believed itself to be in possession of final, absolute truth could
ever conclude that it had reason to put an end to human life, and
only generations that recognized the limits to their own wisdom

and virtue would be likely to subordinate their interests and dreams to the as yet unformed interests and undreamed dreams of the future generations, and let human life go on.

From the foregoing, it follows that there can be no justification for extinguishing mankind, and therefore no justification for any nation ever to push the world into nuclear hostilities, which, once inaugurated, may lead uncontrollably to a full-scale holocaust and to extinction. But from this conclusion it does not follow that any action is permitted as long as it serves the end of preventing extinction. The grounds for these two propositions become clearer if we consider the nature of ethical obligation. It seems especially important to consider the ethical side of the question, because the other common justification for military action—self-interest—obviously can never justify extinction, inasmuch as extinction would constitute suicide for the perpetrator; and suicide, whatever else it may be, is scarcely in the interest of the one who commits it.

I shall let the behavior of Socrates at his trial in Athens, in the fourth century b.c., on charges of corrupting youth and denigrating the gods, stand as a model of ethical behavior. His example has a special, direct relevance to the nuclear question, because every attempt to justify the use of nuclear weapons has been based on some variation of the conviction, first given full expression by him, in words that still sound with their full force, that the highest good is not life itself—mere survival—but the moral life. The possible application of the Socratic principle to the question of extinction is obvious: if under certain circumstances it is the duty of the individual to sacrifice his life for something higher than his life, might it not be the obligation of mankind under certain circumstances to do the same? The philosopher Karl Jaspers, for one, thought so, and was one of the few who have had the courage to state such a belief outright. In his book "The Future of Mankind," published in 1958, he writes, concerning the nuclear question, "Man is born to be free, and the free life that he tries to save by all possible means is more than mere life. Hence, life in the sense of existence—individual life as well as all life—can be staked and sacrificed for the sake of the life that is worth living." He asks, "And if no such way [to the life worth living] is found, does the substance of humanity then lie where failure is no longer an objection—where indeed man's ultimately real, truly serious purpose is his doom?" To which he answers, "It could be necessary only as a sacrifice made for the sake of eternity." I have suggested, though, that doom can never be a human purpose at all, truly serious or otherwise, but, rather, is the end of all human purposes, none of which can be fulfilled outside of human life.

Jaspers's opposite conclusion, I believe, depends on an application to the species as a whole of a canon of morality that properly applies only to each individual person. Ethical commandments have often been regarded as "absolute" for the individual (and thus as justifying any sacrifice made in their name), and, in a certain sense, Socrates regarded them in that light, too. He even claimed that a "voice," or "God," sometimes commanded him not to do certain things. The commands were absolute in two ways. First, once the voice, which we may take to be the voice of conscience, had spoken, he could not be released from it by appeal to any outside authority, such as the majority voice of the community. Second, the commands were absolutely binding on him, and had to be followed even unto death. Therefore, when the city of Athens put him on trial he was not at liberty to abandon the dictates of his conscience and to save his life. Instead, he chided the jury for "trying to put an innocent man to death," and added, for good measure, that since to commit such an injustice would be in his opinion a worse fate than to suffer it, then "so far from pleading on my own behalf, as might be supposed, I am really pleading on yours." In these bold words and actions, which cost him his life, Socrates asserted the absolute sovereignty of his conscience over his actions. But, having asserted that sovereignty, he did not go on to suppose that he had thereby won the right to exercise a similar sovereignty over others. On the contrary, it was of the essence of his conduct at the trial and at the execution that he placed himself wholly at the service of his community, and that

131

his belief in the worth of his actions in fact consisted in this. His radical assertion of the independence of his conscience was thus inseparable from a no less radical subordination of his interests to the good of his city. This subordination was evident in his decision to stand trial, in his decision after the trial to stay in Athens and suffer the death penalty rather than flee (as friends advised him to do), and in the words that he spoke throughout the proceedings. He persisted in dedicating himself to the service of his community even though the community might kill him for his pains. In this devotion, he resembled Christ, of course, who appeared on earth to be "a servant of all," and gave up His life for the sake of the people who put Him to death.

In the present context, the point is that if Socrates is taken as the example, there are no ethics apart from service to the human community, and therefore no ethical commandments that can justify the extinction of humanity. Ethical obligation begins with the assumption that we are naturally inclined to look out for our own interests, and asks that we pay regard to the interests of others— that we do unto them as we would have them do unto us. But since extinction annihilates the community of others it can never be an ethical act, and to say that it could be is like saying that to kill the children in a school would be an educational experience for them, or to starve a country to death would be a beneficial economic measure for it. And even if all the people in the world somehow managed to persuade themselves that their death was justified (thus overlooking the question of for what or for whom it was justified), this suicidal action would still be wrong, because it would also cancel the unconsulted and completely innocent future generations. (Can anybody be more innocent than they are?) In actuality, of course, no one is proposing the voluntary suicide of everyone on earth; on the contrary, what is being claimed is that one or two countries have the right to jeopardize all countries and their descendants in the name of certain beliefs. Hence, those who, to defend risking extinction, start with the moral obligation of "individual life" to sacrifice itself and generalize from that to an obligation of "all life" to sacrifice itself (in Jaspers's phrases) in fact pass from a principle of individual self-sacrifice to a principle of aggression by a few against all—"all" in this case including the unborn generations.

The question remains whether there might be some superethical, ultramundane principle, perhaps of religious inspiration, that could justify the destruction of the world. Is it possible, for example, that one day it might be our obligation to set both human interests and human morality aside and destroy the species for the sake of God? There is a long history of wars waged in the name of one god or another, but in the possible justifications for a nuclear holocaust theological principles could play a role of special importance, because they might seem to offer something to "fight" for that would not itself be destroyed in a holocaust. For example, the extinction of an "evil" mankind might be regarded as acceptable or pleasing to a wrathful God—or, at least, as representing the fulfillment of some plan of His (as in the identification by some Christian fundamentalists of a holocaust with Armageddon). When armies take up the banner of God, the "absolute" sovereignty of each person's individual conscience over his own actions is transmuted into a claim of absolute sovereignty over other people; and the absolute submission owed by each person to the voice of conscience is transmuted into a claim of submission owed by other people to those who, as representatives of religious orthodoxy, have taken it on themselves to speak for God. Then the Christian commandment to sacrifice oneself for one's neighbor at God's command is transformed into permission to sacrifice one's neighbor for God's sake. In the pre-nuclear world, the assumption of these claims led to considerable slaughter; in the nuclear world, it could lead to the end of the species. But all this is infinitely remote from the teaching of Christ, at least, who taught people not to kill their enemies but to love them, and who died rather than lift His hand in violence against His tormentors. It speaks powerfully against any Christian justification for destroying the world that when the Christian God appeared on earth in human form not only did He not sacrifice a single human being for His sake but He suffered a lonely, anguishing, degrading human death so that the world might be saved.

In no saying of His did Christ ever suggest that the two great commandments—to love God and to love one's neighbor—could in any way be separated, or that the former could be used as a justification for violating the latter. In fact, He explicitly stated that religious faith that is divorced from love of human beings is empty and dangerous. For example, He said, "If thou bring thy gift to the altar, and there rememberest that thy brother hath aught against thee; Leave there thy gift before the altar, and go thy way; first be reconciled to thy brother, and then come and offer thy gift." We who have planned out the deaths of hundreds of millions of our brothers plainly have a great deal of work to do before we return to the altar. Clearly, the corpse of mankind would be the least acceptable of all conceivable offerings on the altar of this God.

If there is nothing in the teachings of either Socrates or Christ that could justify the extinction of mankind—nothing, in fact, that could teach us to do anything in regard to this act but hold back from performing it—neither is there anything that would justify the commission of crimes in order to prevent extinction. In the teachings of both men, a person's obligation is to answer even the utmost evil not with more evil but with good. This refusal to be goaded by evil into evil may be the closest thing to an "absolute" that there is in their teachings. (I wonder whether it might not have been this absolute refusal to participate in evil which was in the back of Jaspers's mind when he said that in order to avoid certain evils it was permissible to perpetrate extinction.) Rather, the altogether un-Socratic and un-Christian teaching that the end justifies the means is the basis on which governments, in all times, have licensed themselves to commit crimes of every sort; the *raison d'état* of governments, in fact, enshrines the opposite of the Socratic principle, for it holds that states may do virtually anything whatever in the name of survival. Extinction nullifies the ends-means justification by destroying every end that might justify the means (the *raison d'état* is not well served if the nation is biologically exterminated), but the goal of *preventing* extinction, if it ever became operative as an end, could lend to this expedient line of thinking an immensely enlarged scope, since if the end justifies the means, and the end is human survival, then any means short of human extinction can be countenanced. Herein lies another peril of the nuclear predicament—albeit a lesser one by far than extinction itself, since any political system, no matter how entrenched, is subject to change and decline, whereas extinction is eternal. In most countries, "national security" is found to be justification enough for abusing every human right, and we can only imagine what governments might feel entitled to do once they had begun to claim that they were defending not just national but human survival.

It has not been the mistake of governments of our time to lay too much emphasis on the imperative of human survival, yet in the period of détente between the United States and the Soviet Union the world was given a glimpse of policies in which the aim of avoiding extinction was offered as a justification for repression. Both superpowers, while hardly abandoning the defense of their national interests, made a disturbingly smooth transition between using national interests to rationalize repression and using human survival to rationalize it. In the Soviet Union, a totalitarian country, it was not long before the authorities were supplementing their usual list of charges against critics of the regime by calling them "wreckers of détente," and the like. And in the United States, a democracy, but one that was presided over at the time by an Administration with a criminal and authoritarian bent, President Nixon was quick to invite the public to accept his usurpations and violations of the Constitution as a small price for the country to pay for the grandiose "structure of peace" that he believed he was building together with the Soviets. This incipient alliance of the champions of peace in repression went a step further when the Soviet leaders emerged as vocal defenders of Nixon's constitutional abuses in the Watergate crisis. It is noteworthy also that the Nixon Administration was conspicuously silent about abuses of human rights in the Soviet Union. Regrettably, it may be that the cause of peace can be used no less readily than war as a justification for repression. There is even a superficial resemblance between peace and repression—both tend to be quiet—which should put us on our guard. In the period of détente, the first, tentative steps were taken toward nuclear-arms control (only to stall subsequently), but the totalitarian murk around the world thickened noticeably.

Having said that each generation has an obligation to survive, so that the future generations may be born, I would like to guard against a possible misinterpretation. It has become fashionable recently to suggest that in circumstances of extreme evil—including, especially, imprisonment in concentration camps—personal survival becomes a moral principle, and one that, indeed, takes precedence over the obligation to treat others decently. If this notion were accepted, then the Socratic message that mere survival is empty, and only an honorable life is worth living, would be overruled, and each person would be invited to treat other people however he liked as long as he survived. It might be thought that the obligation of the species to survive adds weight to this point of view. However, each generation's obligation to survive does not in fact lead to a similar obligation on the part of the individual, any more than the individual's obligation to sacrifice himself implies an obligation of self-sacrifice on the part of the species. On the contrary, the species' obligation to survive lays on each individual a new obligation to set aside his personal interest in favor of the general interest. (After all, his personal survival, which cannot last beyond the natural span of his life in any case, in no way aids the survival of the species, since the world's peril does not stem from any shortage of people.) For whereas there is no principle, whether practical, ethical, or divine, that overarches mankind and would offer a justification for its self-destruction, mankind still overarches each person, as it always has done, and summons him, at times, to act in favor of something larger than he is.

Implicit in everything that I have said so far about the nuclear predicament there has been a perplexity that I would now like to take up explicitly, for it leads, I believe, into the very heart of our response—or, rather, our lack of response—to the predicament. I have pointed out that our species is the most important of all the things that, as inhabitants of a common world, we inherit from the past generations, but it does not go far enough to point out this superior importance, as though in making our decision about extinction we were being asked to choose between, say, liberty, on the one hand, and the survival of the species, on the other. For the species not only overarches but contains all the benefits of life in the common world, and to speak of sacrificing the species for the sake of one of these benefits involves one in the absurdity of wanting to destroy something in order to preserve one of its parts, as if one were to burn down a house in an attempt to redecorate the living room, or to kill someone to improve his character. But even to point out this absurdity fails to take the full measure of the peril of extinction, for mankind is not some invaluable object that lies outside us and that we must protect so that we can go on benefitting from it; rather, it is we ourselves, without whom everything there is loses its value. To say this is another way of saying that extinction is unique not because it destroys mankind as an object but because it destroys mankind as the source of all possible human subjects, and this, in turn, is another way of saying that extinction is a second death, for one's own individual death is the end not of any object in life but of the subject that experiences all objects. Death, however, places the mind in a quandary. One of the confounding characteristics of death—"tomorrow's zero," in Dostoevski's phrase—is that, precisely because it removes the person himself rather than something in his life, it seems to offer the mind nothing to take hold of. One even feels it inappropriate, in a way, to try to speak "about" death at all, as though death were a thing situated somewhere outside us and available for objective inspection, when the fact is that it is within us—is, indeed, an essential part of what we are. It would be more appropriate, perhaps, to say that death, as a fundamental element of our being, "thinks" in us and through us about whatever we think about, coloring our thoughts and moods with its presence throughout our lives.

Extinction is another such intangible, incomprehensible, yet all-important presence, surrounding and pervading life without ever showing its face directly. Extinction is, in truth, even less tangibly present than death, because while death continually strikes down those around us, thereby at least reminding us of what death is, and reminding us that we, too, must die, extinction can, by definition, strike only once, and is, therefore, entirely hidden from our direct view; no one has ever seen extinction and no one ever will. Extinction is thus *a human future that can never become a human present.* For who will suffer this loss, which we somehow regard as supreme? We, the living, will not suffer it; we will be dead. Nor will the unborn shed any tears over their lost chance to exist; to do so they would have to exist already. The perplexity underlying the whole question of extinction, then, is that although extinction might appear to be the largest misfortune that mankind could ever suffer, it doesn't seem to happen *to* anybody, and one is left wondering where its impact is to be registered, and by whom.

Lucretius wrote, "Do you not know that when death comes, there will be no other you to mourn your memory, and stand above you prostrate?" And Freud wrote, "It is indeed impossible to imagine our own death: and whenever we attempt to do so, we can perceive that we are in fact still present as spectators." Thought and feeling try to peer ahead and catch a glimpse of death, but they encounter their own demise along the way, for their death is what death is. In the same way, when we try to picture extinction we come up against the fact that the human faculties with which someone might see, hear, feel, or understand this event are obliterated in it, and we are left facing a blankness, or emptiness. But even the words "blankness" and "emptiness" are too expressive—too laden with human response—because, inevitably, they connote the *experience* of blankness and emptiness, whereas extinction is the end of human experience. It thus seems to be in the nature of extinction to repel emotion and starve thought, and if the mind, brought face to face with extinction, descends into a kind of exhaustion and dejection it is surely in large part because we know that mankind

cannot be a "spectator" at its own funeral any more than any
individual person can.

It might be well to consider for a moment the novel shape of the
mental and emotional predicament that the nuclear peril places
us in—a predicament that exists not because of a psychological
failing or the inadequacy of the human mind but because of the
actual nature of the thing that we are trying to think about. Strange
as it may seem, we may have to teach ourselves to think about
extinction in a meaningful way. (This seems less strange when we
recall that whereas people may have a natural aversion to death
no similar instinct moves them to ward off extinction—although
most people's spontaneous reaction to the idea is hardly favorable,
either. Like the peril of extinction itself, recognition of the peril
and understanding of it can come only as a product of our life
together in the common world—as a product, that is, not of instinct
but of civilization. Other species not only do not resist extinction
but are completely unaware that it is happening; the last passenger
pigeon had no way of knowing that it *was* the last passenger pigeon,
much less of doing anything about it.) On first looking into the
consequences of a nuclear holocaust, one is struck by the odd fact
that, beyond a certain point, the larger the imagined attack is,
the less there is to say about it. At "low" levels of attack—the tens
or hundreds of megatons—there is the complexity of the countless
varieties of suffering and social and ecological breakdown to reflect
on. But at higher levels—the thousands of megatons—the complexity steadily gives way to the simplicity and nothingness of
death. Step by step, the "spectators" at the "funeral"—the sufferers
of the calamity, in whose eyes it retains a human reality, and in
whose lives it remains a human experience—dwindle away, until
at last, when extinction is reached, all the "spectators" have themselves gone to the grave, and only the stones and stars, and whatever algae and mosses may have made it through, are present to
witness the end.

Yet no matter how poor and thin a thing for imagination to grasp extinction may be, it seems to be in imagination alone that it can be grasped at all. Lacking the possibility of experience, all we have left is thought, since for us extinction is locked away forever in a future that can never arrive. Like the thought "I do not exist," the thought "Humanity is now extinct" is an impossible one for a rational person, because as soon as *it* is, *we* are not. In imagining any other event, we look ahead to a moment that is still within the stream of human time, which is to say within a time in which other human beings will exist, and will be responding to whatever they see, looking back to our present time and looking forward to future times that will themselves be within the sequence of human time. But in imagining extinction we gaze past everything human to a dead time that falls outside the human tenses of past, present, and future. By adopting a coldly scientific frame of mind, we can imagine that inert scene, but the exercise is oddly fruitless, and seems to hold no clue to the meaning of extinction. Instead, we find that almost everything that might engage our attention or stir our interest—even if only to repel us—has passed away. Struggling in this way to grasp the meaning of extinction, we may be led to wonder whether it can be grasped at all, and begin to suspect that nature provided an instinctual drive for the perpetuation of the species because it knew that our consciousness and will were so poorly equipped to deal with this task.

Given the special role of our mental faculties in any attempt to come to terms with extinction, it is not very surprising that a great deal of the writing that has been done about nuclear strategy is characterized by a highly abstract tone. The atmosphere in which this work goes forward is perfectly suggested by the nickname for the sort of institution in which much of it takes place: "the think tank." This term, evoking a hermetic world of thought, exactly reflects the intellectual circumstances of those thinkers whose job it is to deduce from pure theory, without the lessons of experience, what might happen if nuclear hostilities broke out. But, as Herman Kahn, the director of one of these think tanks (the Hudson Institute), and the author of "Thinking About the Unthinkable," among other works on nuclear strategy, has rightly said, "it will do no good to inveigh against theorists; in this field, everyone is a theorist." Hence, while in one sense Kahn is right to call a nuclear holocaust "unthinkable," it is also true, as his remark suggests, that when it comes to grasping the nature of this peril thinking about it is all that we *can* do.

The intellectual and affective difficulties involved in trying to understand the nuclear predicament have no precedent (unless one is to count individual death as a precedent), but they were foreshadowed in at least some respects by certain barriers that have impeded understanding of other sudden revolutionary developments of the modern age. In "Democracy in America," Tocqueville, speaking of the democratic revolution of his times, wrote, "Although the revolution that is taking place in the social condition, the laws, the opinions, and the feelings of men is still very far from being terminated, yet its results already admit of no comparison with anything that the world has ever before witnessed. I go back from age to age up to the remotest antiquity, but I find no parallel to what is occurring before my eyes; as the past has ceased to cast its light upon the future, the mind of man wanders in obscurity." But if in Tocqueville's day the past had ceased to cast its light upon the future, the present—what was occurring before his eyes—could still do so. Although the democratic revolution had not "terminated," it was nevertheless in full swing, and democratic America provided Tocqueville with enough factual material to fill the two thick volumes of his book. Drawing on this material, he was able to cast so much light on the future that we still see by it today.

The radical novelty of events became an even more troubling impediment to the understanding of totalitarian revolutions of our century. Arendt, who, more than anyone else, performed the offices of a Tocqueville in casting light on totalitarianism, wrote, "The gap between past and future ceased to be a condition peculiar only to the activity of thought and restricted as an experience to those few who made thinking their primary business. It became a tangible reality and perplexity for all; that is, it became a fact of political relevance." The totalitarian regimes, of course, made active attempts to revise or erase the factual record of both the past and the present. Yet these attempts have not been successful, and, in spite of the sense of unreality we feel when we confront the acts of the totalitarian regimes, totalitarianism is for us today something that has left its bloody marks on history, and these events, when we are told of them by credible witnesses, fill us with active revulsion. In Hitler's Germany and Stalin's Russia, horrifying events of dreamlike incredibility occurred, and pure, everyday common sense might reject their very possibility if the historical record were not there. In Arendt's "Eichmann in Jerusalem," we read the following description of the gassing to death by the Nazis of Jews in Poland:

> This is what Eichmann saw: The Jews were in a large room; they were told to strip; then a truck arrived, stopping directly before the entrance to the room, and the naked Jews were told to enter it. The doors were closed and the truck started off. "I cannot tell [how many Jews entered, Eichmann said later], I hardly looked. I could not; I could not; I had had enough. The shrieking, and . . . I was much too upset, and so on, as I later told Müller when I reported to him; he did not get much profit out of my report. I then drove along after the van, and then I saw the most horrible sight I had thus far seen in my life. The truck was making for an open ditch, the doors were opened, and the corpses were thrown out, as though they were still alive, so smooth were their limbs. They were hurled into the ditch, and I can still see a civilian extracting the teeth with tooth plyers."

We don't want to believe this; we find it all but impossible to believe this. But our wishful disbelief is stopped cold by the brute historical fact that it *happened*: we are therefore forced to believe. But extinction *has not happened*, and hides behind the veil of a future time which human eyes can never pierce. It is true that the testimony of those who survived the bombings of Hiroshima and Nagasaki offers us a vivid record of devastation by nuclear arms, but this record, which already seems to exhaust our powers of emotional response, illumines only a tiny corner of a nuclear holocaust, and, in any case, does not reach the question of extinction, which, instead of presenting us with scenes of horror, puts an end to them, just as it puts an end to all other scenes that are enacted by human beings. After several centuries of bringing a variety of nightmarish futures into existence, we have now invented one so unbelievable and overwhelming that it cannot come to pass at all. ("Come to pass" is a perfect phrase to describe what extinction cannot do. It can "come," but not "to pass," for with its arrival the creature that divides time into past, present, and future—the creature before whose eyes it would "pass"—is annihilated.) Deprived of both past and present experience to guide us as we try to face the nuclear predicament, we are left in the unpromising position of asking the future to shed light on itself.

As we look ahead to the possibility of extinction, our secret thought, which is well founded in the facts of the case, may be that since everyone will then be dead no one will have to worry about it, so why should we worry about it now? Following this unacknowledged but logical line of thinking, we may be led to the shrug of indifference that seems to have characterized most people's conscious reaction to the nuclear peril for the last thirty-six years. If extinction is nothing, we may unconsciously ask ourselves, may not no reaction be the right one? By contrast, our thoughts and feelings experience no such defeat when we consider a privation of future generations which falls short of denying them their existence—when we imagine, for example, that their supply of oil will run out, or that their supply of food will grow short, or that their civilization will go into decline. Then, through the widest possible extension of our respect for individual life, we can picture their plight, sympathize with their suffering, and perhaps take some action to forestall the evil. In effect, we are still following the ethical precept of doing unto others as we would have them do unto us, now expanding our understanding of who the others are

143

to include the unborn, as Burke did. This comes naturally to us, as Burke pointed out, because a moment's reflection reveals to us the debt of gratitude that we owe past generations. However, in extending our sympathetic concern in this way, of course, we make the tacit assumption that there will *be* future generations, taking it for granted that nature, acting in and through us, will bring them forth, as it always has done. And in the pre-nuclear world, before it was in our power to extinguish the species, this confidence was warranted. But now the creation of new human beings is just the thing that is in question; and, in our attempt to grasp not the suffering and death of future generations but their failure to come into existence in the first place, a sympathetic response is inappropriate, for sympathy can extend only to living beings, and extinction is the foreclosure of life. The shuddering anticipation that we may feel on behalf of others when we realize that they are threatened with harm is out of place, because the lack of any others is the defining feature of extinction.

In removing the sufferer and his suffering with one blow, extinction again shows its resemblance to death. Montaigne writes, "Death can put an end, and deny access, to all our other woes," and adds, "What stupidity to torment ourselves about passing into exemption from all torment!" Extinction likewise brings not suffering but the end of suffering. Among feelings, suffering and joy are opposites, but both, like all feelings, are manifestations of life, and, as such, are together opposites of either death or extinction. Never having faced the end of human life before, we are led by mental habit to try to respond to it as though it were a disaster of one kind or another, in which people were going to be harmed or bereaved. But in doing so we strain for a reaction that, to our puzzlement, perhaps, does not come, for the excellent reason that in extinction there is no disaster: no falling buildings, no killed or injured people, no shattered lives, no mourning survivors. All of that is dissolved in extinction, along with everything else that goes on in life. We are left only with the ghostlike cancelled future generations, who, metaphorically speaking, have been waiting through all past time to enter into life but have now been turned back by us.

The distinction between harm to people in the world and the end of the world—or even the end of *a* world, such as occurred to European Jewry under Hitler—may give us some clue to the nature of what Arendt, borrowing a phrase of Kant's in order to describe the unparalleled crimes of Hitler's Germany and Stalin's Soviet Union, has called "radical evil." The "true hallmark" of radical evil, "about whose nature so little is known," she says, is that we do not know either how to punish these offenses or how to forgive them, and they therefore "transcend the realm of human affairs and the potentialities of human power, both of which they radically destroy wherever they make their appearance." By crimes that "transcend the realm of human affairs and the potentialities of human power," she means, I believe, crimes so great that they overwhelm the capacity of every existing system of jurisprudence, or other organized human response, to deal with them adequately. She goes on to say, "Here, where the deed itself dispossesses us of all power, we can indeed only repeat with Jesus: 'It were better for him that a millstone were hanged about his neck, and he cast into the sea.'"
I would like to suggest that evil becomes radical whenever it goes beyond destroying individual victims (in whatever numbers) and, in addition, mutilates or destroys the *world* that can in some way respond to—and thus in some measure redeem—the deaths suffered. This capacity of evil was demonstrated on a large scale in modern times by the totalitarian regimes, which, in a manner of speaking, attempted to tear gaping, unmendable holes in the fabric of the world—holes into which entire peoples or classes would sink without a trace—but now it has fully emerged in the capacity of the species for self-extinction, which, by ending the world altogether, would "dispossess us of all power" forever. When crimes are of a certain magnitude and character, they nullify our power to respond to them adequately because they smash the human context in which human losses normally acquire their meaning for us. When an entire community or an entire people is destroyed, most of those who would mourn the victims, or bring the perpetrators to justice, or forgive them, or simply remember what occurred, are themselves destroyed. When that community is all mankind, the loss of the

145

human context is total, and no one is left to respond. In facing this deed, we will either respond to it before it is done, and thus avoid doing it, or lose any chance to respond, and pass into oblivion.

If this interpretation is correct, every episode of radical evil is already a small extinction, and should be seen in that light. Between individual death and biological extinction, then, there are other possible levels of obliteration, which have some of the characteristics of extinction. The "end of civilization"—the total disorganization and disruption of human life, breaking the links between mankind's past and its future—is one. Genocide—the destruction of a people—which can be seen as an extinction *within* mankind, since it eliminates an element in the interior diversity of the species is another; in fact, genocide, including, above all, Hitler's attempt to extinguish the Jewish people, is the closest thing to a precursor of the extinction of the species that history contains. What the end of civilization, genocide, and extinction all have in common is that they are attacks not merely on existing people and things but on either the biological or the cultural heritage that human beings transmit from one generation to the next; that is, they are crimes against the future. The connection between genocide and extinction is further suggested by the fact that what the superpowers *intend* to do if a holocaust breaks out (leaving aside the unintended "collateral effects" for the moment) is to commit genocide against one another—to erase the other side as a culture and as a people from the face of the earth. In its nature, human extinction is and always will be without precedent, but the episodes of radical evil that the world has already witnessed are warnings to us that gigantic, insane crimes are not prevented from occurring merely because they are "unthinkable." On the contrary, they may be all the more likely to occur for that reason. Heinrich Himmler, a leading figure in the carrying out of the destruction of the Jews, assured his subordinates from time to time that their efforts were especially noble because by assuming the painful burden of making Europe "Jewfree" they were fighting "battles which future generations will not have to fight again." His remark applies equally well to a nuclear holocaust, which might render the earth "human-free." This is another "battle" (and the word is as inappropriate for a nuclear holocaust as it was for the murder of millions of Jews) that "future generations will not have to fight again."

If our usual responses to disasters and misfortunes are mismatched to the peril of extinction, then we have to look in some other quarter of our being to find its significance. Individual death once more offers a point of departure. We draw closer to death throughout our lives, but we never arrive there, for just as we are about to arrive we are gone. Yet although death thus always stands outside life, it nevertheless powerfully conditions life. Montaigne writes, "You are in death while you are in life; for you are after death when you are no longer in life. Or, if you prefer it this way, you are dead after life; but during life you are dying; and death affects the dying much more roughly than the dead, and more keenly and essentially." We are similarly "in extinction" while we are in life, and are after extinction when we are extinct. Extinction, too, thus affects the living "more roughly" and "more keenly and essentially" than it does the nonliving, who in its case are not the dead but the unborn. Like death, extinction is felt not when it has arrived but beforehand, as a deep shadow cast back across the whole of life. The answer to the question of who experiences extinction and when, therefore, is that we the living experience it, now and in all the moments of our lives. Hence, while it is in one sense true that extinction lies outside human life and never happens to anybody, in another sense extinction saturates our existence and never stops happening. If we want to find the meaning of extinction, accordingly, we should start by looking with new eyes at ourselves and the world we live in, and at the lives we live. The question to be asked then is no longer what the features and characteristics of extinction are but what it says about us and what it does to us that we are preparing our own extermination.

Because the peril is rooted in basic scientific knowledge, which is likely to last as long as mankind does, it is apparently a permanent one. But in the presence of that peril opposite poles of response, both in feeling and, above all, in action, are possible, and the quality of the lives we live together is conditioned in opposite ways according to which response we choose. The choice is really between two entire ways of life. One response is to decline to face the peril, and thus to go on piling up the instruments of doom year after year until, by accident or design, they go off. The other response is to recognize the peril, dismantle the weapons, and arrange the political affairs of the earth so that the weapons will not be built again. I remarked that we do not have two earths at our disposal—one for experimental holocausts and the other to live on. Neither do any of us have two souls—one for responding to the nuclear predicament and the other for living the rest of our lives. In the long run, if we are dull and cold toward life in its entirety we will become dull and cold toward life in its particulars—toward the events of our own daily lives—but if we are alert and passionate about life in its entirety we will also be alert and passionate about it in its dailiness.

It is a matter of record that in our thirty-six years of life in a nuclear-armed world we have been largely dead to the nuclear peril, and I would like to consider more closely what this failure of response seems to have been doing to our world. Pascal, taking note of the cerebral character of the condition of mortality, once observed that "it is easier to endure death without thinking about it than to endure the thought of death without dying." His observation perfectly describes our response so far to the peril of extinction: we have found it much easier to dig our own grave than to think about the fact that we are doing so. Almost everyone has acknowledged on some level that the peril exists, but the knowledge has been without consequences in our feelings and our actions, and the superpowers have proceeded with their nuclear buildups, in the recent words of George Kennan, "like the victims of some sort of hypnotism, like men in a dream, like lemmings heading for the sea."

For a very short while before and after the first bomb was produced, a few men at and near the top of the American government seemed prepared to deal with the nuclear predicament at its proper depth. One of them was Secretary of War Henry Stimson, who knew

of the Manhattan Project and, in March of 1945—four months before
the Trinity test, at Alamogordo—confided to his diary an account of
a discussion he had had about the new weapon with Harvey Bundy,
his closest personal assistant. "Our thoughts," he wrote, "went right
down to the bottom facts of human nature, morals, and governments, and it is by far the most searching and important thing that
I have had to do since I have been here in the Office of the Secretary of War because it touches matters which are deeper even than
the principles of present government." Yet those deep thoughts
somehow did not take root firmly enough in the hearts of the American leaders or of the world at large, and the old ways of thinking
returned, in the teeth of the new facts. The true dimensions of the
the nuclear peril, and of its significance for mankind, had been
glimpsed, but then the awareness faded and the usual exigencies of
international political life—including, shortly, the Cold War between the United States and the Soviet Union—laid claim to people's passions and energies. The nuclear buildup that has continued to this day began, and the nuclear question, having emerged
abruptly from the twofold obscurity of scientific theory and governmental secrecy, was almost immediately thrust into the new obscurity of the arcane, abstract, denatured world of the theorists in the
think tanks, who were, in effect, deputized to think the "unthinkable" thoughts that the rest of us lacked the will to think.

Thus began the strange double life of the world which has
continued up to the present. On the one hand, we returned to business as usual, as though everything remained as it always had been.
On the other hand, we began to assemble the stockpiles that could
blow this supposedly unaltered existence sky-high at any second.
When the scientists working on the Manhattan Project wanted to
send word to President Truman, who was at the Potsdam Conference, that the detonation near Alamogordo had been successful,
they chose the horrible but apt code phrase "Babies satisfactorily
born." Since then, these "babies"—which are indeed like the offspring of a new species, except that it is a species not of life but of
anti-life, threatening to end life—have "proliferated" steadily under
our faithful care, bringing forth "generation" after "generation" of

weapons, each more numerous and more robust than the last, until they now threaten to do away with their creators altogether. Yet while we did all this we somehow kept the left hand from knowing —or from dwelling on—what the right hand was doing; and the separation of our lives from awareness of the doom that was being prepared under us and around us was largely preserved.

It is probably crucial psychologically in maintaining this divorce that, once Hiroshima and Nagasaki had been pushed out of mind, the nuclear peril grew in such a way that while it relentlessly came to threaten the existence of everything, it physically touched nothing, and thus left people free not to think about it if they so chose. Like a kindhearted executioner, the bomb permitted its prospective victims to go on living seemingly ordinary lives up to the day that the execution should suddenly and without warning be carried out. (If one nuclear bomb had gone off each year in one of the world's cities, we can well imagine that public attitudes toward the nuclear peril would now be quite different.) The continuity, however illusory, between the pre-nuclear world and the nuclear world which was made possible by these years of not using nuclear weapons was important in preserving the world's denial of the peril because it permitted a spurious normality to be maintained—although "normality" was at times embraced with a fervor that betrayed an edge of hysterical insecurity. The spectacle of life going on as usual carried with it a strong presumption that nothing much was wrong. When we observed that no one seemed to be worried, that no one was showing any signs of alarm or doing anything to save himself, it was hard to resist the conclusion that everything was all right. After all, if we were reasonable people and we were doing nothing how could there be anything the matter? The totality of the peril, in particular, helped to disguise it, for, with everyone and everything in the world similarly imperilled, there was no flight from imperilled things to safe things—no flow of capital from country to country, or migration of people from one place to another. Thoughts of the nuclear peril were largely banned from waking life, and relegated to dreams or to certain fringes of society, and open, active concern about it was restricted to certain "far-out" people, whose ideas were on the whole not so much rejected by the supposedly sober, "realistic" people in the mainstream as simply ignored. In this atmosphere, discussion of the nuclear peril even took on a faintly embarrassing aura, as though dwelling on it were somehow melodramatic, or were a sophomoric excess that serious people outgrew with maturity.

It was not unless one lifted one's gaze from all the allegedly normal events occurring before one's eyes and looked at the executioner's sword hanging over everyone's head that the normality was revealed as a sort of mass insanity. This was an insanity that consisted not in screaming and making a commotion but precisely in *not* doing these things in the face of overwhelming danger, as though everyone had been sedated. Passengers on a ship who are eating, sunning themselves, playing shuffleboard, and engaging in all the usual shipboard activities appear perfectly normal as long as their ship is sailing safely in quiet seas, but these same passengers doing these same things appear deranged if in full view of them all their ship is caught in a vortex that may shortly drag it and them to destruction. Then their placidity has the appearance of an unnatural loss of normal human responses—of a pathetic and sickening acquiescence in their own slaughter. T. S. Eliot's well-known lines "This is the way the world ends/Not with a bang but a whimper" may not be literally correct—there will decidedly be a very big bang—but in a deeper sense it is certainly right; if we do end the world, the sequence is likely to be not a burst of strong-willed activity leading to a final explosion but enervation, dulled senses, enfeebled will, stupor, and paralysis. Then death.

Since we have not made a positive decision to exterminate ourselves but instead have chosen to live on the edge of extinction, periodically lunging toward the abyss only to draw back at the last second, our situation is one of uncertainty and nervous insecurity rather than of absolute hopelessness. We know that we may fall into the abyss at any moment, but we also know that we may not. So life proceeds—what else should it do?—but with a faltering and hesitant step, like one who gropes in darkness at the top of a tall precipice. Intellectually, we recognize that we have prepared ourselves for self-extermination and are improving the preparations every day, but emotionally and politically we have failed to respond. Accordingly, we have begun to live *as if* life were safe, but living *as if* is very different from just living. A split opens up between what we know and what we feel. We place our daily doings in one compartment of our lives and the threat to all life in another compartment. However, this split concerns too fundamental a matter to remain restricted to that matter alone, and it begins to influence the rest of life. Before long, denial of reality becomes a habit—a dominant mode in the life of society—and unresponsiveness becomes a way of life. The society that has accepted the threat of its utter destruction soon finds it hard to react to lesser ills, for a society cannot be at the same time asleep and awake, insane and sane, against life and for life.

To say that we and all future generations are threatened with extinction by the nuclear peril, however, is to describe only half of our situation. The other half is that we are the authors of that extinction. (For the populations of the superpowers, this is true in a positive sense, since we pay for extinction and support the governments that pose the threat of it, while for the peoples of the non-nuclear-armed world it is true only in the negative sense that they fail to try to do anything about the danger.) Like all those who are inclined to suicide, we approach the action in two capacities: the capacity of the one who would kill and that of the one who would be killed. As when we dream, we are both the authors and the sufferers of our fate. Therefore, when we hide from ourselves the immense preparations that we have made for our self-extermination we do so for two compelling reasons. First, we don't want to recognize that at any moment our lives may be taken away from us and our world blasted to dust, and, second, we don't want to face the fact that we are potential mass killers. The moral cost of nuclear armament is that it makes of all of us underwriters of the slaughter of hundreds of millions of people and of the cancellation of the future generations—an action whose utter indefensibility is not altered in the slightest degree by the fact that each side contemplates performing it only in "retaliation." In fact, as we shall see, this retaliation is one of the least justified actions ever contemplated, being wholly pointless. It is another nonsensical feature of the nuclear predicament that while each side regards the population of the other side as the innocent victims of unjust government, each proposes to punish the other government by annihilating that already suffering and oppressed population. Nor is there any exoneration from complicity in this slaughter in the theoretical justification that we possess nuclear arms not in order to use them but in order to prevent their use, for the fact is that even in theory prevention works only to the degree that it is backed up by the plausible threat of use in certain circumstances. Strategy thus commits us all to actions that we cannot justify by any moral standard. It introduces into our lives a vast, morally incomprehensible—or simply immoral—realm, in which every scruple or standard that we otherwise claim to observe or uphold is suspended. To be targeted from the cradle to the grave as a victim of indiscriminate mass murder is degrading in one way, but to target others for similar mass murder is degrading in another and, in a sense, a worse way. We endeavor to hold life sacred, but in accepting our roles as the victims and the perpetrators of nuclear mass slaughter we convey the steady message—and it is engraved more and more deeply on our souls as the years roll by—that life not only is not sacred but is worthless; that, somehow, according to a "strategic" logic that we cannot understand, it has been judged acceptable for everybody to be killed.

As it happens, our two roles in the nuclear predicament have been given visual representation in the photographs of the earth that we have taken with the aid of another technical device of our time, the spaceship. These pictures illustrate, on the one hand, our mastery over nature, which has enabled us to take up a position in the heavens and look back on the earth as though it were just one more celestial body, and, on the other, our weakness and frailty in the face of that mastery, which we cannot help feeling when we see the smallness, solitude, and delicate beauty of our planetary home. Looking at the earth as it is caught in the lens of the camera, reduced to the size of a golf ball, we gain a new sense of scale, and are made aware of a new relation between ourselves and the earth: we can almost imagine that we might hold this earth between the giant thumb and forefinger of one hand. Similarly, as the possessors of nuclear arms we stand outside nature, holding instruments of cosmic power with which we can blot life out, while at the same time we remain embedded in nature and depend on it for our survival.

Yet although the view from space is invaluable, in the last analysis the view that counts is the one from earth, from within life—the view, let us say, from a bedroom window in some city, in the evening, overlooking a river, perhaps, and with the whole colored by some regret or some hope or some other human sentiment. Whatever particular scene might come to mind, and whatever view and mood might be immediately present, from this earthly vantage point another view—one even longer than the one from space—opens up. It is the view of our children and grandchildren, and of all the future generations of mankind, stretching ahead of us in time—a view not just of one earth but of innumerable earths in succession, standing out brightly against the endless darkness of space, of oblivion. The thought of cutting off life's flow, of amputating this future, is so shocking, so alien to nature, and so contradictory to life's impulse that we can scarcely entertain it before turning away in revulsion and disbelief. The very incredibility of the action protects it from our gaze; our very love of life seems to rush forward to deny that we could do this. But although we block out the awareness of this self-posed threat as best we can, engrossing ourselves in life's richness to blind ourselves to the jeopardy to life, ultimately there is no way that we can remain unaffected by it. For finally we know and deeply feel that the ever-shifting, ever-dissolving moments of our mortal lives are sustained and given meaning by the broad stream of life, which bears us along like a force at our backs. Being human, we have, through the establishment of a common world, taken up residence in the enlarged space of past, present, and future, and if we threaten to destroy the future generations we harm ourselves, for the threat we pose to them is carried back to us through the channels of the common world that we all inhabit together. Indeed, "they" are we ourselves, and if their existence is in doubt our present becomes a sadly incomplete affair, like only one word of a poem, or one note of a song. Ultimately, it is subhuman.

Because the weight of extinction, like the weight of mortality, bears down on life through the mind and spirit but otherwise, until the event occurs, leaves us physically undisturbed, no one can prove that it alters the way we live. We can only say that it hardly stands to reason that the largest peril that history has ever produced —a peril in which, indeed, history would swallow itself up—should leave the activities of life, every one of which is threatened with dissolution, unaffected; and that we actually do seem to find life changing in ways that might be expected. Since the future generations are specifically what is at stake, all human activities that assume the future are undermined directly. To begin with, desire, love, childbirth, and everything else that has to do with the biological renewal of the species have been administered a powerful shock by the nuclear peril. The timeless, largely unspoken confidence of the species that although each person had to die, life itself would go on—the faith that on earth life was somehow favored, which found one of its most beautiful expressions in Christ's admonition "Consider the lilies of the field, how they grow; they toil not, neither do they spin: And yet I say unto you, That even Solomon in all his glory was not arrayed like one of these"—has been shaken, and with it the also largely unspoken confidence that people had in their own instinctual natures has been upset. It seems significant that Freud, who pioneered our century's self-consciousness in sexual matters, should have been one of the first observers to warn that humanity was headed down a path of self-destruction. In the last paragraph of "Civilization and Its Discontents," published in 1930, he wrote: ·

The fateful question for the human species seems to me to be whether and to what extent their cultural development will succeed in mastering the disturbance of their communal life by the human instinct of aggression and self-destruction. It may be that in this respect precisely the present time deserves a special interest. Men have gained

control over the forces of nature to such an extent that
with their help they would have no difficulty in exterminating one another to the last man. They know this, and
hence comes a large part of their current unrest, their un-
happiness and their mood of anxiety. And now it is to be
expected that the other of the two "Heavenly Powers,"
eternal Eros, will make an effort to assert himself in the
struggle with his equally immortal adversary [death].
But who can foresee with what success and with what
result?

It is as though Freud perceived that the balance between man's
"lower," animal, and instinctual nature, which had historically been
so much feared and despised by religious men and philosophers as
a disruptive force in man's spiritual development, and his "higher,"
rational nature had tipped in favor of the latter—so that now the
greater danger to man came not from rampant, uncontrolled instinct breaking down the restraining bonds of reason and self-
control but from rampant reason oppressing and destroying instinct
and nature. And rampant reason, man found, was, if anything, more
to be feared than rampant instinct. Bestiality had been the cause
of many horrors, but it had never threatened the species with extinction; some instinct for self-preservation was still at work. Only
"selfless" reason could ever entertain the thought of self-extinction.
Freud's merciful, solicitous attitude toward the animal in our nature
foreshadowed the solicitude that we now need to show toward the
animals and plants in our earthly environment. Now reason must sit
at the knee of instinct and learn reverence for the miraculous instinctual capacity for creation.

It may be a symptom of our disordered instinctual life that,
increasingly, sexuality has lost its hiding place in the privacy of the
bedroom and been drawn into the spotlight of public attention,
where it becomes the subject of debate, advice, and technical instruction, just like any other fully public matter. In Freud's day,
open discussion of sexual questions helped to free people from a
harshly restrictive Victorian morality, but in our day it appears that

sex, which no longer suffers from that traditional suppression, is drawn into the open because something has gone wrong with it and people want to repair it. By making it a public issue, they seem to acknowledge indirectly that our instincts have run up against an obstacle, as indeed they have, and are in need of public assistance, as indeed they are. Odd as it may seem, the disorder of our private, or once private, lives may require a political solution, for it may not be until the human future has been restored to us that desire can again find a natural place in human life.

The biological continuity of the species is made into a fully human, worldly continuity by, above all, the institution of marriage. Marriage lends permanence and a public shape to love. Marriage vows are made by a man and a woman to one another, but they are also made before the world, which is formally present at the ceremony in the role of witness. Marriage *solemnizes* love, giving this most inward of feelings an outward form that is acknowledged by everyone and commands everyone's respect. In swearing their love in public, the lovers also let it be known that their union will be a fit one for bringing children into the world—for receiving what the Bible calls "the grace of life." And the world, by insisting on a ceremony, and by attending in the role of witness, announces its stake in its own continuity. Thus, while in one sense marriage is the most personal of actions, in another sense it belongs to everybody. In a world that is perpetually being overturned and plowed under by birth and death, marriage—which for this reason is rightly called an "institution"—lays the foundation for the stability of a human world that is built to house all the generations. In this sense as well as in the strictly biological sense and the emotional sense, love creates the world.

The peril of extinction surrounds such love with doubt. A trembling world, poised on the edge of self-destruction, offers poor soil for enduring love to grow in. Everything that this love would build up, extinction would tear down. "Eros, builder of cities" (in Auden's phrase, in his poem eulogizing Freud on the occasion of his death) is thwarted. Or, to put it brutally but truthfully, every generation that holds the earth hostage to nuclear destruction holds

157

a gun to the head of its own children. In laying this trap for the species, we show our children no regard, and treat them with indifference and neglect. As for love itself, love lives in the moment, but the moment is dying, as we are, and love also reaches beyond its moment to dwell in a kind of permanence. For

> Love's not Time's fool, though rosy lips and cheeks
> Within his bending sickle's compass come;
> Love alters not with his brief hours and weeks,
> But bears it out even to the edge of doom.

But if doom's edge draws close, love's vast scope is narrowed and its resolve may be shaken. The approach of extinction drives love back into its perishable moment, and, in doing so, tends to break up love's longer attachments, which now, on top of all the usual vicissitudes, have the weight of the whole world's jeopardy to bear.

There is, in fact, an odd resemblance between the plight of love and the plight of war in the nuclear world. Military hostilities, having been stopped by dread of extinction from occurring on the field of battle, are relegated to a mental plane—to the world of strategic theory and war games, where the generals of our day sit at their computer terminals waging shadow wars with the ostensible aim of making sure that no real hostilities ever happen. Love, too, although it has not been prevented altogether, has in a way lost its full field of action—the world that included the future generations—and so has tended to withdraw to a mental plane peculiarly its own, where it becomes an ever more solitary affair: impersonal, detached, pornographic. It means something that we call both pornography and nuclear destruction "obscene." In the first, we find desire stripped of any further human sentiment or attachment—of any "redeeming social value," in the legal phrase. In the second, we find violence detached from any human goals, all of which would be engulfed in a holocaust—detached, that is, from all redeeming social value.

The Japanese used to call the pleasure quarters of their cities "floating worlds." Now our entire world, cut adrift from its future and its past, has become a floating world. The cohesion of the social realm—the dense and elaborate fabric of life that is portrayed for us in the novels of the nineteenth century, among other places, inspiring "nostalgic" longing in us—is disintegrating, and people seem to be drifting apart and into a weird isolation. The compensation that is offered is the license to enjoy life in the moment with fewer restrictions; but the present moment and its pleasures provide only a poor refuge from the emptiness and loneliness of our shaky, dreamlike, twilit world. The moment itself, unable to withstand the abnormal pressure of expectation, becomes distorted and corrupted. People turn to it for rewards that it cannot offer—certainly not when it is ordered to do so. Plucked out of life's stream, the moment—whether a moment of love or of spiritual peace, or even of simple pleasure in a meal—is no longer permitted to quietly unfold and be itself but is strenuously tracked down, manipulated, harried by instruction and advice, bought and sold, and, in general, so roughly manhandled that the freshness and joy that it can yield up when it is left alone are corrupted or destroyed.

It is fully understandable that in the face of the distortion and disintegration of human relationships in a doom-ridden world a "conservative" longing for a richer, more stable, and more satisfying social existence should spring up. Unfortunately, however, this longing, instead of inspiring us to take political measures that would remove the world from jeopardy, and thus put life on a solid footing again, all too often takes the form of a simple *wish* that the world would stop being the way it is now and return to its former state, with what are often called "the old values" intact. Rather than take cognizance of the radical causes of the world's decline, with a view to doing something about them, these would-be upholders of the past tend to deny the existence of our new situation. It is only one more part of this denial—the most dangerous part—to imagine that war, too, still exists in its traditional form, in which one's enemies can be defeated on the field of battle without bringing an end to everything. Conservatism in personal and social questions has often gone together with militarism in the past, but now the combination is far more perilous than ever before. It represents a denial of what the world has now become which could lead to the end of the world. If a nation indulges itself in the illusion that, even with nuclear arms, war is possible, and that "victory" can be won with them, it risks bringing about its own and the world's extinction by mistake. Alert and realistic conservatives, by contrast, would see that everything that anyone might wish to conserve is threatened by nuclear weapons, and would recognize in them a threat not only to "the old values" but to any values whatever. And instead of dreaming of the vanished wars of past times they would place themselves in the forefront of a movement for disarmament.

Politics, as it now exists, is even more thoroughly compromised than personal and social life by the peril of extinction. Marriage lays down its map of hereditary lines across the unmarked territory of generational succession, shaping the rudiments of a common world out of biological reproduction, which without marriage would continue anyway, as it did before civilization was born, and does still among animals. Marriage is thus half submerged in the unconscious, instinctual, biological life of the species, and only half emergent into the "daylight" (in Hegel's term) of history and the common world. Politics, on the other hand, is wholly the creature of the common world, and could have no existence without it. (If people did not have reason and language, they could still reproduce but they could not set up a government among themselves.) There is no political "moment," as there is a sensual moment, to fall back on in an attempted retreat from the futility of a jeopardized common world. Politics, accordingly, is fully stuck with the glaring absurdity that with one hand it builds for a future that with the other hand it prepares to destroy. Each time a politician raises his voice to speak of making a better world for our children and grandchildren (and this is an intrinsic part of what politics is about, whether or not it happens to be explicitly stated), the peril of extinction is there to gainsay him with the crushing rebuttal: But there may *be* no children or grandchildren. And when, far more ridiculously, politicians let us know of their desire for a "place in history," it is not only their swollen vanity that invites anger but their presumption in trying to reserve a place in a history whose continued existence their own actions place in doubt.

Since Aristotle, it has often been said that the two basic aims of political association are, first, to assure the survival of members of society (that is, to protect life) and, second, to give them a chance to fulfill themselves as social beings (that is, to enable them to lead a noble or a good life). The threat of self-extermination annuls both of these objectives, and leaves the politics of our day in the ludicrous position of failing even to aim at the basic goals that have traditionally justified its existence. If our economy were to produce a wonderful abundance of silverware, glasses, and table napkins but no food, people would quickly rebel and insist on a different system. The world's political arrangements, which now aim at providing some accoutrements of life but fail to lift a finger to save life itself, are in no less drastic need of replacement. People cannot for long place confidence in institutions that fail even to recognize the most urgent requirement of the whole species, and it is therefore not surprising that, more and more, people do actually look on politicians with contempt, though perhaps without having quite figured out why.

As long as politics fails to take up the nuclear issue in a determined way, it lives closer than any other activity to the lie that we have all come to live—the pretense that life lived on top of a nuclear stockpile can last. Meanwhile, we are encouraged not to tackle our predicament but to inure ourselves to it: to develop a special, enfeebled vision, which is capable of overlooking the hugely obvious; a special, sluggish nervous system, which is conditioned not to react even to the most extreme and urgent peril; and a special, constricted mode of political thinking, which is permitted to creep around the edges of the mortal crisis in the life of our species but never to meet it head on. In this timid, crippled thinking, "realism" is the title given to beliefs whose most notable characteristic is their failure to recognize the chief reality of the age, the pit into which our species threatens to jump; "utopian" is the term of scorn for any plan that shows serious promise of enabling the species to keep from killing itself (if it is "utopian" to want to survive, then it must be "realistic" to be dead); and the political arrangements that keep us on the edge of annihilation are deemed "moderate," and are found to be "respectable," whereas new arrangements, which might enable us to draw a few steps back from the brink, are called "extreme" or "radical." With such fear-filled, thought-stopping epithets as these, the upholders of the status quo defend the anachronistic structure of their thinking, and seek to block the revolution in thought and in action which is necessary if mankind is to go on living.

Works of art, history, and thought, which provide what Arendt calls the "publicity" that makes an intergenerational common world possible, are undermined at their foundations by the threat of self-extermination. Each such work is a vessel that bears the distillation of some thought, feeling, or experience from one generation to another. In his 1970 Nobel Prize acceptance speech, Solzhenitsyn said, "Woe to that nation whose literature is disturbed by the intervention of power. Because that is not just a violation against 'freedom of print,' it is the closing down of the heart of the nation, a slashing to pieces of its memory." In reminding us that totalitarian governments seek to break the connections between generations, which are so inconvenient to all monomaniacal campaigns, Solzhenitsyn might well have been demonstrating that totalitarianism is indeed one of the precursors of the peril of extinction, which puts an end to all the generations. (The difference is that whereas totalitarianism destroys the memories, extinction destroys all the rememberers.) A work of art will often celebrate the most evanescent thing—a glance, a vague longing, the look of a certain shadow—but as soon as the artist picks up his brush or his pen he takes up residence in the immortal common world inhabited by all generations together. As the poets have always told us, art rescues love and other mortal things from time's destruction. And it is not only the artists who reach beyond their own lifetimes with art; it is also the readers, listeners, and viewers, who while they are in the presence of a work of art are made contemporary with it and, in a way, with all other readers, listeners, and viewers, in all ages. Through art, we "are able to break bread with the dead, and without communion with the dead a fully human life is impossible" (Auden). The timeless appeal of the greatest works of art, in fact, testifies to our common humanity as few other things do, and is one of the strongest grounds we have for supposing that a political community that would embrace the whole earth and all generations is also possible.

The other side of art's communion with the dead (which is the basis for Camus's lovely remark "As an artist . . . I began by admiring others, which in a way is heaven on earth") is its communion with the unborn. In nothing that we do are the unborn more strongly present than in artistic creation. It is the very business of artists to speak to future audiences, and therefore it is perhaps not surprising that they—probably more than any other observers, at least in the modern age—have been gifted with prophetic powers. (In our century, the name of Kafka, who seemed to foresee in so many particulars the history of our time, inevitably comes to mind.) Indeed, great works of art are often so closely attuned to the future that it takes the world a few decades to understand them. There is no doubt that art, which breaks into the crusted and hardened patterns of thought and feeling in the present as though it were the very prow of the future, is in radically altered circumstances if the future is placed in doubt. The ground on which the artist stands when he turns to his work has grown unsteady beneath his feet. In the pre-nuclear world, an artist who hoped to enable future generations to commune with his time might be worried that his work would be found wanting by posterity and so would pass into oblivion, but in the nuclear world the artist, whose work is still subject to this danger, must also fear that even if he produces nothing but timeless masterpieces they will fall into oblivion anyway, because there will be no posterity. The masterpieces cannot be timeless if time itself stops. The new uncertainty is not that one's work will be buried and forgotten in the tumult of history but that history, which alone offers the hope of saving anything from time's destruction, will itself be buried in the indifference of the nonhuman universe, dragging all human achievements down with it. The two fates, which now constitute a double jeopardy for artistic creation, are utterly different. In the first, it is life—the "onslaught of the generations," in Arendt's phrase—that undoes the work while itself surviving. In the second, it is death that swallows up both life and the work. The first peril makes us feel our individual mortality more keenly, but, for that very reason, makes us feel the common life of the species more strongly, and both feelings may inspire us to increase our efforts to accomplish whatever it is that we hope to offer the world before we die. The second peril threatens not each individual work but the world to which all works are offered, and makes us feel that even if we did accomplish our individual aims it would be pointless, thus undercutting our will to accomplish anything at all.

It would be futile to try to prescribe to art what it "can" and "cannot" do, as though we in the present had a visionary capacity to foresee art's future forms and, like an omniscient critic, accept some while ruling out others; but it is possible to reflect on what has already occurred, and to wonder what role political and other events in the world may have played in this or that development. Bearing in mind the irreducible mysteriousness of artistic creativity, we may note that some of the developments in art in recent decades have the look of logical, if unconscious, adjustments to the newly imperilled condition of the species. The art critic and social and political observer Harold Rosenberg has spoken of a "de-definition" of art, by which he meant a blurring of the boundary lines that have traditionally separated artistic creation from other human activities. Among the distinctions that have been lost—or deliberately breached —are the ones between the artist and his work of art and between the work of art and its audience. Rosenberg found the first breach in Action painting, in which the meaning of the work came to reside in the act of painting rather than in the finished canvas, and he found the second in all those artistic events that are called "happenings," in which the audience is more or less dispensed with and the "aesthetic effects are given by the event itself, without intervention on the part of the spectator-participant." In trying to do away with the enduring, independently existing art product and its audience, and concentrating on the act of creation, these artists, who "left art behind," seemed to be working toward an art that would fulfill itself—like the sexual act that is isolated from the past and the future—in the moment, thus giving up on communion with the dead and with the unborn: doing away, in fact, with art's whole dependence on the common world, which assumes the existence of the human future. If art could manage this, of course, it would escape the futility of trying to communicate with generations that now may never arrive. Politics is simply powerless to cut itself off from the future and compress itself into a highly charged present (although some of the radical students of the nineteen-sixties seemed at times to be making the attempt), but art may have more leeway for experimentation, perhaps because, as the traditional rescuer of fleeting things from oblivion, it starts off being closer to life in the moment. Whether these experiments can produce much that is worthwhile is another question. Rosenberg spoke of "all those ruses of scrutinizing itself and defiantly denying its own existence" by which art has survived in recent decades, but he held out little hope that these devices could sustain art much longer. Looked at in terms of the predicament of the species as a whole, art appears to be in a quandary. Art attempts both to reflect the period in which it was produced and to be timeless. But today, if it wishes to truthfully reflect the reality of its period, whose leading feature is the jeopardy of the human future, art will have to go out of existence, while if it insists on trying to be timeless it has to ignore this reality —which is nothing other than the jeopardy of human time—and so, in a sense, tell a lie. Art by itself is powerless to solve its predicament, and artists, like lovers, are in need of assistance from statesmen and ordinary citizens.

By threatening to cancel the future generations, the nuclear peril not only throws all our activities that count on their existence into disorder but also disturbs our relationship with the past generations. We need the assurance that there will be a future if we are to take on the burden of mastering the past—a past that really does become the proverbial "dead past," an unbearable weight of millennia of corpses and dust, if there is no promise of a future. Without confidence that we will be followed by future generations, to whom we can hand on what we have received from the past, it becomes intolerably depressing to enter the tombs of the dead to gather what they have left behind; yet without that treasure our life is impoverished. The present is a fulcrum on which the future and the past lie balanced, and if the future is lost to us, then the past must fall away, too.

Death lies at the core of each person's private existence, but part of death's meaning is to be found in the fact that it occurs in a biological and social world that survives. No one can be a spectator at his own funeral, but others can be there, and the anticipation of their presence, which betokens the continuity of life and all that that means for a mortal creature, is consolation to each person as he faces his death. Death suffered in the shadow of doom lacks this consolation. It is a gap that threatens soon to be lost in a larger gap —a death within a greater death. When human life itself is over-hung with death, we cannot go peacefully to our individual deaths. The deaths of others, too, become more terrible: with the air so full of death, every death becomes harder to face. When a person dies, we often turn our thoughts to the good he did while he was alive—to that which he gave to the world, and which therefore out-lasts him in the world's affection. (When someone who did great harm to the world dies, we feel that death has had a more thorough victory, since there is so little of his that the world wishes to pre-serve. Rather, it may wish to bury him even more thoroughly than any grave can.) But when the whole world, in which the dead in a sense live on, is imperilled, this effort at remembrance and preser-vation seems to lose its point, and all lives and deaths are threatened with a common meaninglessness.

There have been many deaths in our century that in certain re-spects resembled those that would be suffered in a nuclear holo-caust: the deaths of the millions of people who died in the concen-tration camps of the totalitarian regimes, which sought not only to kill their victims but to extirpate their memory from the historical record. Because the camps threatened people not only with death but with oblivion, remembrance has become for some survivors a passion and a sacred obligation. When Solzhenitsyn accepted the Nobel Prize, he was at pains to remind the world that he spoke on behalf of millions who had not survived, and his whole historical reconstruction of the Soviet camp system is pitted against totalitarian forgetfulness. Likewise, the command "Never forget," so often heard in connection with the Nazis' genocidal attack on the Jews, is important not only because it may help the world to prevent any repetition but because remembering is in itself an act that helps to defeat the Nazis' attempt to send a whole people into oblivion. Just because genocide, by trying to prevent the future generations of people from being born, commits a crime against the future, it lays a special obligation on the people of the future to deal with the crime, even long after its perpetrators are themselves dead. The need to bear witness and then to remember was felt first by the inmates of the camps and only later by the world at large. The French journalist David Rousset, a survivor of several camps, including Buchenwald, has written of his experiences in those camps:

> How many people here still believe that a protest has even historic importance? This skepticism is the real masterpiece of the S.S. Their great accomplishment. They have corrupted all human solidarity. Here the night has fallen on the future. When no witnesses are left, there can be no testimony. To demonstrate when death can no longer be postponed is an attempt to give death a meaning, to act beyond one's own death. In order to be successful, a gesture must have social meaning. There are hundreds of thousands of us here, all living in absolute solitude.

Thanks to a few heroic witnesses, and to the existence outside the totalitarian world of a nontotalitarian world, which could find out about what happened and then remember it, the connections between the camp victims and the rest of humanity were never altogether severed. There *was* testimony, the "historic importance" of the events in the camps *was* preserved, "human solidarity" *was* partly maintained, however tragically late, and the "masterpiece" of the S.S. was spoiled. Indeed, if we read the testimony of those in the camps deeply enough it may help us in our effort to avoid our extinction. Arendt, writing in her classic study "The Origins of Totalitarianism," made the connection:

Here [in the camps], there are neither political nor historical nor simply moral standards but, at the most, the realization that something seems to be involved in modern politics that actually should never be involved in politics as we used to understand it, namely all or nothing—all, and that is an undetermined infinity of forms of human living-together, or nothing, for a victory of the concentration-camp system would mean the same inexorable doom for human beings as the use of the hydrogen bomb would mean the doom of the human race.

Yet we must insist, I think, that in fact extinction by nuclear arms would be the more profound oblivion, since then the very possibility of remembrance or renewal—of the existence of a Solzhenitsyn or Rousset to bear witness, or of an Arendt to reflect on their testimony, or of readers to ponder what happened and take it to heart—would be gone. In extinction, and only in extinction, the connections between the victims and the rest of humanity would really be severed forever, and the "masterpiece" of the mass murderers would be perfected, for the night would have "fallen on the future" once and for all. Of all the crimes against the future, extinction is the greatest. It is the murder of the future. And because this murder cancels all those who might recollect it even as it destroys its immediate victims the obligation to "never forget" is displaced back onto us, the living. It is we—the ones who will either commit this crime or prevent it—who must bear witness, must remember, and must arrive at the judgment.

A nuclear holocaust would destroy the living and cancel the unborn in the same blow, but it is possible, as I mentioned earlier, at least to imagine that, through sterilization of the species, the future generations could be cancelled while the living were left unharmed. Although the condition of being extinct is by definition beyond experience this remnant—the living cells of the dead body of mankind—would, like a prisoner who knows that he is condemned to die on a certain day, be forced to look extinction in the face in a way that we, who can always tell ourselves that we may yet

escape extinction, are not. To them, the futility of all the activities
of the common world—of marriage, of politics, of the arts, of learning, and, for that matter, of war—would be driven home inexorably.
They would experience in their own lives the breakdown of the ties
that bind individual human beings together into a community and a
species, and they would feel the current of our common life grow
cold within them. And as their number was steadily reduced by
death they would witness the final victory of death over life. One
wonders whether in these circumstances people would want to go
on living at all—or whether they might not choose to end their own
lives. By killing off the living quickly, extinction by nuclear arms
would spare us those barren, bitter decades of watching and feeling
the end close in. As things are, we will never experience the approach of extinction in that pure form, and are left in an irremediable uncertainty. Nevertheless, the spectre of extinction hovers
over our world and shapes our lives with its invisible but terrible
pressure. It now accompanies us through life, from birth to death.
Wherever we go, it goes, too; in whatever we do, it is present. It
gets up with us in the morning, it stays at our side throughout the
day, and it gets into bed with us at night. It is with us in the
delivery room, at the marriage ceremony, and on our deathbeds.
It is the truth about the way we now live. But such a life cannot go
on for long.

Because the unborn generations will never experience their cancellation by us, we have to look for the consequences of extinction
before it occurs, in our own lives, where it takes the form of a spiritual sickness that corrupts life at the invisible, innermost starting
points of our thoughts, moods, and actions. This emphasis on us,
however, does not mean that our only reason for restraining ourselves from elimination of the future generations is to preserve
them as auxiliaries to *our* needs—as the audience for our works of
art, as the outstretched hands to receive our benefactions (and so to
bring our otherwise frustrated charitable impulses to fulfillment),
as the minds that will provide us with immortality by remembering

169

our words and deeds, and as the successors who will justify us by carrying on with the tasks that we have started or advanced. To adopt such an expedient view of the future generations would be to repeat on a monumental scale the error of the philanthropist who looks on the needy only as a convenient prop with which he can develop and demonstrate his moral superiority, or the more familiar and more dangerous figure of the politician who looks on the public only as a ladder on which he can climb to power. It would also put us in the company of those who, in pursuit, very often, of visionary social goals, make the opposite but closely related error of regarding the *present* generations only as auxiliaries—as the expendable bricks and mortar to be used in the construction of a glorious palace in which the future generations will take up residence. (We have merely to remember how many people have been murdered so that "history" might "go forward" to be reminded how great the costs of this mistake have been.) Whether we were subordinating the living or the unborn generations, this reduction of human beings to a supporting role in the completion of cross-generational tasks would suggest that we had come to place a higher value on the achievements of life than we did on life itself, as though we were so dazzled by the house man lives in that we had forgotten who lives there. But no human being, living or unborn, should be regarded as an auxiliary. Although human beings have their obligations to fulfill, they are not to be seen as beasts of burden whose purpose in existing is to carry on with enterprises that are supposedly grander and more splendid than they are. For in the last analysis these enterprises, which together make up the common world, are meant to serve life, not to be served by it. Life does not exist for the sake of the governments, the buildings, the books, and the paintings; all these exist for the sake of life. The works of man are great, but man himself is greater.

The reason that so much emphasis must be laid on the living generations is not that they are more important than the unborn but only that at any given moment they, by virtue of happening to be the ones who exist, are the ones who pose the peril, who can feel the consequences of the peril in their lives, and who can respond to the peril on behalf of all other generations. To cherish life—whether one's own or someone else's, a present life or an unborn life—one must already be in life, and only the living have this privilege. The question that the peril of extinction puts before the living, however, is: Who would miss human life if they extinguished it? To which the only honest answer is: Nobody. That being so, we have to admit that extinction is no loss, since there cannot be loss when there is no loser: and we are thus driven to seek the meaning of extinction in the mere anticipation of it by the living, whose lives this anticipation corrupts and degrades. However, there is another side to the entire question. For while it is true that extinction cannot be felt by those whose fate it is—the unborn, who would stay unborn—the same cannot be said, of course, for extinction's alternative, survival. If we shut the unborn out of life, they will never have a chance to lament their fate, but if we let them into life they will have abundant opportunity to be glad that they were born instead of having been prenatally severed from existence by us. The idea of escaping extinction before one was born is a strange one for us, since it is so new, but to generations that live deep in nuclear time, and who know that their existence has depended on the wisdom and restraint of a long succession of generations before them, we can be sure that the idea will be familiar.

Of every other bequest that the present makes to the future it can be said that that which would be gratefully received if it was given would also be sorely missed if it was withheld. Of life alone is it the case that while its receipt can be welcomed, its denial cannot be mourned. The peril of extinction, by bringing us up against this reality, concentrates our attention in a new way on the simple and basic fact that before there can be good or evil, service or harm, lamenting or rejoicing there *must be life*. (Even those who wish to exploit and harm other human beings must first want human beings to exist.) In coming to terms with the peril of extinction, therefore, what we must desire first of all is that people be born, for their own sakes, and not for any other reason. Everything else—our wish to serve the future generations by preparing a decent world for them to live in, and our wish to lead a decent life ourselves in a common world made secure by the safety of the future generations—flows from this commitment. Life comes first. The rest is secondary.

To recapitulate: In a nuclear holocaust great enough to extinguish the species, every person on earth would die; but in addition to that, and distinct from it, is the fact that the unborn generations would be prevented from ever existing. However, precisely because the unborn are not born, they cannot experience their plight, and its meaning has to be sought among the living, who share a common world with the unborn as well as with the dead, and who find that if they turn their backs on the unborn, and deny them life, then their own lives become progressively more twisted, empty, and despairing. On the other hand, if instead of asking what the act of extinction means we ask what the act of survival means—and in the nuclear world survival has, for the first time, become an act—we find that the relationship between the generations is reconstituted, and we can once again ask what the meaning of our actions will be for the people directly affected by them, who now, because they are presumed to exist, can be presumed to have a response. By acting to save the species, and repopulating the future, we break out of the cramped, claustrophobic isolation of a doomed present, and open a path to the greater space—the only space fit for human habitation —of past, present, and future. Suddenly, we can think and feel again. Even by merely imagining for a moment that the nuclear peril has been lifted and human life has a sure foothold on the earth again, we can feel the beginnings of a boundless relief and calm—a boundless peace. But we can open this path only if it is our desire that the unborn exist for their own sake. We trace the effects of extinction in our own world because that is the only place where they can ever appear, yet those sad effects, important as they are, are only the side effects of our shameful failure to fulfill our main obligation of valuing the future human beings themselves. And if at first we find these future people to be somewhat abstract we have only to remind ourselves that we, too, were once "the future generation," and that every unborn person will be as vivid and important to himself as each of us is to himself. We gain the right perspective on extinction not by trying to peer into the inhuman emptiness of a

post-human universe but by putting ourselves in the shoes of someone in the future, who, precisely because he has been allowed to be
born, can rejoice in the fact of being alive.

With the generation that has never known a world unmenaced by
nuclear weapons, a new order of the generations begins. In it, each
person alive is called on to assume his share of the responsibility for
guaranteeing the existence of all future generations. And out of the
new sense of responsibility must come a worldwide program of
action for preserving the species. This program would be the guarantee of existence for the unborn and the measure of the honor and
the humanity of the living. Its inauguration would mark the foundation of a new common world, which would greatly transcend the old,
pre-nuclear common world in importance and in the strength of its
ties. Without such a program in place, nothing else that we under-
take together can make any practical or moral sense. Thus, the
nuclear peril, while for the first time in history placing the whole
common world in jeopardy, at the same time draws into that common world much that was formerly left out, including, above all,
the terrestrial biological inheritance. Through the jeopardy of our
biological substance, even the things that belong to what Arendt
called the "private realm" are affected, so that ultimately it is not
only the institutions, arts, and sciences—the enduring, heavy structure of the world—whose meaning is changed but also the fleeting
things: sensation, desire, "the summer lightning of individual happiness" (Alexander Herzen). Against the background of the new
double mortality of life, the fleeting things seem even more flicker-
ing, and more to be protected and cherished.

By threatening life in its totality, the nuclear peril creates new
connections between the elements of human existence—a new min-
gling of the public and the private, the political and the emotional,
the spiritual and the biological. In a strikingly pertinent remark,
Arendt, speaking of the individual's capacity for action, writes,
"With word and deed we insert ourselves into the human world,
and this insertion is like a second birth, in which we confirm and

173

take upon ourselves the naked fact of our original physical appearance." Now the whole species is called on literally to take on itself the naked fact of its original physical appearance—to protect our being through an act of our will. Formerly, the future was simply given to us; now it must be achieved. We must become the agriculturalists of time. If we do not plant and cultivate the future years of human life, we will never reap them. This effort would constitute a counterpart in our conscious life of reason and will of our instinctual urge to procreate. And in so doing it would round out and complete the half-finished common world of pre-nuclear times, which, by the time nuclear weapons were invented, had enabled mankind to learn and to suffer but not to act as one.

In asking us to cherish the lives of the unborn, the peril of extinction takes us back to the ancient principle of the sacredness of human life, but it conducts us there by a new path. Instead of being asked not to kill our neighbors, we are asked to let them be born. If it is possible to speak of a benefit of the nuclear peril, it would be that it invites us to become more deeply aware of the miracle of birth, and of the world's renewal. "For unto us a child is born." This is indeed "good news." Yet when we turn from extinction, which silences us with its nothingness, to the abundance of life, we find ourselves tongue-tied again, this time by the fullness of what lies before our eyes. If death is one mystery, life is another, greater one. We find ourselves confronted with the essential openness, unfathomability, and indefinability of our species. (Auden has observed that human nature is indefinable because definition is a historical act that can upset the human reality it seeks to define.) We can only feel awe before a mystery that both is what we are and surpasses our understanding.

Without violating that mystery, we can perhaps best comprehend the obligation to save the species simply as a new relationship among human beings. Because the will to save the species would be a will to let other people into existence rather than a will to save oneself, it is a form of respect for others, or, one might say, a form of love. (By contrast, the will to avoid the holocaust, which would kill off every living person, involves self-interest, and would grow, in part, out of fear. Thus, as we face the nuclear predicament in its entirety, both love and fear are present, but they are inspired by threats to different things.) This love, I believe, would bear a resemblance to the generative love of parents, who in wanting to bring children into the world have some experience of what it is to hope for the renewal of life. They know that when a child is born the whole world is reborn with it, as in a sunrise, since it is only in the mind, heart, and spirit of each human being that the human world has existence. If the ideal for the relationship among living people is brotherhood, then the ideal for the relationship of the living to the unborn is parenthood. Universal brotherhood, which seeks to safeguard lives that are already in existence, embodies the solicitude and protectiveness of love, and its highest command, therefore, is "Thou shalt not kill." Universal parenthood, which would seek to bring life into existence out of nothing, would embody the creativity and abundant generosity of love, and its highest commandment, therefore, would be "Be fruitful and multiply." But this commandment is not the strictly biological one. The nuclear peril makes all of us, whether we happen to have children of our own or not, the parents of all future generations. Parental love, which begins even before any child exists, is unconditional. It does not attach to any quality of the beloved; it only wants him to be. But then all love, when it is deep, has something in it of this character, and is ready to forgive every particular failing in the beloved. Shakespeare says that "love is not love which alters when it alteration finds," and we know from the Bible that "love keeps no accounts."

The common world itself can be seen as a product of the superabundance of life's fruitfulness. It is like a surplus, beyond what each generation can use for itself, that is passed on in a steadily growing accumulation, enabling all the generations to participate in a *life* of mankind which transcends individual life and is not undone by individual death. Extinction is a second death, and this second life is the life that it destroys.

Since the future generations will surely do and suffer wrong, it is part of the work of this love to come to terms with evil. Love is given Job's task: to accept and affirm the creation even in the full knowledge of the unspeakable injustice and suffering that it contains. Thus, while our capacity for sympathizing with the suffering of others is of no help in understanding extinction, because there is no suffering (or any other human experience) in it, it would not be right to say that the question of suffering does not come up, for *in saving* the future generations we will bring them every kind of suffering that life holds (together with every other human experience). The fact that it is not extinction but life that brings suffering, and even death, is the clearest proof that extinction is misconceived as a disaster in any ordinary sense. On the contrary, survival means disaster—endlessly, as long as life is beset by accident and folly. In the pre-nuclear common world, our aim was to spare all generations every particular evil that it was in our power to resist, but now our determination must be first to give the future generations all the evils, which are as much a part of life as breathing, and only then to set about mitigating them. Fortunately or unfortunately, we cannot pick and choose which experiences of life to give the future generations. Either we keep them out of life completely or we get them in for all of it.

To favor life on these terms is difficult, but it is not inhuman. We find this affirmation in one form in parental love and we find it in another form in religious faith, as the example of Job attests. Augustine wrote that after his introduction to Christianity "no more did I long for better things, because I thought of all things, and with a sounder judgment I held that the higher things are indeed better than the lower, but that all things together are better than the higher things alone." And he wrote, "All things, by the very fact that they *are*, are good." A Japanese Buddhist monk seems to have been saying the same thing even more simply when he said, "Every day is a good day." A similar affirmation runs through the ceremonial words of Christian sacramental occasions. Marriage vows, in which the couple swear to love one another in sickness and in health and "for better for worse," seem to signify an affirmation not only of the married condition but of the whole human condition. And in the words sometimes spoken in burial services the affirmation is

176

made outright: "Ashes to ashes, dust to dust. The Lord gave, and the Lord hath taken away; blessed be the name of the Lord."

The first principle of life in the new common world would be respect for human beings, born and unborn, based on our common love of life and our common jeopardy in the face of our own destructive powers and inclinations. This respect would grow out of each generation's gratitude to past generations for having permitted it to exist. Each generation would look on itself as though it were a delegation that had been chosen by an assembly of all the dead and all the unborn to represent them in life. The living would thus look on the gift of life the way any political representative should look on election to office—as a temporary trust to be used for the common good. For if the surface of the globe is the breadth of the world, time, which politics is now called on to guarantee, is its depth, and we cannot expect the world to cohere horizontally if it is not joined together vertically as well. In this new world, the people of the present generations, if they acquit their responsibility, would be the oldest of the grandfathers, and their role would be that of founders.

A second principle of life in the nuclear common world would be respect for the earth. This is nothing but a full realization of the ecological principle, according to which the earth's environment is seen not merely as a surrounding element in which it is more or less pleasant to live but as the foundation of human as of other life. The oneness of the earth as a system of support for life is already visible around us. Today, no matter how strenuously statesmen may assert the "sovereign" power of their nations, the fact is that they are all caught in an increasingly fine mesh of global life, in which the survival of each nation depends on the survival of all. There is no "sovereign" right to destroy the earthly creation on which everyone depends for survival (although such a right is exactly what each superpower now claims for itself). More and more, the earth is coming to resemble a single body, or, to use Dr. Thomas's metaphor, a single cell, which is inhabited by billions of separate intelligences and wills. In these circumstances, the use of violence is like the left hand attacking the right, or like both hands attacking the throat. We want to maintain the independence of each person's mind and will—for our liberty consists in this—but in doing so we must not kill the one terrestrial body in which we are all incarnated together.

A third principle would be respect for God or nature, or whatever one chooses to call the universal dust that made, or became, us. We need to remember that neither as individuals nor as a species have we created ourselves. And we need to remember that our swollen power is not a power to create but only a power to destroy. We can kill all human beings and close down the source of all future human beings, but we cannot create even one human being, much less create those terrestrial conditions which now permit us and other forms of life to live. Even our power of destruction is hardly our own. As a fundamental property of matter, nuclear energy was nature's creation, and was only discovered by us. (What is truly our own is the knowledge that has enabled us to exploit this energy.) With respect to creation, things still stand as they have always stood, with extra-human powers performing the miracle, and human beings receiving the fruits. Our modest role is not to create but only to preserve ourselves. The alternative is to surrender ourselves to absolute and eternal darkness: a darkness in which no nation, no society, no ideology, no civilization will remain; in which never again will a child be born; in which never again will human beings appear on the earth, and there will be no one to remember that they ever did.

III.
THE CHOICE

Four and a half billion years ago, the earth was formed. Perhaps a half billion years after that, life arose on the planet. For the next four billion years, life became steadily more complex, more varied, and more ingenious, until, around a million years ago, it produced mankind—the most complex and ingenious species of them all. Only six or seven thousand years ago—a period that is to the history of the earth as less than a minute is to a year—civilization emerged, enabling us to build up a human world, and to add to the marvels of evolution marvels of our own: marvels of art, of science, of social organization, of spiritual attainment. But, as we built higher and higher, the evolutionary foundation beneath our feet became more and more shaky, and now, in spite of all we have learned and achieved—or, rather, because of it—we hold this entire terrestrial creation hostage to nuclear destruction, threatening to hurl it back into the inanimate darkness from which it came. And this threat of

181

self-destruction and planetary destruction is not something that we will pose one day in the future, if we fail to take certain precautions; it is here now, hanging over the heads of all of us at every moment. The machinery of destruction is complete, poised on a hair trigger, waiting for the "button" to be "pushed" by some misguided or deranged human being or for some faulty computer chip to send out the instruction to fire. That so much should be balanced on so fine a point—that the fruit of four and a half billion years can be undone in a careless moment—is a fact against which belief rebels. And there is another, even vaster measure of the loss, for stretching ahead from our present are more billions of years of life on earth, all of which can be filled not only with human life but with human civilization. The procession of generations that extends onward from our present leads far, far beyond the line of our sight, and, compared with these stretches of human time, which exceed the whole history of the earth up to now, our brief civilized moment is almost infinitesimal. And yet we threaten, in the name of our transient aims and fallible convictions, to foreclose it all. If our species does destroy itself, it will be a death in the cradle—a case of infant mortality. The disparity between the cause and the effect of our peril is so great that our minds seem all but powerless to encompass it. In addition, we are so fully enveloped by that which is menaced, and so deeply and passionately immersed in its events, which are the events of our lives, that we hardly know how to get far enough away from it to see it in its entirety. It is as though life itself were one huge distraction, diverting our attention from the peril to life. In its apparent durability, a world menaced with imminent doom is in a way deceptive. It is almost an illusion. Now we are sitting at the breakfast table drinking our coffee and reading the newspaper, but in a moment we may be inside a fireball whose temperature is tens of thousands of degrees. Now we are on our way to work, walking through the city streets, but in a moment we may be standing on an empty plain under a darkened sky looking for the charred remnants of our children. Now we are alive, but in a moment we may be dead. Now there is human life on earth, but in a moment it may be gone.

Once, there was time to reflect in a more leisurely way on our predicament. In August, 1945, when the invention of the bomb was made known through its first use on a human population, the people of Hiroshima, there lay ahead an interval of decades which might have been used to fashion a world that would be safe from extinction by nuclear arms, and some voices were in fact heard counselling deep reflection on the looming peril and calling for action to head it off. On November 28, 1945, less than four months after the bombing of Hiroshima, the English philosopher Bertrand Russell rose in the House of Lords and said:

> We do not want to look at this thing simply from the point of view of the next few years; we want to look at it from the point of view of the future of mankind. The question is a simple one: Is it possible for a scientific society to continue to exist, or must such a society inevitably bring itself to destruction? It is a simple question but a very vital one. I do not think it is possible to exaggerate the gravity of the possibilities of evil that lie in the utilization of atomic energy. As I go about the streets and see St. Paul's, the British Museum, the Houses of Parliament, and the other monuments of our civilization, in my mind's eye I see a nightmare vision of those buildings as heaps of rubble with corpses all round them. That is a thing we have got to face, not only in our own country and cities, but throughout the civilized world.

Russell and others, including Albert Einstein, urged full, global disarmament, but the advice was disregarded. Instead, the world set about building the arsenals that we possess today. The period of grace we had in which to ward off the nuclear peril before it became a reality—the time between the moment of the invention of the weapons and the construction of the full-scale machinery for extinction—was squandered, and now the peril that Russell foresaw is upon us. Indeed, if we are honest with ourselves we have to admit that unless we rid ourselves of our nuclear arsenals a holocaust not only *might* occur but *will* occur—if not today, then tomorrow; if

183

not this year, then the next. We have come to live on borrowed time: every year of continued human life on earth is a borrowed year, every day a borrowed day.

In the face of this unprecedented global emergency, we have so far had no better idea than to heap up more and more warheads, apparently in the hope of so thoroughly paralyzing ourselves with terror that we will hold back from taking the final, absurd step. Considering the wealth of our achievement as a species, this response is unworthy of us. Only by a process of gradual debasement of our self-esteem can we have lowered our expectations to this point. For, of all the "modest hopes of human beings," the hope that mankind will survive is the most modest, since it only brings us to the threshold of all the other hopes. In entertaining it, we do not yet ask for justice, or for freedom, or for happiness, or for any of the other things that we may want in life. We do not even necessarily ask for our personal survival; we ask only that we *be survived*. We ask for assurance that when we die as individuals, as we know we must, mankind will live on. Yet once the peril of extinction is present, as it is for us now, the hope for human survival becomes the most tremendous hope, just because it is the foundation for all the other hopes, and in its absence every other hope will gradually wither and die. Life without the hope for human survival is a life of despair.

The death of our species resembles the death of an individual in its boundlessness, its blankness, its removal beyond experience, and its tendency to baffle human thought and feeling, yet as soon as one mentions the hope of survival the similarities are clearly at an end. For while individual death is inevitable, extinction can be avoided; while every person must die, mankind can be saved. Therefore, while reflection on death may lead to resignation and acceptance, reflection on extinction must lead to exactly the opposite response: to arousal, rejection, indignation, and action. Extinction is not something to contemplate, it is something to rebel against. To point this out might seem like stating the obvious if it were not that on the whole the world's reaction to the peril of extinction has been one of numbness and inertia, much as though extinction were as inescapable as death is. Even today, the official response to the sickening reality before us is conditioned by a grim fatalism, in which the hope of ridding the world of nuclear weapons, and thus of surviving as a species, is all but ruled out of consideration as "utopian" or "extreme"—as though it were "radical" merely to want to go on living and to want one's descendants to be born. And yet if one gives up these aspirations one has given up on everything. As a species, we have as yet done nothing to save ourselves. The slate of action is blank. We have organizations for the preservation of almost everything in life that we want but no organization for the preservation of mankind. People seem to have decided that our collective will is too weak or flawed to rise to this occasion. They see the violence that has saturated human history, and conclude that to practice violence is innate in our species. They find the perennial hope that peace can be brought to the earth once and for all a delusion of the well-meaning who have refused to face the "harsh realities" of international life—the realities of self-interest, fear, hatred, and aggression. They have concluded that these realities are eternal ones, and this conclusion defeats at the outset any hope of taking the actions necessary for survival. Looking at the historical record, they ask what has changed to give anyone confidence that humanity can break with its violent past and act with greater restraint. The answer, of course, is that everything has changed. To the old "harsh realities" of international life has been added the immeasurably harsher new reality of the peril of extinction. To the old truth that all men are brothers has been added the inescapable new truth that not only on the moral but also on the physical plane the nation that practices aggression will itself die. This is the law of the doctrine of nuclear deterrence—the doctrine of "mutual assured destruction"— which "assures" the destruction of the society of the attacker. And it is also the law of the natural world, which, in its own version of deterrence, supplements the oneness of mankind with a oneness of nature, and guarantees that when the attack rises above a certain level the attacker will be engulfed in the general ruin of the global ecosphere. To the obligation to honor life is now added the sanction that if we fail in our obligation life will actually be taken away from us, individually and collectively. Each of us will die, and as we die we will see the world around us dying. Such imponderables as the sum of human life, the integrity of the terrestrial creation, and the meaning of time, of history, and of the development of life on earth, which were once left to contemplation and spiritual understanding, are now at stake in the political realm and demand a political response from every person. As political actors, we must, like the contemplatives before us, delve to the bottom of the world, and, Atlas-like, we must take the world on our shoulders.

The self-extinction of our species is not an act that anyone describes as sane or sensible; nevertheless, it is an act that, without quite admitting it to ourselves, we plan in certain circumstances to commit. Being impossible as a fully intentional act, unless the perpetrator has lost his mind, it can come about only through a kind of inadvertence—as a "side effect" of some action that we do intend, such as the defense of our nation, or the defense of liberty, or the defense of socialism, or the defense of whatever else we happen to believe in. To that extent, our failure to acknowledge the magnitude and significance of the peril is a necessary condition for doing the deed. We can do it only if we don't quite know what we're doing. If we did acknowledge the full dimensions of the peril, admitting clearly and without reservation that any use of nuclear arms is likely to touch off a holocaust in which the continuance of all human life would be put at risk, extinction would at that moment become not only "unthinkable" but also undoable. What is needed to make extinction possible, therefore, is some way of thinking about it that at least partly deflects our attention from what it is. And this way of thinking is supplied to us, unfortunately, by our political and military traditions, which, with the weight of almost all historical experience behind them, teach us that it is the way of the world for the earth to be divided up into independent, sovereign states, and for these states to employ war as the final arbiter for settling the disputes that arise among them. This arrangement of the political affairs of the world was not intentional. No one wrote a book proposing it; no parliament sat down to debate its merits and then voted it into existence. It was simply there, at the beginning of recorded history; and until the invention of nuclear weapons it remained there, with virtually no fundamental changes. Unplanned though this arrangement was, it had many remarkably durable features, and certain describable advantages and disadvantages; therefore, I shall refer to it as a "system"—the system of sovereignty. Perhaps the leading feature of this system, and certainly the most important one in the context of the nuclear predicament, was the apparently indissoluble connection between sovereignty and war. For without sovereignty, it appeared, peoples were not able to organize and launch wars against other peoples, and without war they were unable to preserve their sovereignty from destruction by armed enemies. (By "war" I here mean only international war, not revolutionary war, which I shall not discuss.) Indeed, the connection between sovereignty and war is almost a definitional one—a sovereign state being a state that enjoys the right and the power to go to war in defense or pursuit of its interests.

It was into the sovereignty system that nuclear bombs were born, as "weapons" for "war." As the years have passed, it has seemed less and less plausible that they have anything to do with war; they seem to break through its bounds. Nevertheless, they have gone on being fitted into military categories of thinking. One might say that they appeared in the world in a military disguise, for it has been traditional military thinking, itself an inseparable part of the traditional political thinking that belonged to the system of sovereignty, that has provided those intentional goals—namely, national interests—in the pursuit of which extinction may now be brought about unintentionally, or semi-intentionally, as a "side effect." The system of sovereignty is now to the earth and mankind what a polluting factory is to its local environment. The machine produces certain things that its users want—in this case, national sovereignty —and as an unhappy side effect extinguishes the species.

The ambivalence resulting from the attempt to force nuclear weapons into the preëxisting military and political system has led to a situation in which, in the words of Einstein—who was farseeing in his political as well as in his scientific thought—"the unleashed power of the atom has changed everything save our modes of thinking, and we thus drift toward unparalleled catastrophes." As Einstein's observation suggests, the nuclear revolution has gone quite far but has not been completed. The question we have to answer is whether the completion will be extinction or a global political revolution—whether the "babies" that the scientists at Alamogordo brought forth will put an end to us or we will put an end to them. For it is not only our thoughts but also our actions and our institutions—our global political arrangements in their entirety—that we have failed to change. We live with one foot in each of two worlds. As scientists and technicians, we live in the nuclear world, in which whether we choose to acknowledge the fact or not, we possess instruments of violence that make it possible for us to extinguish ourselves as a species. But as citizens and statesmen we go on living in the pre-nuclear world, as though extinction were not possible and sovereign nations could still employ the instruments of violence as instruments of policy—as "a continuation of politics by other means," in the famous phrase of Karl von Clausewitz, the great philosopher of war. In effect, we try to make do with a Newtonian politics in an Einsteinian world. The combination is the source of our immediate peril. For governments, still acting within a system of independent nation-states, and formally representing no one but the people of their separate, sovereign nations, are driven to try to defend merely national interests with means of destruction that threaten not only international but intergenerational and planetary doom. In our present-day world, in the councils where the decisions are made there is no one to speak for man and for the earth, although both are threatened with annihilation.

The peril that the scientists have brought into our lives stems from hitherto unknown properties of the physical universe, but it is not an external, self-propelled peril—as though they had discovered that forces in the interior of the earth were one day going to blow it up, or that a huge asteroid was one day going to collide with it. Rather, the peril comes from our own actions—from within us—and if we had never sought to harm one another the energy latent in matter would have remained locked up there, without posing any threat to anybody. Thus, the peril of extinction by nuclear arms is doubly ours: first, because we have it in our power to prevent the catastrophe, and, second, because the catastrophe cannot occur unless, by pursuing our political aims through violence, we bring it about. Since military action is the one activity through which we deliberately threaten to employ our new mastery over nature to destroy ourselves, nothing could be more crucial to an understanding of the practical dimensions of the nuclear predicament than a precise understanding of what nuclear weapons have done to war, and, through war, to the system of sovereignty of which war has traditionally been an indispensable part. All war is violent, but not all violence is war. War is a violent means employed by a nation to achieve an end, and, like all mere means, is subject to Aristotle's rule "The means to the end are not unlimited, for the end itself sets the limit in each case." The possible ends of war are as varied as the desires and hopes of men, having ranged from the recovery of a single beautiful woman from captivity to world conquest, but every one of them would be annihilated in a nuclear holocaust. War is destructive, but it is also a human phenomenon—complex, carefully wrought, and, in its way, fragile and delicate, like its maker—but nuclear weapons, if they were ever used in large numbers, would simply blow war up, just as they would blow up everything else that is human.

One of the respects in which war is unique among the uses to which mankind's steadily increasing technical skills have been put is that in war no benefit is obtained and no aim achieved unless the powers involved exert themselves to the limit, or near-limit, of their strength. In the words of Clausewitz: "War is an act of violence pushed to its utmost bounds; as one side dictates to the other, there arises a sort of reciprocal action which logically must lead to an extreme." For only at the extremes are victory and defeat—the results of war—brought about. Even when victory and defeat are not absolute, the terms of the disengagement are determined by the nearness of one side to defeat. In this case, the antagonists, like chess players near the end of the game, see the inevitable outcome and spare themselves the trouble of actually going through the final moves. As Clausewitz writes, "everything is subject to a supreme law: which is the *decision by arms*." Therefore, "all action . . . takes place on the supposition that if the solution by force of arms which lies at its foundation should be realized, it will be a favorable one." For "the decision by arms is, for all operations, great and small, what cash payment is in bill transactions," and "however remote from each other these relations, however seldom the realization may take place, still it can never entirely fail to occur." Nuclear arms ruin war by making the decision by arms impossible. The decision by arms can occur only when the strength of one side or the other is exhausted, or when its exhaustion is approached. But in nuclear "war" no one's strength fails until *both* sides have been annihilated. There cannot be a victor without a vanquished, the collapse of whose military efforts signals the end of the hostilities, permitting the victor to collect his spoils. But when both adversaries have nuclear arms that moment of collapse never comes, and the military forces—the missiles—of both countries go on "fighting" after the countries themselves have disappeared. From the point of view of a power contemplating war in the pre-nuclear world, war appeared to depend on the possession of great strength, since the side that possessed the greater strength had the better chance of being victorious. But when war is seen from the point of view of the nuclear world it becomes clear that as an institution—as the mechanism with which sovereign states settled their disputes—war depended, above all, on weakness: the weakness of the defeated party, whose collapse made the decision by arms (the whole purpose of war) possible. And this weakness, in turn, depended on the presence of certain technical limitations on the ability of mankind in general to avail itself of natural forces for destructive purposes. When science made the energy in mass available to man, the crucial limits were removed, for everybody, forever, and the exhaustion of the defeated party—and so the triumph of the victor—was rendered impossible. War itself has thus proved to be a casualty of the tremendous means that were put at its disposal by science. We are now in a position to see that helplessness has always been the specific product of war, and weakness its essential ingredient. War has never been anything but unilateral disarmament—the disarmament of one side by the other. But now, before the exhaustion of either party can be reached, everyone will be dead, and all human aims—the aims pursued in the "war" and all others—will have been nullified. In a nuclear conflict between the United States and the Soviet Union—the holocaust—not only the adversaries but also the world's bystanders will vanish. In this "war," instead of one side winning and the other losing, it is as though all human beings lost and all the weapons won. Clausewitz writes, "War can never be separated from political intercourse, and if, in the consideration of the matter, this is done in any way, all the threads of the different relations are, to a certain extent, broken, and we have before us a senseless thing without an object." War can, for example, decline into mere looting or banditry or some other form of aimless violence. But, of all the "senseless things" that can ever occur when war's violence (its means) is severed from its political purposes (its ends), a nuclear holocaust is the most senseless. To call this senseless thing "war" is, in fact, simply a misnomer, and to go on speaking of "nuclear war," and the like, can only mislead and confuse us. Thus, while the Soviet Union and the United States are perfectly free to fire their thousands of nuclear weapons at one another, the result would not be war, for no end could be served by it. It would be comprehensive destruction—a "senseless thing." With the invention of nuclear weapons, it became impossible for violence to be fashioned into war, or to achieve what war used to achieve. Violence can no longer break down the opposition of the adversary; it can no longer produce victory and defeat; it can no longer attain its ends. It can no longer be war.

It must be emphasized that what nuclear weapons have ruined is not only "nuclear war" but all war (that is, all war between nuclear powers). "Conventional war," which in fact encompasses everything that deserves to be called war, is ruined because as long as nuclear weapons are held in reserve by the combatants, in accordance with the supposedly agreed-upon rules of some "limited war," the hostilities have not run to that extreme of violence at which the essential helplessness of one side or the other has been produced. If a decision were to be reached while the "defeated" party held potentially decisive means of violence in its possession, then that decision would be not "by arms" but by something else. We have to imagine that this power would accept its defeat while knowing that the use of its bombs would reverse it. A current example illustrates how little willingness there is among nuclear powers to accept such an outcome. For some time, it has been widely believed that the Soviet Union enjoys a preponderance in conventional forces over the NATO powers in Europe, and the United States has reserved for itself the right to resort to nuclear weapons in Europe rather than accept a conventional defeat there. Thus, the United States has already publicly discarded the notion of abiding by any rules of "limited war" if those rules should prove to mean a defeat for the United States. And there is certainly very little reason to suppose that the Soviet Union is any more willing to volunteer for defeat than the United States. That being the likely state of things, there seems little chance that a conventional war between nuclear powers could stay limited. And this means that a conventional war between nuclear powers must not even be begun, since it threatens the same holocaust that the limited use of nuclear weapons threatens. As a practical matter, this rule has up to now been followed by the statesmen of the nuclear world. Disregarding theoretical treatises on the possibility of "limited war" between nuclear powers, including "limited nuclear war," they have held back from any war; thus, in our thirty-six years of experience with nuclear weapons no two nuclear powers have ever entered into even conventional hostilities. The same cannot be said, of course, of hostilities between nuclear powers and non-nuclear powers, such as the Vietnam War or the Soviet-Afghanistan war. These remain possible—although, for reasons that I shall not go into here, they are not, it would seem, profitable.

It is often said that nuclear arms have made war obsolete, but this is a misunderstanding. Obsolescence occurs when a means to some end is superseded by a new and presumably better means—as when it was discovered that vehicles powered by internal-combustion engines were more efficient than vehicles pulled by horses at transporting people and goods from one place to another. But war has not been superseded by some better means to its end, which is to serve as the final arbiter of disputes among sovereign states. On the contrary, war has gone out of existence without leaving behind any means at all—whether superior or inferior—to that end. The more than three decades of jittery peace between the nuclear super-powers which the world has experienced since the invention of nuclear weapons is almost certainly the result of this lack. There is thus no need to "abolish war" among the nuclear powers; it is already gone. The choices don't include war any longer. They consist now of peace, on the one hand, and annihilation, on the other. And annihilation—or "assured destruction"—is as far from being war as peace is, and the sooner we recognize this the sooner we will be able to save our species from self-extermination.

When nuclear weapons were invented, it was as though a battlefield on which two armies had been fighting for as long as anyone could remember had suddenly been bisected in an earthquake by a huge chasm, so that if the armies tried to rush at one another in order to engage in battle they would plunge into this chasm instead, pulling their nations in with them. And it was as though, further, the generals of these armies, having spent their lifetimes fighting this war and hearing about their forebears' exploits in it, periodically forgot about the existence of the chasm, and therefore from time to time sent their armies into the field—only to discover that the chasm was still there.

The disabling of war is in itself something to be welcomed (although not if the price is extinction, or even the perpetual threat of extinction), but the system of sovereignty was bereft by it. The ultimate purpose of military forces in the system of sovereignty—the defense of one's nation by combating and defeating the attacking forces of the enemy—was nullified in a stroke, for there could be no defense against nuclear weapons. The "final arbiter" had been taken away, and nations, now living in terror of their annihilation but also terrified of being taken over by their enemies, were left to figure out some new means of securing their survival and of pursuing their aims in the world. In effect, the system of sovereignty faced a breakdown. The world now had to decide whether to reject sovereignty and "war" (which, suddenly, no longer was war) and institute global political arrangements that would arbitrate international disputes or to try to shore up sovereignty with the use or deployment of nuclear weapons. Lord Russell and a few other people favored the first course, but a larger number favored the second. Still others favored the first course in the abstract but turned out to be unwilling in practical terms to make the radical political changes that were called for. It was easy to say, as many did, that in a nuclear world mankind had to live in peace or perish; it was a far different matter to make actual political sacrifices that would permit the nuclear peril to be lifted. The present-day United Nations is the empty husk of those irresolute good intentions. But, whatever people said, or ineffectually hoped for, the world in fact chose the course of attempting to refashion the system of sovereignty to accommodate nuclear weapons.

The doctrine that resulted was the doctrine of nuclear deterrence: the forbidding political and intellectual product of our attempt to live simultaneously in the two worlds—the nuclear, scientific world and the pre-nuclear military and political one. Since the doctrine is the means by which the world now endeavors to escape its doom from moment to moment, it deserves our most searching examination. In its intellectual, emotional, and moral tone as well as in its content, the doctrine was something new. Not surprisingly, the people in charge of framing this doctrine and putting it into practice seem at times to suffer from double vision, as though at some moments they recognized that we live in a nuclear world, in which the life of the species is at stake, but at other times forgot this, and believed that wars could still be fought without the risk of self-extermination. It is a symptom of the schism between what Einstein called our "thinking" and the reality around us that when our

194

strategists set out to think their "unthinkable" thoughts they feel
obliged to quite deliberately leave the rest of their human equipment—their feelings, their moral sense, their humanity—behind. For
the requirements of strategy in its present form force them to plan
actions that from any recognizable moral point of view are indefen-
sible. One strategic thinker, in a striking inversion of the usual
understanding of ethical obligation, has said that an "iron will" is
required if one is to recommend the slaughter of hundreds of millions of people in a nuclear attack—a point of view that is uncom-
fortably close to that of Heinrich Himmler, who told the com-
manders of the SS that in order to carry out the extermination of
the Jews they had to be "superhumanly inhuman." In both statements, it is not obedience to our moral feelings but resistance to
those feelings that is presented as our obligation, as though moral
feeling were a siren call that it would be weak to give in to and
that it is our duty to resist. Once the "strategic necessity" of planning the deaths of hundreds of millions of people is accepted, we
begin to live in a world in which morality and action inhabit two
separate, closed realms. All strategic sense becomes moral nonsense,
and vice versa, and we are left with the choice of seeming to be
either strategic or moral idiots. The feeling of unreality that present strategic thinking arouses is compounded by the fact, itself a
unique feature of life in the nuclear world, that the strategist must
incessantly plan for future attacks and counterattacks whose prevention is supposedly the planning's whole purpose. Strategic thinking thus refers to a reality that is supposed never to come into
existence. Therefore, not only is morality deliberately divorced from
"thinking" but planning is divorced from action. The result of all
these novel mental operations is a fantastic intellectual construct—
the body of strategic theory built up over more than thirty years—
in which ratiocination, unrestrained either by moral feelings or by
facts, has been permitted to run wild in a riot of pure theory. On
this "thinking" almost no bounds are set, and the slaughter of whole
populations and the extinction of man become all too "thinkable."
But the divorce of thought from feeling, of strategy from morality,
and of planning from action are all only manifestations of the more

195

fundamental divorce between the pre-nuclear basis of our whole approach to political life and the reality of our nuclear world. The reason we cannot bear emotionally and morally to face the actions that we "think" about and plan and the reason the aim of all our strategic planning must be to prevent the actions we are planning to take are the same: the actions we have in mind, which risk the termination of our species, are irredeemably senseless. And as long as we continue to accept the underlying assumptions of this strategy we will be condemned to go on sketching "scenarios" for futures that must never be, while neglecting all planning for futures that *can* be, and that would permit us to be.

The central proposition of the deterrence doctrine—the piece of logic on which the world theoretically depends to see the sun rise tomorrow—is that a nuclear holocaust can best be prevented if each nuclear power, or bloc of powers, holds in readiness a nuclear force with which it "credibly" threatens to destroy the entire society of any attacker, even after suffering the worst possible "first strike" that the attacker can launch. Robert McNamara, who served as Secretary of Defense for seven years under Presidents Kennedy and Johnson, defined the policy, in his book "The Essence of Security," published in 1968, in the following terms: "Assured destruction is the very essence of the whole deterrence concept. We must possess an actual assured-destruction capability, and that capability also must be credible. The point is that a potential aggressor must believe that our assured-destruction capability is in fact actual, and that our will to use it in retaliation to an attack is in fact unwavering." Thus, deterrence "means the certainty of suicide to the aggressor, not merely to his military forces, but to his society as a whole." Let us picture what is going on here. There are two possible eventualities: success of the strategy or its failure. If it succeeds, both sides are frozen into inaction by fear of retaliation by the other side. If it fails, one side annihilates the other, and then the leaders of the second side annihilate the "society as a whole" of the attacker, and the earth as a whole suffers the consequences of a full-scale holocaust, which might include the extinction of man. In point of fact, neither the United States nor the Soviet Union has ever adopted the "mutual-assured-destruction" doctrine in pure form; other aims, such as attempting to reduce the damage of the adversary's nuclear attack and increasing the capacity for destroying the nuclear forces of the adversary, have been mixed in. Nevertheless, underlying these deviations the concept of deterring a first strike by preserving the capacity for a devastating second strike has remained constant. The strategists of deterrence have addressed the chief issue in any sane policy in a nuclear-armed world—the issue of survival—and have come up with this answer: Salvation from extinction by nuclear weapons is to be found in the nuclear weapons themselves. The possession of nuclear weapons by the great powers, it is believed, will prevent the use of nuclear weapons by those same powers. Or, to put it more accurately, the threat of their use by those powers will prevent their use. Or, in the words of Bernard Brodie, a pioneer in nuclear strategy, in "The Absolute Weapon: Atomic Power and World Order," a book published in 1946: "Thus far, the chief purpose of our military establishment has been to win wars. From now on its chief purpose must be to avert them. It can have almost no other useful purpose." Or, in the classic, broad formulation of Winston Churchill, in a speech to the House of Commons in 1955: "Safety will be the sturdy child of terror, and survival the twin brother of annihilation."

This doctrine, in its detailed as well as its more general formulations, is diagrammatic of the world's failure to come to terms with the nuclear predicament. In it, two irreconcilable purposes clash. The first purpose is to permit the survival of the species, and this is expressed in the doctrine's aim of frightening everybody into holding back from using nuclear weapons at all; the second purpose is to serve national ends, and this is expressed in the doctrine's permitting the defense of one's nation and its interests by threatening to use nuclear weapons. The strategists are pleased to call this clash of two opposing purposes in one doctrine a paradox, but in actuality it is a contradiction. We cannot both threaten ourselves with something and hope to avoid that same thing by making the threat—both intend to do something and intend not to do it. The head-on contradiction between these aims has set up a crosscurrent of tension within the policies of each superpower. The "safety" that Churchill mentions may be emphasized at one moment, and at the next moment it is the "terror" that comes to the fore. And since the deterrence doctrine pairs the safety and the terror, and makes the former depend on the latter, the world is never quite sure from day to day which one is in the ascendant—if, indeed, the distinction can be maintained in the first place. All that the world can know for certain is that at any moment the fireballs may arrive. I have said that we do not have two earths, one to blow up experimentally and the other to live on; nor do we have two souls, one for reacting to daily life and the other for reacting to the peril to all life. But neither do we have two wills, one with which we can intend to destroy our species and the other with which we can intend to save ourselves. Ultimately, we must all live together with one soul and one will on our one earth.

For all that, the adoption of the deterrence doctrine represented a partial recognition that the traditional military doctrine had become an anachronism—a doctrine that was suited well enough to the pre-nuclear world but lost all application and relevance when the first nuclear bomb flashed over the New Mexico desert. In assessing the advance made by deterrence, we must acknowledge how radically it departed from traditional military doctrine. Traditional military doctrine and nuclear doctrine are based on wholly different factual circumstances, each set of which corresponds to the technical realities of its period. Traditional military doctrine began, as I have suggested, with the premise that the amounts of force available to the belligerents were small enough to permit one side or the other to exhaust itself before both sides were annihilated. Nuclear doctrine, on the other hand, begins with the premise that the amounts of force are so great that both sides, and perhaps all mankind, will be annihilated before either side exhausts its forces. Like postulates in geometry, these two premises determine the entire systems of thought that follow, and no discussion of military strategy can make any sense unless one clearly specifies which premise one is starting from. But, as I pointed out at some length at the outset of these observations, there is no longer room for doubt that in our time the second premise is the correct one.

The chief virtue of the doctrine of nuclear deterrence is that it begins by accepting this basic fact of life in the nuclear world, and does so not only on the rhetorical plane but on the practical plane of strategic planning. Hence, it acknowledges that victory can no longer be obtained in a contest between two well-armed nuclear powers, such as the United States and the Soviet Union. Senator Barry Goldwater wrote a book, published in 1962, whose title was "Why Not Victory?" To this question the strategists of deterrence have a decisive answer: Because in the present-day, nuclear world "victory" is oblivion. From this recognition flows the conclusion, arrived at by Brodie in 1946, that the sole purpose of possessing nuclear strategic arms is not to win war but to prevent it. The adoption of the aim of preventing rather than winning war requires the adoption of other policies that fly in the face of military tradition. One is abandonment of the military defense of one's nation—of what used to be at the center of all military planning and was the most hallowed justification of the military calling. The policy of deterrence does not contemplate doing anything in defense of the homeland; it only promises that if the homeland is annihilated the aggressor's homeland will be annihilated, too. In fact, the policy goes further than this: it positively requires that each side leave its population open to attack, and make no serious effort to protect it. This requirement follows from the basic logic of deterrence, which is that safety is "the sturdy child of terror." According to this logic, the safety can be only as great as the terror is, and the terror therefore has to be kept relentless. If it were to be diminished—by, for example, building bomb shelters that protected some significant part of the population—then safety would be diminished, too, because the protected side might be tempted to launch a holocaust, in the belief that it could "win" the hostilities. That is why in nuclear strategy "destruction" must, perversely, be "assured," as though our aim were to destroy, and not to save, mankind.

In strategic terms, the requirement that the terror be perfected,

THE FATE OF THE EARTH

and never allowed to deteriorate toward safety, translates into the requirement that the retaliatory force of both sides be guaranteed—first, by making sure that the retaliatory weapons cannot be destroyed in a first strike, and, second, by making sure that the society of the attacking power *can* be destroyed in the second strike. And since in this upside-down scheme of things the two sides will suffer equally no matter which one opens the hostilities, each side actually has an interest in maintaining its adversary's retaliatory forces as well as its own. For the most dangerous of all the configurations of forces is that in which one side appears to have the ability to destroy the nuclear forces of the other in a first strike. Then not only is the stronger side theoretically tempted to launch hostilities but—what is probably far more dangerous—the other side, fearful of completely losing its forces, might, in a crisis, feel compelled to launch the first strike itself. If on either side the population becomes relatively safe from attack or the retaliatory strike becomes vulnerable to attack, a temptation to launch a first strike is created, and "stability"—the leading virtue of any nuclear balance of power —is lost. As Thomas Schelling, the economist and noted nuclear theorist, has put it, in "The Strategy of Conflict," a book published in 1960, once instability is introduced on either side, both sides may reason as follows: "He, thinking I was about to kill him in self-defense, was about to kill me in self-defense, so I had to kill him in self-defense." Under deterrence, military "superiority" is therefore as dangerous to the side that possesses it as it is to the side that is supposedly threatened by it. (According to this logic, the United States should have heaved a sigh of relief when the Soviet Union reached nuclear parity with it, for then stability was achieved.) All these conclusions follow from the deterrence doctrine, yet they run so consistently counter to the far simpler, more familiar, and emotionally more comprehensible logic of traditional military thinking —not to mention instinct and plain common sense, which rebel against any such notion as "assuring" our own annihilation—that we should not be surprised when we find that the deterrence doctrine is constantly under challenge from traditional doctrine, no matter how glaringly at odds with the facts traditional doctrine may be.

The hard-won gains of deterrence, such as they are, are repeatedly
threatened by a recrudescence of the old desire for victory, for
national defense in the old sense, and for military superiority, even
though every one of these goals not only would add nothing to our
security but, if it should be pursued far enough, would undermine
the precarious safety that the deterrence doctrine tries to provide.

If the virtue of the deterrence policy lies in its acceptance of
the basic fact of life in the nuclear world—that a holocaust will bring
annihilation to both sides, and possibly the extinction of man as
well—its defect lies in the strategic construct that it erects on the
foundation of that fact. For if we try to guarantee our safety by
threatening ourselves with doom, then we have to mean the threat;
but if we mean it, then we are actually planning to do, in some
circumstance or other, that which we categorically must never do
and are supposedly trying to prevent—namely, extinguish ourselves.
This is the circularity at the core of the nuclear-deterrence doctrine;
we seek to avoid our self-extinction by threatening to perform the
act. According to this logic, it is almost as though if we stopped
threatening ourselves with extinction, then extinction would occur.
Brodie's formula can be reversed: if the aim of having nuclear forces
is to avert annihilation (misnamed "war" by him), then we must
cling for our lives to those same forces. Churchill's dictum can be
reversed, too: If safety is the sturdy child of terror, then terror is
equally the sturdy child of safety. But who is to guarantee which of
the children will be born? And if survival is the twin brother of
annihilation, then we must cultivate annihilation. But then we may
get annihilation. By growing to actually rely on terror, we do more
than tolerate its presence in our world: we place our trust in it. And
while this is not quite to "love the bomb," as the saying goes, it
decidedly is to place our faith in it, and to give it an all-important
position in the very heart of our affairs. Under this doctrine, instead
of getting rid of the bomb we build it ever more deeply into our
lives.

The logical fault line in the doctrine runs straight through the
center of its main strategic tenet—the proposition that safety is
achieved by assuring that any nuclear aggressor will be annihilated

in a retaliatory strike. For while the doctrine relies for its success on a nuclear-armed victim's resolve to launch the annihilating second strike, it can offer no sensible or sane justification for launching it in the event. In pre-nuclear military strategy, the deterrent effect of force was a useful by-product of the ability and willingness to wage and win wars. Deterrence was the shadow cast by force, or, in Clausewitz's metaphor, the credit that flowed from the ability to make the cash payment of the favorable decision by arms. The logic of pre-nuclear deterrence escaped circularity by each side's being frankly ready to wage war and try for victory if deterrence failed. Nuclear deterrence, however, supposedly aims solely at forestalling any use of force by either side, and has given up at the outset on a favorable decision by arms. The question, then, is: Of what object is nuclear deterrence the shadow? Of what cash payment is it the credit? The theoretical answer, of course, is: The retaliatory strike. Yet since in nuclear-deterrence theory the whole purpose of having a retaliatory capacity is to deter a first strike, one must ask what reason would remain to launch the retaliation once the first strike had actually arrived. Nuclear deterrence requires one to prepare for armed conflict not in order to "win" it if it breaks out but in order to prevent it from breaking out in the first place. But if armed conflict breaks out anyway, what does one do with one's forces then? In pre-nuclear times, the answer would have required no second thought: it would have been to strive for the decision by arms—for victory. Yet nuclear deterrence begins by assuming, correctly, that victory is impossible. Thus, the logic of the deterrence strategy is dissolved by the very event—the first strike—that it is meant to prevent. Once the action begins, the whole doctrine is self-cancelling. In sum, the doctrine is based on a monumental logical mistake: one cannot credibly deter a first strike with a second strike whose *raison d'être* dissolves the moment the first strike arrives. It follows that, as far as deterrence theory is concerned, there is no reason for either side not to launch a first strike.

What seems to be needed to repair the doctrine is a motive for retaliation—one that is not supplied by the doctrine itself and that lies outside its premises—but the only candidates are those belonging to traditional military doctrine; namely, some variation of victory. The adherents of nuclear victory—whatever that would be—have on occasion noted the logical fallacy on which deterrence is based, and stepped forward to propose their solution: a "nuclear-war-fighting" capacity. Thus, the answer they give to the question of what to do after the first strike arrives is: Fight and "win" a "nuclear war." But victory does not suddenly become possible simply because it offers a solution to the logical contradiction on which the mutual-assured-destruction doctrine rests. The facts remain obdurately what they are: an attack of several thousand megatons will annihilate any country on earth many times over, no matter what line of argument the strategists pursue; and a "nuclear exchange" will, if it is on a large scale, threaten the life of man. Indeed, if victory were really possible there would have been no need for a deterrence strategy to begin with, and traditional military strategy would have needed no revision. This "solution" is therefore worse than the error it sets out to remedy. It resolves the contradiction in the deterrence doctrine by denying the tremendous new reality that the doctrine was framed to deal with, and that all of us now have to deal with on virtually every level of our existence. Consequently, this "solution" could lead us to commit the ultimate folly of exterminating ourselves without even knowing what we were doing. Aiming at "victory," we would wind up extinct.

In the last analysis, there can be no credible threat without credible use—no shadow without an object, no credit without cash payment. But since use is the thing above all else that we don't want, because it means the end of all of us, we are naturally at a loss to find any rationale for it. To grasp the reality of the contradiction, we have only to picture the circumstances of leaders whose country has just been annihilated in a first strike. Now their country is on its way to becoming a radioactive desert, but the retaliatory nuclear force survives in its silos, bombers, and submarines. These leaders of nobody, living in underground shelters or in "doomsday" planes that could not land, would possess the means of national defense but no nation to defend. What rational purpose could they have in launching the retaliatory strike? Since there was no longer a nation, "national security" could not be the purpose. Nor could defense of other peoples be the purpose, since the retaliatory strike might be the action that would finally break the back of the ecosphere and extinguish the species. In these circumstances, it seems to me, it is really an open question whether the leaders would decide to retaliate or not.

This conclusion is not one that is likely to be breathed aloud by anyone in or near power in either the Soviet Union or the United States. Since deterrence depends fully as much on one's adversary's perception of one's "unwavering" will to retaliate as on one's technical ability to do it, an acknowledgment that retaliation is senseless would in a way amount to unilateral disarmament by verbal means. The doctrine of nuclear deterrence thus deters debate about itself, and this incidental "deterrence" may have been no small factor in the sharp limits placed on the definition of "respectable," so-called "realistic" thinking about nuclear strategy. Nevertheless, the contradiction at the heart of the doctrine has occasioned considerable indirect intellectual twisting and turning among the nuclear theorists, and the resulting recommendations lead one into byways of the maze of strategic theory which stand out as bizarre and frightening even for the catalogues of nuclear strategic "options." The commonest solution to the problem of the missing motive for retaliation is to suggest that the policymakers try to cultivate an appearance of unreason, for if one is insane one doesn't need to supply any motive for retaliating—one might do it simply out of madness. The nuclear theorist Herman Kahn, for example, suggests that "it might best deter the attack" by an *"appearance* of irrationally inexorable commitment." Kahn first wonders whether it might not be enough merely to "pretend" to be irrationally committed, but he concludes that a pretense of unreason is not reliable, and that one must *"really intend to do it."* The prescription, then, which he calls the policy of "the rationality of irrationality," is to coolly resolve to be crazy. How statesmen are to go about this, Kahn does not say. Another solution, quite closely related, is to try to create either the appearance or the reality of being out of control. Uncontrol, like insanity, removes the need for a rational motive in

204

retaliating, this time by arranging for the retaliation to occur "by accident." Thomas Schelling, addressing the general question "How can one commit himself in advance to an act that he would in fact prefer not to carry out in the event?," suggests the tactic either of pretending that the crucial decisions will be in part up to "chance" or of actually arranging things so that this is true, thus adding to Kahn's concept of reasoned insanity the planned accident. With this strategy in effect, he writes, "the brink is not . . . the sharp edge of a cliff, where one can stand firmly, look down, and decide whether or not to plunge." Rather, "the brink is a curved slope that one can stand on with some risk of slipping." Therefore, "brink-manship involves getting onto the slope where one may fall in spite of his own best efforts to save himself, dragging his adversary with him." That these astonishing remedies are no less consequential in the real world than the doctrinal illogicality they try to remedy is testified to by, among other things, a statement in the memoirs of President Richard Nixon's chief of staff H. R. Haldeman that Nixon believed in the "Madman Theory" of the Presidency, according to which the nation's foes would bow to the President's will if they believed that he had taken leave of his senses and was ready to risk a holocaust in order to secure some limited national gain. Whether or not Nixon had read the writings of Kahn and Schelling, he was following their counsel to the letter.

The recommendation of these tactics naturally raises the questions of whether, with the life of our species at stake, we want our nuclear decision-makers to be cultivating irrationality and uncontrol, and whether a slippery slope over the nuclear abyss is where we all want to be. But these questions, which I think must be answered with a resounding "no," come up only as a consequence of our reliance on "terror" to provide "safety," and on the threat of "annihilation" to provide "survival." For it is in an effort to strengthen and shore up the terror and make annihilation more certain that the strategists and statesmen are forced into these appalling postures. Their problem is to find a way of appearing "inexorably" resolved to do things that can never make any sense or ever be justified by any moral code, and irrationality and uncontrol fulfill

205

the requirements for the very reason that they represent the abandonment of morality and sense. Adopted as policy, they lend credibility to actions that are—conveniently for strategic purposes, if not for the safety of mankind—immoral and insane.

It must be added that there is another extreme solution, which would entirely remove the defect in the doctrine of nuclear deterrence. This solution, described (but not recommended) by Kahn, would be to construct a literal doomsday machine, which would blow up the whole world as soon as an adversary engaged in some activity that had previously been defined as "unacceptable" by the machine's possessor. Kahn, who estimated in 1960 that a doomsday machine might be built for as little as ten billion dollars, points out that the machine would eliminate any doubt concerning the retaliatory strike by making it fully automatic. The retaliatory strike would still be senseless, but this senselessness would no longer cloud its "credibility," since the action would have been predetermined: the foundation would have been provided for a fully consistent policy of nuclear deterrence, under which nations would be deterred from launching nuclear attacks by the prearranged certainty that their own countries would perish in the ensuing global annihilation. But Kahn is also quick to point out a disadvantage of the doomsday machine which makes its construction immediately repugnant and intolerable to anyone who thinks about it: once it is in place, "there is no chance of human intervention, control, and final decision." And behind this objection, we may add, is an even simpler and more basic one: the chief reason we don't want a doomsday machine is that we don't want doom—not in any circumstances. Doom doesn't become any more acceptable because it comes about as someone's "final decision." And, of course, even though no enemy attack has been launched, in a moment of computer confusion the doomsday machine might make its own "final decision" to go off.

Because deterrence, on which we all now rely for whatever safety we have, is a psychological strategy, which aims at terrorizing the adversary into holding back from attacking us, it might seem that the discovery in one or the other command center of the logical absurdity of the policy would lead to the breakdown of the system—or, at least, to the abandonment of the doctrine. That this has not occurred is an indication that, even in the abstruse realm of nuclear doctrine, theory and practice, thought and reality are still different. In the real world, there are several stand-ins for the missing motive for the crucial retaliatory strike. The first stand-in is revenge, which, even though retaliation is not a rational action, might cause it to be carried out anyway. According to the emotional logic of revenge, the living act to right the wrong inflicted on the unjustly slain, who, being dead, cannot themselves realign the unbalanced scales of justice. Revenge is neither sensible nor constructive—especially not in a nuclear holocaust—but it is human, and the possibility that it would well up in the breasts of the leaders of a country that has just been effaced from the earth can by no means be ruled out by an aggressor; he has to consider that, even without any irrationality of the planned sort, a "rational" response to a nuclear attack can hardly be counted on. The second, and perhaps more important, stand-in for the missing motive is the irreducible unpredictability of events once the nuclear threshold is crossed. At this verge, with the survival of the species at stake, the human mind falters. The leaders of the nuclear powers have no choice, as they stare into McNamara's "vast unknown," but to assume that the stakes are total. Certainly there is no need for anyone to strain to appear irrational, as Kahn suggests, or out of control, as Schelling suggests: a world that has embarked on a holocaust is in its nature irrational and out of control.

Our experience of nuclear crises leads us to believe that when the leaders of nuclear powers are forced to contemplate the reality of a holocaust at close quarters they have looked on it in this light. That is, they have assumed that if limited nuclear war, or even conventional war between the superpowers, breaks out, a holocaust is the likely result. Michael Mandelbaum, in his history of nuclear strategy and experience, "The Nuclear Question," published in 1979, observes that when the Soviet and American leaders confronted one another in the Cuban missile crisis they discovered that the fearful nature of a holocaust, which during the days of the crisis partly emerged from abstraction and unreality to become almost palpable in people's emotions, strongly deterred them from inaugurating hostilities at no matter how minor a level. Brought face to face with the beast, both sides realized that "there was no way to fight a nuclear war." Thus, "in striving to avoid having to fight a nuclear war they took great care not to start a war of any kind, which they feared would become nuclear." This lesson of experience offered some complementary lessons. One was that although no one had decided to establish a doomsday machine, people had to act as though one were in place. They had to assume that one misstep could be the misstep that ended the world. The notion that there was a middle ground of "tactical" nuclear hostilities of a limited kind, or even of conventional hostilities, disappeared under the awful pressure of the crisis. The doorway to the "vast unknown" seemed always right at hand, and all the scenarios of "limited war" and the like tended to crumble.

A final "deterrent," which, although fallible, is both rational and human, but which goes unmentioned in deterrence theory, is the humanity of the leaders of the nuclear powers. History is crowded with ruthless, berserk actions, yet there are none that have attained the horror and insanity of a nuclear holocaust, and very few that have gone as far as the worst crime of which we do have experience—genocide. I believe that without indulging in wishful thinking we can grant that the present leaders of both the Soviet Union and the United States are considerably deterred from launching a nuclear holocaust by sheer aversion to the unspeakable act itself.

The inconsistencies that bedevil the doctrine of nuclear deterrence —the reliance upon a second strike that has no explicable purpose, the need to cultivate irrationality and uncontrol to remedy this and other defects, the reliance upon the logic of the doomsday machine combined with the failure to carry the logic through to its conclusion, and many others that might be mentioned—are all consequences of the larger, inherent inconsistency of reliance upon preparations for annihilation to prevent annihilation. The result of relying on this contradictory system for our survival is our present half-numb, half-terror-stricken world, in which growing mountains of nuclear weapons are supposed to improve the world's safety, and in which we do not know from one moment to the next whether we will survive or be exploded back into our original atoms. Reflecting on the frightful effects of this arrangement—effects that, even without a holocaust, corrupt our lives—we are led to wonder why it should be necessary to seek safety in terror, survival in annihilation, existence in nothingness, and to wonder why we shouldn't resort to the more straightforward measure of disarmament: of seeking survival by banning the instruments of death.

Even to put this question, however, is to reveal that in Churchill's and Brodie's formulations, which have been echoed with great regularity, in many versions, by the statesmen who have been in charge of the world's nuclear arsenals (President Kennedy, for example, said in his Inaugural Address, "Only when our arms are certain beyond doubt can we be certain beyond doubt that they will never be used"), an essential part of the truth is being left out. The missing element is the political aim of strategy. For the fact is that the nuclear powers do *not*, as the statesmen so often proclaim, possess nuclear weapons with the sole aim of preventing their use and so keeping the peace; they possess them also to defend national interests and aspirations—indeed, to perpetuate the whole system of sovereign states. But now, instead of relying on war for this enforcement, as nations did in pre-nuclear times, they rely on the threat of extinction. The proposition based on the aim of survival is that one prepares for extinction only in order to secure survival; however, the aim of holding on to the system of sovereignty introduces a much less reassuring, much less frequently voiced, and much less defensible proposition, which is that one prepares for extinction in order to protect national interests. This threat not only makes no sense in its own terms, since actual execution of the threat would eradicate any national interest in whose pursuit the hostilities were launched, but also undercuts the policy of deterrence, by continually propelling nations to threaten to bring about the holocaust whose avoidance is supposedly the policy's main justification. For while the aim of survival causes statesmen to declare regularly that no purpose could ever be served by a holocaust, and that the aim of nuclear policy can only be to prevent such insanity, the pursuit of national objectives forces them to declare in the next breath that they are unwaveringly resolved to perpetrate exactly this unjustifiable and insane action if some nation threatens a "vital interest" of theirs.

Thus, the peril of extinction is the price that the world pays not for "safety" or "survival" but for its insistence on continuing to divide itself up into sovereign nations. Without this insistence, there would be no need to threaten annihilation in order to escape annihilation, and the world could escape annihilation by disarming, as Russell, Einstein, and others recommended as early as the mid-nineteen-forties. Churchill's aphorism thus needs revision to read, "National sovereignty will be the sturdy child of terror and the twin brother of annihilation." This is less pithy and less palatable than the original, but it is the truth about our present nuclear arrangements. Or, to be exact, and to give those arrangements their due, the statement should read, "Safety will be the sturdy child of terror, and survival the twin brother of annihilation, *provided that nations respect one another's vital interests; otherwise, we end the world.*" But, no matter how one phrases it, the fact, which is rarely, if ever, mentioned either in the cold, abstract language of the theorists or in the ringing tones of the statesmen, is that the nuclear powers put a higher value on national sovereignty than they do on human survival, and that, while they would naturally prefer to have both, they are ultimately prepared to bring an end to mankind in their attempt to protect their own countries.

That we have let extinction replace war as the final protector of national interests is concealed to a certain extent by the fact that so far nuclear threats have been used, broadly speaking, for defensive purposes, to preserve rather than upset the status quo. For example, no one has attempted simply to conquer other countries through the threat or the use of nuclear weapons. Our reliance on extinction to thus freeze the world more or less in its present state is, in a sense, flushed out of hiding in times of crisis, when the status quo is challenged. At these moments—the Berlin crisis, the Cuban missile crisis, the American mining of Haiphong Harbor in 1972, the Soviet invasion of Afghanistan in 1979, among others— the world suddenly glimpses how far the superpowers are ready to go in pursuit of their interests. When calm returns, however, we are permitted to forget this ugly fact about the nuclear world, and to indulge ourselves again in the illusion that we possess nuclear arms solely in order to prevent their use.

As I have noted earlier, the crisis brought about by the Soviet invasion of Afghanistan serves to illustrate the contradictory pressures that operate on statesmen in any nuclear crisis. When the Soviet Union began the airlift of thousands of troops into Afghanistan, early in December of 1979, and, a few weeks later, oversaw the murder of the country's leader, President Hafizullah Amin (an extreme leftist who had fallen out of favor with Moscow), and installed its own man, Babrak Karmal, in his place, the American reaction was immediate and strong, but it involved neither the use nor the threat of force. President Carter sharply curtailed the sale of grain and certain other items to the Soviet Union, asked the United States Olympic Committee not to participate in the Olympics in Moscow in the summer of 1980 (the request was honored), and announced that he was asking the Senate to delay consideration of the SALT II treaty, which he and Brezhnev had already signed. The lack of military action, or even a threat of such action, against the Soviets in Afghanistan signalled that, while the American government was greatly disturbed by the invasion, it did not regard it as menacing the "vital interests" of the United States. The same could not be said, however, of a possible invasion of Afghanistan's neighbor Iran, which supplied oil in large quantities to the West, or of nearby Saudi Arabia, which has the largest oil reserves of any country in the world. The independence of these nations was indeed considered to be a vital interest of the United States, because the nations of the Western alliance and Japan had come to depend on Middle Eastern oil for the functioning of their economies; and it was a growing fear that the Soviet Union might next threaten these countries that gave the crisis a nuclear dimension. The fact was that the United States was worried not so much about Afghanistan and its people as about Western oil supplies. And to counter that perceived peril the United States did resort to a military threat, which took the form of Carter's statement, in his State of the Union address, in January, that "an attempt by any outside force to gain control of the Persian Gulf region will be regarded as an assault on the vital interests of the United States of America," and that "such an assault will be repelled by any means necessary, including military force." And shortly afterward any ambiguity about the meaning of the threat was dispelled by the story in the *Times* concerning a Defense Department "study" (apparently leaked by the Administration) that found that in the event of a Soviet invasion of northern Iran the United States should consider the use of nuclear weapons. However, just as everyone knew that the Soviet Union had conventional superiority in the Persian Gulf, everyone also knew that the Soviet Union possessed nuclear weapons and would be perfectly capable of using them in retaliation if the United States used them first. No one could suppose that the Soviet Union would advance into Iran only to give up and go home once the United States had used nuclear weapons against its troops. Rather, it was thought, the Soviet Union would either hold off from such an invasion in the first place or have some plan in mind for responding to an American nuclear attack. Furthermore, it was clear to all observers that neither side could expect to "win" a nuclear "war" in the Middle East. Only after all the missiles were fired—not only at targets in the Middle East but at targets throughout the world—would any outcome be reached, but that outcome, of course, would be mutual annihilation. Since these elementary facts were well known to both sides, and had certainly been rehearsed countless times in "war games" and the like, both sides were well aware that President Carter in threatening to use "any means necessary" to defend the Persian Gulf was in effect invoking the ultimate sanction: the threat of pushing the world into a nuclear holocaust. I shall not deal here with the question of whether or not Carter was correct in his judgment that the Soviet Union was considering the conquest of the Persian Gulf countries, and thus needed to be deterred from doing so. I only wish to observe that in the present global political system a leader of a nuclear power who comes to believe that his nation's vital interests are being threatened by another nuclear power faces a pair of alternatives that never confronted any statesman of pre-nuclear times: he can acquiesce in the aggression—a policy that, if it were to be followed consistently, could leave his nation at the adversary's mercy—or he can threaten, as Carter did, to unleash a holocaust in which the life of mankind might be lost, his hope being, of course, that the threat alone will deter the enemy from its aggressive action.

We are left to wonder what Carter would have done if the Soviets had ignored his threat and invaded Iran or Saudi Arabia, just as we are left to wonder what any Soviet or American leaders would do if an "unacceptable" move against the "vital interests" of their countries ever actually materialized—if, for example, the Soviet Union invaded West Germany, or the NATO forces invaded East Germany. This is what the world had to ask itself during the Cuban missile crisis, and what it has to ask itself whenever the interests of the superpowers clash in any part of the world. (And the question also comes up now in Sino-Soviet disputes—as it did when the Chinese recently engaged in a border war against the Soviet-backed Vietnamese. The divide that defines "the brink" now runs between the Soviet Union and China as well as between the Soviet Union and the United States.) As in the case of the retaliatory strike in deterrence theory, we encounter the disparity between the supposed rationality of *threatening* the use of nuclear weapons and the irrationality of actually *using* them if the threat should fail. For while it arguably makes sense to *deter* the foe from some action with the threat of a holocaust, it can never make sense to *launch* the holocaust if the foe is not deterred, since there is no human purpose that can justify extinction. And yet the success of the deterrence doctrine depends on the credibility of the threat of this unjustifiable use. Would Carter—a dedicated Christian—have risked extinction in the attempt to hold on to Middle Eastern oil? When he made his threat, did he consider his obligation to all of mankind and to the numberless future generations of human beings? Would he have plunged the world into the "vast unknown"? And did Brezhnev consider those obligations when he jarred the peace of the world by sending his armies across Soviet borders to subjugate one of the earth's sovereign peoples? Would Brezhnev, who has stated that to launch a nuclear holocaust would be "suicide," commit that suicide if he believed that the West was about to gain control of Eastern Europe? Would Deng Xiaoping take that risk to keep hold of a piece of Inner Mongolia? Did Khrushchev weigh the importance of the earth and the human species when he sent into Cuba missiles capable of carrying nuclear warheads? And did Kennedy weigh the importance of those things when he blockaded Cuba and then, according to his brother, waited to find out whether events over which "he no longer had control" would lead the world into a holocaust? These are the questions that hang in the air over our nuclear world, leaving us perpetually uncertain whether the next moment may not be the world's last.

When one great power adopts a strategic theory, it becomes a doctrine; when two rival great powers adopt it, it becomes a system; and when those rivals more or less abide by the rules of the system, and even hold negotiations aimed at strengthening it (I am thinking of SALT), and are prepared to see new nations enter it as they develop the necessary technical equipment, the system can be described as entrenched. This is the point at which the system of deterrence has arrived today. In essence, it is, as we have seen, a system of sovereign nation-states presided over by a hedged, or qualified, doomsday machine, with which we hope to reap the deterrent benefits of the threat of doom without clearly committing ourselves to doom if deterrence should fail—as we know that it well may, especially with the number of nuclear powers in the world growing. The basic dictate of the system is that if in the opinion of any nuclear power any other nuclear power seriously breaks the rules, then all powers are to be annihilated. Since in a holocaust the consequences may be the same for the aggressor, its punisher, and bystanders, the distinction between friendly and hostile nuclear forces has lost most of its meaning, and the nuclear arsenals of the world are effectively combined by policy into one great arsenal, which is looked to by all powers equally for their "safety." By the same token, even conventionally armed nations have the potential of blowing the world up, for they may draw the superpowers into one of their wars. We can picture this system in simple form if we imagine it as a doomsday machine possessed jointly by all nuclear powers. It is as though a number of people, each one possessing certain valuables that the others want and, furthermore, think they have a right to, are grouped in a room around a single bomb that is large enough to kill them all if it goes off. Each person holds in his hands a switch with which he can detonate the bomb. Every once in a while, a new person enters, also holding a switch. These people constantly reassure one another that the purpose of the whole system is to frighten everyone into inaction and let everyone enjoy in peace the valuables he has, and that for anyone to pull the switch would be suicidal and insane. Yet whenever a dispute breaks out over which valuables rightfully belong to whom, those same people hotly declare that enjoyment of their valuables is more important to them than everyone's life, their own included, and declare their "unwavering" and "inexorable" determination to set off the bomb if they cannot have their way. To this description we must add that some of the people in the room are not quite sure that the system works the way they have been told it does, and suspect that if they are the ones to set off the bomb they may be spared and only the others killed.

Examined in theoretical terms, the deterrence system emerges as a monstrous hybrid, stuck halfway between what the political philosophers call a "state of nature," in which individuals live together without founding any central authority among them, and the so-called "civil state," in which such an authority has been founded. In the passage from the state of nature to the civil state, each individual surrenders his capacity for violence to the central authority, which then employs the gathered resources, according to a system of laws, in the service of the common good. In the deterrence system, the individuals have combined their forces into a single force—the machine that will punish everyone with annihilation if anyone breaks the rules—but have failed to establish any central authority to preside over it. Thus, they have centralized the means of violence while leaving the decision-making decentralized —in effect, delegating to each member of the community a veto power over the continued survival of the species. It is no overstatement to say that if any society organized its affairs in this way, giving to each citizen the power to kill all the others, it would be regarded as deranged. (The system is even worse than anarchy, in which the evil that each person can do is at least limited by the limits of his own strength.) But, for some reason, when it comes to organizing the whole world, and providing for its survival, we regard such a system as a masterpiece of prudent statesmanship.

The dilemma of the nation that in order to protect its national sovereignty finds that it must put the survival of mankind at risk is a trap from which there is no escape as long as nations possess arsenals of nuclear weapons. The deterrence doctrine seeks to rationalize this state of affairs, but it fails, because at the crucial moment it requires nations to sacrifice mankind for their own interests—an absurdity as well as a crime beyond reckoning. Indeed, the deterrence doctrine actually almost *compels* the world to live perpetually on the brink of doom, for any nation that took a step or two back would put its interests and, ultimately, its independence at the mercy of the military forces of its adversaries. And although, for any number of reasons, an adversary might not press its advantage (as, for example, the United States did not right after the Second World War, when it possessed a monopoly on nuclear weapons), no nation has yet volunteered to put itself at this competitive disadvantage. It appears that the only way to escape from the trap is to change the system, and take away from nuclear weapons the responsibility for defending nations. But unless one supposes that, in a global spread of quietism, nations and people in general are going to give up the pursuit of their interests and their ideals and become wholly inactive, this separation can be achieved only if a new way—a nonviolent way—of making and guaranteeing these decisions is found.

In the decades since nuclear arms first appeared in the world, the doctrine of nuclear deterrence has commanded the sincere respect and adherence of many people of good will—especially when they found themselves arguing, as they so often did, with the adherents of traditional military doctrine, who even today, in the face of extinction itself, go on arguing for "military superiority," and the like. And if one once accepts the existence of the doomsday machine, then deterrence theory, however flawed, does offer the hope of certain benefits, the main one being a degree of "stability." Therefore, the perpetual struggle of its adherents against the sheer lunacy of "fighting a nuclear war" is a creditable one. But the fundamental truth about the doctrine and about its role in the wider political—and, it must be added, biological—scheme of things also has to be recognized. For the doctrine's central claim—that it deploys nuclear weapons only in order to prevent their use—is simply not true. Actually, it deploys them to protect national sovereignty, and if this aim were not present they could be quickly dismantled. The doctrine, then, has been the intellectual screen behind which the doomsday machine was built. And its deceptive claim that only by building nuclear weapons can we save ourselves from nuclear weapons lent the doomsday machine a veneer of reason and of respectability—almost of benevolence—that it should never have been given. For to build this machine at all was a mistake of the hugest proportions ever known—without question the greatest ever made by our species. The only conceivable worse mistake would be to put the machine to use. Now deterrence, having rationalized the construction of the machine, weds us to it, and, at best, offers us, if we are lucky, a slightly extended term of residence on earth before the inevitable human or mechanical mistake occurs and we are annihilated.

Yet the deterrence policy in itself is clearly not the deepest source of our difficulty. Rather, as we have seen, it is only a piece of repair work on the immeasurably more deeply entrenched system of national sovereignty. People do not want deterrence for its own sake; indeed, they hardly know what it is, and tend to shun the whole subject. They want the national sovereignty that deterrence promises to preserve. National sovereignty lies at the very core of the political issues that the peril of extinction forces upon us. Sovereignty is the "reality" that the "realists" counsel us to accept as inevitable, referring to any alternative as "unrealistic" or "utopian." If the argument about nuclear weapons is to be conducted in good faith, then just as those who favor the deterrence policy (not to speak of traditional military doctrine) must in all honesty admit that their scheme contemplates the extinction of man in the name of protecting national sovereignty, so must those who favor complete nuclear and conventional disarmament, as I do, admit that their recommendation is inconsistent with national sovereignty; to pretend otherwise would be to evade the political question that is central to the nuclear predicament. The terms of the deal that the world has now struck with itself must be made clear. On the one side stand human life and the terrestrial creation. On the other side stands a particular organization of human life—the system of independent, sovereign nation-states. Our choice so far has been to preserve that political organization of human life at the cost of risking all human life. We are told that "realism" compels us to preserve the system of sovereignty. But that political realism is not biological realism; it is biological nihilism—and for that reason is, of course, political nihilism, too. Indeed, it is nihilism in every conceivable sense of that word. We are told that it is human fate—perhaps even "a law of human nature"—that, in obedience, perhaps, to some "territorial imperative," or to some dark and ineluctable truth in the bottom of our souls, we must preserve sovereignty and always settle our differences with violence. If this is our fate, then it is our fate to die. But must we embrace nihilism? Must we die? Is self-extermination a law of our nature? Is there nothing we can do? I do not believe so. Indeed, if we admit the reality of the basic terms of the nuclear predicament—that present levels of global armament are great enough to possibly extinguish the species if a holocaust should occur; that in extinction every human purpose would be lost; that because once the species has been extinguished there will be no second chance, and the game will be over for all time; that therefore this possibility must be dealt with morally and politically as though it were a certainty; and that either by accident or by design a holocaust can occur at any second—then, whatever political views we may hold on other matters, we are driven almost inescapably to take action to rid the world of nuclear arms. Just as we have chosen to make nuclear weapons, we can choose to unmake them. Just as we have chosen to live in the system of sovereign states, we can choose to live in some other system. To do so would, of course, be unprecedented, and in many ways frightening, even truly perilous, but it is by no means impossible. Our present system and the institutions that make it up are the debris of history. They have become inimical to life, and must be swept away. They constitute a noose around the neck of mankind, threatening to choke off the human future, but we can cut the noose and break free. To suppose otherwise would be to set up a false, fictitious fate, molded out of our own weaknesses and our own alterable decisions. We are indeed fated by our acquisition of the basic knowledge of physics to live for the rest of time with the knowledge of how to destroy ourselves. But we are not for that reason fated to destroy ourselves. We can choose to live.

In this book, I have not sought to define a political solution to the nuclear predicament—either to embark on the full-scale reëxamination of the foundations of political thought which must be undertaken if the world's political institutions are to be made consonant with the global reality in which they operate or to work out the practical steps by which mankind, acting for the first time in history as a single entity, can reorganize its political life. I have left to others those awesome, urgent tasks, which, imposed on us by history, constitute the political work of our age. Rather, I have attempted to examine the physical extent, the human significance, and the practical dimensions of the nuclear predicament in which the whole world now finds itself. This predicament is a sort of cage that has quietly grown up around the earth, imprisoning every person on it, and the demanding terms of the predicament—its durability, its global political sweep, its human totality—constitute the bars of that cage. However, if a description of the predicament, which is the greatest that mankind has ever faced, cannot in itself reveal to us how we can escape, it can, I believe, acquaint us with the magnitude and shape of the task that we have to address ourselves to. And it can summon us to action.

To begin a summary with the matter of war: By effectively removing the limits on human access to the forces of nature, the invention of nuclear weapons ruined war, which depended for its results, and therefore for its usefulness, on the exhaustion of the forces of one of the adversaries. War depended, above all, on the weakness of human powers, and when human powers came to exceed human and other earthly endurance—when man as master of nature grew mightier than man as a vulnerable, mortal part of nature—war was ruined. Since war was the means by which violence was fashioned into an instrument that was useful in political affairs, the ruin of war by nuclear weapons has brought about a divorce between violence and politics. I submit that this divorce, being based on irreversible progress in scientific knowledge, not only is final but must ultimately extend across the full range of political affairs, and that the task facing the species is to shape a world politics that does not rely on violence. This task falls into two parts—two aims. The first is to save the world from extinction by eliminating nuclear weapons from the earth. Just recently, on the occasion of his retirement, Admiral Hyman Rickover, who devoted a good part of his life to overseeing the development and construction of nuclear-powered, nuclear-missile-bearing submarines for the United States Navy, told a congressional committee that in his belief mankind was going to destroy itself with nuclear arms. He also said of his part in the nuclear buildup that he was "not proud" of it, and added that he would like to "sink" the ships that he had poured so much of his life into. And, indeed, what everyone is now called on to do is to sink all the ships, and also ground all the planes, and fill in all the missile silos, and dismantle all the warheads. The second aim, which alone can provide a sure foundation for the first, is to create a political means by which the world can arrive at the decisions that sovereign states previously arrived at through war. These two aims, which correspond to the aims mentioned earlier of preserving the existence of life and pursuing the various ends of life, are intimately connected. If, on the one hand, disarmament is not accompanied by a political solution, then every clash of will between nations will tempt them to pick up the instruments of violence again, and so lead the world back toward extinction. If, on the other hand, a political solution is not accompanied by complete disarmament, then the political decisions that are made will not be binding, for they will be subject to challenge by force. And if, as in our present world, there is neither a political solution nor disarmament, then the world will be held perpetually at the edge of doom, and every clash between nuclear powers will threaten to push it over the edge.

The significance of the first aim—disarmament—which, without being paradoxical, we can describe as a "strategic" aim, can be clarified if we extend to its logical conclusion the reasoning that underlies the doctrine of deterrence. At present, the world relies on nuclear weapons both to prevent the use of nuclear weapons and to regulate the behavior of nations; but let us go a step—a very large step—further, and suppose, for a moment, that the world had established a political means of making international decisions and thus had no further need for nuclear or any other weapons. In order for such a thing to happen, we may ask, would the doctrine of deterrence and the fears on which it is based have to evaporate in the warmth of global good will? They would not. On the contrary, fear of extinction would have to increase, and permeate life at a deeper level: until it was great enough to inspire the complete rearrangement of world politics. Indeed, only when the world has given up violence does Churchill's dictum that safety is the sturdy child of terror actually become true. (At present, as we have seen, it is not safety but sovereignty that is the sturdy child of terror.) Under the current deterrence doctrine, one might say, safety is only the frail, anemic child of terror, and the reason is precisely that the terror is not yet robust enough to produce a sturdy offspring. For we still deny it, look away from it, and fail to let it reach deep enough into our lives and determine our actions. If we felt the peril for what it is—an urgent threat to our whole human substance—we would let it become the organizing principle of our global collective existence: the foundation on which the world was built. Fear would no longer dictate particular decisions, such as whether or not the Soviet Union might place missiles in Cuba; rather, it would be a moving force behind the establishment of a new system by which every decision was made. And, having dictated the foundation of the system, it would stand guard over it forever after, guaranteeing that the species did not slide back toward anarchy and doom.

This development would be the logical final goal of the doctrine of nuclear deterrence. In the pre-nuclear world, the threat of war, backed up by the frequent practice of war, served as a deterrent to aggression. Today, the threat of extinction, unsupported, for obvious reasons, by practice but backed up by the existence of nuclear arms and the threat to use them, serves as the ultimate deterrent. Thus, in today's system the actual weapons have already retired halfway from their traditional military role. They are "psychological" weapons, whose purpose is not to be employed but to maintain a permanent state of mind—terror—in the adversary. Their target is someone's mind, and their end, if the system works, is to rust into powder in their silos. And our generals are already psychological soldiers—masters of the war game and of the computer terminal but not, fortunately, of the battlefield. In this cerebral world, strategy confronts strategy and scenario battles scenario, the better to keep any of them from ever actually unfolding. But we need to carry this trend further. We need to make the weapons *wholly* cerebral—not things that sit in a silo ready to be fired but merely a thought in our minds. We need to destroy them. Only then will the logical fallacy now at the heart of the deterrence doctrine be removed, for only then will the fear of extinction by nuclear arms be used for the sole purpose of preventing extinction, and not also for the pursuit of national political aims. In a perfected nuclear deterrence, the knowledge in a disarmed world that rearmament potentially means extinction would become the deterrent. Now, however, it would be not that each nuclear-armed country would deter its nuclear-armed adversary but that awareness of the peril of extinction would deter all mankind from reëmbarking on nuclear armament. All human beings would join in a defensive alliance, with nuclear weapons as their common enemy. But since that enemy could spring only from our own midst, deterrer and deterred would be one. We thus arrive at the basic strategic principle of life in a world in which the nuclear predicament has been resolved: *Knowledge is the deterrent.* The nuclear peril was born out of knowledge, and it must abide in knowledge. The knowledge in question would be, in the first place, the unlosable scientific knowledge that enables us to build the weapons and condemns us to live forever in a nuclear world. This knowledge is the inexpungible minimum presence that the nuclear peril will always have in the life of the world, no matter what measures we adopt. In the second place, the knowledge would be the full emotional, intellectual, spiritual, and visceral understanding of the meaning of extinction—above all, the meaning of the unborn generations to the living. Because extinction is the end of mankind, it can never be anything more than "knowledge" for us; we can never "experience" extinction. It is *this* knowledge—this horror at a murderous action taken against generations yet unborn, which exerts pressure at the center of our existence, and which is the whole reality of extinction insofar as it is given to us to experience it—that must become the deterrent.

In a disarmed world, we would not have eliminated the peril of human extinction from the human scene—it is not in our power to do so—but we would at least have pitted our whole strength against it. The inconsistency of threatening to perpetrate extinction in order to escape extinction would be removed. The nuclei of atoms would still contain vast energy, and we would still know how to extinguish ourselves by releasing that energy in chain reactions, but we would not be lifting a finger to do it. There would be no complicity in mass murder, no billions of dollars spent on the machinery of annihilation, no preparations to snuff out the future generations, no hair-raising lunges toward the abyss.

The "realistic" school of political thinking, on which the present system of deterrence is based, teaches that men, on the whole, pursue their own interests and act according to a law of fear. The "idealistic" school looks on the human ability to show regard for others as fundamental, and is based on what Gandhi called the law of love. (Whereas the difference between traditional military thinking and nuclear strategic thinking lies in the different factual premises that they start from, the difference between the "realistic" and the "idealistic" schools of political philosophy lies in different judgments regarding human nature.) Historically, a belief in the necessity of violence has been the hallmark of the credo of the "realist"; however, if one consistently and thoroughly applies the law of fear in nuclear times one is driven not to rely on violence but to banish it altogether. This comes about as the result not of any idealistic assumption but of a rigorous application to our times of the strictly "military" logic of traditional war. For today the only way to achieve genuine national defense for any nation is for all nations to give up violence together. However, if we had begun with Gandhi's law of love we would have arrived at exactly the same arrangement. For to one who believed in nonviolence in a pre-nuclear setting the peril of extinction obviously adds one more reason—and a tremendous one, transcending all others—for giving up violence. Moreover, in at least one respect the law of love proves to fit the facts of this peril better than the law of fear. The law of fear relies on the love of self. Through deterrence—in which anyone's pursuit of self-interest at the expense of others will touch off general ruin that will destroy him, too—this self-love is made use of to protect everyone. However, self-love—a narrow, though intense, love—cannot, as we have seen, extend its protection to the future generations, or even get them in view. They still do not have any selves whose fear of death could be pooled in the common fund of fear, and yet their lives are at stake in extinction. The deterrence doctrine is a transaction that is limited to living people

—it leaves out of account the helpless, speechless unborn (while we can launch a first strike against them, they have no forces with which to retaliate)—and yet the fate of the future generations is at the heart of extinction, for their cancellation is what extinction is. Their lives are at stake, but their vote is not counted. Love, however, can reach them—can enable them to be. Love, a spiritual energy that the human heart can pit against the physical energy released from the heart of matter, can create, cherish, and safeguard what extinction would destroy and shut up in nothingness. But in fact there is no need, at least on the practical level, to choose between the law of fear and the law of love, because ultimately they lead to the same destination. It is no more realistic than it is idealistic to destroy the world.

In supposing for a moment that the world had found a political means of making international decisions, I made a very large supposition indeed—one that encompasses something close to the whole work of resolving the nuclear predicament, for, once a political solution has been found, disarmament becomes a merely technical matter, which should present no special difficulties. And yet simply to recognize that the task is at bottom political, and that only a political solution can prepare the way for full disarmament and real safety for the species, is in itself important. The recognition calls attention to the fact that disarmament in isolation from political change cannot proceed very far. It alerts us to the fact that when someone proposes, as President Carter did in his Inaugural Address, to aim at ridding the world of nuclear weapons, there is an immense obstacle that has to be faced and surmounted. For the world, in freeing itself of one burden, the peril of extinction, must inevitably shoulder another: it must assume full responsibility for settling human differences peacefully. Morever, this recognition forces us to acknowledge that nuclear disarmament cannot occur if conventional arms are left in place, since as long as nations defend themselves with arms of any kind they will be fully sovereign, and as long as they are fully sovereign they will be at liberty to build nuclear weapons if they so choose. And if we assume that wars do break out and some nations find themselves facing defeat in the conventional arena, then the reappearance of nuclear arms, which would prevent such defeat, becomes a strong likelihood. What nation, once having entrusted its fortunes to the force of arms, would permit itself to be conquered by an enemy when the means of driving him back, perhaps with a mere threat, was on hand? And how safe can the world be while nations threaten one another's existence with violence and retain for themselves the sovereign right to build whatever weapons they choose to build? This vision of an international life that in the military sphere is restricted to the pre-nuclear world while in the scientific realm it is in the nuclear world is, in fact, thoroughly implausible. If we are serious about nuclear disarmament—the minimum technical requirement for real safety from extinction—then we must accept conventional disarmament as well, and this means disarmament not just of nuclear powers but of all powers, for the present nuclear powers are hardly likely to throw away their conventional arms while non-nuclear powers hold on to theirs. But if we accept both nuclear and conventional disarmament, then we are speaking of revolutionizing the politics of the earth. The goals of the political revolution are defined by those of the nuclear revolution. We must lay down our arms, relinquish sovereignty, and found a political system for the peaceful settlement of international disputes.

The task we face is to find a means of political action that will permit human beings to pursue any end for the rest of time. We are asked to replace the mechanism by which political decisions, whatever they may be, are reached. In sum, the task is nothing less than to reinvent politics: to reinvent the world. However, extinction will not wait for us to reinvent the world. Evolution was slow to produce us, but our extinction will be swift; it will literally be over before we know it. We have to match swiftness with swiftness. Because everything we do and everything we are is in jeopardy, and because the peril is immediate and unremitting, every person is the right person to act and every moment is the right moment to begin, starting with the present moment. For nothing underscores our common humanity as strongly as the peril of extinction does; in fact, on a practical and political plane it establishes that common humanity. The purpose of action, though, is not to replace life with politics. The point is not to turn life into a scene of protest; life is the point.

Whatever the eventual shape of a world that has been re-invented for the sake of survival, the first, urgent, immediate step, which requires no deep thought or long reflection, is for each person to make known, visibly and unmistakably, his desire that the species survive. Extinction, being in its nature outside human experience, is invisible, but we, by rebelling against it, can indirectly make it visible. No one will ever witness extinction, so we must bear witness to it before the fact. And the place for the rebellion to start is in our daily lives. We can each perform a turnabout right where we are—let our daily business drop from our hands for a while, so that we can turn our attention to securing the foundation of all life, out of which our daily business grows and in which it finds its justification. This disruption of our lives will be a preventive disruption, for we will be hoping through the temporary suspension of our daily life to ward off the eternal suspension of it in extinction. And this turnabout in the first instance can be as simple as a phone call to a friend, a meeting in the community.

However, even as the first steps are taken, the broad ultimate requirements of survival must be recognized and stated clearly. If they are not, we might sink into self-deception, imagining that inadequate measures would suffice to save us. I would suggest that the ultimate requirements are in essence the two that I have mentioned: global disarmament, both nuclear and conventional, and the invention of political means by which the world can peacefully settle the issues that throughout history it has settled by war. Thus, the first steps and the ultimate requirements are clear. If a busload of people is speeding down a mountainside toward a cliff, the passengers do not convene a seminar to investigate the nature of their predicament; they see to it that the driver applies the brakes. Therefore, at a minimum, a freeze on the further deployment of nuclear weapons, participated in both by countries that now have them and by countries that do not yet have them, is called for. Even better would be a reduction in nuclear arms—for example, by cutting the arsenals of the superpowers in half, as George Kennan suggested recently. Simultaneously with disarmament, political steps of many kinds could be taken. For example, talks could be started among the nuclear powers with the aim of making sure that the world did not simply blunder into extinction by mistake; technical and political arrangements could be drawn up to reduce the likelihood of mechanical mistakes and misjudgments of the other side's intentions or actions in a time of crisis, and these would somewhat increase the world's security while the predicament was being tackled at a more fundamental level. For both superpowers— and, indeed, for all other powers—avoiding extinction is a common interest than which none can be greater. And since the existence of a common interest is the best foundation for negotiation, negotiations should have some chance of success. However, the existence of negotiations to reduce the nuclear peril would provide no reason for abandoning the pursuit of other things that one believed in, even those which might be at variance with the beliefs of one's negotiating partner. Thus, to give one contemporary example, there is no need, or excuse, for the United States not to take strong measures to oppose Soviet-sponsored repression in Poland just because it is engaged in disarmament talks with the Soviet Union. The world will not end if we suspend shipments of wheat to the Soviet Union. On the other hand, to break off those talks in an effort to help the Poles, who will be as extinct as anyone else if a holocaust comes about, would be self-defeating. To seek to "punish" the other side by breaking off those negotiations would be in reality self-punishment. All the limited aims of negotiation can be pursued in the short term without danger if only the ultimate goal is kept unswervingly in mind. But ordinary citizens must insist that all these things be done, or they will not be.

If action should be concerted, as it eventually must be, in a common political endeavor, reaching across national boundaries, then, just as the aim of the endeavor would be to hold the gates of life open to the future generations, so its method would be to hold its own gates open to every living person. But it should be borne in mind that even if every person in the world were to enlist, the endeavor would include only an infinitesimal fraction of the people of the dead and the unborn generations, and so it would need to act with the circumspection and modesty of a small minority. From its mission to preserve all generations, it would not seek to derive any rights to dictate to the generations on hand. It would not bend or break the rules of conduct essential to a decent political life, for it would recognize that once one started breaking rules in the name of survival no rule would go unbroken. Intellectually and philosophically, it would carry the principle of tolerance to the utmost extreme. It would attempt to be as open to new thoughts and feelings as it would be to the new generations that would think those thoughts and feel those feelings. Its underlying supposition about creeds and ideologies would be that whereas without mankind none can exist, with mankind all can exist. For while the events that might trigger a holocaust would probably be political, the consequences would be deeper than any politics or political aims, bringing ruin to the hopes and plans of capitalists and socialists, rightists and leftists, conservatives and liberals alike. Having as the source of its strength only the spontaneously offered support of the people of the earth, it would, in turn, respect each person's will, which is to say his liberty. Eventually, the popular will that it marshalled might be deployed as a check on the power of whatever political institutions were invented to replace war.

Since the goal would be a nonviolent world, the actions of this endeavor would be nonviolent. What Gandhi once said of the spirit of nonviolent action in general would be especially important to the spirit of these particular actions: "In the dictionary of nonviolent action, there is no such thing as an 'external enemy.'" With the world itself at stake, all differences would by definition be "internal" differences, to be resolved on the basis of respect for those with whom one disagreed. If our aim is to save humanity, we must respect the humanity of every person. For who would be the enemy? Certainly not the world's political leaders, who, though they now

menace the earth with nuclear weapons, do so only with our permission, and even at our bidding. At least, this is true for the democracies. We do not know what the peoples of the totalitarian states,
including the people of the Soviet Union, may want. They are
locked in silence by their government. In these circumstances, public opinion in the free countries would have to represent public
opinion in all countries, and would have to bring its pressure to bear,
as best it could, on all governments.

At present, most of us do nothing. We look away. We remain
calm. We are silent. We take refuge in the hope that the holocaust
won't happen, and turn back to our individual concerns. We deny
the truth that is all around us. Indifferent to the future of our kind,
we grow indifferent to one another. We drift apart. We grow cold.
We drowse our way toward the end of the world. But if once we
shook off our lethargy and fatigue and began to act, the climate
would change. Just as inertia produces despair—a despair often so
deep that it does not even know itself as despair—arousal and action
would give us access to hope, and life would start to mend: not just
life in its entirety but daily life, every individual life. At that point,
we would begin to withdraw from our role as both the victims and
the perpetrators of mass murder. We would no longer be the de-
stroyers of mankind but, rather, the gateway through which the
future generations would enter the world. Then the passion and will
that we need to save ourselves would flood into our lives. Then the
walls of indifference, inertia, and coldness that now isolate each of
us from others, and all of us from the past and future generations,
would melt, like snow in spring. E. M. Forster told us, "Only connect!" Let us connect. Auden told us, "We must love one another or
die." Let us love one another—in the present and across the divides
of death and birth. Christ said, "I come not to judge the world but
to save the world." Let us, also, not judge the world but save the
world. By restoring our severed links with life, we will restore our
own lives. Instead of stopping the course of time and cutting off the
human future, we would make it possible for the future generations
to be born. Their inestimable gift to us, passed back from the future
into the present, would be the wholeness and meaning of life.

The Choice

Two paths lie before us. One leads to death, the other to life. If we choose the first path—if we numbly refuse to acknowledge the nearness of extinction, all the while increasing our preparations to bring it about—then we in effect become the allies of death, and in everything we do our attachment to life will weaken: our vision, blinded to the abyss that has opened at our feet, will dim and grow confused; our will, discouraged by the thought of trying to build on such a precarious foundation anything that is meant to last, will slacken; and we will sink into stupefaction, as though we were gradually weaning ourselves from life in preparation for the end. On the other hand, if we reject our doom, and bend our efforts toward survival—if we arouse ourselves to the peril and act to forestall it, making ourselves the allies of life—then the anesthetic fog will lift: our vision, no longer straining not to see the obvious, will sharpen; our will, finding secure ground to build on, will be restored; and we will take full and clear possession of life again. One day—and it is hard to believe that it will not be soon—we will make our choice. Either we will sink into the final coma and end it all or, as I trust and believe, we will awaken to the truth of our peril, a truth as great as life itself, and, like a person who has swallowed a lethal poison but shakes off his stupor at the last moment and vomits the poison up, we will break through the layers of our denials, put aside our fainthearted excuses, and rise up to cleanse the earth of nuclear weapons.

INDEX

Dolan, Philip J. (*cont.*)
   "Effects of Nuclear Weapons,
      The"
doom, *see* annihilation; extinction;
   holocaust; self-destruction
"doomsday clock," 108–9
doomsday machine, 206, 208, 214,
   215, 217
Dostoevsky, Fëdor Mikhailovich, 137
Dulles, John Foster, 31
dust, lofting of, 20, 51, 89

earth:
   as cell (analogy), 77, 112, 177
   cooling of, from dust in strato-
      sphere, 20, 89
   experimentation on, precluded, 76,
      77, 198
   habitability of, 21, 73–4
   knowledge/ignorance of, 75, 76–8,
      93
   and mankind, relationship, 75;
      changed in favor of humans'
      power, 94, 109–10, 111, 113–14;
      and power of death, increased,
      111–12; respect, in new common
      world, 177–8
   nuclear effects on, 7, 23, 73–4, 78
   photographs of, from space, 153–4
   and sovereignty, relationship, 187
   see also ecosphere
economy:
   effect of holocaust on, 65–7, 69–70
   effects on ecosphere, 110
ecosphere:
   balance and reciprocity of, 77,
      91–3, 111–12, 185
   and economy, 110
   "gross simplification" of, 64, 65
   and mankind, *see* earth: and
      mankind, relationship
   nuclear effects on, 19–20, 22–3, 78,
      81–2, 84–96, 110–14
   and ultraviolet radiation, 81–8
      passim
   see also climate; earth; ozone layer
"Effects of Nuclear War, The"
   (report, 1979), 4
"Effects of Nuclear Weapons, The,"
   see Glasstone, Samuel, and
   Philip J. Dolan

Einstein, Albert, 10, 12–13, 187–8,
   194–5
   formula, $E=mc^2$, 10–11, 13, 101
   as pacifist and scientist, 104–5
Eisenhower, Dwight David, 6
electromagnetic pulse, 17–18, 22, 75
Eliot, Thomas Stearns, 151
energy in mass, 9–12
   discovered (only), by humans, 178
   and nuclear peril, 106–7
environment, *see* animals; climate;
   earth; ecosphere; oceans; plants
epidemic(s), 68, 78
error, as start of holocaust, 26–7, 182,
   205, 228
escape from devastation zone (nuclear), 40–3 *passim*, 50, 57, 70
escape from earth, 106
escape from nuclear peril, *see* denial
   of nuclear peril; extinction:
   prevention of
Europe:
   nuclear hostilities in, 72, 192, 214
   nuclear vulnerability of, 29, 65
evacuation, 34, 59–60
evil:
   humanity as, 133
   and love, 175–6
   provocation by, 134
   "radical," 145–6
evolution of species, 92–3, 112–13,
   181
   and ozone, 79–81
   and possible reappearance of
      mankind, 114
extinction:
   as abstraction, 140
   and concentration camps, 168
   vs. death, 117, 119, 137–8, 144;
      individual's, 112, 117, 118, 119,
      127–8, 137, 147, 166, 184
   effect on life and the living, 147,
      155
   escape from, by unborn, 171
   ethical considerations, 130–6
   fear of, as deterrent, 221–5
   and generations (connections be-
      tween), 162; *see also* genera-
      tions, future
   and genocide, 146
   God as author of, 127

Glasstone, Samuel, and Philip J.
Dolan: "Effects of Nuclear
Weapons, The," 4–5, 14, 20–1,
36, 47, 53, 59, 79
global conditions and effects, *see*
climate; earth; ecosphere
goals, *see* purposes, human
God:
and Adam and Eve, 115
commandments of, as conscience
(Socrates), 131
as justification for destruction of
world, 133
man's usurpation of omniscience of,
126
respect for, in new common world,
178
as threatening extinction, 127
and Tower of Babel, 103
governments:
and control of science, 105
ends-means justification used by,
134–5
justify repression, 134–6
national defense, *see* defense of
national interests
secrecy about nuclear weapons,
101, 107, 149
see also sovereignty, national;
superpowers
grasses, and radiation, 63–5
greenhouse effect, 88–9, 92, 110
ground burst:
and fallout, 18–19, 44, 66, 67
on New York, 50–2, 53–4
on power plant, 60–1
on U.S., 58–9

Hachiya, Michihiko, 42–3
Haldeman, H. R., 205
Hegel, Georg Wilhelm Friedrich,
101–2, 160
Hersey, John, 41, 43
Herzen, Alexander, 173
Himmler, Heinrich, 146, 195
Hiroshima, 23, 36–45, 46
survivors' testimony, 38–43 *passim*,
142–3
"Hiroshima and Nagasaki," 5, 45
Hitler, Adolf, 146–7

holocaust, nuclear:
as Armageddon, 127, 133
"benefits" of, 7
consequences of: difficulty of
imagining, 139–40; range of,
6–7; studies on, 4–5; *see also*
ecosphere: nuclear effects on;
extinction; weapons, nuclear:
destructive effects of
effect on economy, 65–7, 69–70
effect on ecosphere, 19–20, 22–3,
78, 81–2, 84–96, 110–14
effect on individuals, 22, 23, 24, 26
effect on society, 19, 22–3, 45, 73;
see also extinction
emotional responses to, 7–9
error as start of, 26–7, 182, 205,
228
and extinction, *see* extinction
precipitation of, *see* hostilities,
nuclear: precipitating events
"recovery" from, 68, 73, 84; *see
also* survival
suddenness of, 34, 37, 182, 198
uncertainty about effects of, 25,
72–8 *passim*, 207
as "unthinkable," 4, 8, 32, 141
see also hostilities, nuclear;
weapons, nuclear: destructive
effects of
hostilities, nuclear:
extent of, 71–2
justification for, 130
"limited" war, 31–2, 33, 66, 192,
207–8
precipitating events, 26–30; error
as, 26–7, 182, 205, 228; inadvertence, 186; limited war, 207–
208; "reasoned insanity," 204–5
sequence of, possible, 30–2
theoretical nature of, 158; *see also*
strategy, nuclear
between U.S. and Soviet Union, 27,
71–2, 191, 192
"victory" in, 159–60, 190, 199,
202, 203
see also holocaust, nuclear
Hsiao, Ting H., 86
human beings, *see* mankind
human extinction, *see* death, second

McElroy, Michael, 80, 81–2, 91–2
McNamara, Robert, 33, 196, 207
"Military Balance, The," 55
military doctrine, traditional:
    and deterrence doctrine, 200–201,
        202, 217
    and nuclear weapons, 187, 198
military targets, 55–6
mistake, as start of holocaust, 26–7,
    182, 205, 228
Montaigne, Michel Eyquem de, 144,
    147
Mumford, Lewis, 120
mushroom cloud, 18, 49, 51, 53, 57;
    see also fallout, radioactive
mutations and abnormalities, genetic,
    45, 71, 90

Nachtwey, D. Stuart, 86–7
Nagasaki, 23, 44, 49, 142–3
N.A.S. report (1975), 5, 75, 78, 79,
    81, 84, 86, 88, 89, 90–1
National Academy of Sciences:
    interim report (1977), 74
National Academy of Sciences:
    "Long-Term Worldwide Effects
    of Multiple Nuclear-Weapons
    Detonations," *see* N.A.S. report
    (1975)
nations:
    belligerent, *see* hostilities, nuclear;
        superpowers; war
    defense of, *see* defense of national
        interests
    governments of, *see* governments
    with nuclear weapons, *see*
        weapons, nuclear: countries
        armed with
nature, *see* earth; ecosphere
Nazism, 142
    and Jews, 146–7, 167, 195
New York City:
    one-megaton bomb: air-burst over,
        47–50; ground-burst on, 50–2
    20-megaton bomb: air-burst over,
        52–3; ground-burst on, 53–4
Nixon, Richard Milhous, 135, 205
nonproliferation, 108, 227–8; *see also*
    disarmament efforts

oceans, 78, 86–8; *see also* fish
Office of Civil Defense: "Survival of
    Food Crops and Live-
    stock . . . ," 5, 62–4 *passim*
oil supply, and nuclear policy, 29–
    30, 211–13
overkill, 56, 58, 65
overpressure(s), 47, 50, 55
ozone layer, 79–81, 91–2
    depletion/destruction of, 20–1,
        110; abiotic results, 79–88; and
        climate, 88–90; from nuclear
        weapons, 75, 81–2
    and ultraviolet radiation, 20–1,
        79, 80, 91

parenthood, universal, and the unborn,
    175
Pascal, Blaise, 148
Pericles, 121–2
peril, nuclear, *see* predicament,
    nuclear
Persian Gulf region, 29–30, 211–13
philosophy, *see* thought and reason
physics:
    in nineteenth century, 9
    in twentieth century, 9–13; as
        foundation of nuclear peril,
        100–108
    as villain among sciences, 104
plants, and radiation, 61–2, 63–5, 78,
    85–6
plutonium, 13, 16–17, 90
Plutarch, 109
politics:
    compromised by nuclear peril,
        160–2
    and disarmament, 221, 222–8
        passim
    "realistic" *vs.* "idealistic," 224
    and science, 105
    as solution to nuclear peril, 108,
        219, 220, 225–6, 227, 228
    and violence, 220
    see also conservatism; govern-
        ments; revolutions; society;
        sovereignty, national
population centers:
    evacuation of, 34, 59–60
    as targets, 52, 55–6, 66

power plant(s), nuclear, 60–1
predicament, nuclear:
  basis in scientific knowledge,
    100–108, 147, 188
  denial of, *see* denial of nuclear
    peril
  as ecological peril, 111–14; *see
    also* ecosphere
  permanence of, 109, 147
  and politics, 108, 160–2, 219, 220,
    225–6, 227, 228
  responses to, *see* responses to
    nuclear peril
  and unborn, *see* generations, future
  see also extinction
preëmptive strike, 27–8, 202–4
    passim
proliferation of nuclear weapons, 54,
    94, 107, 148, 149–50, 183–4,
    209; *see also* nonproliferation
"publicity" (Arendt's term), 119–20,
    162
pulse, *see* electromagnetic pulse;
    thermal pulse
purposes, human:
  extinction as end of, 131
  vs. life as totality, 123–4
  and peril of extinction, 95

rad (roentgen absorbed dose), 62;
    see also radiation, nuclear: doses
Radford, Edward, 71
radiation, nuclear, 12
  and animals, 61–2
  delayed effects of, 44–5, 60–1
  doses: acute, 51; from attack on
    power plant, 60–1; from attacks
    on U.S., 51–2, 53–4, 57–8, 59;
    at "hot spots," 90; lethal, 19,
    63–4; and mutation, genetic, 71;
    per-capita, 12; *see also* rad; rem
  duration of, 20
  genetic vulnerability to, 12, 45, 71,
    90
  initial, 17, 46
  longterm effects of, 70–1
  and plants, 61–2, 63–5
  see also fallout, radioactive;
    radiation sickness

radiation, ultraviolet, *see* ultraviolet
    radiation
radiation sickness, 19, 42, 43–4, 51–2,
    60
radioactivity, *see* fallout, radioactive;
    radiation, nuclear; radiation
    sickness; rain, black/radioactive
rain, black/radioactive, 37, 44, 49
reason, *see* thought and reason
"recovery" from holocaust, 68, 73, 84
relativity, 10–11
rem (roentgen equivalent in man),
    51; *see also* radiation, nuclear:
    doses
reproductive capacity (human), vul-
    nerability to radiation, 45; *see
    also* mutations and abnormalities,
    genetic; sexuality, human
responses to nuclear peril:
  in action, 148, 188, 220
  denial, *see* denial of nuclear peril
  emotional, 139, 141, 147–8, 152
  failure of, 4, 136–7, 150–2, 161–2,
    230
  indifference, 143
  intellectual, 151–2, 187–8
  "normality" maintained, 150, 151
  political, 25, 148, 152, 161–2, 188
  recognition, 148, 149, 183, 222; in
    deterrence theory, 199, 201
retaliation, 152–3, 200–204 *passim*
  and doomsday machine, 206
  out of "reasoned insanity," 204–5
  and revenge, 207
  see also deterrence, nuclear
    (theory)
revolutions:
  democratic (Tocqueville), 141
  political (nonviolent), 226–7
  scientific *vs.* social, 100–101, 103–4
  totalitarian, 141–2
Rickover, Adm. Hyman, 220
Rilke, Rainer Maria, 128–9
Roosevelt, Franklin Delano, 105
Rosenberg, Harold, 164–5
Rousset, David, 167
Ruderman, Malvin A., 75
Russell, Bertrand Arthur William,
    3d Earl Russell, 183, 194
Russia, *see* Soviet Union

sacrifice, of individual life and of
human species, 125, 130–3
Schelling, Thomas, 200, 205
science:
  collective nature of, 102–3
  knowledge of: as basis of nuclear
    peril, 100–108, 147, 188;
    permanence of, 102–3, 105–6,
    147, 219, 223
  revolutions in, *vs.* social revolu-
    tions, 100–101, 103–4
  social aims and applications of,
    104–5
  uncertainty factor in research,
    104–5
  see also physics
secrecy about nuclear weapons, 101,
  107, 149
self-destruction, 94, 103, 122–3,
  181–2
  denial of possibility, 152
  Freud on, 155–6
  inadvertent, 186
  justification for, 132, 136
  permanence of capacity for, 109,
    147, 219
  as predetermined, 218–19
  as radical evil, 145–6
  see also death, second (*i.e.* of
    mankind); extinction; suicide
sexuality, human, 156–7; *see also*
  reproductive capacity, human
Shakespeare, William, 158, 175
shelter(s), 34–6, 59, 60, 61, 67–8
society:
  cohesion of, disintegrating, 158–9
  and denial of nuclear peril, 150–2
  impact of holocaust on, 19, 22–3,
    45, 73
  objectives of, *vs.* scientific aims,
    104–5
  revolutions in, *vs.* scientific
    revolutions, 100–101, 103–4
  see also generations; politics
Socrates, 130–2, 134
Solzhenitsyn, Alexander, 121, 162,
  166–7
sovereignty, national, 186
  and disarmament, 218
  and earth, relationship, 187

and international disputes, 186–7,
  188, 193–4, 225–9
and national defense, *see* defense
  of national interests
and war, 186–7, 189–93
see also governments; politics
Soviet Union:
  invasion of Afghanistan (1979),
    211
  nuclear attack on U.S., 55–9
  nuclear capabilities of, 31, 34, 52,
    54, 192
  nuclear conflict with U.S., 27, 71–2,
    191, 192
  and Persian Gulf region, 211–13
  and precipitation of nuclear
    hostilities, 29, 212, 214
  survival of U.S. attack on, 65
  see also superpowers
standards of worth, 124–30
starvation, after holocaust, 69, 84
Stern, Vernon M., 63
Stimson, Henry, 148–9
Strategic Arms Limitation Talks, 108
strategy, nuclear:
  and civil defense, 35–6
  as justification for nuclear arma-
    ment, 152–3
  and military doctrine, traditional,
    187, 198
  and moral sense, 195–6, 205–6
  and precipitation of hostilities,
    26–30
  and sequence of nuclear attack,
    30–3
  theoretical nature of, 140–1, 149,
    158, 195
  see also deterrence, nuclear
    (theory); limited war; retaliation
strong-force reactions, 9, 11–12, 14,
  16
strontium-90, 62
suffering:
  and extinction, 144
  of future generations, 176
suicide, 152
  and deterrence doctrine, 196
  extinction as, 130, 132
  see also self-destruction
superpowers:
  awareness of nuclear peril, 6

superpowers (*cont.*)
  Cold War between, 149
  détente between, 135–6
  and deterrence doctrine, 196–8
  leaders' humanity, 208
  and nuclear hostilities: extent of,
    71–2; precipitation of, 27,
    210–11, 214–15
  responsibility for nuclear peril, 107,
    152
  and weapons, nuclear: buildup of,
    see proliferation; parity of, 200;
    reduction of, *see* disarmament
    efforts
  see also Soviet Union; United
    States
survival, 21, 172–3
  in deterrence doctrine, 197
  future generations' relation to, 171
  hope for, 184
  and human aggressiveness, 185
  vs. human purposes, 123–4
  imagined, as denial of peril, 126
  moral value of, 130, 172–3
  of nuclear attack on U.S., 60,
    65–71
  as obligation, 136, 231
  personal, *vs.* that of species, 136
  and suffering, 176
  as way of life, 109
  see also civil defense; extinction:
    prevention of; holocaust,
    nuclear: "recovery" from
"Survival of Food Crops and Livestock . . . ," 5, 62–4 *passim*
survivors, *see* escape from devastation zone (nuclear); Hiroshima:
  survivors' testimony; "recovery"
  from holocaust; shelter(s);
  survival
sympathy:
  with suffering, 176
  for unborn, 143–4
Szilard, Leo, 107

targets, nuclear, 33, 55–6
  hard and soft, 55
  industrial, 56, 66
  military, 55–6
  population centers, 52, 55–6, 66

terrorism, nuclear, 61
testing, nuclear:
  at Bikini Atoll, 53, 59, 74–5
  and knowledge of weapons' effects,
    22, 36
  and ozone layer, 75
  radiation from, 12, 62, 74–5
  at Trinity site, N.M., 3
thermal pulse, 18
  at Hiroshima, 37
  from nuclear attack on: New York,
    49, 50, 53; U.S., 56–7, 58
  and plants, 64
  of 12½- and 20-megaton bombs, 46
thermonuclear reaction, *see* bomb,
  hydrogen; fusion, atomic
think tank(s), 140–1, 149
Thomas, Lewis, 73, 93
  analogy of earth as cell, 77, 112,
    177
thought and reason:
  and common world, 120
  vs. instinct, 156
  permanence of, 102
  in response to nuclear peril, 151–2,
    187–8
  threatened by nuclear peril, 162
  see also earth: knowledge/igno-
    rance of; science: knowledge of
Tocqueville, Alexis Charles Henri
  Maurice Clérel de, 141
totalitarianism:
  breaks connections between gener-
    ations, 162, 166–7
  and détente, 136
  difficulty in accepting, 141–2
  and radical evil, 145
  revolutions of, 141–2
  see also Nazism
Tower of Babel, 103
trees, and radiation, 63–4
Truman, Harry S, 11
Tsipis, Kosta, 60–1, 84

ultraviolet radiation:
  abiotic effects of, 79–88 *passim*
  and evolution, 79–81
  human vulnerability to, 83–4
  and ocean life, 86–8
  and ozone layer, 20–1, 79, 80, 91

243

THE
ABOLITION

*I dedicate this book
with love to William Shawn.*

CONTENTS

I.
DEFINING THE
GREAT PREDICAMENT

I N A SPEECH given in Hiroshima in February of 1981, Pope John Paul II said, "In the past, it was possible to destroy a village, a town, a region, even a country. Now it is the whole planet that has come under threat. This fact should fully compel everyone to face a basic moral consideration: from now on, it is only through a conscious choice and then deliberate policy that humanity can survive." The Pope's deceptively simple statement contains an invaluable anatomy of the challenge that the invention of nuclear weapons has placed before mankind. In distinguishing between "a conscious choice" and "deliberate policy," he defines two stages— one individual and spiritual, the other public and political—that we must pass through if we are to resolve the nuclear predicament. Because by building large nuclear arsenals we threaten to extinguish ourselves as a species, each of us is called on to do something that no member of any generation before ours has had

to do: to assume responsibility for the continuation of our kind—
to *choose* human survival. There is nothing perfunctory or easy
about making this choice. For example, it is wholly inadequate for
us to remind ourselves that "nuclear war is horrible," and to assure
ourselves that we are not "for" extinguishing mankind. The potential extermination of the human species by nuclear arms presents,
like every monumental crime—Hitler's genocidal attack on the
Jewish people being the most monstrous in memory—a challenge
to the human spirit, and not one that we can be at all sure in
advance that we are up to meeting. But even among monumental
crimes the extermination of the species is unique. For the risk of
extinction is not just one more item on the agenda of issues that
faces us. Embracing, as it does, the life and death of every human
being on earth and every future human being, it embraces and
transcends all other issues. It is the ground in which they and
every issue that might arise in the future have their significance
and their being. But even to say that it is a life-and-death matter
does not go far enough, because while the individual person may
choose to give his life for causes that he considers to be greater and
more important than his own life, including the cause of saving the
lives of others, the extinction of mankind would destroy not only
every person's life but also every larger cause, including the lives
of all others, for which a person might be willing to give up his life.
Extinction therefore threatens not so much each person's life
(which is threatened at the same time by many other things, and
will one day end anyway) as the *meaning* of our lives. It threatens
life with meaninglessness as individual death never can. In doing
so, it not only encompasses all human life but reaches deep into
each life, requiring each of us to make this business his own.
Sometimes it is suggested that it is ignoble to give the highest
priority to our effort to save mankind from destruction, because
in doing so we supposedly place our animal wish to stay alive
above our higher, more specifically human obligation to live a
morally decent life. But just the opposite is the case. It is precisely
all those things *for which* people have throughout history been
willing to sacrifice their lives that we have, indecently, now

4

placed, in their entirety, at risk. And it is our desire to save those things—not merely the desire to save our own necks—which moves us to choose to save our species. It is also sometimes suggested that fear will inspire us to combat the nuclear peril, but that reasonable-sounding idea seems to me equally mistaken. Fear, a more or less reflexive response that we share with other species, drives each of us, as an individual, to save himself in the face of danger. Fear cannot distinguish between a fire in one's own house and a nuclear holocaust—between one's own death and the end of the world—and is therefore useless even to begin to suggest to us the meaning of the nuclear peril. Its meaning can be grasped only to the extent that we feel the precise opposite of fear, which is a sense of responsibility, or devotion, or love, for other people, including those who have not yet been born. In Germany, the peace movement has inverted the traditional Biblical admonition "Fear not" to say "You must fear." But the original version was the right one, for nuclear matters as for others. Fear isolates. Love connects. Only insofar as the latter is strong in us are we likely to find the resolve to prevent our extinction.

The conscious choice to take responsibility for the continuation of human life is further complicated and confused by the fact, which also is peculiar to the nuclear peril, that we are able to respond to it only before it happens. Since after extinction no one will be present to take responsibility, we have to take full responsibility now. It follows that we incur the full burden of guilt for extinguishing our species merely by preparing to do the deed, even without actually pushing the button. Sometimes it is suggested that while it would be a crime to extinguish mankind we are blameless if we intend—and threaten—to do so, provided that some laudable goal is being served by the threat. But if we absolve ourselves of responsibility for the intent, then we in effect evade responsibility altogether, since we can hardly assume responsibility after we are all dead. Therefore, insofar as we are going to take any responsibility whatever, we must in fact take it for the intent alone. To combine strategic with Christian terminology, we must adopt a policy of preemptive repentance. We must repent the

5

crime before we commit it, and in that repentance find the will
not to commit it. This displacement of repentance from the aftermath of the crime to the time preceding it would be, to paraphrase
William James, the moral equivalent of deterrence. The only difference between it and the strategic sort is that whereas in strategic deterrence we are deterred by what the enemy may do to us,
in moral deterrence we are deterred by what we may do to him
—and to countless innocents, including all potential future generations of human beings. Or, to put it simply, we are not only fearful
at the thought of suffering a nuclear holocaust but repelled by the
thought of perpetrating one. Still, it would be misleading, perhaps,
to try to distinguish too sharply between our fearful, selfish impulses and our altruistic, selfless ones. The holocaust itself will
make no such distinctions. The fallout will fall on the just and the
unjust alike. After the Cuban missile crisis, Premier Nikita Khrushchev remarked that the smell of burning flesh was in the air. But,
in truth, that smell is never far from our nostrils now. The world's
nuclear arsenals threaten to annihilate everyone in response to a
transgression or mistake by any one party. That is how the doctrine of deterrence is designed. In consenting to live under it, we
bear responsibility not only for the lives of the people whom "we"
may kill but also for the lives of those whom "they" would kill;
namely, our families, our friends, and our other fellow-citizens.
Through the balance of terror, we all come to hold a dagger to the
hearts of those nearest and dearest to us as well as to threaten
those far away, down to the uttermost generations of human beings. The parent threatens the child, the lover the lover, the friend
the friend, the citizen the citizen. Our acceptance of nuclear
weapons is in that sense a default of parenthood, of love, of friendship, of citizenship, in which we all, like hijackers of airplanes, take
one another hostage and threaten to kill one another. In acquiesc-
ing in the balance of terror, we become irresponsible parents,
coldhearted lovers, faithless friends, and apathetic citizens. And in
making a "conscious choice" to lift the nuclear peril we resolve to
escape this pervasive corruption of our lives. We resolve to clear
the air of the smell of burning flesh.

6

In making the choice, however, one decides nothing about the *means* of attaining the goal. That task is left to the second stage: framing the "deliberate policy." In fact, one has not even determined whether the goal of bringing the species to safety is attainable. If it is not, then our situation is tragic in the full sense of the word. Then our species, while willing to live, would be fated to die. And, indeed, there are many distinguished observers today who, while they do not write off the human species, believe that its safety cannot be very much improved. In particular, they rule out the abolition of nuclear weapons as impossible. For example, a *New York Times* editorial critical of the recent pastoral letter of the National Conference of Catholic Bishops on war and peace, in which the bishops advocated the eventual abolition of nuclear weapons, stated, "Fundamentally, the American bishops' approach falters on the assumption that the nuclear dilemma can eventually be resolved by eliminating rather than controlling nuclear weapons. But there is no known way to get rid of The Bomb, no way to guard against all possible production or concealments of warheads." And in *Living with Nuclear Weapons,* a book written at the request of Derek Bok, the president of Harvard, by five professors and a graduate student associated with Harvard—Albert Carnesale, Paul Doty, Stanley Hoffmann, Samuel P. Huntington, Joseph S. Nye, Jr., and Scott D. Sagan, and published in 1982 —it is stated that a world without nuclear weapons is "a fictional utopia," and "humanity has no alternative but to hold this threat at bay and to learn to live with politics, to live in the world we know: a world of nuclear weapons, international rivalries, recurring conflicts, and at least some risk of nuclear crisis." In the closing paragraph of the Harvard book, there is a memorable sentence, which the authors apparently thought important enough to make use of for their title. It reads, "Living with nuclear weapons is our only hope." This sentence could be engraved on our currency, alongside "In God we trust," or perhaps replacing it, for it reflects accurately the faith of our time. We truly not only "live with" nuclear weapons but place our hope for the future in them. And now some of us have apparently arrived at a point at which we profess to have lost all hope without them. Yet if a nuclear-free world is really "a fictional utopia," and if there is really "no known way to get rid of The Bomb"—not even "eventually"—then one must wonder what hope there is for mankind. Given the incurable fallibility of men and machines, doesn't it follow that sooner or later the bomb will get rid of us?

In the last few years, much of the public, having very largely ignored the nuclear peril for almost four decades, has been discovering a different faith. To express it in the Pope's terms, these people have been making their conscious choice: they have been choosing human survival. This long-delayed but deep and powerful public response is, like the predicament it addresses, a unique phenomenon, and familiar terms have to be stretched or altered to describe it, or even to name it. For example, it is both more and less than a "peace movement"—the usual, and probably inescapable, term for it. It is more because the word "movement" suggests something of a political character, whereas this response was born and has gathered strength outside politics. It has begun as a pre-political stocktaking, in which people have been reexamining life itself, and every activity in life, in the light of the present peril to all life. This psychological and spiritual process, which is the very substance of the conscious choice, might be described as an awakening rather than a movement. The response is less than a traditional movement for much the same reason: though it stands poised at the edge of the political arena, and has already intervened, or tried to intervene, in certain decisions (the deployment of the new American missiles in Europe, for example), it has yet to find full political expression. That is, it has decided that it wants man to survive, but it has not (as its critics are quick to point out) settled on a "deliberate policy" for reaching its goal. Thus, it might be described as an awakening seeking to become a movement. This awakening is new, and its extent and its consequences are still uncertain, but it promises to be one of those great changes of heart in mankind—such as the awakening to the evil of slavery in the nineteenth century—that alter the psychological and spiritual map of the world, and, first acting outside politics, sweep into it with decisive effect. If politics is the art of the possible, then deep changes in opinion of this kind extend the boundaries of what the possible includes. (The political process in a democracy is broader than is sometimes supposed. When politicians speak of what is "possible" or "impossible," they are often referring to nothing more than what is or is not acceptable to current public opinion. What they often really mean when they say that something is "impossible" is that they cannot win the next election if they advocate it. But if public opinion changes, then their opinion changes, too, and all of a sudden yesterday's impossible thing is possible.)

Just what may have triggered the new movement is a matter for speculation, but several circumstances and events are usually mentioned. They include the large buildup of nuclear arms by the Soviet Union in the last two decades, which has brought it up to the level of nuclear parity with the United States; the breakdown of the Strategic Arms Limitation Talks and the stalemate of the Strategic Arms Reduction Talks that succeeded them; the collapse of a mood of "détente" between the United States and the Soviet Union; the growing deployment by both the Soviet Union and the United States of missiles with the power to achieve a first strike against at least some missiles of the other side; the decision by the North Atlantic Treaty Organization to deploy intermediate-range nuclear missiles in Europe; and many provocative or ignorant-seeming statements regarding nuclear arms by officials of the Reagan Administration—statements such as one by T. K. Jones, the Deputy Under-Secretary of Defense for Research and Engineering, Strategic and Theatre Nuclear Forces, that "if there are enough shovels to go around, everybody's going to make it" through a nuclear holocaust, and, most important, the statement, in a top-secret Department of Defense planning document obtained by the *Times*, that the United States not only is planning for "prolonged" nuclear war but has as its aim to "prevail" in it— in plain language, to win it. But standing in the background of all

9

these circumstances and events, I believe, is a development so simple and elementary that it is often overlooked. It is the fact that the doomsday machine—that immense collaborative undertaking of the United States and the Soviet Union, with minor assistance from other countries—has, over the last thirty-nine years, been assembled, with the finishing touches perhaps having been put on by the Soviet buildup. What was once merely a phrase in books is now actuality. And the real doomsday machine, lowering over the world, looks, feels, and is different in innumerable ways from the theoretical article. Of course, the doomsday machine didn't spring into existence all at once. The superpowers held no unveiling ceremony to announce to mankind that the preparations for the annihilation of the human species were now complete. Yet when people turned their attention to the nuclear peril they tended to see it all at once, with astonishment and horror, as though they had suddenly turned around and found themselves looking at a ferocious beast in the room with them. But looking at the nuclear peril was unlike any other looking. Because people were looking at things that they already in a sense knew about (the existence of nuclear arms had never been a secret), and not at some facts that had just been brought to light by reporters, it was a kind of looking within—a kind of introspection. And because these things that everyone already knew about were sickening and almost unbelievable, and because each person doing the looking was himself both implicated in and condemned by the evil, this looking within was anguishing. It seems not to be given to human beings to hold great horrors unremittingly before their mind's eye, and particularly not when the beholder is himself the potential perpetrator of the horror. We falter. We need respite. We forget. Then perhaps we look again. Alertness and stupor alternate. And we seem to lack any way of picturing extinction. The recent television film *The Day After* performed a public service by portraying Kansas after a nuclear attack. But no film can ever show the full consequences of a holocaust. It would have to display nothingness on the screen, and last forever. Even to try to understand the notion of extinction requires both intellectual and emotional effort. The boundlessness, the invisibility, and the emptiness of extinction are confounding. Extinction lacks the intricacy and detail that would permit our intellects to take hold of it—to analyze, to draw distinctions, to judge. Yet it is important to try to achieve an intellectual understanding of it, if only because by holding that in our mind we can sustain our effort and maintain our resolve without being dependent on the uncertainties of emotion. And, of course, as we strive, daily life in all its profusion goes on making its claims, introducing an at times comical disproportion in our lives between the immensity of our thoughts about the life and death of man and the smallness of our preoccupations with a particular personal quarrel, or meal, or financial worry, that may be absorbing us at a given moment. Weighing these incommensurables—deciding, for example, how much effort to expend to save the human species for all time as against how much to expend on, say, buying a sofa —is itself a considerable feat of balance and judgment.

Looking within themselves at the nuclear peril prepared people for action, and also was in itself a kind of action, albeit action taken within the privacy of each person's soul. Because this preparatory action—this coming to grips as a human being with the altered human situation—was not yet a political action, and prescribed no political course, it seemed to some as if it were nothing. That may be one reason the public awakening caught so many politicians and so much of the press by surprise: it had come about in domains of existence—the moral and spiritual—in which they ordinarily take little professional interest. That may also be the reason that, insofar as the movement has had leaders (a peculiar characteristic of it, apparently related to its grass-roots origin, has been its lack of conspicuous political leadership), they have tended to be doctors, including psychiatrists, and clergymen—people ordinarily concerned not with politics but with disturbances in the body, the psyche, and the soul. The new disturbances were, in fact, seismic. Suddenly, people were awash in fathomless questions of human existence. How did it happen, people started to ask themselves, that we have become the underwriters of the slaughter of billions of innocent people? Can such slaughter ever be justified?

How? What is the meaning of human life on earth? What would its extermination mean? What does it mean about us that we have built the equipment with which to carry out that extermination, and are apparently prepared to perform the act? What does it mean that we—one link in the chain of the generations—are prepared to cut the chain, and set adrift in darkness all the future generations of human beings? What is our responsibility to these unborn people, and how can we fulfill it?

These questions are no newer than the technical invention that propelled them into the thick of history: they were raised in 1945, in the stunned aftermath of the Hiroshima bombing. Yet before long they receded from people's thoughts, as though they were too shocking for people to take to heart on such short notice. We who are alive today, however, thirty-nine years into the nuclear world, stand on different historical ground. Some of us have moved through the years of our lives in the shadow of the peril—have grown up, come of age, married, had children, worked, and approached death in the knowledge that before long all mankind may die. In one sense, our experience of the peril is oblique (no nuclear blast has been directed against human beings since Nagasaki), but in another sense it is fundamental, since if mankind destroys itself with nuclear weapons no one will experience our disappearance after the fact, and our experience of that fate now, before it happens, is all the experience of it that anyone will ever get. It *is* the experience of extinction. What we feel, therefore, is not so much fear of a future event, such as we feel when we realize that one day something terrible may happen to us, as it is disgust at the debasement of life right now because it is threatened by and threatens the extinction of man.

To make the choice is essential, for without it we are simply becalmed—as we were until very recently. If the inner landscape of our souls does not change, the outer landscape of the world will not change, either. And once the choice has been made it must, like every profound moral and spiritual decision, be continually refreshed and renewed. Since the beginning of history, human beings have stood in wonder at the blessing of life within them and around them. But now, for the first time, that wonder implies a political obligation. Every beautiful morning, every note of song, every infant's smile must propel us into action. Making and sustaining the conscious choice is a labor that has an integrity of its own, independent of what we may propose to do about the nuclear predicament. Just as in medicine the diagnosis precedes the prescription, and lays the basis for it, the conscious choice must precede the deliberate policy. But then we must frame the deliberate policy. If we fail, the cost to us—even if it happens that we do not stumble into oblivion—is that our wonder at life and our joy in it will be progressively diminished and corrupted. The choice must be made so that the policy can follow; but if the policy does not follow—if, instead, we sink back into stupefaction and complacency—the choice itself will be undone. Worse, it will, in effect, be reversed: by default, we will have chosen annihilation. In these pages, I propose to address the question of deliberate policy—specifically, the question of how we might abolish nuclear arms—but first, as a way of framing the policy question, I would like, by sketching out the chief features of our predicament (including, briefly, the facts that underlie the peril itself, some of which have come to light only recently), and by discussing some of the responses to the predicament over the years, to describe the elements of what appears to be a historic impasse, in which the world has now been stuck for almost four decades.

As citizens, we would like to know what the consequences of a nuclear holocaust at various levels of nuclear armament would be. We would like to know how many weapons of what size would kill how many people; how many weapons would be necessary to annihilate a particular country (our own, for example); and how many would be necessary to destroy our whole species. In search of answers to these questions, we naturally turn to scientists. But when we do we find that they can offer us only a portion of the information that either they or we need in order to make a firm judgment. That this should be so is not the fault of today's scientists, who have made impressive strides in understanding the natural world. Rather, it is due to humanity's still having only a rudimentary over-all comprehension of the living systems whose destruction or mutilation is in question; namely, human societies, ecosystems, and, ultimately, the earth itself—which is to say life itself, insofar as it has been given to human beings to know life. What is known about the earth is awesome—as readers of the September, 1983, issue of *Scientific American,* for example, which takes the workings of the earth as its subject, can appreciate. Yet what remains unknown is more awesome still. What is known seems towering until one looks at how much there remains to find out, and then it seems minuscule.

The crucial role of uncertainty in assessing the consequences of a nuclear holocaust needs some emphasis, because it is often overlooked or misunderstood by people who, for understandable reasons, would like simple and clear factual answers. The scientists can speak with great confidence about the properties of the weapons, which they invented and have observed in tests. But as soon as they begin to speak about the effects of those weapons on the surrounding world uncertainty sets in. For instance, it is known that land-surface nuclear explosions would create large amounts of radioactive fallout. Yet there has never been a true land-surface explosion of a bomb with a yield of more than one kiloton. The farther we get from the simple, immediate effects of the weapons —the initial nuclear radiation, the electromagnetic pulse, the thermal pulse, the blast wave, the local fallout—the more speculative our knowledge becomes. Maximum uncertainty is reached when we get to the question of extinction. Nuclear weapons threaten our species with extinction not because every last person on earth would be blown up or irradiated in a nuclear holocaust (something that could conceivably come close to happening in the targeted nations, though not in all the nations of the earth) but because a holocaust might so drastically alter the ecosphere that the earth would become uninhabitable by human beings.

The story of the advances that have been made in our understanding of the effects of a holocaust implies the unfinished state of our present knowledge of the total effects. That story has been one of continual surprises. The first surprise was the atomic bomb itself, which not ten years before its invention had been declared by many eminent scientists to be an unlikelihood bordering on an impossibility. Even Albert Einstein is reported to have remarked in 1935 that to split the atom would be akin to shooting birds in the dark in a country where there were few birds. Perhaps the next surprise, which came as a result of atmospheric testing, was the huge amount and range of radioactive fallout; its extent was unsuspected until it began falling on Pacific islanders and American servicemen after the American test on Bikini Atoll, in 1954. A further surprise that came during testing was the electromagnetic pulse—a gigantic surge of electricity that is generated by gamma radiation acting on air. The electromagnetic pulse of just one big nuclear bomb, if it is detonated high above the United States, may, it is now believed, damage solid-state electrical circuits throughout the continental United States and in parts of Canada and Mexico. A more recent surprise was the discovery, made in the early 1970s, of a danger to the ozone layer—one that in terms of global damage could be the most serious of the dangers that had been discovered up to that time. A report by the National Academy of Sciences in 1975 on *Long-Term Worldwide Effects of Multiple Nuclear-Weapons Detonations* found that after a holocaust in which ten thousand megatons were detonated ozone reduction might be as high as seventy per cent in the Northern Hemisphere (where all the detonations were assumed to have occurred) and forty per cent in the Southern Hemisphere. The formation of an ozone layer is believed to have been a precondition for the emergence of multicellular life, and of life on land, because ozone blocks out wavelengths of ultraviolet light that are harmful to many forms of life, and while reductions in the ozone of the magnitudes mentioned in the report would not eliminate all organisms with more than one cell or drive life back into the sea they could pervasively harm both plant and animal life, and their ultimate consequences for the earth's varied ecosystems are unforeseeable. Weighing these effects of a nuclear holocaust, scientists gave us

15

warning that extinction was a possibility. For example, in March of 1982, in support of a proposal for joint hearings by the House Foreign Affairs Committee and the Senate Foreign Relations Committee on the effects of a holocaust, a number of scientists made statements on the subject. Marvin Goldberger, the president of the California Institute of Technology, said, "Full-scale war would eliminate humanity to all intents and purposes. Survival itself would be questionable." Paul Marks, the president of the Memorial Sloan-Kettering Cancer Center, said, "Nuclear war would wipe out the [human] race where the war was fought, and it could exterminate the entire race. It would make half the world uninhabitable. I'm not sure of the effect on the other half. It would probably make it uninhabitable, too." Other scientists who were quoted in favor of the proposal placed greater stress on the chances for survival. For example, Lewis Thomas, president emeritus of Sloan-Kettering, said, "Nuclear war would almost surely destroy human society. We would lose all of what we call culture. U.S.–U.S.S.R. conflict would eliminate the Northern Hemisphere for all practical purposes. The Southern Hemisphere might survive. I doubt that all humans would be exterminated." But whether they were pessimistic or optimistic about the chances for human survival the scientists surrounded their opinions with appropriate expressions of doubt, saying that extinction was "possible," or that the Southern Hemisphere "might" survive. Their common ground was uncertainty.

The wisdom of these scientists' reluctance to make final judgments became abundantly clear late last year, when, at a conference in Washington called "The World After Nuclear War," another group of eminent scientists revealed the latest surprise in the unfolding and obviously unfinished story of the effects of a nuclear holocaust. They had concluded that in a holocaust soil and dust from the explosions and smoke from fires set by the explosions would create a dark cloud over the earth which would largely block out sunlight, turning day into twilight or night, and drastically lowering the temperature, to create a "nuclear winter." The way in which this discovery was made is instructive of the unex-

16

pected ways in which science moves forward. One important new element in the discovery was space travel. In 1971, Mariner 9—the first spacecraft to go into orbit around another planet—began to circle Mars. Aboard was an infrared interferometric spectrometer —an instrument that could measure temperatures on the surface of Mars and at various heights in the atmosphere above it. As it happened, Mars was enveloped in a global dust storm when Mariner 9 arrived. The spectrometer showed that the atmosphere of Mars was considerably warmer than it usually was, and the surface considerably cooler: the dust in the atmosphere was absorbing sunlight, thus warming the atmosphere, and was blocking it from reaching the surface, thus cooling the surface. A group of scientists concerned with parallels between the earth and other planets— Richard Turco, an atmospheric physicist in Marina del Rey, California; Owen Toon, Thomas Ackerman, and James Pollack, all from the National Aeronautics and Space Administration's Ames Research Center; and Carl Sagan, the director of the Laboratory for Planetary Studies at Cornell—set about applying these findings to terrestrial questions. Their interest was spurred by a recently advanced hypothesis that the extinction of the dinosaurs at the end of the Cretaceous period, sixty-five million years ago, might have resulted from a drop in light and temperature brought about when an asteroid crashed into the earth, lofting a cover of dust into the terrestrial atmosphere.

Meanwhile, two other scientists—Paul Crutzen, of the Max Planck Institute for Chemistry, in Mainz, Germany, and John Birks, of the University of Colorado—had calculated that smoke generated by the fires that would be started by nuclear explosions would greatly decrease the sunlight reaching the earth. (In fact, the smoke would be more important than the dust in blocking sunlight.) The earth—its cities and its forests in particular—is like a well-laid fire. If you light it with enough nuclear matches, it will burn, and as it burns it will fill the atmosphere with smoke and plunge much of the world into a frigid darkness for several months. These findings, which were published in 1982, and the findings from Mars led Turco and his colleagues to conduct a study

17

that they eventually called *Nuclear Winter: Global Consequences of Multiple Nuclear Explosions.* They concluded that within two weeks after a holocaust in which five thousand megatons were used had occurred in the Northern Hemisphere the cloud of smoke would circle the hemisphere. A deep gloom would have gathered, and land temperatures would be falling. Also, a toxic smog, loaded with hydrogen cyanide and other debris of the burned cities, could cover the hemisphere. A few weeks later, the cloud would penetrate the Southern Hemisphere, and land temperatures there would also begin to fall. After a holocaust in which ten thousand megatons were used (the study estimated this to be about three-quarters of what is available in present strategic arsenals, whose exact megatonnage is unknown), temperatures at the center of continents in the Northern Hemisphere could sink as low as twenty-three degrees below zero Fahrenheit, even in summer. Near coastlines, the temperatures would be more moderate, because of the warming influence of the sea, but violent, monsoon-like storms caused by the difference between inland and ocean temperatures could be expected. After a period lasting from several months to a year, the cloud would have largely dissipated, and sunlight, now unfortunately including the biologically harmful ultraviolet light let in by the ozone loss, would reach the surface again. In the Southern Hemisphere, the drops in temperature and the other effects would be less severe. One of the most surprising findings of the study was that as little as a hundred megatons—less than one per cent of the world's arsenals—could, if it were to be targeted on urban centers, trigger a less severe but still catastrophic nuclear winter, in which temperatures could drop more than fifty degrees Fahrenheit. Thus, there appears to be a threshold—determined by the number of explosions it would take to set a significant number of cities on fire—above which the major features of this climatic catastrophe would occur.

The human and biological consequences of the nuclear winter literally defy representation. Some are gross and obvious. People would freeze. They would find it difficult to see what they were doing. Crops wouldn't grow, so they would starve. Other animals would freeze and starve. If the holocaust occurred during the growing season, then "virtually all land plants in the Northern Hemisphere would be damaged or killed," in the words of Paul Ehrlich, professor of biological sciences at Stanford University, who presented a report to the conference on the biological consequences of the nuclear winter. "In the oceans, the darkness would inhibit photosynthesis in the tiny green plants (algae) that form the base of all significant marine food chains," Ehrlich said. "Tropical forests could largely disappear." The combined consequences of the nuclear winter, coming on top of the other effects, which in themselves could kill or wound billions of people and would shatter the elementary equipment of civilization by which modern man survives, lie far beyond our power of prediction, but they could, in words of Ehrlich's that, in the light of the new discoveries, add urgency to the words of warning we had already had from other scientists, "entrain the extinction of humanity."

The question of whether nuclear weapons might extinguish mankind first came up in the 1940s, in a context slightly different from the present one. As the team of scientists at Los Alamos was preparing for the detonation of the first bomb, it occurred to someone that the heat of the explosion might be so great that it would ignite the earth's atmosphere and burn it up, ending not only human life but all life on earth. Robert Oppenheimer, the director of the project, took the danger seriously enough to ask a group of scientists on the team to figure out whether or not this would happen. The group found not only that the temperature of the bomb would be insufficient to set the atmosphere on fire but that the temperature needed to do that was so high that it could never be reached by any nuclear explosion. Armed with this assurance, the Los Alamos team went ahead and set off the bomb. (In social, if not in scientific, terms, the group's calculation may be described as the most important ever made by scientists.) One wonders whether the team would have done so if the group had come back with a less reassuring answer—if, for example, it had said that there was a one-in-a-hundred chance that the bomb would set the atmosphere on fire. Whatever the team might have

19

done then, now that more than fifty thousand nuclear weapons stand ready to be detonated in the world's arsenals no such assurance regarding the survival of our species in the event of a holocaust is, or can be, forthcoming from responsible scientists. The physicist Theodore Taylor has said, "The consequences of nuclear war are unpredictable. The extinction of the species forever cannot be ruled out by any process of scientific investigation." We will gain more knowledge. (Already, a Russian scientist at the "World After Nuclear War" conference has suggested that the warming of the upper atmosphere by the smoke and soot from a holocaust will melt glaciers and snows in high mountain ranges, creating floods "of continental magnitude.") But our knowledge will never be complete. To accept uncertainty is essential in facing the nuclear peril honestly, and to learn to make judgments, and to act on them, in the midst of uncertainty is the beginning of wisdom in dealing with the nuclear predicament. It is especially important to avoid all false assurances and pseudo certainty. These, unfortunately, are rife, and include not only baseless, dogmatic judgments about the ultimate effects of a holocaust but also a large array of doubtful "strategic" predictions concerning precisely what moves and countermoves might be made in a holocaust.

Once the citizen has gone to the scientists and received the information that they have available, he must, without further professional help, take counsel with himself. The scientists can tell what they know; they can tell what they suspect; and they can guess with the rest of us about how much there may still be to find out. In putting his questions to the scientists, the citizen has already in a way asked them to venture beyond the proper limits of their disciplines, for he has asked them not for the proved results of experimentation but for speculation that is unprovable, unless we blow up the earth in search of answers. Because of the importance of the issue, the scientists oblige us with their best answers while candidly confessing the uncertainty and incompleteness of their findings. It would obviously be a mistake for the citizen to do what the scientists have warned against, and treat educated speculation as hard, scientific fact. The most valuable thing that the citizen carries away from the scientists' report, I suggest, is not any particular estimate—the percentage of ozone reduction, for example, or the level of temperature drop in the nuclear winter—for most of these estimates have been revised many times in the past and may be revised again in the future, and are, in any case, almost certainly an incomplete catalogue of effects. It is, rather, a broad sense of the power of a nuclear holocaust to throw the ecosphere as a whole into catastrophic disorder.

As the citizen takes stock of the perils, at least two considerations that lie outside the range of scientific evidence must come into play. The first is that effects of a nuclear holocaust will not fail to occur merely because they haven't been predicted. It may be that, say, only fifty per cent of them have been discovered, but a hundred per cent of them will occur. Unless—like the advocates of Newtonian physics at the end of the nineteenth century, who thought that with the scientific achievements of their time the edifice of physics had essentially been completed—we have the arrogance to believe that our present knowledge of the earth is perfect, we have no choice but to assume that the list of surprises is not complete. It should help us to preserve modesty in making judgments about the effects of a nuclear holocaust to recall that if we had sought in, say, 1950 to make a final judgment about those effects we would have seriously underestimated or left entirely out of account what are perhaps the three most important global effects that have been discovered so far: the extent of fallout; ozone loss; and the nuclear winter. The second consideration is that from a human point of view our extinction is an unlimited consequence. It would not only put an end to the living genera· tions but foreclose all future generations, down to the end of time. It would mark the defeat of all human strivings, all human hopes, all human ideals, past and future. For now human beings, engaged, as always, in the ambitions and disputes of their particular place and time, can end the human story in all places for all time. The eternal has been placed at stake in the temporal realm, and the infinite has been delivered into the care of finite human beings. It is because of this special nature of the peril, I believe, that the very existence of uncertainty about whether or not a holocaust would extinguish our species should lead us to treat the issue morally and politically *as though* it were a certainty. That is, when we turn to the nuclear predicament we should muster all the commitment that loyalty to our species can inspire. In my book *The Fate of the Earth* (1982), I wrote a passage that emphasizes the importance of uncertainty, and I repeat it here to clarify the reason for treating the uncertainty *as though* it were certainty:

> We know that a holocaust may not occur at all. If one does occur, the adversaries may not use all their weapons. If they do use all their weapons, the global effects, in the ozone and elsewhere, may be moderate. And if the effects are not moderate but extreme, the ecosphere may prove resilient enough to withstand them without breaking down catastrophically. These are all substantial reasons for supposing that mankind will not be extinguished in a nuclear holocaust, or even that extinction in a holocaust is unlikely, and they tend to calm our fear and to reduce our sense of urgency. Yet at the same time we are compelled to admit that there *may* be a holocaust, that the adversaries *may* use all their weapons, that the global effects, including effects of which we are as yet unaware, *may* be severe, that the ecosphere *may* suffer catastrophic breakdown, and that our species *may* be extinguished. We are left with uncertainty.

I concluded, "Once we learn that a holocaust *might* lead to extinction we have no right to gamble, because if we lose, the game will be over, and neither we nor anyone else will ever get another chance. Therefore, although, scientifically speaking, there is all the difference in the world between the mere possibility that a holocaust will bring about extinction and the certainty of it, morally they are the same, and we have no choice but to address the issue of nuclear weapons as though we knew for a certainty that their use would put an end to our species." It is in this spirit that

I continue here to speak of nuclear weapons as an issue of life or death for mankind.

The totality of the peril (in the sense just defined) is, of course, the most important feature of the nuclear predicament. It must inevitably shape and color all our thinking on the subject, including our thinking on what we should do about the predicament. A second, less often mentioned feature, which is of importance to the policy question, is the abruptness with which the peril arrived. Great changes had occurred in the conditions of life before, but they had arrived gradually. The industrial revolution, for example, transformed the way people lived, but it was made up of innumerable technical innovations that were released into the world over centuries, so that people had time to make their adjustments. The industrial revolution would offer a closer analogy if all the inventions made between, say, 1700 and 1945 had somehow arrived at once, in 1700. The nuclear predicament—the result of the invention of a *single* device—sprang into the world full-fledged, offering little time for reflection or adjustment. (There did remain the time required to build up the arsenals—a sort of grace period—but it was very short, and, in any case, has been squandered.) Slavery offers another analogy. It was there at the beginning of history, and it took mankind millennia to finally confront the practice and abolish it. But when nuclear weapons were invented a brand-new evil was suddenly created, as though slavery had been lowered into our midst in an instant. And we did not have the luxury of millennia in which to react. The peril was immediate, and called on us to act right away.

A third feature of the predicament, which is also of importance·to the policy question, is the peril's apparent everlastingness. While nuclear weapons can, I believe, one day be eliminated, the knowledge of how to make them, which is rooted in our century's fundamental discoveries in physics, appears likely to be with us forever, and since that is so the possibility that nuclear arsenals

23

will be rebuilt and used cannot be ruled out. We are not condemned to live always in a world armed with nuclear weapons,
but we shall always live in a nuclear world. In that respect, nuclear
energy is like a new sun that has risen over the earth—a sun that
will beam its bleak light on human affairs as long as the sun in the
sky will. We speak of "the nuclear age," but since, strictly speaking, that "age," like the period "after Christ," has no end in view,
it would be more appropriate to speak, in the Latin phrase, of "a
new order of the ages." But perhaps if we optimistically suppose
that nuclear weapons (though not the knowledge of how to make
them) will one day be abolished we can call the period up to then
"the nuclear age"—and pray that it will be short.

As if it were not enough that the threat posed by the nuclear
peril was unlimited in its scope, instantaneous in its appearance,
and everlasting in its staying power, a fourth key feature of the
predicament is that nuclear weapons immediately lodged themselves at the very heart of international decision-making, and so
carried revolutionary global political implications. Given all the
rest, it might seem that the revolutionary political implications
would hardly need mention, but the fact is that one can imagine
perils on an equal scale physically whose political solution would
be relatively simple. For example, it was discovered some years
ago that certain types of spray cans release gases which, like the
products of nuclear explosions, can rise into the stratosphere,
where they decompose, and that their components erode the
ozone layer. Let us suppose that scientists had discovered (as in
fact they have not) that at present levels of spray-can use the
erosion of the ozone layer would go far enough to doom all land
animals in ten years. We can have little doubt that the nations of
the earth would quickly sign a treaty abolishing spray cans. Or let
us suppose that scientists had discovered (as, again, they have not)
that, beyond a certain threshold, the burning of fossil fuels would
trigger a runaway "greenhouse effect" in the atmosphere, in
which the temperature of the earth would rise to lethal levels.
(Scientists suspect that a runaway greenhouse effect may be responsible for the seven-hundred-degree surface temperature of

24

Venus. They also suspect that a greenhouse effect produced by the burning of fossil fuels will warm the earth by several degrees in the next hundred years.) Once again, it is hard to doubt that, despite the importance of fossil fuels, the nations of the earth would quickly sign a treaty bringing their use under control. For it would surely very soon become clear to people everywhere that they valued humanity more than they valued fossil fuels. Or if we imagine that one day we were attacked by creatures from space whose aim was to destroy mankind and take over the planet, it is again hard to doubt that the nations of the earth would unite to defend their planet. (The Soviet Union and the United States even managed to unite to defeat the earthly peril of Nazi Germany.) Yet when it comes to saving the earth from the peril of a nuclear holocaust the necessary agreements are not arrived at so easily— as the history of the last thirty-nine years attests. And for this failure there is a substantial cause that would not be a factor in any of the foregoing, imagined situations. The solution of each of those threats would require us to give something up—spray cans, fossil fuels, the immediate pursuit of earthly rivalries. But if we ask what it is that we would have to give up in order to resolve the nuclear predicament we find that it is nothing less than the whole present structure of international affairs. For the very first effect of the invention of nuclear weapons—which occurred even without their going off—was to fatally undermine the institution of war.

It may seem odd to speak of war, the nemesis of human institutions, as an institution itself, liable to change and decline like any other, yet we are now in a position to see that it has been just that: a particular kind of organization of human affairs, with a particular character, a particular technical foundation, and particular uses. Its preeminent use has been to serve as what has been called since Roman times "the final arbiter" of disputes among nations—as the world's means of last resort for getting things settled. But when nuclear weapons entered the arsenals of nations war could no longer arbitrate anything, because the levels of force available would destroy every prize that a nation might want either to seize or to defend. Nations bent on achieving some aim by the use of force, whether the aim was their own survival or another country's subjugation, could not hope to succeed in a nuclear-armed world. To be sure, nuclear-armed nations could still attack one another (if they were foolish enough), but at the end of the road only their "mutual assured destruction" now awaited them. This would not be war—once defined as "the continuation of politics by other means"—but only suicide, which is the continuation of nothing.

It's worth noting that the point in the nuclear buildup at which mutual assured destruction became possible (and victory in war impossible) is different from the point at which extinction became possible. Perhaps because both results are absurd, the two are sometimes lumped together. The difference becomes obvious if we imagine that two small countries, each of which can be annihilated with just a few dozen nuclear weapons, are faced off against one another. Each would destroy the other long before the two together could extinguish the species. When the countries are large, however, the gap between mutual assured destruction and extinction is narrower, and the new conclusion that even "limited nuclear war" might trigger the nuclear winter narrows this gap still further. In a general holocaust, the mutual destruction of the belligerents would be only a minor absurdity within the major, unlimited absurdity of the end of humanity. Nevertheless, the potential for mutual assured destruction needs to be underscored, because it is precisely *this* minor absurd outcome—which does not depend on the presence of a peril of extinction—that spoils war as a rational instrument of national policy, and forces nations to look for a substitute. (The possibility of extinction, above and beyond mutual assured destruction, gives their search a transcendent importance.)

To avoid misunderstanding: When I say that war has been spoiled as a means of settling international disputes, I mean that it has been spoiled in those theatres of potential conflict in which the rivals are abundantly armed with nuclear weapons, as the United States and the Soviet Union are. In other theatres, in which one or both powers lack nuclear weapons, nations can and do go on fighting wars. To avoid further misunderstanding: What has been ruined is, precisely, war—no more and no less. Violence between nuclear-armed states is still possible on any scale, from terrorist acts right up to the end of the world, but none of this would, properly speaking, be war. For war is not just violence; it is violence shaped to achieve state ends. But all these ends would be unattainable by "war" as it exists today, for by the time anyone had "won" the "war" both sides would have been annihilated.

In sum, the underlying *human* question that the invention of nuclear weapons confronts us with is whether we will live or die as a species, but the underlying *political* question, which must be tackled before the human question can be favorably resolved, is how disputes among nations are to be handled in a world in which war has been spoiled as an instrument of state policy. Nuclear weapons are radical biologically and spiritually because they threaten our species with extinction, but they are radical politically because they have spoiled war. For traditionally the political character of our world has been determined in large part by the outcome of wars—by whether the Romans or the Carthaginians, Napoleon or Wellington, the Axis or the Allies, were victorious. At stake, therefore, *in addition* to the life or death of mankind, is everything that nations are and everything that they stand for, since it is through war that nations in the past have sought ultimately to protect their existence. How, we are now forced to ask, are we to defend the things that we believe in—or, on a more prosaic level, that we merely want? (For the United States, and for the Western alliance, the chief question of this sort is, perhaps, how we can protect our liberties and, by a reasonable extension, liberty in the world as a whole.) How are nations to respond to aggression? Or should there any longer even *be* nations, which, continuing their historical reliance on the resort to force in pursuit of their parochial interests, now menace the survival of all mankind? At issue is *who* is going to decide international disputes and *how*—and these are, of course, the fundamental issues of politics. Should nations decide through violence, as in the past? Should an international authority decide? Is there another way of deciding? No proposal that fails to give an answer to this underlying question

27

can inspire confidence, and only a proposal that deals with it to the world's satisfaction seems likely to stand a chance of finally resolving the nuclear predicament.

There is a strong temptation to underestimate either the biological or the political dimension of the peril, because then the job of finding a solution is much simplified. For example, if we choose to disregard the radical nature of the political issue, then, responding without impediment to the totality and immediacy of the peril, we are free to imagine that we can "ban" nuclear weapons without further ado—without, that is, having to account for how, politically, a nuclear-free world would work, what would be likely to happen in it, and whether or not it would be likely to stay nuclear-free. On the other hand, if, duly impressed by the intractability of the political challenge, we choose instead to play down the physical immediacy and totality of the peril, we may complacently and unconscionably leave our species at risk of annihilation. Such, I believe, is our present condition.

The difficulty of taking all the features of the nuclear predicament into account was made clear in the first attempts to discover solutions. Sheer thought, of course, was able to see its way to a solution quite easily. The steps in the reasoning were simple ones. If war now meant nuclear war—and no one could doubt that it did—and nuclear war meant, at best, the mutual assured destruction of the belligerents and, at worst, human extinction, then war no longer made any sense and would have to be given up. But if war was given up, then some other means would have to be found to resolve the disputes that war had always resolved. A means was not hard to find—at least, on the purely intellectual plane. It was government—world government. The rule of law would supplant the rule of force, and what had once been decided by violence would now be decided by courts, parliaments, and all the other institutions of civil society. In the early days of the nuclear age, many people, including, notably, many scientists, were swayed by this compelling logic, and soon set to work to bring a world government into existence. Preeminent among them, perhaps, was Albert Einstein, who, at the beginning of the century, had first revealed that energy and matter are the same. As early as September 29, 1945—less than two months after the bomb was dropped on Hiroshima, on August 6—he wrote:

> The pathetic attempts made by governments to achieve what they consider to be international security have not the slightest effect on the present political structure of the world, nor is it recognized that the real cause of international conflicts is due to the existence of competing sovereign nations. Neither governments nor people seem to have learned anything from the experiences of the past and appear to be unable or unwilling to think the problem through. The conditions existing in the world today force the individual states, out of fear for their own security, to commit acts which inevitably produce war.
>
> At the present high level of industrialization and economic interdependence, it is unthinkable that we can achieve peace without a genuine supranational organization to govern international relations.

At about the same time, Einstein was one of the signatories of a letter, published in the *New York Times,* that said, in part:

> We have learned, and paid an awful price to learn, that living and working together can be done in one way only—under law. There is no truer and simpler idea in the world today. Unless it prevails, and unless by common struggle we are capable of new ways of thinking, mankind is doomed.

And in June of 1946 he told an interviewer:

> Our defense is not in armaments, nor in science, nor in going underground. Our defense is in law and order.

Einstein knew very well that the political climate of his time was hostile to his proposal, and he knew that many people regarded it as, in his words, "illusory, even absurd." Nevertheless, in a reply to critics, he asked:

> Is it really a sign of unpardonable naiveté to suggest that those in power decide among themselves that future conflicts must be settled by constitutional means rather than by the senseless sacrifice of great numbers of human lives? Once such a firm decision has been reached, nothing will be "impossible." . . .
>
> A "sophisticated" person might well comment: We have been working toward the same goal by means of small, patient steps, which, in view of human psychology, is the only possible method. But I, the so-called "idealist," regard this attitude as a fatal illusion. There is no *gradual* way to secure peace. As long as nations have no real security against aggression, they will, inevitably, continue to prepare for war. And, as history has proven conclusively, preparation for war always leads to actual war. When the North American Colonies united and created a central government in Washington, it came about not through a slow process but through a resolute and creative act.

In interviews, articles, letters, and public statements, Einstein, continuing to state his case with his customary clarity, modesty, simplicity, and passion, advocated this position until the end of his life, in April, 1955.

Einstein's view that the nuclear predicament could be resolved and mankind saved only if the world renounced force and adopted peaceful political means for the settlement of its disputes possessed a straightforward logic that no one ever refuted and that was apparently irrefutable. (His view that the only such means possible was world government was more debatable.) But what logic called for and what the world was prepared to accept were two different things. Einstein set out to change minds. He knew, as few other men did, what the measure of the peril was, and he worked tirelessly to impart that knowledge to others. As a scientist, he was used to thinking a problem through to its end, and he thought the political implications of the nuclear predicament through to their end, too. He placed his faith in reason—in people's ability to learn, and to act on what they have learned. He had changed the world through scientific thought, and now he wanted to change it further through political thought. In that sense, world government was a scientists' *sort* of idea. Using reason, scientists analyzed the problem, came up with a formula that would solve it, and then invited the world to apply that formula. Einstein wrote, "Just as we have changed our thinking in the world of pure science to embrace newer and more useful concepts, so we must now change our thinking in the world of politics and law. It is too late to make mistakes." And, even more simply, "Past thinking and methods did not succeed in preventing world wars. Future thinking *must* prevent wars." But politics was different from science, and thinking turned out not to have the effectiveness in world affairs that it had had in the laboratory. In politics, the process was different and the tempo was different. Political ideas moved at a slower pace than scientific ones from one mind to the minds of many, and from the minds of many into action.

Certainly one cause of the world's apparent indifference to the nuclear peril, and of the short shrift it gave the idea of world government, was the peril's all-or-nothing character, which removed it from people's direct experience. Most evils arrive in the world a little bit at a time, so that in pushing people into action the bite of painful experience is added to the voice of pure reason. If a factory is polluting the water supply, for example, deadly poison doesn't suddenly start running from the tap; the pollution appears gradually, and people are driven to do something before a catastrophe occurs. But after Hiroshima and Nagasaki the nuclear peril turned out to leave the world physically untouched, and the field was left to "thinking" alone. There can be little doubt that if in the last thirty-nine years one Hiroshima-sized nuclear weapon had gone off each day in a city somewhere in the world (thus releasing, in all, only about one per cent of the explosive power of today's arsenals) Einstein's proposal, or something of an equally radical nature, would have found acceptance by now. As it was, the nuclear weapons fortunately stayed unexploded (while unfortunately multiplying in the world's arsenals), and people were not impelled to think or do very much about them.

The stronger reasons for the rejection of the sweeping changes that Einstein wanted, however, were unquestionably political. Arrayed against his argument was not so much counterargument as brute fact—everything that comes under the heading of political "reality," which in the short run, at least, has a weight and an inertia that are independent of argument and the light of reason. On the immediate level, reality was two great powers— the United States and the Soviet Union—whose systems of government were wholly antithetical. While it was quite conceivable that these two powers could live together without war—that is, "coexist"—there seemed little or no possibility that they could fuse into a single government. Reality was, in addition, the countless unresolved struggles that went on, and go on, among the less powerful nations of the world, dividing Arab from Jew, Irishman from Englishman, Turk from Greek, and so on. On the deepest level, however, reality was the entire political organization of the world. Standing in the way of Einstein's "thinking," that is, was nothing less than the world's political institutions as they had existed throughout history—the entire system of independent states, whose defense now threatened extinction. The invention of nuclear weapons brought basic physical and biological reality, now radically transformed by the revolution in scientific thought, into head-on collision with basic political reality, where no similar revolution appeared likely soon. And the collision was not just a clash of styles, or a failure of scientists and politicians to speak one another's language; it was objective and real. Science had moved with the speed of thought to alter physical reality and to give technical man the ability to place the whole world in peril of annihilation, but the political thinkers were powerless to perform a comparable miracle in political affairs. Political affairs, weighted with tradition and habit—in this case, a way of doing things which had lasted throughout history—moved with a ponderous gait of their own, and were not to be hurried. The nuclear predicament had emerged in an instant from the laboratory, but the resolution of the predicament could not emerge from any laboratory. It would have to be born in its own time, in the hearts of the billions of the earth's people.

The disparity between the swiftness of science in presenting the peril (a swiftness much accentuated, from the world's point of view, by the governmental secrecy out of which the bomb sprang) and the seemingly built-in slowness of the world's thinking and the world's institutions to adjust to it presented the world, in effect, with a monumental problem of timing. While the predicament might not be inherently beyond resolution, the mismatch between the immediacy of the peril and the magnitude of the psychological, spiritual, and political work required for mankind to make an adequate response—which might conceivably take generations—could in itself prove fatal. The proposal for world government therefore engendered as much discouragement as hope. Many people believed that a solution might lie there, but they could not see how to arrive at it soon enough to respond to the pressing emergency in which the species found itself. Nor did sovereignty show any signs of expiring on its own. If anything, it was tightening its hold—especially in the Third World, where patriotic feeling was showing itself to be an almost irresistible force, against which the great colonial empires of the West were proving powerless.

In those circumstances, it was anything but surprising that a second school of thought about how to handle the nuclear predicament soon emerged—a school that was ready to accept the unwillingness of nations to surrender their sovereignty and enter into a world government. In 1946, in a book called *The Absolute Weapon*, by a group of academics at the Yale Institute of International Studies, there appeared two chapters written by the politi-

33

cal scientist Bernard Brodie, which have come to be considered a founding document of American nuclear strategy, and which we may take as representative of the second school of thought. Brodie begins by accepting as given the continuation of the sovereign state—the very thing whose abolition Einstein saw as the only hope for survival in the nuclear world. As befits someone stating a premise, Brodie does not so much argue the point as simply assert it, saying, with light irony, that "the wholesale conversion of mankind away from those parochial attitudes bound up in nationalism is a consummation devoutly to be wished" but "the mere existence of the bomb does not promise to accomplish it at an early enough time to be of any use." If the existence of the nation-state is a given, then the possibility of the use of force becomes another given, because it is through the use of force that nations have ultimately sought to assure their survival. And if the possibility of the use of force is a given, then the existence of nuclear weapons becomes still another given, because nuclear weapons are the most powerful instruments of force available. Thus, while it may be true that, as Einstein said, if you want to rid the world of nuclear weapons you will have to establish a world government, neither of these things, in Brodie's view, can be accomplished, and the truly important and interesting question, therefore, is what policy to adopt in a world in which both sovereign states and nuclear weapons are present. Significantly, Brodie does not see this task as an end in itself; rather, he sees it as a way of buying time while more radical solutions, of the Einsteinian variety, are worked on. He wants merely to "transmute what appears to be an immediate crisis into a long-term problem," so as to give society the opportunity it needs to adjust its politics to its physics. His answer to the problem of mismatched timing is to work within the realm of the politically "possible" for the present, and postpone more ambitious efforts. It is noteworthy, though, that while he and the other authors of *The Absolute Weapon* acknowledge the need to find radical solutions sometime in the future they have no suggestions to offer about how to proceed with this work. The "short term" occupies them completely.

It is in framing policy for a world in which nuclear weapons are a given that Brodie shows his prescience and his originality. He begins with an unsparing description of the destructive power of the atomic bomb—a description that Einstein, for one, would surely have approved of. He points out that to destroy any city in the world, from one to ten atomic, or fission, bombs will suffice (the hydrogen, or fusion, bomb, which can be thousands of times as powerful as the fission bomb, and so can do the job much more efficiently, had, of course, not yet been invented); that no defense against the bomb is possible; and that therefore "it is now physically possible for air forces no greater than those existing in the recent war to wipe out all the cities of a great nation in a single day." He then notes that some "scientists and laymen" who have a "passionate" preoccupation with "proposals for 'world government' " have concluded from these admittedly terrifying facts that "the safeguards to security formerly provided by military might are no longer of any use," and that the bomb must therefore be regarded as "the apotheosis of aggressive instruments." And he quotes J. Robert Oppenheimer as saying that the bomb "is a weapon for aggressors, and the elements of surprise and of terror are as intrinsic to it as are the fissionable nuclei." Brodie disagrees. In a key paragraph, he says, "The truth of Professor Oppenheimer's statement depends on one vital but unexpressed assumption: that the nation which proposes to launch the attack will not need to fear retaliation. If it must fear retaliation, the fact that it destroys its opponent's cities some hours or even days before its own are destroyed may avail it little." The would-be aggressor, who knew that he faced retaliation, Brodie thinks, would very likely give up its aggression. "Multilateral possession of the bomb," therefore, will discourage, not encourage, aggression, provided that it is "as nearly certain as possible that the aggressor who uses the bomb will have it used against him."

Here, in a nutshell, and without the jargon and intellectual adornment of the "strategic theory" that unfolded luxuriantly in later years, is the doctrine of nuclear deterrence—although Brodie did not use that word. From Brodie's observations flowed the basic tenets of the doctrine of deterrence: that nuclear weapons offer nations effectively unlimited force; that winning a nuclear war is impossible; that it is imperative, therefore, to stop such a war from ever beginning; that the weapons themselves play the crucial role in that effort; that an invulnerable retaliatory force is of particular importance; that there is a special danger inherent in any capacity, on either side, for destroying the nuclear forces of the other side in a first strike; and that "perceptions" and "psychology" play an essential role in convincing the adversary that any aggression by him will lead only to his annihilation, and so in maintaining the "stability" of the whole arrangement. Summing up in a way that must have been jarring to military sensibilities at that time, Brodie wrote, "The writer . . . is not for the moment concerned about who will *win* the next war in which atomic bombs are used. Thus far the chief purpose of our military establishment has been to win wars. From now on its chief purpose must be to avert them. It can have almost no other useful purpose." The policy of deterrence did not, of course, remove the peril of nuclear annihilation. On the contrary, it deliberately and firmly increased it (by sanctioning a buildup of nuclear arms), in the hope that the immediacy of the threat, felt by each side in the face of the other side's nuclear arsenals, would produce a stalemate in which the world would live on the very edge of the abyss but for precisely that reason would take special care not to lose its balance. The great advantage of deterrence was not the high degree of safety that it offered—for under it a single miscalculation could tip the world into the abyss—but its immediate practicability. For while it was doubtful in the extreme that the world would soon put together a world government, there was little doubt that in the absence of such a step the world's great powers could and would build large nuclear arsenals and threaten one another with them. To be sure, once the Soviet Union had acquired nuclear weapons, and the nuclear stalemate had been established, no one in either Washington or Moscow needed any political scientists to tell him that a nuclear attack might be met with retaliation in kind, and was, for that reason, among others, a bad idea. But it was

the distinction of Brodie and his fellow-strategists to foresee this
in 1946, when only one power possessed the bomb. His discovery
was that a balance of nuclear forces might make possible a world
more stable than any before it in our century. While he agreed
with the advocates of world government that the bomb could not
be defended against, he saw, as many of them did not, that the
threat of retaliation could play the role that defenses had played
in the past, and that in this threat there might lie a measure of
safety for a nuclear-armed world.

The argument between the Einsteinian school and the Brodiean
school reflected not just a split in opinion but a split in the world
itself. For the arrival of nuclear weapons in the world had at a
stroke opened a fissure down the center of human life, placing
whole realms of human existence at odds with one another. The
traditional demands of man's international political existence,
rooted in sovereignty and pursued through the use of force, were
suddenly at variance with the demands of man's existence pure
and simple, which was now mortally endangered. Political man
held a knife to the throat of biological man, but since politics, like
every other human activity, is possible only where there are
human beings, political man also held a knife to his own throat. At
the same time, the demands of man's moral existence, which were
meaningless if they did not call on us to hold back at all costs from
slaughtering billions of people and perhaps putting our species to
death, were at variance with those of man's political existence,
which seemed to require that we threaten to do just that, on pain
of military defeat by our enemies if we did not. Einstein and
Brodie, in a manner of speaking, took up positions on opposite
sides of the gap, with Einstein standing alongside trembling, imperilled biological man and asking political man to yield, and Brodie standing alongside dug-in, unbudgeable political man and asking biological man to endure the peril. And each, of course, had
a compelling reason for standing where he did, since no one could
deny, on the one hand, that the peril was great—indeed, unlim-

ited—and its urgency extreme or, on the other, that the immediate top-to-bottom transformation of international political life was, at the very least, doubtful. A bystander looking for guidance was left to contemplate two conclusions, each of which had apparently been established incontrovertibly by experts: (1) that the nature of physical reality as it had now been revealed by physics made a swift revolution in global politics necessary if human survival was to be assured, and (2) that the nature of political reality as it had revealed itself throughout history made such a revolution impossible.

People of Einstein's persuasion came to be called "idealists," as he had noted, while those of Brodie's persuasion came to be called "realists," but in fact both camps were characterized by a spirit of realism. This was not a debate in which there was reality on one side and a mistaken idea on the other. Rather, there were two opposed realities: the reality of the peril of extinction by nuclear arms, and the reality of the existing political institutions of the world. The two schools of thought therefore did not so much clash irreconcilably as fail even to join the argument; it was as though each were addressing a different "nuclear predicament" —and, in a way, each was. Einstein took as his point of departure his knowledge of the laws of physics and of the peril they defined; he went on to ask what had to be done to remove the peril, and concluded that the whole political realm had to be revolutionized. Since not only politics but everything human was in danger of "being disintegrated someday into atoms and swept up into the atmosphere," as he put it, revolution in just one department of life seemed to him a small price to pay. Brodie, by contrast, took as his point of departure his knowledge of the laws of politics and of the existing political world, and concluded that for the immediate future the peril would have to be lived with. Rarely in a great debate had each side had so many seemingly incontestable points to make. Could anyone seriously doubt that, as a supporter of Einstein's views said, quoting Alexander Hamilton, "to look for a continuation of harmony between a number of independent, unconnected sovereignties situated in the same neighborhood would be to disregard the uniform course of human events, and to set at defiance the accumulated experience of ages"? On the other hand, could anyone argue with William T. R. Fox, one of the authors of *The Absolute Weapon,* when, in the final chapter of that book, he observed, "It would be very dangerous to create a machine of central force before one created a machinery of central justice. For a machinery of central justice to work satisfactorily, its judgments would have to be based upon a worldwide community of values. That community of values does not exist today"? Wasn't it a fact that, as Einstein said, "today the atomic bomb has altered profoundly the nature of the world as we know it, and the human race consequently finds itself in a new habitat to which it must adapt its thinking"? But wasn't it also a fact that, as Fox noted, a Soviet commentator had just called the idea of world government a smoke screen for "renunciation of the basis of the struggle against fascist aggression"; and that the United States was also "unwilling to surrender a degree of control over its own destinies sufficient to permit a world authority to enforce its declared policy against any challenger"?

Einstein and Brodie, each rooted firmly in the reality he knew best, were unable to find common ground. Einstein, the proponent of what was necessary for survival, could not persuade the world that it was politically possible. Brodie, the definer of what was politically possible, could not enlarge his conception of it to encompass what was necessary for survival. The world was offered two problematic proposals: one that would solve the problem but could not be brought into being, and one that could be brought into being but did not solve the problem. The gap between them—between imperilled biological man and entrenched political man; between the irresistible force of nuclear weapons and the immovable object of the world's political institutions (immovable, that is, except by nuclear weapons, which could move them right out of existence in an instant); between a resolution of the broad human crisis of the peril of extinction and a resolution of the political crisis of how the world was to be organized without war; between the laws of science and the laws of history; between the dictates of conscience and the dictates of policy; between "idealism" and "realism"; between the "long term" and the "short term"; between the necessary and the possible; between the slowness of political change and the swiftness of the approach of doom—remained unbridged. And it has remained so to the present day.

Whoever may have had the better of the debate between the two schools, it was, of course, the deterrence doctrine that eventually became official policy. People couldn't, or wouldn't, or just did not, establish world government, and they turned to the only prominent alternative. Before that happened, however, the United States launched an initiative at the United Nations to prevent a nuclear-arms race and abolish nuclear weapons. The initiative failed, but in failing it threw a spotlight on the mountainous political obstacles to a solution of the nuclear problem. The initiative originated, in January of 1946, with the appointment by Secretary of State James Byrnes of a committee headed by Under-Secretary of State Dean Acheson whose work would be to frame a proposal for nuclear disarmament which the United States would make at a forthcoming meeting of the Atomic Energy Commission of the United Nations. Acheson proceeded to appoint a board of consultants, under the chairmanship of David E. Lilienthal, who was then the director of the Tennessee Valley Authority, and including Robert Oppenheimer. On March 17, after intense labors, the committee and the board of consultants concluded their deliberations and embodied them in a document commonly known as the Acheson–Lilienthal report, which was transmitted to Byrnes the following day. At the heart of the committee's recommendations was a proposal that nuclear activities be placed under international control. The report had arrived at an ingenious solution (which may yet prove useful to the world one day) to the thorny problem arising from the need for inspection under any agreement by nations to forgo the production and possession of nuclear arms. Impressed by the political difficulties that would face teams charged with inspecting a large number of independent, national nuclear facilities, the report recommended that all "dangerous" nuclear activities—from uranium mining to the construction of nuclear reactors—be placed under the direct ownership of an international authority associated with the United Nations. (Individual nations would be licensed by the authority to carry out certain "safe" nuclear activities.) This authority, they reasoned, could readily inspect that which it was doing itself.

On March 18, President Truman announced the appointment of Bernard Baruch, a financier who served as an adviser to several Presidents, to represent the United States at the disarmament talks at the United Nations, and Baruch was given the Acheson–Lilienthal report. Much to the dismay of the report's authors, Baruch turned out to have many reservations about it, including its assumption that major violations of the proposed system of international controls would ultimately come before the United Nations Security Council, whose decisions could be nullified by a veto by any one of five nations: the United States, the Soviet Union, England, France, and China. It was the Soviet veto that worried Baruch. He recommended that the veto power in the Security Council be abolished for decisions having to do with atomic energy. And, in a second major departure from the report, he recommended that penalties be established for violations of the agreement concerning atomic energy. (The report had not proposed any penalties.) Without these, he said, the proposal as a whole would amount to nothing more than a warning system, which would put the world on notice if nuclear arming began but would be unable to do anything about it. In short, he had noted the lack in the report of any means for dealing with the underlying political question of how disputes among nations—in this case, disputes concerning the life-and-death matter of atomic energy— were to be decided, and his recommendations were designed to repair the omission: the Security Council would decide. What he recommended was not world government, but it contained something like the essence of world government: an authority with the power to make and enforce decisions concerning the most critical element of military power. President Truman agreed with Baruch and adopted his recommendations.

In June, Baruch presented the proposal to the United Nations, and it was immediately turned down by Andrei Gromyko, the Soviet representative at the arms negotiations. The Soviet Union had substantial reasons for turning it down. The United Nations, which did not yet include most of the hundred-odd nations that make up what we now call the Third World, could be counted on in those days to vote in favor of Western proposals, and the Soviet Union's veto in the Security Council was its only means of undoing the results. To accept an international authority that controlled mining rights in the Soviet Union and held a monopoly on nuclear energy could thus mean accepting not only a large measure of American control over Soviet nuclear energy but also American intervention in Soviet life—an idea as repugnant to the Soviet Union as the converse would have been to the United States if the Soviet Union had enjoyed majority support at the United Nations. Besides, the Soviet Union was at the time well on its way to getting the bomb. (It succeeded in 1949.) However, the Soviet Union went far beyond rejecting the repeal of the veto. It also denounced inspection, as a breach of national sovereignty. Gromyko stated, "When the Charter of the United Nations was prepared by the conference at San Francisco, the question of sovereignty was one of the most important questions considered. This principle of sovereignty is one of the cornerstones on which the United Nations structure is built; if this were touched the whole existence and future of the United Nations would be threatened." But Gromyko did not go on to suggest ways in which the Baruch plan could be made acceptable. Instead, he made a proposal that seemed almost designed to be unacceptable to the United States—as we may suspect that it was, given the Soviet Union's strong interest in developing the bomb for itself, and its imminent ability to do so. Gromyko called for an international convention to ban the production of nuclear weapons, which was to be followed some time later by the establishment of two committees at the United Nations—one for an exchange of scientific information, and the other to fashion safeguards for the abolition agreement. In short, the United States was *first* to give up its atomic monopoly, and *then* the Soviet Union would consent to *discuss* inspection and international control. The predictable United States rejection came quickly.

The amendment of the Acheson–Lilienthal report by Baruch, and then the rejection of the Baruch proposal by the Soviet Union —accompanied by a wholly unacceptable proposal of its own— illustrated the likely fate of any plan, however brilliant, that did not take into account the political questions at the outset. Once again—this time in action rather than in theory—the world had reached the impasse that seemed to block any radical or full solution of the nuclear predicament. The Acheson–Lilienthal committee had repaired to the relatively uncontroversial ground of technology, and offered a technical solution to the problem. But the problem could not in fact be divorced from the political issue, which meant at bottom how the world was going to be making its decisions in the international arena from then on, and the two governments, whose very business was politics, had no choice but to put politics back into the negotiations. When they did that, however, the proposal foundered, because there was no willingness on either side to make the radical political concessions that alone could have put the two sides on negotiable ground. It was as though in the course of the negotiations they had recognized the validity of Einstein's conviction that the predicament could be resolved only if a global authority with real power was established. But the plain truth, as William T. R. Fox had noted in *The Absolute Weapon,* was that neither side wanted a real international authority—not presiding over nuclear matters, and not presiding over any other matters, either—whose actions it could neither control nor derail. (When the United States lost its majority support at the United Nations, it quickly lost its enthusiasm for the idea that any binding decisions should be made by that body.) Both sides preferred a nuclear-arms race, with the United States hoping to use

43

its technical superiority to increase its lead, and the Soviet Union hoping to catch up. (As was virtually inevitable, the latter is what eventually happened.)

The arms race began. Other proposals for full nuclear disarmament were made, but they never occupied the center of the political stage. Much of what Brodie and other advocates of deterrence had foreseen for a nuclear-armed world came to pass. In the succeeding decades, no war, conventional or nuclear—much less a third world war—broke out between the great nuclear powers. Whether war was avoided because of the balance of terror or for some other reason we cannot know (a negative is impossible to prove), but it is only common sense to suppose that the fear of nuclear destruction, while it was not the only factor involved, contributed heavily to the resolve of the great powers to remain at peace. However, another of Brodie's hopes went unfulfilled— his hope that deterrence would serve as a stopgap to buy time in which the world could find its way to the long-term political solution he saw as ultimately necessary. For many years, deterrence continued to be explained as a time-buying measure. As late as 1960, for example, Herman Kahn, a prominent theorist of nuclear strategy, was arguing for a policy of deterrence by saying, "We must take seriously the problem of reaching 1975." The possibility of a long-term solution still seemed real to him, and in 1962 he wrote:

> We probably must accept the notion that the world as we know it is passing from the stage of history, and that attempts to preserve this five-hundred-year-old nation-state system would probably be as futile as the earlier attempts of some of the small German or Italian states to stave off the unification of their countries. If we wish to influence these coming changes, we simply must learn much more about existing and potential international orders—and learn fast.

But none of the sweeping changes occurred, or even began to occur—not after 1946, not after 1960, and not after the world had made it to 1975. The short term had a way of stretching on indefinitely and the long term a way of receding into the future. Deterrence had been presented as a sort of trailer that mankind would live in while the permanent home of a full political resolution of the nuclear predicament was being constructed. But what happened as the years passed was that the trailer was built up and elaborated, while the home went unstarted.

The failure of the long term ever to arrive was no small defect in the justification for the doctrine of deterrence, inasmuch as it had been in considerable measure by presenting deterrence as a short-term, time-buying device that its advocates had answered objections to the doctrine's glaring shortcomings: that it held mankind perpetually dangling over the nuclear abyss, suspended on the slender thread of whatever wisdom the statesmen, all of them fallible, and many of them extremely so, might happen to possess at a given instant; that by defining safety in terms of possessing nuclear arsenals it not only permitted but actually encouraged their proliferation; that it kept us all in the intolerable position of standing ready to slaughter billions of our fellow human beings; and, in general, that it required us all to rely for our safety on the criminal and absurd "threat" to blow our species off the face of the earth forever. What the world actually experienced was not the hoped-for slow progress toward a full solution but steady retrogression, in the form of the arms race and the proliferation of nuclear weapons, which were developed by more and more countries. Sometimes our performance in the postwar period is called a great success, on the ground that we have so far avoided a nuclear holocaust, and much of the credit for the success is given to the policy of deterrence. What this reckoning overlooks is that in that same period the world has built up arsenals of more than fifty thousand nuclear warheads—in short, that behind the screen of our deterrence policy we have built the means of our annihilation. Seen in the best possible light, this self-endangerment of our species was a tragic necessity. Seen less forgivingly—and, I be-

lieve, more justly—it was the greatest collective failure of responsibility by any generation in history. But, whichever of these it
was, self-congratulation is certainly out of order. If someone climbs
out on the ledge of a high building and threatens to jump off, we
do not stand around congratulating him on his wisdom and restraint in not having jumped yet, and expounding on how safe a
place the ledge of a building must be; we seek to pull him in at
the earliest possible opportunity.

Part of the nuclear buildup was sanctioned—in fact, required
—by the doctrine of deterrence, which founded the world's safety
not on Einstein's "law and order" but on terror. To that extent,
deterrence must share in the blame for our suicidal preparations.
But the nuclear buildup—apparently fuelled by a tremendous
internal momentum—went far, far beyond what was required
under that doctrine. Strictly speaking, the deterrence doctrine
should have set a limit on the number of bombs required by a
nation. It would have been the number needed to guarantee the
destruction of the adversary's society in a retaliatory strike. Brodie
wrote in 1946, "It appears that for any conflict a specific number
of bombs will be useful to the side using it, and anything beyond
that will be a luxury. . . . We can say that if two thousand bombs
in the hands of either party is enough to destroy entirely the
economy of the other, the fact that one side has six thousand and
the other two thousand will be of relatively small significance."
This is another idea of Brodie's that went unnoticed. Instead of
stopping the arms race when several thousand Hiroshima-sized
weapons had been stockpiled on each side, the superpowers invented the hydrogen bomb and went on to build tens of thousands
of those, giving each side the preposterously redundant capacity
for raining down hundreds of thousands of Hiroshimas on the
adversary. Deterrence theory, it seemed, was competent to start
an arms race but not to stop one.

There was a retrogression in thinking as well. While the nuclear arsenals grew to tower up to the sky around us, people
seemed to forget that anyone had ever hoped for any other kind
of world. People got accustomed to life in the trailer and forgot

about the permanent home they were supposed to have had. Intellectual horizons narrowed and hopes dimmed. The vision of a world without nuclear weapons all but died. People's eyes became adjusted to the nuclear darkness, in a sort of moral equivalent of the nuclear winter. The time that Brodie had hoped to win was won, but it had not been used to achieve the ends he had had in mind. Instead, the champions of deterrence lost their former modesty and began to advance their makeshift as a permanent solution. The journalist Thomas Powers has spoken in the past few years to many of the military men who are responsible for carrying out the nuclear policies of the United States, and he has made a special point of asking them how they view the future. In his recent book *Thinking About the Next War,* he reports that he found two convictions to be nearly universal: first, that even with the arsenals in place—in fact, *because* the arsenals are in place— nuclear weapons will *never* be used and, second, that the military men "*know* we shall never get rid of nuclear weapons": that their abolition not only is "not on the horizon" but is not even "*over* the horizon." That is also the view of the Harvard authors of *Living with Nuclear Weapons,* who ask, "Why not abolish nuclear weapons? Why not cleanse this small planet of these deadly poisons?" They answer categorically, "Because we cannot," and go on to explain that the discovery of nuclear weapons "lies behind us" and "cannot be undone." In this prognosis, the hope of abolishing nuclear weapons has been extinguished, and the short-term stopgap of deterrence has completely usurped the place of full nuclear disarmament, which is frankly ruled out.

The doctrine of deterrence reigned supreme in official circles in the United States for the better part of the postwar period, during which the public, for its part, showed only sporadic interest in nuclear matters—being only too willing, it seemed, to hand the whole sickening business over to the specialists. Then, toward the end of the 1970s, this wide consensus—consisting, on the one hand, of widespread doctrinal agreement among government officials and, on the other, of public acceptance of their stewardship—was unexpectedly shattered by two upheavals: one in public opinion, in the form of the new peace movement, and the other in government policy, in the form of a subtle but profound and many-sided crisis in the doctrine of deterrence itself, which is now in a state of confusion amounting almost to disintegration. And this confusion, in turn, forced the world to face once again the elemental questions that Brodie and Einstein, among many others, had confronted, but not resolved, in the first days of the nuclear age. Even as the doctrine's theorists were elevating it to the position of dogmatic truth, support for it was beginning to erode. As so often seems to happen in the history of both men and ideas, the moment of apotheosis was the signal for decline. The crisis in the doctrine emerged into full public view under the Reagan Administration, but cracks had been appearing in it for at least half a decade before that. As the balance prescribed by deterrence was attained (with lots of overkill thrown in for good measure), contradictions that had always underlain the doctrine but had gone largely unremarked on before began to emerge into prominence. These contradictions all had to do, in one way or another, with the central, unresolvable contradiction of "defending" one's country by threatening to use weapons whose actual use would bring on the annihilation of one's country and possibly of the world as well. And the emergence of the contradictions was in turn propelled, I believe, by a recognition—this time on the part of nuclear strategists rather than citizens at large—of what a doomsday machine really is, and what it means to intend, in certain circumstances, to use one. This gigantic new reality, which has quietly grown up behind our backs in the decades since the weapons were invented, is, I suggest, the underlying cause of both the crisis in public confidence and the crisis in policy, and so in that sense they are part of a single, deeper crisis. Both, in their different ways, are responses to the fantastic, horrifying, brutal, and absurd fact that we human beings have actually gone ahead and wired our planet for its and our destruction. Whereas for the public, which was not much interested in the subtleties of doctrine, the crisis appeared in the stark form of the over-all senselessness and horror of the species' highly advanced preparations to commit suicide, for the strategists it took the form of a thousand inconsistencies, anomalies, and logical faults that kept cropping up irrepressibly in the details of nuclear policies and in their justifications. Yet when these various internal faults are looked at closely they turn out to be symptoms of the larger absurdity that is upsetting the public.

According to strict deterrence theory, the attainment of parity over the years should have had a stabilizing effect, for only then did the deterrence system become fully operational. The world should have breathed easier. Superiority on either side, theory decreed, lessens the security of both, because it creates an incentive on the stronger side to strike first, which, in turn, creates an incentive on the weaker side to avoid that first strike by itself striking first, and so on. When the strategists actually found themselves looking at parity, however, they discovered that it made them nervous. For one thing, parity put in question several American policies of long standing, perhaps the most important being the policy for the defense of Europe, where, in the opinion of many experts, the Soviet Union enjoyed superiority in conventional forces. In the event of a Soviet conventional attack in Europe, the American plan was—and still is—to make up for NATO's possible conventional inferiority by resorting to nuclear weapons early in the hostilities. (The American reliance on nuclear weapons to defend Europe goes back to the first years of the postwar period, when the United States had a monopoly on nuclear weapons and, in response to strong public demand, had partly demobilized the conventional forces that had been fighting in the Second World War.) As long as the United States possessed clear nuclear superiority, it could be argued that this plan had a certain plausibility—or "credibility," to use the favored term— because it was at least possible to imagine that if the Soviet Union was faced with a nuclear attack in Europe it would refrain from responding in kind, for fear of coming off worse in a general holocaust. But when the Soviet Union reached nuclear parity with the United States this thinking no longer obtained. Then there

49

remained no basis (in deterrence theory, at any rate) for believing that the Soviet Union would hold back from nuclear retaliation if the United States had used nuclear weapons first. And if after that Soviet retaliation the United States attacked again, at a higher level of force, there was no reason to suppose that the Soviet Union would not retaliate in kind again, and so on up the line, until both sides' arsenals were depleted and both sides were annihilated. While one supposed virtue of nuclear superiority was that with it you could get an advantage in a war, it also had another theoretical virtue, which was that it might supply a stopping point in any hostilities that got going—the point at which the weaker side, foreseeing the unfavorable consequences to itself of continuing, gave up. But when the forces became equal that point would never be arrived at and the escalation would climb smoothly to oblivion. In the succinct (if ungrammatical) words of Henry Kissinger in an address in Brussels in 1979, which were quoted recently by former Secretary of Defense Robert McNamara in an article on NATO's nuclear policy, and on the role of nuclear weapons in general, in *Foreign Affairs*, "the European allies should not keep asking us to multiply strategic assurances that we cannot possibly mean, or if we do mean, we should not want to execute because if we execute, we risk the destruction of civilization." And, in Mr. McNamara's own words in the article, "if deterrence fails and conflict develops, the present NATO strategy carries with it a high risk that Western civilization, as we know it, will be destroyed"—to which one can add that *Homo sapiens* in its entirety may be destroyed into the bargain.

At the outset of a crisis, it is true, the President may not have to make the final, drastic choice. The policy of "flexible response" —of responding to each level of attack with a comparable level of retaliation—offers him less drastic steps to take. And certainly we should hope that even after the madness has begun it can somehow be stopped. (One excellent proposal that has been made recently is for a joint Soviet-American control center, where in the event of a crisis information could be exchanged, so that the two powers wouldn't miscalculate one another's intentions.) However, flexible response, even if it works, can only postpone, not evade, that final decision. If the foe is determined—and we have to assume that he is if he has launched a nuclear war against a nuclear-armed adversary—then the moment will still come, after the "limited" salvos have been fired, when a choice must be made between defeat and annihilation. But that moment may come well before some of the scenarists of nuclear war imagine that it will come, for there is good reason to doubt whether the limited attacks supposedly made available by flexible response will stay limited. The hope that nuclear hostilities, once they are started, can be limited depends on at least four very doubtful assumptions: that the leaders on both sides will retain control over their forces and that their orders will be obeyed (if, that is, the leaders survive); that the adversary will grasp one's "limited" intent even as he sees nuclear bombs tearing up his armies and his country; that if he does grasp this he will, in the interests of restraint all around, forgo the real or imagined advantages of a full-scale preemptive strike; and, finally, that the two sides, showing a wisdom in the midst of a nuclear holocaust which they failed to show in the days and hours leading up to it, while the world was intact, will come to their senses, establish diplomatic contact, and agree to halt the descent into the abyss in mid-course. No one knows how diplomacy would fare halfway to the end of the world, but it seems unwise to rely on it very heavily. In any case, the conclusion that the nuclear winter may descend after only a fraction of the world's present arsenals have been detonated may have made the distinction between "limited" and "total" nuclear war academic. "Limited war" itself has turned out to have potentially unlimited consequences.

In an effort to remedy the flaws in the American plan for the defense of Europe, the NATO governments hit on a plan that turned out only to exacerbate the underlying tensions. If the American threat to defend Europe with nuclear weapons was losing credibility, the NATO planners feared, then the Soviet leaders might start to believe that they could conquer or intimidate Europe without encountering an American response. This fear was increased when the Soviet Union began to withdraw its one-warhead SS-4 intermediate-range missiles that it had targeted on Europe and replace them with more modern, three-warhead SS-20 missiles. What was needed, the NATO planners decided—both to "reassure" the Europeans and to frighten the Russians—was a way of binding the defense of Europe more tightly to the defense of the United States. The upshot was the Euromissiles—intermediate-range ballistic and cruise missiles that would be based in Europe and would be capable of striking the Soviet Union. Their deployment, it was believed, would convince the Soviet Union once and for all that the Americans were serious about the defense of Europe. The problem was that a mere change in the place of deployment—from the United States to Europe—of American missiles capable of reaching Soviet territory did little to cure the incredibility of the threat of their use. In Mr. McNamara's words, "for the same reason that led Henry Kissinger to recognize that a U.S. President is unlikely to initiate the use of U.S.-based strategic nuclear weapons against the U.S.S.R., so a President would be unlikely to launch missiles from European soil against Soviet territory." Meanwhile, a large segment of the European citizenry was anything but reassured by the plan. On the contrary, it was frightened. People in Europe felt that they were becoming all too dependent on the United States, and they feared that the United States might drag them against their will into a holocaust of its own making. They believed that they were becoming (in the recent words of Rudolf Augstein, the publisher of *Der Spiegel*) a "computer component" in a broader superpower game, over which they had no control. Furthermore, unconvinced that the Euromissiles, which were to be under the sole control of the United States, would bind the fortunes of Europe and the United States closer together, they feared that the missiles might be used to try to fight a "limited" nuclear war in Europe alone, sparing the United States. (These fears were fanned when President Reagan opined at a briefing for news editors in October of 1981 that a limited nuclear war might indeed be possible.) Before long, a very large number of these people began to make their apprehensions known in demonstrations throughout Europe.

Meanwhile, in the United States four Americans with long experience in government—George Kennan; McGeorge Bundy; Gerard Smith, head of the delegation that negotiated the SALT I agreement; and Robert McNamara—had a quite different solution to suggest to the problem of the defense of Europe. They recommended that the United States consider adopting a policy of no first use of nuclear weapons in Europe while building NATO conventional forces to whatever level was necessary to achieve a balance with Warsaw Pact conventional forces. As they saw it, a policy of no first use would improve on the existing policy in a number of ways: it would add to the credibility of an American response to Soviet conventional attack (since at least the initial American response would no longer have to be suicidal); it would remove from the United States the responsibility and the onus of actually planning to be the first to use nuclear weapons (the Soviets have already declared a no-first-use policy); it would, by giving the United States something better to do in the event of aggression in Europe than start a nuclear holocaust, somewhat reduce the chances of a holocaust. These benefits, all of which appear to be real and substantial, are perhaps reason enough to adopt the policy of no first use, yet that policy would nevertheless fall short of fully resolving the contradiction that underlies the American plan for the defense of Europe. In conventional war, there is no guarantee of success in any engagement—and certainly not when the opposing forces are, by design, evenly balanced. Hence, in the event that a conventional war broke out in Europe it is quite possible that, even if there should be a conventional balance in place, the NATO forces would begin to lose, and so would be forced to decide anyway between defeat and a first use of nuclear weapons—or, if the Warsaw Pact started to lose, it would face the decision. In either case, there seems to be a fair chance that nuclear weapons would be used. Conventional defeat is the Achilles' heel of no first use. A policy of no first use thus can never really live up to its name. There is always an invisible asterisk attached, referring us to a footnote that reads, "Unless we start to lose." Without this qualification, a policy of no first use would really be a form of unilateral nuclear disarmament by verbal means, in which the foe was invited to take what he could, provided only that he did it with conventional forces. (If he used nuclear forces, nuclear deterrence would come into play.)

This limitation of no first use, of which the authors of the proposal were well aware, is worth mentioning not because it discredits the recommendation (it does not) but because it points to the contradiction at the heart of deterrence itself. The underlying problem, which both citizens and policymakers are now wrestling with, is that, given the difficulty of limiting nuclear war, and given the extreme consequences even if the war *is* limited, *any* actual use of nuclear weapons is likely to be self-defeating and senseless. For whether or not there is a policy of no first use, and whether or not the hostilities begin with the use of conventional weapons, there is, ultimately, no way to spare the President (if it is he who faces the decision) from having to make the final, terrible choice between defeat and annihilation. This is the moment at which the President has to decide whether or not actually to carry out the notorious "threat of suicide"—also known as the "threat to end the world"—with which the two great nuclear powers ultimately hope to deter one another from aggression. (Deployment of the Euromissiles commits him to making it earlier rather than later.) The crux of the matter is that while there may be a benefit in making the threat it can never make sense to carry it out, no matter what the circumstances. For how can it make sense to "save" one's country by blowing it to pieces? And what logic is there in staving off a limited defeat by bringing on unlimited, eternal defeat? Nuclear deterrence is like a gun with two barrels, of which one points ahead and the other points back at the gun's holder. If a burglar should enter your house, it might make sense to threaten him with this gun, but it could never make sense to fire it.

The dilemma is even more sharply defined if one turns from Europe, where the West has conventional forces in place with which to at least try to repel possible Soviet aggression, to the Middle East, where it has almost none and, furthermore, has no

chance of dispatching enough in time to make a military difference. The fault line in the doctrine here is wider. In the Middle
East, the military policy is either one of nuclear first use or nothing. The United States is making provision for a rapid-deployment
force that could be sent to the Middle East in a crisis, but in the
face of a full-scale Soviet conventional attack it could do no more
than be a trip wire for the American launching of nuclear weapons. Yet the Soviet Union can retaliate with nuclear weapons in
the Middle East just as easily as it can in Europe, and the ladder
of escalation climbs up just as smoothly from the Persian Gulf as
it does from the plains of Germany. The President appears to have
no way to "protect" Middle Eastern oil militarily other than by
launching nuclear weapons. But for whose use will the oil have
been protected if everyone winds up dead in the process of protecting it?

If the threat of nuclear war is irrational, one might ask, why do
nations go on making it, and why do they bother even to build
nuclear weapons instead of, say, building more conventional
weapons, which, according to some theorists, they might sensibly
use? Why doesn't the absurdity of "defending" one's country by
threatening suicide lead to the collapse or abandonment of the
policy? The answer, of course, is that the minute a nation gives up
nuclear weapons it puts itself militarily at the mercy of its nuclear-
armed foes, for no one has yet devised a successful defense against
nuclear attack. Rather than be put in this position, nations prefer
to make irrational threats—and hope never to be forced to decide
whether or not to carry them out. As for the problem of credibility,
in the real world—as opposed to the world of logic and theory—
the irrationality of the threat to commit suicide probably doesn't
do a great deal to reduce its effectiveness. There has been enough
insanity in history to lend credibility to even the maddest threats,
and for governments to threaten to do something irrational is
quite enough to get everybody to believe they will do it. (It is one
of the humiliating aspects of our nuclear policy that if rationality

ever prevailed in the world our policy would become untenable.) Another point in favor of the deterrence doctrine is its probable descriptive honesty. It discards all dubious assumptions regarding the likelihood of limiting a nuclear holocaust; or, at the very least, it acknowledges that no sensible statesman can *count on* these assumptions, and therefore invites statesmen to look on the use of nuclear weapons as the beginning of the end. The morality of the doctrine of mutual assured destruction has been assailed on the ground that it calls for the mass slaughter of innocents, as indeed it does. But this immorality is inherent in the very possession of tens of thousands of nuclear weapons, whatever the doctrine. There is no conceivable way that these can be used without mass slaughter on an incalculable scale, and no theoretical sophistry can eliminate this basic fact. The doctrine of mutual assured destruction is in that sense not so much a policy as an acknowledgment of reality. It brings us—statesman and citizen alike—face to face with the way things really are in a nuclear-armed world.

In an article in *The New York Review of Books*, in June of 1983, McGeorge Bundy proposed a policy of what he called "existential deterrence," in which we would make political use of some of the inherent qualities of nuclear arsenals. One of these qualities is uncertainty. He observes that "the existing systems on both sides are now so powerful and varied that no political leader can have or hope to have any clear idea of what would in fact happen 'if deterrence failed'—that is, if nuclear war began." And he goes on to remark that "scenarios" that pretend to predict what would happen "reflect nothing more than the state of mind of their authors." Our knowledge of the immense destructive power of nuclear weapons and our incurable ignorance of the exact course that that destruction would take are, he suggests, irreducible, "existential" properties of our nuclear arsenals, and he suggests that we can count on these properties to deter a foe, even without spelling out our murderous retaliatory intentions in detail. The reason for this uncertainty is, of course, the same as the reason for our uncertainty concerning our survival as a species "if deterrence failed": we have never had any experience with nuclear holocausts. The new finding that limited war could cause nuclear winter adds extremely important support to "existential" deterrence. This finding shows that an attacker might even destroy himself with his own first strike. Now, therefore, our own missiles are not only figuratively but literally pointed at ourselves. But there is, of course, no cause for rejoicing in this, because while it is true that the new finding may make statesmen more reluctant than before to launch nuclear hostilities this gain is won at the cost of an increase in the danger of an accidental or inadvertent extinction of mankind.

Because of the "existential" properties of large nuclear arsenals, deterrence overcomes its cracked logical foundations and "works"; that is, it inspires a well-justified terror in the minds of our adversaries, just as their arsenals inspire a reciprocal terror in us. The illogic of deterrence does not lead to a direct weakening of the fear that it inspires. No statesman in his right mind is so foolish as to stake his country's existence on the surmise that if he launches a nuclear attack against his foe the foe, guided by pure reasonableness and logic, will sit back and endure the attack without responding. The consequences of the doctrine's illogic are to be found somewhere else: in another audience, in ourselves. This audience very much includes the people who make up the new peace movement—people who are increasingly repelled by the idea of putting mankind to the sword because some crisis in Europe or Lebanon or the Falkland Islands, or wherever, has got out of hand. But before the peace movement arose another group, closer to power and more influential, had begun to ponder the dilemma. Its members were, and are, the strategists of "counterforce" and "nuclear-war-fighting," some of whom now guide the policies of the Reagan Administration. Having in many cases spent their lives studying nuclear strategy, they were well aware of the contradiction between the benefits of threatening to start a nuclear war and the senselessness of actually doing so. These people took theory seriously, and they took the contradiction seriously. They were not reassured by the uncertainty in nuclear affairs which restored the credibility that logic undermined, or by any of the other "existential" properties of nuclear arsenals. But what worried them chiefly was not, as with the peace movement, that a small crisis could bring on the end of the world; it was that the Soviet Union—counting on the reluctance of the United States to commit suicide by launching a nuclear attack—might go ahead with some act of aggression, including even a limited nuclear attack, hoping that there would be no response. But, having identified in deterrence the same inconsistency that the peace movement had identified, they struck off in an entirely different direction, embarking on a critique of mutual assured destruction from a new angle. The new strategists wanted to repair American credibility, and in order to do it they set out to find some rational goal for the United States to pursue "if deterrence failed." How would the adversary be deterred, they asked, if there was no sensible or reasonable threat to deter him with? Their solution—which marked a radical shift in strategic thought—was the idea of actually fighting and winning a nuclear war, just as though it were a conventional war. If the United States could fight and win a nuclear war, then the *threat* to use nuclear weapons would no longer be a suicide threat, and would become credible again. Once the new thinking had found wide acceptance in the Reagan Administration, the Administration, without rejecting the doctrine of deterrence outright, began to make statements and take actions that could be interpreted only as part of a war-fighting, or war-winning, strategy. Navy Secretary John Lehman said, "You have to have a war-winning capability if you are to succeed." Secretary of Defense Caspar Weinberger said, "You show me a Secretary of Defense who's planning not to prevail [in a war], and I'll show you a Secretary of Defense who ought to be impeached." And, as I have mentioned, a top-secret plan stated that the United States should prepare to fight "a prolonged" nuclear war and to be able to "prevail" in it and "force the Soviet Union to seek earliest termination of hostilities on terms favorable to the United States."

A decision to "prevail" in the event of nuclear war necessarily wreaked havoc on the traditional tenets of deterrence. Deterrence called for equality of forces, but prevailing required superiority; deterrence was upset by the power of either side to destroy the forces of the other side in a first strike, but prevailing required such a power; deterrence acknowledged the impossibility of an effective defense against a nuclear attack, but prevailing required such a defense; deterrence sought stability and was consistent with arms-control agreements based on equality, but prevailing, since it required superiority, was inconsistent with such agreements. And the Reagan Administration set out to achieve the objectives required for prevailing. The President called for the development and deployment of first-strike weapons. His Administration proposed ambitious programs both for civil defense and for space-based defense against Soviet ballistic missiles. All the while, it kept up a barrage of rhetoric against the Soviet Union more bellicose than anything heard from any other Administration in the postwar period.

As it happened, technical developments had for some time abetted the development by the United States of first-strike, nuclear-war-fighting weapons. One of these developments was the invention, in the mid-1960s, of the Multiple Independently Targeted Reentry Vehicle (MIRV), which permitted one missile to be equipped with many warheads, each of them guided to a different target. If the targets were the silos of enemy missiles, then just one missile fired offensively could menace many missiles sitting defensively in their silos. Another destabilizing technical development was a revolution in accuracy, which improved the chances that the warheads, multiplied or not, would actually reach the silos they were aimed at. The doctrine of deterrence had always rested on the twin foundations of the vulnerability of civilian populations to nuclear attack and the invulnerability of nuclear forces to nuclear attack. But now offensive capacity was improving to a point at which nuclear forces were beginning to become vulnerable. Although bombers in the air and submarines at sea still remained safe from a first strike, the safety of land-based missiles was dwindling. Meanwhile, the Soviet Union, too, although its public statements were more restrained than those of the United States had become, was developing weapons with a first-strike capacity. The

United States had been the first to deploy MIRVs but the Soviet Union was the first to place them on giant land-based missiles capable of carrying ten warheads apiece. (The MX, which will carry as many as ten warheads, is an attempt to match this dangerous achievement.) The move on both sides to build first-strike weapons shows the vulnerability of the nuclear balance in general to technical advances. The arms race is always, in effect, afloat on a stream of technical discovery, which can upset its most carefully laid plans. It is always as much a race against the scientific unknown as against the adversary per se. This aspect of the race—the qualitative, rather than the quantitative—has nothing to do with any malign influence of scientists. Rather, it is inherent in an arms race in a world in which experience has shown that the greatest advantages are to be gained not so much by mounting gigantic industrial efforts as by fishing new devices out of the unknown. At bottom, it stems from each side's well-justified fear that the other side will arrive at an advantageous discovery first. (An example would be a device that could detect the positions of submarines from a great distance.)

The debate between the mutual-assured-destruction school and the new nuclear-war-fighting school happens to have been encapsulated in an exchange of letters between the writer Theodore Draper and Secretary of Defense Weinberger in *The New York Review of Books*. (In entering into correspondence with Draper, Weinberger, as Draper acknowledged, showed a respect for the views of a private citizen—and, by implication, a sense of accountability to the public—that is all too often lacking in public officials.) It gives us a portrait in miniature of the stresses that are now tearing deterrence apart. The occasion for the exchange was an open letter written by Weinberger which appeared in *The New York Review* in November of 1982. In an "open reply," Draper takes note of the top-secret document parts of which were obtained by the *New York Times*—"Fiscal Year 1984–1988 Defense Guidance," which was approved by Weinberger and provides general strategic direction over a five-year period for America's armed services—which states that American nuclear forces "must prevail and be able to force the Soviet Union to seek earliest termination of hostilities on terms favorable to the United States," and he goes on to accuse the Administration of planning to try to "win" a nuclear war. In a letter to Draper, Weinberger denies the charge, saying, "We believe neither side could win," and he also denies that the Administration hopes to "prevail" in a protracted nuclear war. But, going on to broach the question that has occasioned the rise of the nuclear-war-fighting school—namely, what the United States should actually do with its nuclear weapons "if deterrence fails"—he says, "U.S. contingency planning, to serve deterrence, must also envision the possible employment of nuclear weapons." The answer of the mutual-assured-destruction school to the question of what to do if deterrence fails is that one goes ahead with mutual assured destruction. This answer Weinberger rejects, explaining that "it would be militarily, politically and morally unsound to confine the President to resorting either to capitulation or massive retaliation." Then, giving his own formulation of what to do, he says, "Our policy requires that, if necessary, we prevail in denying victory to the Soviets and in protecting the sovereignty and continued viability of the United States and of the Western democracies as free societies." But this goal—with its "viability of the United States," its preserved "sovereignty," its intact "free societies," and its "denying victory" to the Soviet Union—has about it a suspicious look of prevailing, not to say winning.

Weinberger's tortured and evasive formulation gives Draper his opening to respond. In a second letter, he accuses Weinberger of rejecting the goal of prevailing at the beginning of his letter "only to reinstate it in a peculiarly negative form"—in which the phrase "terms favorable to the United States" mentioned in the "Defense Guidance" plan has been replaced by the less provocative "denying victory to the Soviet Union." Draper then accuses Weinberger of both "denying the aim to 'prevail' and affirming the plan to prevail." Weinberger, in a final letter, seems to have

61

little to say in rebuttal of this point. He writes that American military policy as a whole is "defensive," as though Draper had accused the Administration of planning aggression (he had not), and then, once more addressing the crucial question of what the American plan should be if deterrence fails, merely comes up with a slightly milder and even more euphemistic version of his previous answer. This time, he says that the United States should seek to "terminate the conflict quickly at the lowest level of destruction possible, to restore deterrence, and to protect the sovereignty and continued viability of the United States and of the Western democracies as free societies with fundamental institutions and values intact." But then he shifts from defense of Administration policies to criticism of the policy supported by Draper, who believes that the United States should possess enough nuclear forces to annihilate the Soviet Union in a retaliatory strike and then stop. "Although . . . you believe massive response against the Soviet population is the response necessary to provide for deterrence, for political, military, and, yes, moral reasons, we do not target civilian populations as such," Weinberger writes. "If we are forced to retaliate and can only respond by destroying population centers, we invite the destruction of our own population. Such a deterrent strategy could lack conviction, particularly as a deterrent to nuclear—let alone conventional—attack on an ally." In other words, he articulates the nuclear-war-fighters' complaint against mutual assured destruction: that suicide is not a very plausible threat.

Now it is Draper's turn to lack an answer. In fact, in his next letter he fails to take up the question of what he proposes that the United States should do if deterrence breaks down; instead he concentrates more fire on Weinberger's unconvincing answers to the same question. Weinberger's charge that to unleash mutual assured destruction is senseless as an action and implausible as a threat is permitted to stand. In short, in responding (or, in Draper's case, failing to respond) to the question of what to do "if deterrence fails," each man succeeds in demonstrating the senselessness of the other man's plan and does not succeed in defending his own plan. It's a case of mutual assured destruction. And both are right. Draper succeeds in showing that Weinberger really wants to win a nuclear war, and that this hope is utterly illusory, but he cannot find any justification for actually carrying out the mutual assured destruction that he supports. He is reduced to saying, in effect, that deterrence *won't* fail. Thus, in his second letter he says that the only "effective use" of nuclear weapons is to "prevent their use" in the first place. But that answer begs the question under discussion, which is what to do with them *if prevention fails* and nuclear bombs are landing on one's soil. In other words, there is no deterrence without a threat. The question is: Threat of what? As Weinberger points out, the answer given to *this* question by policymakers *now*, before any attack has been made, theoretically bears on whether prevention itself will work, since under the deterrence doctrine it is fear of retaliation that keeps the first strike from being launched. Weinberger, for his part, succeeds in showing that mutual assured destruction is a senseless action and therefore an unconvincing threat, but he cannot demonstrate that in the nuclear war he apparently has in mind we can actually preserve our "institutions and values intact" or "force" the Soviet Union to accept "terms favorable to the United States," or achieve any of the other things he promises in his long string of euphemisms for victory.

The truth that neither man wants to face up to is that there is nothing that it would make sense to do "if deterrence fails"— nothing, that is, but to get on the hot line and try to stop the whole debacle as soon as possible. But that intention cannot be spelled out in advance by government officials as their "response" to nuclear attack, because deterrence requires that they threaten devastating retaliation of one kind or another, be it attempted nuclear-war-fighting or straight mutual assured destruction. When the President is asked what the United States will do if it is subjected to nuclear attack by the Soviet Union, he cannot answer, "I will immediately call up the Soviet Premier and ask him to please stop." He cannot tell the world that if we suffer nuclear attack our retaliation will be a phone call. For the instant he gave that answer deterrence would dissolve. Once again, we arrive at the very core of what is wrong with deterrence, which can be stated very simply: it commits us in certain circumstances to do what we must never do in any circumstances—plunge into a nuclear holocaust, in which our species could be destroyed and the human story ended forever. Deterrence theory is indeed a marvel of circularity and contradiction. To obtain the benefit of the policy, we must threaten to perform an insane action. But the benefit we seek is precisely *not* to perform that action. We thus seek to avoid performing an act by threatening to perform it. As long as the policy succeeds, of course, everyone is happy. But the moment it fails we would like to scrap the whole thing, because then we find ourselves committed to performing an insane action—to doing the very thing whose avoidance was the purpose of the policy. But if, looking ahead to this terrible moment, we admit now that once the breakdown occurs (and Soviet troops are flooding into Western Europe, for example) we don't want to perform the insane act of shoving the world into the abyss of doom we lose the pre-breakdown benefits that we now enjoy. So we don't admit it—perhaps not even to ourselves—and continue to stand ready to perform the act.

Draper and Weinberger have their separate ways of evading this terrible truth of our time. Draper simply declines to acknowledge the illogic of making a threat whose execution would be senseless. Weinberger, in an apparent step forward, acknowledges the illogic, but then, in his attempt to repair it, takes two steps backward, by taking leave of the reality that gave rise to the whole problem in the first place—the reality of the overwhelming destructive force of the weapons, which are more than a match for any institutions we have, not to speak of "values." (It's when *we* annihilate *them* that our "values" are destroyed.) In effect, he and the Administration he speaks for have escaped from illogic into fantasy. Of the two defects, the illogic, as I have noted, is preferable, in part because it is compensated for by the "existential" qualities of the arsenals, including the impenetrable uncertainty that, in the real world, must reside in the minds of all sensible people regarding what would happen once a nuclear holocaust actually started. If there must be nuclear weapons, then this uncertainty, and not the iron resolve to annihilate the adversary and suffer annihilation oneself, in mutual assured destruction, or the supposed ability to defeat him in a "nuclear war," is the strongest buttress of such stability as our jeopardized world now enjoys. The necessity of relying on uncertainty, however—on our *in*ability to control or predict our actions—is only one more demonstration that there is no truly rational or humanly justifiable way either to use or to threaten to use nuclear weapons, and that only their abolition can return our lives to sanity and normality.

In 1946, Bernard Brodie and a number of other strategic thinkers devised the doctrine of deterrence as a means of gaining time for the world while it worked on a true solution to the nuclear problem. But the world, instead of using the time won in this way, chose to forget the underlying issues and to elevate the temporary expedient into a dogma. An improvisation became orthodoxy. Meanwhile, the world, lulled into a false sense of reassurance, in effect went to sleep. In the decades following the invention of the bomb, the doctrine of deterrence achieved a seemingly unchallengeable dominance. Its triumphant progress perhaps reached its apogee in the early 1970s, when the first nuclear-arms-control agreements between the United States and the Soviet Union were signed. So widely accepted in our country had the doctrine become that some likened it to a religious faith, and referred to its experts as a "priesthood"—a priesthood that might argue back and forth in specialized journals over the fine points of theology but was united on the basic articles of the faith. It even had its paradoxes and mysteries (such as what to do if deterrence failed)—an essential ingredient in any theology worth the name. And when the arms-control agreements were signed it seemed that the faith had spread from Washington to Moscow. If all this was "élitist," it was also reassuring. A doctrine was in place that promised "stability" in the world. The two great nuclear adversaries seemed to subscribe to it. (The sheer fact of agreement on *something* was important.) What was better, under its guidance they had reached agreements that promised to be only the first in a long series—a series in which the weapons would be, if not abolished, at least "managed." The direction the two powers were moving in seemed to be the right one. And yet within a few years this solid-seeming edifice had disintegrated. The doctrine of deterrence on which it was based had come apart, the priesthood was scattered, the arms-control "process" was at a standstill, the two great nuclear powers were exchanging insulting and menacing remarks, and the arms race, unguided now by any coherent philosophy on either side—much less by one shared by the two sides—was spiralling out of control.

Deterrence had not been assailed from without. No enemy had challenged it. No consistent new doctrine had taken its place in men's minds. ("Nuclear-war-fighting" remained an uncertain and ambivalent mishmash of atavistic military impulses and abstruse theorizing presented in the teeth of the most elementary facts of the nuclear age.) Rather, deterrence was unraveling from within; it was a victim of its own contradictions, which were seized upon in large measure by its own practitioners. Yet when the contradictions were looked at unblinkingly it turned out that they were inherent in the existence of the doomsday machine itself. For the truth was that there was nothing wrong with the doctrine of deterrence which was not wrong simply with the possession of vast nuclear arsenals—with or without the doctrine of deterrence. The reason that no repair of the doctrine was possible was that the problem did not lie in doctrine. It lay in the world's possession of nuclear arsenals—in their "existential" features, if you like. For, whatever government spokesmen might say about possessing nuclear weapons only to prevent their use, the inescapable truth was that possession inevitably implied use, and use was irredeemably senseless, since it threatened to bring about the destruction of whatever one might think one was trying to defend: if you tried to reject deterrence while holding on to the weapons, you only wound up with nuclear-war-fighting. Thus, at bottom, the crisis in doctrine stemmed from the reliance on nuclear arms. Indeed, deterrence was probably the least obnoxious and most sensible doctrine consistent with the absurd situation of possessing the arsenals. Most important, it was based on an acknowledgment of the true extent of the peril. Furthermore, it renounced the aggressive use of the weapons, and sought stability rather than military advantage from them. It endeavored to increase the element of *threat* to the maximum while reducing the risk of *use* to the minimum. If this effort was self-contradictory—since the threat was credible only insofar as use was a real possibility—and was in that sense like trying to make use of the shadow of an object without having the object itself, it was certainly better than imagining that after a nuclear holocaust we would wind up with our societies and "values" intact.

It was against this background of official confusion and international discord that the new peace movement arose. But while the movement may have been triggered in part by the crisis in the deterrence doctrine it has not taken the restoration of deterrence as its goal. To be sure, some members of the old nuclear priesthood have come to the defense of their beleaguered doctrine, but only to find real priests challenging it, in the bishops' pastoral letter. It turned out that while the nuclear-war-fighters were looking at the contradictions of deterrence and worrying about a loss of credibility people on the outside were looking at those same contradictions and worrying about the loss of mankind itself. Having made their conscious choice in favor of human survival, they could hardly be content with a policy that left mankind perched on the edge of doom and prescribed that in certain not altogether unlikely circumstances we jump. And when the proponents of deterrence began to present the arrangement as permanent, and to rule out full nuclear disarmament even in the long run, the doctrine came to seem an abomination. It began to look like a death sentence for the human race. Yet while extreme dissatisfaction with deterrence was implicit in making the "conscious choice" to try to preserve the human species a critique of deterrence was not yet a deliberate policy of the peace movement.

The world was awakening, but what it was awakening *to* was not a ready solution to the nuclear predicament but, rather, the impasse that the world had reached in the first years of the nuclear age. When the world woke up, it was therefore only to find itself manacled to the bed on which it was lying, for the "impossibility" of any real relief from the nuclear peril—and the impossibility, in particular, of the abolition of nuclear weapons—had been affirmed by decades of strategic thinking. It was perhaps not surprising, then, that many people wanted to go back to sleep—in effect, saying, "Wake us up again when you have some answers." For trailing after the elemental human questions raised by the peace movement was a whole new set of questions, concerning what should be done. Can the goal of a nuclear-free world actually be reached, or is it in fact impossible—a "fictional utopia," as *Living with Nuclear Weapons* tells us? If the Harvard book is right, what then is the outlook? If it is wrong, and the path is open, what then is the path? Is it unilateral disarmament? If so, what would happen to our independence and our liberties? Or is bilateralism best? If it is, how can we in the West, including both governments and the peace movement, bring our influence to bear on the Soviet Union, where no independent peace movement is permitted? Must political détente precede disarmament? If the superpowers are to get rid of half of their weapons, must they first get rid of half of their political differences? Or can disarmament go ahead with the political differences intact? If so, how far can it go? *Can* they get rid of half of the weapons? Three-quarters? All? Does world government then become necessary? Or will something else do? In addressing these questions, the peace movement finds itself up against the issues that divided Einstein and Brodie; and the old debate on these issues, which has been in abeyance for some time, has been resumed.

Much of it is the same as in 1945. Once again, supposed "realists" tilt against supposed "idealists"; once again, moralists call strategists immoral, and strategists call moralists naïve; once again, the necessary is called impossible, and the impossible is called necessary. In short, rhetorical warfare has broken out afresh along the whole front of the still unbridged divide that the invention of nuclear weapons opened between the world's historical political organization of human life and human life itself. Yet there are some changes in the debate. Perhaps the most significant change is that the political program of the peace movement, in contrast to that of Einstein and his school, has so far been modest and tentative. There is little appetite for sweeping proposals that might resolve the predicament all at once if they were acted upon but that probably would not be acted upon, because they would be unlikely to meet with official or public acceptance. In particular, there are virtually no new calls for world government—a pair of words so thoroughly out of fashion that merely uttering them seems guaranteed to sink in political oblivion any plan connected with them. For Einstein, the boundlessness of the peril of extinction and the sweeping, radical solution of world government were so tightly connected as to be almost two parts of one thought, with the latter simply implicit in the former. For the peace movement of the 1980s, however, the question has been broken into many thoughts, and there has been a sense of a great distance to be crossed, intellectually as well as politically, between an analysis of the problem and an analysis of its resolution. This dissection of the issue—this opening up of its moral and political dimensions, revealing a richer complexity than had previously been recognized —is probably one more result of the world's years of experience of living with the doomsday machine. In 1945, the peril was on the horizon and was approaching quickly, yet it remained distant and abstract. The bombings of Hiroshima and Nagasaki were soon seen as part of a war that was over, not as harbingers of everybody's future. In 1984, the peril, while still in a sense invisible and abstract, nevertheless surrounds and pervades our lives. It is the sky overhead and the ground underfoot. We are immersed in it and permeated by it. In sum, we now live in a *nuclear world,* and our reactions, our thoughts and feelings, conscious and unconscious, have reference to that world. They have a flavor of experience, which the reactions of people in 1945 could not have.

The American bishops' pastoral letter exemplifies both the spirit and the substance of the new movement. It subjects the nuclear policies of the great powers to searching moral and intellectual scrutiny. The question that the bishops start by asking is not so much "What shall we do?" as the more uncomfortable, prior question "What are we doing?" Though their goal is not novelty—they hold established policies up to the light of time-honored standards and principles—their investigation breaks new ground, for hitherto as a society we have permitted our nuclear policies to escape such examination. By insisting that our political and military practices be judged according to traditional ethical standards, the bishops are taking the first step toward making our sundered world whole. This is a fitting effort for the Catholic Church, which over the centuries has made an effort to find and apply moral standards that are appropriate to all domains of life, public and private. Invoking the just-war theory of Catholic teaching, which says that it is at times permissible to kill in defense of one's country, the bishops sanction the existence of a breach of some size between the moral standards for private conduct and the moral standards for governmental conduct. But they draw limits. First, they declare that nuclear weapons must *never* be used against cities. Quoting the Second Vatican Council, they state, "Any act of war aimed indiscriminately at the destruction of entire cities or of extensive areas along with their population is a crime against God and man himself. It merits unequivocal and unhesitating condemnation." Second, they condemn the initiation of nuclear war, finding it "not justified by rational political objectives." Third, they reject the notion of "limited" nuclear war, stating that to cross the nuclear threshold is "to enter a world where we have no experience of control, much testimony against [limited war's] possibility, and therefore no moral justification for submitting the human community to this risk."

Having made these firm and far-reaching moral judgments, the bishops do not go on to make equally firm and far-reaching recommendations for action on the basis of them. Rather, they subscribe to such moderate and partial proposals as the nuclear freeze and no first use. Like the peace movement as a whole, the bishops are diagnostic radicals but prescriptive moderates. They reserve judgment on the deeper political questions, perhaps because they believe (as I do) that it is only on the prior foundation of a solid moral and intellectual understanding of the predicament that a sound political solution can be built. According to this line of thinking, the present system of deterrence, while possessing virtues that should not be overlooked, is a perfect example of a solution built on shaky foundations, and its recent disarray, which is due more to internal disintegration than to assault from without, is a symptom of its basic infirmity. Seen in this light, the political hesitancy of the bishops and of the movement as a whole must be judged a strength, not a weakness. It bespeaks a wise open-mindedness, not a fatal impracticality or a neglect of the realities of political life. It means only that the bishops are addressing the issue in the two stages recommended by the Pope: first the "conscious choice," then the "deliberate policy." Before the nuclear question could be re-answered, it had to be reopened, and they have reopened it. However, if those who have raised the question withhold judgment on the policy question for a prolonged period the strength will become a fatal weakness. Beyond a certain point, a failure to follow up the choice with a policy will breed discouragement. The peace movement, like the world as a whole, is in need of proposals for action which are commensurate with the hopes that it has raised, and are answerable to the moral standards it uses to measure present policies. If no such proposals are forthcoming, the peace movement seems sure to dissipate, just as peace movements in the past have dissipated. In that event, a yet more profound atmosphere of fatalism than people have felt so far seems likely to descend over the world, because people will be convinced that even popular action—previously their one untried hope—is helpless in the face of the nuclear peril, which will then truly take on the final aspect of a doomsday machine: something that has been made by human beings but has slipped beyond human control.

For the time being, the movement has given its backing to proposals that are somewhat more ambitious than those normally considered feasible by the arms-control experts but are still moderate enough to win widespread approval. In the United States, the outstanding proposal of this kind is, of course, the freeze, which from the moment it became widely known enjoyed broad public support. (In Europe, the comparable effort, which has now failed, was to block deployment of the Euromissiles.) In fact, the freeze proposal was adopted by the movement perhaps as much for its political "salability" as for its merits, which I believe are nevertheless great. The freeze answers the urgent need to head off the next advance in the arms race, which promises to be a particularly perilous one. The first-strike weapons already deployed by the Soviet Union and the United States have undermined stability, and the weapons planned for the near future— weapons such as the MX and the Trident D-5 missile—would undermine it further. Another peril to stability is the plan to put arms in space, by developing both anti-satellite weapons and space-based anti-missile weapons. Anti-satellite weapons are destabilizing because they threaten to blind the warning systems and the intelligence-gathering systems of one or both sides in a crisis, and leave the statesmen acting in the dark as nuclear hostilities begin. Space-based anti-missile weapons are destabilizing because they could menace the retaliatory capacity of the other side—a threat that would certainly be met either by a further buildup of missiles or by the development of still other weapons, designed to attack the space-based anti-missile ones, or by both. Still another technical development that threatens stability is the cruise missile, which promises to greatly complicate future arms-control talks. Unlike most ballistic missiles, which are large and relatively easy to spot by satellite, cruise missiles are small—as little as eighteen feet long and twenty-one inches in diameter—and therefore easy to conceal. Moreover, cruise missiles, whose eventual deployment may be in the tens of thousands, can be equipped with either nuclear or conventional warheads, and a rival power cannot always know from the outside which is which. Both this difficulty in determining which of them are nuclear-armed and the ease with which they can be hidden would make the verification of arms-control agreements incomparably more complicated than it is today.

While the freeze is fully defensible as a measure in its own right, virtually none of the advocates of the freeze (or of any of the other moderate measures that have been put forward by the peace movement) present it (or any of the others) as the final goal of their efforts. They are well aware that, as an answer to the question of what mankind should do about the threat of human extinction by nuclear arms, the proposal that one should freeze the doomsday machine in place would, if it were to be offered without promise of a further proposal, be a non sequitur. They all, therefore, regard it as only "a first step." A step, however, implies a direction, and a direction implies a goal. Neither the direction nor the goal has yet been defined. If one asks what "the next step" should be, the answer is very likely to be "reductions," or "deep reductions." But when one asks how far the reductions should go, and what sort of world they would lead to, haziness and ambiguity set in. The goal of complete nuclear disarmament is sometimes mentioned, but in a perfunctory, almost casual way. Few details are offered, and no convincing picture of a nuclear-free world has yet been presented.

These lacks are only part of another lack—the lack of any doctrine that could guide the steps toward the goal of complete nuclear disarmament. A doctrine is a comprehensive policy—or, if you like, a "deliberate policy"—for dealing with an entire issue. It offers both a broad picture of the world and long-term goals to strive toward, so that the short-term measures are not a groping in a void, and do not contradict one another. When the issue is nuclear disarmament, the basic question that a doctrine must address is the underlying political one of how, in a world in which war has become mutual annihilation, the bitterest and most intractable disputes among nations are to be settled. In other words, the issue is nothing less than how the world is to be organized politically. Deterrence deserves to be called a doctrine because it offers an answer—however unsatisfactory one may find it—to the political question. It holds that the disputes among nations which in the past have been resolved through war must now be averted by the maintenance of a balance of terror with huge nuclear arsenals. It invites us to tolerate a degree of risk of extinction as the price for national defense and international stability. The proposal for world government, too, deserves to be called a doctrine, because it also answers the basic question—holding that these disputes must be resolved by civil procedures under a global authority. This solution invites us to revolutionize the politics of the earth as the cost of lifting the peril of extinction. Whatever one thinks of the bargain struck by either of these resolutions of the nuclear predicament, both deserve to be recognized as politically "serious," in the sense that both face the basic political issue without evasion. There have, by contrast, been any number of suggestions that have lacked seriousness in this sense. They may, for example, call for nuclear disarmament, or for total disarmament, but without acknowledging the need for the vast political changes that would enable nations to resolve their disputes bindingly by peaceful means, and without specifying any such means. Sometimes the intent behind such incomplete proposals may be purely rhetorical, as when a politician wishes to end his speech with an uplifting thought, and sometimes genuine political naïveté may be responsible. Inasmuch as the settlement of the disputes that arise among men is of the very essence of politics, these proposals are truly— to use a much-abused term—politically "unrealistic." They simply evade the political dimension of the issue altogether.

So far, the current peace movement has not given any significant backing to proposals that ignore the political dimension of the predicament. Rather, to the extent that it has recommended actions it has largely insisted on political workability throughout, and has chosen the course of backing modest but useful plans of action, such as the freeze, within the framework of existing broad policy, and of leaving the deeper political question open for the time being. Uneasy with deterrence but uninterested in world government, the peace movement seeks to chart a new course, but it has not yet found a way to do it. Lacking any doctrine to call its own, the movement has been driven reluctantly to rely for now on the basic framework of deterrence to justify its moderate proposals. Thus, it defends the freeze in part on the ground that it will stabilize deterrence, and protect the nuclear balance from the technical developments that threaten to destabilize it in the near future. And, in fact, the broad acceptability of the freeze is probably attributable in no small measure to its compatibility with deterrence. (A recent poll showed that seventy per cent of the American public favored a freeze.) Accordingly, in putting forward the freeze the peace movement offers the world a new step to take but borrows an old doctrine to justify it. This borrowing is in itself unexceptionable (since it is a clear benefit to everybody for the present system to be made safer and for future deterioration of its stability to be headed off), but it has a high price attached if it continues for very long. For the premise of the doctrine of deterrence—that safety can be maintained only by the maintenance of large nuclear arsenals—is at odds with the deepest premise of the new movement, which is that we must somehow stop threatening ourselves with annihilation. The bishops' pastoral letter can again serve as an illustration.

The bishops begin by unequivocally condemning the mass slaughter of innocents with nuclear weapons. Yet deterrence requires such slaughter—or, at the very least, cannot promise to avoid it—simply because any large-scale nuclear attack, even if it is aimed at military targets, will involve the mass slaughter of innocents. There is, of course, a policy that would succeed in translating the pastoral letter's ban on nuclear mass slaughter into actual policy. It is unilateral disarmament—and not some unilateral "gesture" or other but the real thing: an immediate declaration by the President that he was dismantling the nation's nuclear

arsenal in the shortest possible time, and that meanwhile he renounced the use of nuclear weapons. Yet if there are two words
that in the present political climate doom a proposal to political
oblivion even more swiftly than "world government" they are
"unilateral disarmament," and the bishops explicitly reject this
course. Nevertheless, they seem at times to steer in its direction.
At one point in the letter, they observe that "the political paradox
of deterrence has also strained our moral conception." Then they
pose a series of questions: "May a nation threaten what it may
never do? May it possess what it may never use? Who is involved
in the threat each superpower makes: Government officials? Or
military personnel? Or the citizenry in whose defense the threat
is made?" This series of questions has the look of an exploratory
probe of dangerous territory—a probe in which the bishops reconnoitre the perilous ground of unilateral disarmament only to veer
away again. For if these questions are answered in a certain way
they make the moral argument for unilateral nuclear disarmament: "A nation may never threaten what it may never do. It must
never possess what it may never use. Not only government officials
and military personnel but also the citizenry in whose defense the
threat is made are involved in the threat." Judged by traditional
ethical standards, including, specifically, the Catholic teaching on
war, this position is not an extreme one. It does not rule out all
killing, for example. It does not even rule out killing on quite a
large scale. It merely spells out the measures necessary if the
injunction against the mass slaughter of innocents is to be more
than exhortation and become policy. The bishops boldly ask us
whether we are willing, under any conceivable circumstances, to
kill countless millions of innocent people, and to this their and our
immediate impulse is to cry out "No!" And, indeed, at one point
the bishops state that we must say a clear "no" to nuclear weapons.
If I may use myself as an example, I know that if the nuclear button
were on my desk and a nuclear attack were launched against the
United States I would be unable to retaliate in kind. I would
utterly lack the "resolve" to do this. In fact, my whole resolve
would be that it not be done. This "retaliation" would seem to me

to be a separate, new, unspeakable crime in its own right, which was in no way an appropriate response to the unspeakable crime that had just been committed against my country. As I see it, it would, in fact, not even *be* retaliation, since most of the people it would kill—innocent citizens, including children—would have had nothing to do with their government's criminally insane decision. Yet I know that this unwillingness of mine would, if it were generalized into a policy, be so far outside the pale politically as to have virtually no acceptance. In that sense, to truly say "no" to nuclear weapons forces one into a position that is politically irrelevant—at least, as far as present policy is concerned. Although I can't speak for others, I suspect that there are many people who want to say a real "no" to nuclear weapons but find that majority opinion is overwhelmingly against them. So, in desperation, they, like the bishops, seek partial and gradual measures that, if they are pursued long enough, may enable us one day not only to say but to practice our "no."

The fissure that nuclear weapons have created between our political selves and our moral selves is precisely delineated by the fact that as long as there are nuclear weapons in the world we are compelled to choose between a position that is politically sound but immoral and one that is morally sound but politically irrelevant. The bishops, who have had the rare courage to articulate the dilemma, oscillate between these two positions and conclude with a compromise. Having begun by condemning the slaughter of innocents with nuclear arms, they appear to catch a glimpse of the political implication of that stand (unilateral disarmament) and reject it, and finally fall back on deterrence, to which they give a "strictly conditioned" acceptance—the condition being that deterrence be recognized as a provisional remedy while full-scale nuclear disarmament is being worked out. (On this point, I find myself in disagreement with the bishops. My unwillingness to support the use or the threat to use nuclear weapons is unconditional. There are simply some means that I think are wrong, no matter what the end pursued, and this is one of them. And if it is wrong in that sense, then it is wrong in all times and places and

77

circumstances, including now, right here, and in our present circumstances. If we are attacked with nuclear weapons, I *want* the retaliation to be a phone call. Thus, unlike the bishops, I cannot support deterrence conditionally, because I think that it is as wrong conditionally as it is eternally. If, while awaiting a full solution to the nuclear problem, we, in obedience to the dictates of deterrence policy, take action that leads to the death of billions of people, they will not be conditionally dead. And if we extinguish mankind it will not be conditionally extinguished. It will be extinguished forever. At the same time, however, precisely because extinction is forever, I believe that moderate steps that fall short of a full solution to the nuclear peril should receive everyone's wholehearted support. We can and must morally boycott evil in this world, but we cannot boycott the world. The purity of an individual person's conduct has immeasurable importance for *the world*. But if in seeking to preserve our purity we let *the world* perish, of what use will our purity be then?) The bishops state that we must say a clear "no" to nuclear weapons. Ultimately, however, their "no" is qualified, and nuclear weapons are accepted, if only temporarily. The bishops articulate the soul's demand that we desist at all costs from carrying out mass murder and the extinction of our species, but they do not find a home for that demand in our present world. Yet the choked-back "no" continues to sound beneath the argumentation and compromise. It becomes the banked moral fire that is needed to keep the idea of disarmament active in our thoughts and efforts.

The bishops' U-turn, in which they criticize but then embrace deterrence, although only provisionally and with barely contained revulsion, reflects the whole peace movement's rejection of the premises of deterrence and its simultaneous reliance on deterrence to justify the moderate and politically popular proposals that it has put forward. Moral and intellectual torment, of which the pastoral letter is a paradigm, is one of the results of that reliance. Another, which has greater practical consequences, is that of leaving the movement without any road map to full nuclear disarmament to offer the world—and, worse, we are all left to rely on a road map that specifically precludes full nuclear disarmament. For while the people of the peace movement have not examined in detail the possibility of nuclear disarmament in the framework of deterrence, the theorists of deterrence have, and they have all but unanimously ruled it out as unattainable—as "a fictional utopia."

The popular notion of a whole series of "steps," which evokes the image of a stairway, encourages the simple but hopeful idea that if enough steps are taken the top of the stairway will be reached and complete nuclear disarmament will be attained. And certainly the usefulness of distinguishing between short-term steps and long-term goals seems obvious and undeniable. It needs to be said—once and for all, one would hope—that there is no need whatever to choose between short-term, moderate "steps" that are within our immediate grasp and long-term, radical goals whose achievement would bring us real safety. Nothing is more arid and fruitless than the abuse-laden exchanges between the champions of these two approaches, with one side saying that the moderate steps are useless because they don't go far enough, and the other side saying that long-term goals should be barred from the discussion because they will distract us from moderate measures that we can really achieve. These arguments are like the wasted breath of two people standing at the bottom of a stairway arguing about whether it is more important to take the first step or the last step to get to the top. Isn't it self-evident that both are needed? The two camps would do well to call a cease-fire and become allies, with the short-term people gaining hope and a sense of direction from a new understanding that long-term goals are both essential and achievable, and the long-term people taking heart from the actual accomplishments of the short-term people. And then, of course, they could pit their combined efforts against the steady retrogression that has been our real record over the last thirty-nine years.

However, an agreement on the obvious point that all the steps —first, middle, and last—must be traversed if one is to get to the top of the stairs would hardly solve the substantive question of just *which* stairway leads to safety (if such a thing is attainable at all in the nuclear world). Close examination of the doctrine of deterrence dashes the hope that *this* doctrine is such a stairway. The problem is inherent in the very nature of deterrence as it is currently practiced. Under deterrence, "safety" lies in the weapons themselves, and in the terror they inspire. More particularly, it lies in the power of each side to destroy the society of the other side after suffering a first strike. If that power is lost, then the balance of terror is lost, and deterrence dissolves. Deterrence thus establishes a level beneath which "reductions" may not go, and the level is the number of weapons necessary to destroy the society of the adversary in a retaliatory strike. This situation is often called "minimum deterrence," and it marks the lower limits of arms reductions under the doctrine of deterrence in its present form. Under deterrence, arms control can theoretically eliminate redundancy, but it must never touch the essential capacity for "assuring" the annihilation of the other side. In other words, it can get rid of the overkill but not the kill—an advance, but not one that offers much relief to people in the targeted countries. Indeed, in the light of the conclusion that even a fraction of the present arsenals could trigger a nuclear winter, it turns out that there might not even be any relief for untargeted nations, whose interests might otherwise be served by a policy of minimum deterrence. From the point of view of a mortal human being, the first time you lose your life is the time that counts, and whether or not your ghost is being stalked through the rubble by further nuclear explosions is a point of small interest. Another problem with minimum deterrence, which was seized on by Weinberger in his argument with Draper (who, however, favors not "minimum" but what he calls "sufficient" deterrence), is that it leaves the statesmen with an all-or-nothing choice as soon as the brink is reached, and deprives them of all flexibility.

Reduction to zero is, of course, ruled out. For, according to the terms of the doctrine, if nations had no nuclear weapons to threaten one another with, deterrence would evaporate. In fact, there is a sense in which even reductions are antithetical to the logic of deterrence: if under this doctrine safety relies on terror, then it may be dangerous—destabilizing—to undermine, or even to "minimize," that terror, because one might at the same time minimize the safety. The only reason to minimize the number of weapons would be to minimize the damage "if deterrence fails," but such minimizing runs directly counter to the essence of the logic of deterrence, which is that everyone will be dissuaded from launching an attack only because everyone knows that the damage to his own society will be the maximum possible. It can even be argued that overkill is useful in producing a deterrent effect. It may eliminate every last shred of doubt on either side that to make war in a nuclear world is to commit suicide. (And the recent statements by our own government officials show how durable the illusion is that one might survive—or even come out on top—in a nuclear war.)

A goal for arms control which does make sense under the doctrine of deterrence is stability, but stability is not necessarily served by reductions; rather, increases to assure "the survivability of the retaliatory force," for example, or to heighten that force's destructive power might in some circumstances be judged necessary. In fact, a minor argument has broken out in the arms-control world between the advocates of reductions and the advocates of stabilization. The former aim at reducing the numbers of nuclear weapons, apparently in the hope that the momentum achieved might lead the world to safety. The latter argue that, given the existence of nuclear arsenals, the numbers are unimportant, and the thing to do is to remove the technical imbalances and the political tensions that could lead to use of the arsenals—whatever their size. (The ultimate stabilization, of course, would be for the Soviet Union and the United States to come to an understanding regarding their international differences.) However, both schools accept the underlying framework of deterrence. Deterrence is a system—a way of organizing the nuclear world. As such, it has an underlying logic (though a flawed one), definite rules and provisions, and definite military and technical requirements. If in order to achieve the abolition, or even the severe reduction, of nuclear weapons this logic is to be abandoned, its rules broken, and its provisions violated, then some other system—some other way of organizing the world—has to be offered in its stead.

The theorists of deterrence do not altogether rule out the abolition of nuclear weapons; they rule it out only as a measure that is possible in a world of sovereign states. If we are to achieve the abolition of nuclear weapons—not to mention complete disarmament—then, they say, we must establish world government. World government, they admit, could at least theoretically replace deterrence. But they reject world government, and, with it, abolition. According to this view, we must choose between a nuclear-armed world of sovereign states and a nuclear-free world ruled by world government. The one thing they see as truly impossible, in the long run as well as the short run, is a world of still sovereign states from which nuclear weapons have been abolished. This is because they see no way that the political question —how disputes among nations are to be resolved—can be answered in such a world. They foresee that if in such a world a dispute arises and diplomatic efforts are unavailing, then one or both countries will shortly rearm, and war will break out. What is worse, in anticipation of such a conflict some nations may secretly stockpile or actually produce nuclear weapons, in undetectable violation of the abolition agreement, so as to have an immediate and overwhelming advantage over their potential adversaries— or, at any rate, to avoid being left at a hopeless disadvantage if it turns out that the adversary has cheated. And the deterrence theorists note, as a clinching argument, that even if it should happen that no one was violating the agreement the knowledge of how to make the weapons would remain in the world, and nations could rebuild nuclear weapons openly as soon as some unresolvable political dispute broke out. Since in this view political disputes are sooner or later inevitable, it would not be long before the whole world had embarked again on a chaotic, pell-mell nuclear-arms race—the worst of all possible results. This line of thinking, though it is no secret, is not widely known among the public, yet among strategic analysts it is broadly accepted. And since it is to the analysts, by and large, that the politicians turn when they wish to translate hopeful rhetoric into action this view stands as a serious obstacle to any plan for full nuclear disarmament—and should so stand unless the points made can be answered. The following are but a few examples of this reasoning. Herman Kahn wrote in 1960:

> It has probably always been impractical to imagine a completely disarmed world, and the introduction of the thermonuclear bomb has added a special dimension to this impracticality. Given the large nuclear stockpiles in the Soviet Union, the United States, and the British Isles, it would be child's play for one of these nations to hide completely hundreds of these bombs. . . . The violator would then have an incredible advantage if the agreement ever broke down and the arms race started again. This surely means that even if all nations should one day agree to total nuclear disarmament, we must presume that there would be the hiding of some nuclear weapons or components as a hedge against the other side doing so. An international arrangement for banishing war through disarmament will not call for total disarmament but will almost undoubtedly include provisions for enforcement that cannot be successfully overturned by a small, hidden force. Otherwise it would be hopelessly unstable. . . .
>
> While total disarmament can be ruled out as an immediate possibility, one can conceive of some sort of international authority which might have a monopoly of war-making capability. . . . However, it is most doubtful in the absence of a crisis or war that a world government can be set up in the next decade.

Living with Nuclear Weapons makes some of these same points:

Complete disarmament would require some form of world government to deter actions of one nation against another. In a disarmed world, without such a government armed with sufficient force to prevent conflict between or among nations, differences in beliefs and interests might easily lead to a renewal of war. But any world government capable of preventing world conflict could also become a world dictatorship. And given the differences in ideology, wealth, and nationalism that now exist in the world, most states are not likely to accept a centralized government unless they feel sure of controlling it or minimizing its intrusiveness.

And the M.I.T. political scientist and arms-control expert George Rathjens, in an essay published in 1977 in which he advocates large reductions in the nuclear arsenals of both sides, writes:

> We reject the possibility of complete nuclear disarmament as being unrealistic for the foreseeable future. This becomes clear as soon as one faces up to the changes in the political environment that would be required. . . .
>
> (a) All states would have to be parties to disarmament agreement. . . .
>
> (b) All would have to accept such intrusive inspection as to preclude weapons manufacture. . . .
>
> (c) To be sure of timely access to any suspected installation where nuclear weapons might be stored or produced, the forces available to the international authority would have to be sufficiently strong to overcome resistance rapidly. . . .
>
> We are, then, for all practical purposes, dealing with the question of the establishment of a world government (or something very close to it), and one with rather extraordinary powers of search and seizure at that.

As it happens, agreement on this point extends even to the advocates of world government. Both see an unbreakable linkage between full nuclear (or total) disarmament and world government. In *World Peace Through World Law,* published in 1958, which is one of the most carefully thought through of the proposals for world government, Grenville Clark and Louis B. Sohn spell out the minimum that they think would be necessary:

> Apart from an effective inspection system to supervise the disarmament process from the outset, it will be indispensable simultaneously to establish an adequate world police force in order that, after complete disarmament has been accomplished, the means will exist to deter or apprehend violators of the world law forbidding any national armaments and prohibiting violence or the threat of it between nations. It will then become equally clear that along with the prohibition of violence or the threat of it as the means of dealing with international disputes, it will be essential to establish alternative peaceful means to deal with all disputes between nations in the shape of a world judicial and conciliation system. It will doubtless also be found advisable, in the interest of a solid and durable peace, to include a World Development Authority, adequately and reliably financed, in order to mitigate the vast disparities between the "have" and the "have not" nations.
>
> The necessity will also be seen for a world legislature with carefully limited yet adequate powers. . . . In addition, it will be necessary to constitute an effective world executive, free from any crippling veto, in order to direct and control the world inspection service and the world police force and to exercise other essential executive functions. Finally, it will follow as surely as day follows night that an effective world revenue system must be adopted.

And, in 1955, Bertrand Russell wrote:

> It would be wholly futile to get an agreement prohibiting the H-Bomb. Such an agreement would not be considered binding after war has broken out, and each side on the outbreak of war would set to work to manufacture as many bombs as possible.

I might add that in *The Fate of the Earth* (in which I sought to define the political task posed by nuclear weapons but did not propose any course of action) I wrote:

> This task [of resolving the nuclear predicament] falls into two parts—two aims. The first is to save the world from extinction by eliminating nuclear weapons from the earth. . . . The second aim, which alone can provide a sure foundation for the first, is to create a political means by which the world can arrive at the decisions that sovereign states previously arrived at through war. These two aims . . . are intimately connected. If, on the one hand, disarmament is not accompanied by a political solution, then every clash of will between nations will tempt them to pick up the instruments of violence again, and so lead the world back toward extinction. If, on the other hand, a political solution is not accompanied by complete disarmament, then the political decisions that are made will not be binding, for they will be subject to challenge by force.

(I take the liberty of quoting myself again only because I wish to acknowledge my former adherence to a point of view with which I now propose to argue.)

These statements, and countless others that might be quoted, form a remarkable consensus. One school favors world government and the other opposes it, yet they agree that if full nuclear disarmament (or total disarmament) is to be achieved world government is necessary. They make different choices, but they agree on what the choices are, and they agree that between the two there is no middle ground. The changeover is from one fundamental organization of the world to another. And each organization has its own logic and fundamental structure, radically different from the other's. Deterrence, as we have seen, cannot countenance any reductions below what is necessary for "minimum deterrence," and even these reductions, it is sometimes argued, may be destabilizing. But world government, as the passage by Clark and Sohn makes clear, has an even more comprehensive and indivisible logic—one that moves from an inspection force to a police force, and from a police force to a court, so that by the time you reach the end of the paragraph you have a "World Development Authority," set up to hand over the money of the "have" nations to the "have not" nations. The real problem with world government, as this passage suggests, is not that it is "impossible," or "utopian"—for if enough people want it they can surely have it— but that if we choose it we get more than we want. The heart sinks at the thought of world government not because it is "unrealistic" but because it is all too real. To use a homely metaphor, it is like one of those mail-order clubs in which to receive an attractive introductory offer of, say, a book or a plant one must accept for the rest of the year a monthly book or plant that one may not want. We want relief from the nuclear peril, but if we sign up for world government as the means of getting it we find that global institution after global institution is inexorably delivered on our doorstep thereafter, each one equipped to meddle in some new area of our lives. We are caught up, seemingly for purely technical reasons, in a whirlwind of political change that, in and of itself, we do not want. (The reason for what seems the illimitably sweeping character of world government is easier to understand when one recalls that it is being instituted as a replacement for war, which was previously the "final arbiter" of *all* international disputes, no matter what their character or origin might be.) We would like world government to make just one decision—to "ban" (as it's often put) nuclear weapons—but we find that in order to do that it must apparently have the power to make almost any decision we can think of. And from this unlimited delegation of power we shrink back. (Most proposals for world government, and particularly those made by Americans or Englishmen, are hedged about with all kinds of restraints, but, while the restraints might indeed work and be useful, experience tells us that they can always break down, and it is hard to place much trust in them.)

In sum, I am suggesting that the reason we have failed to achieve nuclear disarmament in the last thirty-nine years is not merely that we have lacked the fortitude or the will or the moral sensitivity (although we can hardly exonerate ourselves on those counts) but also that even on the purely intellectual level we have been missing a piece of the puzzle: a way of abolishing nuclear weapons that does not require us to found a world government, which the world shows virtually no interest in founding. The requirement for world government as the inevitable price for nuclear disarmament is at the heart of the impasse that the world has been unable to break through in almost four decades of the nuclear age. It stops citizens and government officials alike from clearly advocating the natural and obvious goal of their anti-nuclear efforts: the abolition of nuclear arms. The linkage is in itself paralyzing. Until it is removed—until we find some way of ridding ourselves of nuclear weapons without having to establish world government, or something like it—major relief from the nuclear peril seems unlikely.

Once the early hopes for a nuclear-free world raised by the advocates of world government had, in the late 1940s, been effectively buried, the tone and content of the continuing discussion of the nuclear question in official circles came to be conditioned by a key piece of reasoning. The reasoning ran: If nuclear weapons are to be abolished, there must be world government; world government is impossible; therefore, we must arm ourselves with nuclear weapons. Once this piece of reasoning was accepted, the greatest of the human and moral questions that were raised by nuclear weapons—questions such as whether it was acceptable to annihilate whole nations, or whether it made sense to build the machinery for the self-extermination of mankind—were, in effect, ruled out of order. For if there was only one path—world government—that led to complete nuclear disarmament, and that path was blocked, a nuclear buildup became inevitable. There is moral responsibility only where there is choice, but here no choice was seen, and therefore no responsibility was seen, either. While the necessity for threatening to use, and perhaps one day actually using, nuclear weapons was certainly regrettable, it was suggested that there was no sense in losing sleep over it until someone showed a plausible way of abolishing them. The remaining questions were details: how many millions you had to threaten to kill to make deterrence take effect, how many bombs you needed to do it, how to keep your retaliatory force safe, etc. The underlying logic constituted a license, which has been honored until the present, to "think the unthinkable" without any qualms. And if anyone protested the amoral coldness of this thinking, the burden of proof was on him. Did he propose world government? Did he suppose that it could be established and established in time to prevent a nuclear holocaust? Could he point to some other way of abolishing nuclear weapons? If not, it was said, he should hold his tongue.

In 1961, James Newman, an editor on the staff of *Scientific American*, reviewing Herman Kahn's book *On Thermonuclear War* in that periodical, described it as "a moral tract on mass murder: how to plan it, how to commit it, how to get away with it, how to justify it." Kahn's book was exactly that, but so was every book on nuclear strategy—unless it advocated unilateral disarmament—and if Newman could not show the way to avoid this mass murder, then the question was whether he really had the standing to complain. He could be seen to be just as deeply implicated as Kahn was, the only difference being that Kahn was ready to think about the mass murder and talk about it, while Newman was not. (So firmly rooted was the underlying justification for nuclear strategizing that the theorists of the unthinkable at times assumed an air of martyred dignity, as though they were being held in disrepute for volunteering to take up a necessary but painful burden that the rest of society was too weak or squeamish to shoulder.

And the theorists were absolutely right—as long as everyone agreed that a nuclear-armed world was the only realistic one.)

The new peace movement now finds itself in the same position as James Newman. Its members have exhumed the elemental human and moral questions that are posed by nuclear weapons. They have discovered their revulsion against the idea of enjoying a precarious "safety" at the price of holding hostage the life of every human being on earth and every future, unborn human being. They have awakened with shock and horror to the realization that, like a demented person who has filled the basement of his house with TNT and threatens to set it off, the human family has crammed its planetary home, unmenaced by any outside power, with nuclear weapons. They have rebelled against the belief that mankind's "no" to nuclear slaughter and self-annihilation is untranslatable into action, and must always be blocked by an impenetrable shield of political impossibility. And all this has been essential work, without which mankind would never be able to escape from its self-constructed trap. But now they are asked —and rightly—what plan they have to offer to show the way out of the impasse. If they have none, it is said, they are airing their anguish and indignation before the public for nothing—behavior comparable to running up to someone on death row and shouting "You must die! You must die!" Their challenge, and everyone's challenge, is to unmake the chain of reasoning that locks us in inaction, to break through the shield of political impossibility, and to chart the path that leads back to survival.

II.
A DELIBERATE POLICY

THE CONSENSUS, among so many of those who have thought deeply about the nuclear predicament, that nuclear weapons cannot be abolished unless world government is established seems to find support in traditional political theory: in the distinction between the so-called state of nature, in which men live in anarchy and resolve their disputes among themselves, with war serving as the final arbiter, and the so-called civil state, in which men live under a government and submit their disputes to its final arbitration. In reflecting on the formation of states out of warring tribes or principalities, political thinkers have often observed that the transition from the state of nature to the civil state is usually radical and abrupt, frequently involving some act of conquest or other form of violence, and admits of no partial or halfway solutions, in which, say, a central authority is given the legislative power to "decide" the outcome of disputes but not

93

the executive power to enforce its decisions. We seem to be faced with the same radical, either-or choice in the world as a whole, in which nations, although each constitutes a civil state within its own borders, have, according to the traditional view, always lived in an anarchic state of nature in their relations with each other. The United Nations, which has been helpful in moderating hostilities in our tense and warlike world but has not been empowered to resolve basic disputes among nations, appears to exemplify what halfway measures toward entry into the civil state lead to in the global arena.

The reason that halfway measures toward the civil state never seem to amount to very much is straightforward and basic. Human beings, existing on earth in large numbers and possessed of separate and independent wills, inevitably get into disputes, and government and war are the two immemorial means by which the disputes have been bindingly resolved. Nations do not dare to give up war and disarm until world government, or some equivalent, is in place, because if they did they would be left without any final arbiter for settling disputes. This situation would be inherently unstable, because as soon as a serious dispute arose—concerning, for example, who was to control a certain piece of territory— nations would reach for the instruments of war, and the impotent, halfway civil measures would be ignored or swept aside (as happened, for example, to the League of Nations in the 1930s). That is why the political thinkers of our time have, with rare unanimity, declared that either total disarmament or full nuclear disarmament is impossible without the simultaneous establishment of world government—and we are left with the unfortunate choice between living with a full balance of nuclear terror, which we would like to get away from, and instituting a full global state, which we would like to avoid. (Mere nuclear disarmament is seen as impossible without world government because among the instruments of war nuclear arms overrule all the others. They have the final word.)

The key event in the transition from the state of nature to the civil state is the centralization of power, in which the individual nations (or people) renounce their right to resort to force at their own discretion, yielding it to the central authority, which is then empowered to make and enforce final decisions. Unfortunately, the centralization of power does not necessarily require a shift from "lawlessness" to "law," as advocates of world government sometimes seem to suggest. The central authority can be, in a moral sense, as "lawless" as any individual. When the central authority in question is a world government, this possibility assumes terrifying proportions, which have no precedent in the annals of politics. Moreover, the establishment of a central authority does not necessarily entail a reduction in the levels of violence, as the record of the totalitarian regimes in the first half of our century makes clear (and as the record of the Pol Pot government in Kampuchea has made clear more recently). Governments, we are forced to acknowledge, are fully as capable of slaughtering huge numbers of people as war is. And if a lawless government were to assume control of the world and such slaughter were to be carried out in the global darkness of the oppression of all mankind the horror of the situation would be beyond all imagining.

What the world's entry into the civil state would accomplish, however, is, as everyone acknowledges, an end to war—or, in our time, an end to the possibility of "mutual assured destruction" and human extinction. In war, the level of force used is bid up to the maximum, because victory (if any) goes to the side that keeps on fighting longer. War is, in Clausewitz's words, a form of "reciprocal action" that "must lead to an extreme" in order to reach a conclusion. And for that reason nuclear weapons spoil war as a final arbiter of international disputes: the extreme they run to is total annihilation. Central governments, on the other hand, don't need to run to any extremes of force to carry out even the most extensive slaughter. One bullet for each "subversive," fired into the back of the head, will suffice. In fact, strictly speaking, no active violence at all is necessary. Vast populations can be killed off by simple deprivation. If you place a multitude of people in a camp, force them to work hard, and cut back their rations, you can kill as many of them as you want to. Certainly no nuclear bombs will be necessary to kill them. In that limited, tragic sense, world government, even at its worst, would be a way out of the nuclear predicament. (Of course, if world government were to break down, and civil war were to arise, the nuclear peril might re-arise with it; but just at the moment the peril of a nuclear holocaust resulting from a breakdown of world government is, I should say, the least of our worries.) Even if one regards these worst-case nightmares of world government run amok as unlikely, the prospect of a supreme political power ruling over the whole earth remains chilling. Anarchy is not liberty, yet it could be that in anarchy, with all its violence, the human spirit has greater latitude to live and grow than it would have in the uniform shadow of a global state.

To be sure, for a number of people it is not the attractions of world government that lead them to favor that particular resolution of the nuclear predicament. It is their dismay at what they see as the alternative: an indeterminate period of life on the edge of the abyss, terminated by extinction. The real choice, they say, is not between world government and anarchy but between world government and nothing—"one world or none," as people used to put it. Nevertheless, most people are agreed that the immediate political choice before us is between an anarchic state of nature, in which nations possess nuclear weapons, and the civil state, or world government, in which they would not. (Some people, it is true, have suggested that the world government itself might have to possess nuclear weapons—a prospect that can only increase one's misgivings about this institution.) This definition of the actions open to us is at the heart of an impasse in which the world has been stuck throughout the nuclear age.

In *The Nuclear Revolution: International Politics Before and After Hiroshima*, of 1981, the political scientist Michael Mandelbaum, reflecting the opinion of the consensus—which includes both the advocates of world government and the advocates of our present-day policy of nuclear deterrence—writes, "Relations among sovereign states are still governed by the principle of anarchy. War is still possible." And he goes on:

> A logical way to do away with war among nation-states is to abolish national armaments altogether. This, in turn, requires abolishing the incentives for states to have armaments. They have them because of the insecurity that arises from the anarchical structure of the international system. So the requirement for disarmament is the disappearance of anarchy, in favor of an international system organized along the lines of the state in domestic politics. States must give up sovereignty. This is the political revolution that some anticipated in 1945 but that has not come to pass.

In this view, evidently, our world of nuclear-armed deterrence remains in the traditional anarchic state of nature. I should like to argue, however, that inasmuch as nuclear weapons have spoiled war—the final arbiter in the state of nature—we are mistaken about this, having been misled by the habits of pre-nuclear political thought, which so often lead us astray in the new and strange nuclear world. A deterred world, I believe, is no longer in anarchy—in the traditional state of nature. Nor, of course, is it in the civil state. It is not even quite in between the two but, rather, is in a new state altogether—the deterred state—which has been brought into being by the all-pervasive, deeply rooted, man-made reality of a nuclear-capable world. It was, I believe, an unacknowledged change of this kind that Einstein was referring to when he made his famous remark, "The unleashed power of the atom has changed everything save our modes of thinking, and thus we drift toward unparalleled catastrophe." But if our world, because of the invention of nuclear weapons, has already departed from the traditional state of nature, then the possibility seems to open up that our choices may not be restricted to the either-or one between nuclear-armed anarchy and world government. New and more promising alternatives may be available. I believe that they are. In particular, I believe that within the framework of deterrence itself it may be possible to abolish nuclear weapons. But to understand how this might be so we need to examine deterrence more deeply—its mechanisms, its scientific and technical foundations, and its political goals.

A simple analogy may help to clarify the full novelty of the deterred state. Let us suppose that one day my neighbor comes into my house and starts to carry off my furniture. If he and I live in the civil state, I will call the police, and some organ of government will eventually decide what is to be done. If he and I live in a state of nature, there are no police or organs of government, and it is for me alone to try to stop him—by persuasion, if possible, or, if that fails, by force. Force is my last resort, the final arbiter of my dispute with my neighbor, and what then ultimately decides our dispute is whether it is he or I who lies dead on the ground. It's worth noting, though, that there is nothing inherently violent in the fact of a dispute. My neighbor may have quietly carried off my furniture while I was out. It is as a solution to the dispute that violence—or some alternative—enters the picture. In the civil state, my dispute with my neighbor is arbitrated by government, and in the state of nature it is arbitrated by the fight between him and me (if it comes to that). But when one turns to deterrence one finds that neither of these things is happening. Deterrence arbitrates nothing. Underlying the traditional belief that my neighbor and I must resolve our dispute either by violence or by government was the unstated assumption that the dispute must *be* resolved. Deterrence, however, discovers another possibility—that disputes can be suspended, can be kept in abeyance, without any resolution. It uses terror to prevent disputes from ever coming into being. Under deterrence, I neither call the police nor shoot my neighbor—or even lay hands on him—because he doesn't enter my house to begin with. For under deterrence I have, in anticipation of my neighbor's depredations, filled my house with explosives, wired them to go off the moment any unauthorized person crosses my threshold, and (an essential step) informed my neighbor of what I have done—hoping, of course, that he will then have the good sense to give up any plans he might have for stealing my furniture. Deterrence intervenes at a point in the action quite different from that at which either force or an organ of government intervenes. Force or an organ of government steps in after the dispute has arisen and has reached an impasse, to settle it, whereas deterrence steps in before anyone has made a move, to keep the dispute from taking place.

The mechanism of deterrence is as different from the mechanism of war as its end result is from the end result of war. Deterrence is essentially psychological in its action. It uses terror to produce a mental result—the decision not to act. In the international sphere, its aim is to make government leaders *reflect* before they engage in aggression. When its action is effective, no one lies dead on the ground (although if it fails all do). It relies for its success not on the corpse of the fallen soldier but on the prudence of the live, thinking statesman. War, by contrast, while it has its psychological elements, including an element of deterrence, is in essence physical in its action: it blasts the opponent out of the way, as though he were a thing rather than a person, and his soon to be darkened psyche is of purely secondary interest.

In making deterrence possible, nuclear weapons have thus offered a new answer to the question (which lies at the heart of the nuclear predicament) of how disputes among nations are to be handled—an answer in which the disputes, instead of being arbitrated either by government or by war (or by anything else, for that matter), are kept out of "court" altogether. Because both government and war were ways of settling disputes, the civil state and the state of nature were both states of change. The deterred state, by contrast, is a stalemate. In the sphere of international politics, all is held stationary, in a sort of global-political version of "the freeze"—a version in which it is not arms that are frozen in place but national boundaries—and change is relegated to other spheres, such as the economic, the cultural, and the spiritual, and to domestic turmoil, including revolution. (Revolutionary war escapes incapacitation by nuclear weapons because the enemies—

often belonging to the same families—are too closely intertwined to be able to kill one another by such indiscriminate means. Furthermore, while people have shown themselves willing to consider precipitating the annihilation of their own countries by antagonizing another nuclear power, they have yet to show themselves willing to threaten their own countries with nuclear weapons.)

Whatever may be the advantages or disadvantages of the state of deterrence, its foundations are solid. They are deeply lodged in the nature of things. They lie, in the last analysis, in the structure of matter, which we are powerless to return to its former, Newtonian state—a feat that would require us to forget twentieth-century physics. We are used to thinking of deterrence as a policy, but before it is a policy it is a simple fact of life for nuclear-armed nations. Hand two nations the wherewithal to dip their buckets into the bottomless pools of energy that lie in the heart of matter and a state of deterrence springs up between them, whatever their policies may be. For their leaders, if they are rational, will grasp without the help of theory that if they drop nuclear bombs on their nuclear-armed foe, the foe may drop nuclear bombs on them in return. In the last analysis, victory is ruled out in the nuclear world because the adversaries are matched not against reserves of power that belong in any basic way to either of them individually but against the unlimited, universal power of nuclear energy, which is now more or less available to all. And what human power can hope to defeat the universe? The role of deterrence *policy* is to acknowledge, codify, and shore up this situation, and then seek certain advantages from it.

It would be a mistake, however, to suggest that the deterred state has been added to the two traditional ones, as though we were now free to choose among three states. Rather, the foundations of the traditional state of nature have themselves been altered, so that now we must distinguish between two states of nature—the pre-nuclear one and the nuclear one. The idea of an alteration in nature comes as something of a shock to us, as the very word "nature" suggests that it might. The word suggests the *given*—all that exists, has always existed, and always will exist, independent of human power to alter it. It was not in this realm that we expected alteration. We looked for alteration, on the whole, in the civil state, where our efforts and our will were supposed to make a difference. Whatever else might change, "anarchy" appeared to be a constant—stable, if you will. But we failed to reckon with modern physics (one of the "natural" sciences), which proved capable of transforming nature. Anarchy rested on a shaky base. When the atom was cracked open and its vast energy was spilled into our human world, anarchy's underpinnings were washed away. Thanks to physics, the supposedly changeless physical world was unexpectedly changed, and nations were simply obliged to adjust as best they could. (One of the ironies of our situation is that the natural world has proved to be more changeable than the supposedly flexible political world.)

Of course, the phrase "altering nature" is not literally accurate. In literal fact, nature remains just as it was before we pried into its secrets (as far as we know, neither the detonation of a few tens of thousands of nuclear weapons on our planet nor our disappearance as a species would have the slightest effect on any of the hundred billion or so galaxies in the universe), and what we really mean by the expression is that the physical world in which human beings live and conduct their affairs has been altered. We are not the inventors but only the discoverers of the energy in matter. The universe has always been built this way, and human beings, belonging to a rational and inquiring species, were bound to discover the fact. And then we were bound to try to figure out—as we are now doing—how to survive in such a universe. Nothing now seems more "unnatural" to us than the nuclear peril, and yet in reality nothing is more "natural," inasmuch as the peril is rooted in the basic structure of nature itself.

Whether or not one subscribes to the policy of nuclear deterrence—the threat to strike back with nuclear weapons if one's country is attacked with them or if it starts to lose a conventional war—one has to recognize as an objective fact that the equations of war and peace have had to be rewritten in our nuclear world, and that in those rewritten equations war comes out a suicidal proposition. Not only has war been taken away from us by physics —been "spoiled"—but we can't get it back. Some have tried. Among them are the devotees of "nuclear-war-fighting," who believe that it is possible to fight and survive, and even prevail in, a nuclear war, and who are now in the ascendancy in Washington. But their efforts inevitably founder in the boundless destruction of the more than a million Hiroshimas that are waiting to happen in the world's fifty-thousand-odd nuclear weapons. What these strategists can never explain is how anyone can "prevail" in a "war" after which no one would be left. Their "victories," or restorations of the peace "on terms favorable to the United States," are apparently of an extra-human sort—"victories" in which, after all the people have been killed, our bombs triumph over the other side's bombs. And the strategists' sometimes intricate and ingenious scenarios of nuclear-war-fighting are testimony only to the ability of the human mind, transported by pure abstract theory, to take leave of reality altogether.

In short, under deterrence the passage to a world in which the use of force is given up as the means of settling international differences *has already begun.* In a way, it has been accomplished. In the first days of the nuclear age, it seemed to some "idealists" that the task facing mankind was to abolish war, but "realists" replied that this was impossible—at least, in the short run—because it required the establishment of world government; instead, they proposed the policy of deterrence. However, when one looks at deterrence closely it turns out that war has not been preserved by it. Isn't this what the political scientist Bernard Brodie was getting at when he said, in 1946, in *The Absolute Weapon,* that in the nuclear world the only purpose of military preparations was to avert wars, not to win them? And isn't this what countless statesmen of our time have been telling us in saying that the purpose of their nuclear policies is only to prevent the use of nuclear and other weapons? The statement "War has been spoiled," which stands in such sharp contrast to Mandelbaum's "War is still possible," thus refers not to an idealistic aspiration but to a fait accompli. We cannot abolish war, because nuclear weapons have already done the job for us. What we can and must abolish is mutual assured destruction and the possibility of human extinction, the threat of which we now trade on to keep the peace. Our ambivalence toward this threat, which we try simultaneously to renounce and to exploit for our political ends, defines our new predicament. Just by thinking a little harder, and by looking a little bit more closely at both theory and practice in our nuclear world, we seemingly have already accomplished this "impossible" thing of abolishing war (among nuclear powers, anyway). This is not a mere phrase but a bedrock reality of our time, on which we may rely as we seek elements with which to build the edifice of our future safety. All the debates, carried over from the pre-nuclear age, about whether or not war is moral, and whether or not world government might be preferable, are no doubt extremely interesting, but they are anachronistic, for the world to which they have reference has gone out of existence.

Nuclear weapons, we see, have knocked the sword of war from our hands. Now it is up to us to decide what we will pick up in its place. The question before us shifts from how to abolish war to how to get along in a world from which war has been abolished. And we can start by seeing the first alternative that we have hit on—deterrence—in a new light: not as a continuation of international "anarchy," in which "war is still possible," but as *one* possible system for getting along in a world without war. Without quite recognizing it, we have taken the first steps toward global agreement. It is true that force, while it is no longer the final arbiter, or any sort of arbiter, still plays the central role, as it did in the pre-nuclear state of nature, for a by-product of force, terror, is what holds everybody immobile. Yet it is also true that, as in the civil state, each individual's force, in a kind of tacit agreement, is supposed never to be used. And, as in the civil state, the whole system depends on the recognition by each individual actor of a common interest—survival—that must take precedence over individual interests. Since everybody knows and acknowledges that the use of force by any party may push everybody toward a common doom, all make efforts together to ensure that the "first use" never occurs—although at the same time each side, paradoxically, must constantly bristle with resolve to use force to repel any aggression, should it somehow occur. Moreover, right at the heart of deterrence there is an element of cooperation and consent—a crucial ingredient of every civil state, no matter how oppressive. This is the "psychological" element in deterrence, on which all else depends. For while it is true that sheer terror is the operative force in deterrence it is also true that the statesman on whom it operates must give his consent if it is to work. To be sure, his freedom of action is no greater than that of someone who is being told to do something at gunpoint; nevertheless, he remains a free agent in extremely important ways. His state of mind—his self-interest, his sanity, his prudence, his self-control, his clear-sightedness—is the real foundation of his country's and everyone else's survival. In short, he must *decide* that the world he lives in is not one in which aggression pays off. In all these respects, a deterred world is not a state of anarchy awaiting the imposition of a world order but, rather, already a sort of world order, albeit one that is in many ways contradictory and absurd.

In a deep sense, unless the species does destroy itself our world will remain a deterred world. By this I do not mean that we shall forever maintain nuclear weapons and threaten one another with mutual assured destruction. I mean that whether we possess nuclear weapons or abolish them the terror they inspire will dominate our affairs and dictate the character of our political decisions. Even if mankind were now to enter formally into the civil state, and found a world government to replace war, deterrence would, in a way, still be in effect. In the pre-nuclear world, entry into the civil state would have been a free act, arising out of an abundant faith in humanity and confidence in its betterment. For us, however, who live surrounded by doom, like people in a town at the foot of a rumbling volcano (it is our peculiar distinction not to have built our town next to Vesuvius but to have built Vesuvius next to our town), entry into the civil state would be a compelled act: a measure taken not so much to better life as only to hold on to it —not to bring heaven to earth but only to preserve the earth. Being inspired by terror, entry into the civil state would be a variant of the balance of terror under deterrence—a variant in which nations, instead of deterring each other from starting a nuclear holocaust, would all join together to deter the species as a whole from extinguishing itself. While the shift from multiplicity to unity would require a global political revolution—it would be some equivalent of what Einstein called for—even that revolution would not suspend the underlying transformation of human existence which was brought about by the development of nuclear weapons. We can never recover war. We will always be at risk, somewhere down the road, of extinguishing ourselves. We will always live in a state of deterrence. These changes mark a transformation of our world. And it is this transformed world, not the vanished, pre-nuclear one, that is our true starting point as we face the nuclear peril.

The great aim—the supreme good—that we seek through deterrence is "stability." However, this aim, to which we often refer as though it were single and indivisible, actually comprises two separate and conflicting aims. The first is to preserve the political stalemate—to freeze the status quo. The status quo in question is the one that was more or less fixed in place (at least in the central theatres of superpower rivalry, where the influence of nuclear weapons made itself felt most keenly) in the years immediately following the Second World War. What recommended this status quo as the one in which to freeze the world was not the virtue of its particular arrangements—in fact, terrible injustices, including Soviet domination of Eastern Europe, were institutionalized by it —but only the fact that it *was* the status quo when the nuclear age began, and was thus the logical starting place for a system whose essence was going to be that no changes through military action were permitted. In a broader sense, however, the status quo was

105

the system of independent states, which had existed throughout history but whose continued existence was called into question by the nuclear peril. The second aim is to avert a nuclear holocaust, which the great powers hope to head off by the paradoxical, jujitsulike means of threatening one another (if only in retaliation) with that same holocaust. In other words, the policy seeks to give satisfactory resolutions of the two great issues that were raised by the development of nuclear weapons—*how* man should live (in nation-states or in some other way; under capitalism, Communism, or something else; and so on) and *whether* he would live.

The principle that binds these two aims of deterrent policy together, and whose observance would make them obtainable simultaneously, is the principle of nonaggression. This principle embodies no millennial dreams, yet its realization has been much sought (through the League of Nations and the United Nations, among other organizations) and rarely achieved. Nuclear weapons lend tremendous support to the principle of nonaggression. Traditionally, victory—the light at the end of the tunnel of war—has been the great incentive for aggression; but nuclear weapons have killed this hope in the breasts of all realistic government leaders and have thus robbed aggression of its point. Confusingly—and regrettably—they have robbed defense of *its* point, too, since in a nuclear "war" the defender is as thoroughly annihilated as the aggressor. For both parties, the tunnel of war now leads only to eternal darkness. The development of nuclear weapons has therefore, at least in theory, laid the foundation for a world at peace. And, in fact, ever since the balance of terror was established the great powers have enjoyed the stability promised by deterrence. They have never used military force against one another, although the air has been filled with threats (which are of the essence of deterrence), and although they have felt free to use their forces against non-nuclear powers. No one has liked this stalemate very much, yet people have made do with it. It is "acceptable": we have accepted it.

No one knows what any of the statesmen of our day would really do if, in the moment of truth, they were forced to choose

A Deliberate Policy

between the two goals of deterrence policy, and either suffer military defeat or launch a nuclear holocaust. But there can be no doubt about which course the doctrine of deterrence specifies: it specifies the holocaust. If it doesn't specify the holocaust, then it isn't deterrence but something else. In that sense, deterrence gives a clear priority to national defense over human survival (although government leaders, of course, hope never to have to make the choice). If this weren't so, the resolution of the nuclear predicament would be easy. We could simply "ban the bomb," and let political matters sort themselves out however they might. If human survival had been the world's overriding goal from the time the nuclear threat first presented itself, and *not* to use nuclear weapons had really been the dominant consideration in nuclear policy—that is, if people had been ready to risk or sacrifice their particular ways of life for the sake of life itself (not their individual lives but the survival of the species)—then they would have at least seriously considered either disarming unilaterally or establishing world government, or doing both. Sometimes it is suggested that unilateral disarmament might itself lead to the use of nuclear weapons, because by creating a military imbalance it would invite the very aggression that the disarmers were hoping to head off. This argument, however, holds true only for half-hearted, faltering unilateral disarmament, which would be reversed as soon as an enemy attack materialized. Thoroughgoing, resolute disarmament would not lead to any use of nuclear arms, because the enemy could get what it wanted from the now militarily undefended country simply by walking into it. What unilateral disarmament might really lead to is not a nuclear holocaust but military defeat and foreign occupation. If by "stability" we meant only the absence of war, then unilateral disarmament would be a matchless way of achieving it. Defeat could be entirely "stable."

In the present context, however, the point is not to advocate or oppose either unilateral disarmament or world government but only to make it clear that the rejection of both by just about everybody in favor of a policy of deterrence shows that the principal goal of deterrence is to preserve national sovereignty and everything that goes with sovereignty. At the very heart of the riddle of deterrence sits sovereignty, whose preservation the policy achieves by subjecting mankind to the risk of extinction. Whatever final judgment one might make on this bargain—and it is extreme dissatisfaction with it that has fuelled the new peace movement—the arguments in its favor are substantial enough not to require obfuscation by the misleading claim that we possess nuclear arms chiefly in order to avoid using them. National sovereignty *in itself*—the full political control by local people of their own territories—is, most people would agree, highly desirable. Certainly most people treasure the independence of their own countries. And probably very few even of those whose countries are not defended by nuclear arsenals would like to see either the establishment of a world government or the collapse of the balance of terror through unilateral disarmament. Furthermore, liberty in the world at large may depend on the political survival of a certain number of countries, including, above all, the democracies of the West. The strongest and most honest argument in favor of the possession of nuclear weapons, then—for those who believe in liberty—is that upholding liberty is worth the risk of extinction. (For the Soviet government, of course, the justification would be that socialism is upheld.) The argument is strengthened if one maintains—as the Catholic bishops, in their pastoral letter, and Brodie do but *Living with Nuclear Weapons* does not—that deterrence is a temporary, emergency arrangement, soon to be replaced by some better system, in which we no longer secure our safety by threatening our doom.

Nevertheless, it remains true that, within the limits imposed by the fundamental decision to defend national sovereignty with nuclear arsenals, the mutual-assured-destruction strategists do, as an additional goal, seek to deploy the weapons in such a way as to reduce to a minimum the chance of a holocaust. They do their best to see to it that the threat of annihilation by which sovereignty is preserved also prevents the execution of the threat. Above all, they seek to adopt strategic policies that add to stability—by, for example, building retaliatory rather than first-strike weapons, forgoing attempts at civil defense, establishing hot lines and the like with the adversary, and, of course, entering into arms-control agreements. (It is regarding these measures, which assume the existence of nuclear arsenals, that the sometimes arcane disputes between the advocates of mutual assured destruction and the advocates of nuclear-war-fighting take place, with the mutual-assured-destruction school, on the whole, favoring measures that will stop the holocaust from ever occurring in the first place and the nuclear-war-fighting school favoring measures that would supposedly enable the United States to get some advantage over the Soviet Union if a holocaust did occur.)

Such are the means and ends of the doctrine of deterrence, on which we rely today for the safety of the nuclear world. They present us with a striking disparity. The over-all end—the military stalemate—is modest and conservative. The means, however—two nations' threats to annihilate one another and, perhaps, all mankind—are extreme in a way that gives new meaning to that word. The problem with deterrence is not that it doesn't "work" —it is, I am sure, a very effective (though far from infallible) way of restraining the superpowers from attacking one another, should they be inclined to do so—but that we must pay an inconceivable price if it fails. Regarded as a sort of world order, deterrence is a regime in which every crime is punished by the severest possible penalty, as though the ruler of a state had decreed that if just one of the citizens commits a burglary all the citizens must be put to death. This radical disproportion between ends and means invites us to inquire whether we might not be able to achieve our modest ends by less extreme means—a means by which we did not threaten ourselves with doom. This definition of our task is, of course, quite different from the one in which we were invited to found world government in the midst of "anarchy" or else accept a life lived perpetually on the edge of extinction. Now we would be working within deterrence defined in its broadest sense—as the new "state of nature," brought into being by the very peril that

109

we wish to alleviate. This could come about because deterrence offers us elements to work with that were not available in the pre-nuclear age. Two stand out. The first is the stalemate itself, which was made possible only because of the fearsome destructive power of the military invention that backs it up. The second is the unlosable nature of the knowledge that underlies the invention, and prevents us from ever wholly expunging the possibility of nuclear destruction from our affairs.

Our first step would be to accept the political verdict that has been delivered by deterrence, and formalize the stalemate. The achievement of the stalemate was, in the broadest sense, accidental: conceived as a makeshift for coping in the short term with a sudden peril that the world lacked either the imagination or the will (or both) to tackle head-on, it gradually took shape, over a period of decades, through trial and error. Its creation was the principal work of a generation. The question for that generation (once world government and full nuclear disarmament were jointly ruled out) was whether, given the presence of nuclear weapons in the world, stability could be achieved. It could be. It was. But now, with the answer to that question in hand, we can start with the stability—the stalemate—and invert the question, asking whether, within the new context of our transformed world, there might not be a better means of preserving that same stability: a means with less extreme risk attached. What for the people of the earlier generation was the end point of their efforts can for us be the starting point. For even as we see that deterrence is possible we know, and have felt in our hearts, that the bargain now struck by it is unworthy of human life, because it turns us into potential mass slayers of our species. This lesson, too, is a fruit of our experience in the nuclear age, and it drives us to seek to dismantle the doomsday machine at the earliest possible moment. A deepening awareness of the full meaning of that bargain—frequently and rightly described as "Faustian"—for strategy, for the state of our civilization, and for the state of our souls is what now inspires the world's gathering protest against nuclear arms.

Our method can be to convert into a settlement in principle

the settlement of political differences which we have achieved in fact under the pressure of the nuclear threat. We can, in a manner of speaking, adopt our present world, with all its injustices and other imperfections, as our ideal, and then seek the most sensible and moderate means of preserving it. This effort is consistent with the spiritual task that nuclear weapons have put before us, which is at bottom to awaken ourselves to a new appreciation and gratitude for the world that is given to each of us at birth. For the time being, instead of asking ourselves how, in the light of the peril to all life, we must transform all life, we ask what the best way is to keep everything just the same. Not improvement but mere continuation is our dream. This, of course, is a deeply conservative aim, but then the nuclear peril seems to call on us to be conservative, inasmuch as *conserving* ourselves and our world is the challenge that we now face. To many peoples, the idea of freezing the status quo might seem discouraging, especially if for them the status quo includes intervention in their affairs by a great power. The peoples of Eastern Europe are a case in point. They cannot wish to formalize Soviet domination of their countries. The formalization of the status quo envisioned here, however, would not do that. It would permit those peoples every means to liberate themselves that they now have at their disposal, and would remove only means that they now already lack—Western military intervention in their struggles.

The next question is whether, after formalizing the status quo, we can reduce our reliance on the extreme means by which we now uphold it, and how far a reduction can go. The invaluable lesson of deterrence theory is that in the nuclear age the use of force is self-cancelling. This is the profound truth that the statesmen of our day are struggling to articulate when—expressing, no doubt, their fervent desire, though it is not the actual case—they tell us that they possess nuclear weapons only in order *not* to use them. At first, the simple and almost irresistible implication of that truth for policy seems to be that we can take the whole hateful machinery of force—conventional and nuclear—and clear it out of our lives. The moment we did that, all the paradoxes, contradictions, absurdities, and abominations that we live with under deterrence would evaporate. If the whole doomsday machine is intended only to paralyze itself—to do nothing—why do we need it? Can't we accomplish nothing without threatening suicide? But the very question reveals that after all—semi-covertly and somewhat shamefacedly—we actually rely on the doomsday machine to serve another end: the preservation of our sovereignty. We still exploit the peril of extinction for our political ends. And we don't know how to wean ourselves from that reliance without taking radical steps, such as unilateral disarmament or world government. But while some of us may be ready for radical steps the world as a whole, it is clear, is not, and demands that we preserve the sovereignty of states, even though it requires a risk to our survival. Given this political reality—which shows no sign of changing soon—it appears that, in one form or another, our reliance on the nuclear threat cannot be broken. Nevertheless, even under these terms we have far more flexibility than we have thought. It is a flexibility that, I believe, extends all the way to the abolition of nuclear arms.

On the face of it, there appears to be a contradiction between the two goals we have set for ourselves. It appears that we want to keep the stalemate but to abolish the weapons that make it possible. Yet this contradiction exists in present policy—taking the form of our threatening to use the weapons in order *not* to use them. Either way, paradox is our lot. We seek to preserve a stalemated, purely defensive world but must apparently make use of —or at least make provision for—purely offensive weapons to do it. Indeed, one way of looking at the nuclear predicament is to see it as the final outcome of a competition between offense and defense which has been going on throughout the history of war, in a sort of war within war. The invention of nuclear weapons gave the victory once and for all, it appears, to the offensive side. Although the unpredictability of science prevents a truly definitive judgment, the chances that the defense will ever catch up look vanishingly dim. The entire history of warfare supports this conclusion: although the balance between offense and defense has swung back and forth, the general trend has been unvaryingly toward the increasing destructiveness of offensive war. It is this rising general destructiveness, and not the recent success of one particular offensive weapon in eluding destruction by a defensive counterpart, that has now culminated in the whole planet's being placed in mortal peril. The ultimate vulnerability of human beings is the result of the frailty of nature itself, on which we depend utterly for life; as is now clearer to us than ever before, nature cannot stand up to much nuclear destruction. Given this flood tide of destructive power, which was rising steadily even before nuclear weapons were developed, and has continued since their development (in the fields of chemical and biological warfare, for example), the hopes for defense are not so much slight as beside the point. Most of these hopes rest on weapons that counter not the effects of nuclear weapons but, rather, the nuclear weapons' delivery vehicles. Yet a delivery vehicle is simply anything that gets from point A to point B on the face of the earth. A horse and cart is a delivery vehicle. An army battling its way into enemy territory is a delivery vehicle. A man with a suitcase is a delivery vehicle. There seems little chance that all existing vehicles—not to mention all the vehicles that science will dream up in the future —can be decisively countered. And it is even more unlikely that the devices designed to attack all the delivery vehicles would remain invulnerable to devices that scientists would soon be inventing to attack *them*. The superiority of the offense in a world of uninhibited production of nuclear weapons and their delivery vehicles therefore appears to be something that will last for the indefinite future.

The contradiction between the end we seek and the means of attaining it becomes even clearer when we try to imagine the situation we would have if in 1945 the scientists, instead of handing us the ultimate offensive weapon, had emerged from their laboratory with an ultimate defensive weapon—perhaps one of those impenetrable bubbles with which science-fiction writers like to surround cities. Then a thoroughgoing, consistent defensive world would be possible. Aggressively inclined nations might hurl their most lethal weapons at their neighbors, but the weapons would all bounce off harmlessly, and no one would be hurt. Peoples would then live safely within their own borders, suffering only the torments that they managed to invent for themselves. Under our present circumstances, by contrast, we have not perfect defense but perfect vulnerability.

It was in addressing this contradiction that the strategists came up with the doctrine of deterrence in the first place. Their chief discovery was that the threat of retaliation could substitute for the missing defenses. But while defense and deterrence have the same ends the way they work is nearly opposite. In a defensive system, you rely on your military forces actually to throw the enemy forces back: the swung sword falls on the raised shield without inflicting damage; the advancing foot soldier falls into the moat; the warhead is pulverized by the laser beam. But in a system of deterrence you have given up all hope of throwing the enemy back, and are hoping instead, by threatening a retaliatory attack that *he* cannot throw back, to dissuade him from attacking at all. Deterrence thus rests on the fear of a double offense, in which everyone would destroy everyone else and no one would be defended. The crucial element in deterrence is the foreknowledge by the potential aggressor that if he starts anything this is how it will end. Offensive means are made to serve defensive ends. But in the process the continuation of our species is put in jeopardy.

Inasmuch as the goal we have chosen is to shore up a stalemated, defensive world, one way of defining our task would be to ask whether, having agreed to live with the status quo, we might by further agreement accomplish what we are unable to accomplish through technical efforts; namely, to snatch the victory away from offensive arms and hand it, at least provisionally, back to defensive ones. The question is whether as political and diplomatic actors we could rush into the fray on the side of the defense and turn the tables. I think that, within certain all-important limits, we can. The key is to enter into an agreement abolishing nuclear arms. Nations would first agree, in effect, to drop their swords from their hands and lift their shields toward one another instead. They would agree to have not world government, in which all nations are fused into one nation, but its exact opposite —a multiplicity of inviolate nations pledged to leave each other alone. For nations that now possess nuclear weapons, the agreement would be a true abolition agreement. For those that do not now possess them, it would be a strengthened nonproliferation agreement. (A hundred and nineteen nations have already signed the nonproliferation treaty of 1968.) Obviously, an agreement among the superpowers on both the nature of the status quo and the precise terms of abolition would be the most difficult part of the negotiation. The agreement would be enforced not by any world police force or other organ of a global state but by each nation's knowledge that a breakdown of the agreement would be to no one's advantage, and would only push all nations back down the path to doom. In the widest sense, the agreement would represent the institutionalization of this knowledge. But if nuclear weapons are to be abolished by agreement, one might ask, why not go all the way? Why not abolish conventional weapons and defensive weapons as well? The answer, of course, is that even in the face of the threat of annihilation nations have as yet shown no willingness to surrender their sovereignty, and conventional arms would be one support for its preservation. While the abolition of nuclear arms would increase the margin of mankind's safety against nuclear destruction and the peril of extinction, the retention of conventional arms would permit the world to hold on to the system of nation-states. Therefore, a second provision of the agreement would stipulate that the size of conventional forces be limited and balanced. In keeping with the defensive aim of the agreement as a whole, these forces would, to whatever extent this was technically possible, be deployed and armed in a defensive mode.

There is also another reason for retaining defenses. One of the most commonly cited and most substantial reasons for rejecting the abolition of nuclear arms, even if the nuclear powers should

115

develop the will to abolish them, is that the verification of a nu-clear-abolition agreement could never be adequate. And, as far as I know, it is true that no one has ever devised a system of verifica-tion that could, even theoretically, preclude significant cheating. Like defense, it seems, inspection is almost inherently imperfect. When arsenals are large, the argument runs, a certain amount of cheating on arms-control agreements is unimportant, because the number of concealed weapons is likely to be small in relation to the size of the arsenals as a whole. But as the size of the arsenals shrinks, it is said, the importance of cheating grows, and finally the point is reached at which the hidden arsenals tip the strategic balance in favor of the cheater. According to this argument, the point of maximum—indeed, total—imbalance is reached when, after an abolition agreement has been signed, one side cheats while the other does not. Then the cheater, it is said, has an insuperable advantage, and holds its innocent and trusting co-signer at its mercy. But if anti-nuclear defenses are retained the advantage in cheating is sharply reduced, or actually eliminated. Arrayed against today's gigantic nuclear forces, defenses are help-less. Worse, one side's defenses serve as a goad to further offensive production by the other side, which doesn't want the offensive capacity it has decided on to be weakened. But if defenses were arrayed against the kind of force that could be put together in violation of an abolition agreement they could be crucial. On the one side would be a sharply restricted, untested, and clandestinely produced and maintained offensive force, while on the other side would be a large, fully tested, openly deployed, and technically advanced defensive force. Such a force might not completely nul-lify the danger of cheating (there is always the man with a suit-case), but no one can doubt that it would drastically reduce it. At the very least, it would throw the plans of an aggressor into a condition of total uncertainty. Moreover, as the years passed after the signing of the agreement the superiority of the defense would be likely to increase, because defensive weapons would continue to be openly developed, tested, and deployed, while offensive weapons could not be. Therefore—probably as a separate, third provision of the agreement—anti-nuclear defensive forces would be permitted.

President Reagan recently offered a vision of a world protected from nuclear destruction by defensive weapons, many of which would be based in space. The United States, he said, should develop these weapons and then share them with the Soviet Union. With both countries protected from nuclear attack, he went on, both would be able to scrap their now useless nuclear arsenals and achieve full nuclear disarmament. Only the order of events in his proposal was wrong. If we seek first to defend ourselves, and not to abolish nuclear weapons until after we have made that effort, we will never abolish them, because of the underlying, technically irreversible superiority of the offensive in the nuclear world. But if we abolish nuclear weapons first and then build the defenses, as a hedge against cheating, we can succeed. Abolition prepares the way for defense.

However, none of these defensive arrangements would offer much protection if the agreement failed to accompany them with one more provision. The worst case—which must be taken into account if nations are to have confidence in the military preparations for thwarting aggressors—is not mere cheating but blatant, open violation of the agreement by a powerful and ruthless nation that is determined to intimidate or subjugate other nations, or the whole world, by suddenly and swiftly building up, and perhaps actually using, an overwhelming nuclear arsenal. This possibility creates the all-important limits mentioned earlier. As soon as it happened, the underlying military superiority of the offensive in the nuclear world would again hold sway, and the conventional and anti-nuclear defenses permitted under the abolition agreement would become useless. (Just how soon in this buildup the offensive weapons would eclipse the defensive ones would depend on the effectiveness of the defenses that had been built up.) The only significant military response to this threat would be a response in kind: a similar nuclear buildup by the threatened nations, returning the world to something like the balance of terror as we know it today. But in order to achieve that buildup the threatened nations would probably have to have already in existence considerable preparations for the manufacture of nuclear arms. Therefore, a fourth provision of the abolition agreement would permit nations to hold themselves in a particular, defined state of readiness for nuclear rearmament. This provision would, in fact, be the very core of the military side of the agreement. It would be the definition, in technical terms, of what "abolition" was to be. And it would be the final guarantor of the safety of nations against attack. However, this guarantor would not defend. It would deter. The most important element in this readiness would simply be the knowledge of how to make the weapons—knowledge that nations are powerless to get rid of even if they want to. This unlosable knowledge is, as we have seen, the root fact of life in the nuclear world, from which the entire predicament proceeds. But, just as the potential for nuclear aggression flows from the knowledge, menacing the stability of the agreement, so does the potential for retaliation, restoring the stability of the agreement. Its persistence is the reason that deterrence doesn't dissolve when the weapons are abolished. In other words, in the nuclear world the threat to use force is as self-cancelling at zero nuclear weapons as it is at fifty thousand nuclear weapons. Thus, both in its political ends—preservation of a stalemate—and in its means—using the threat of nuclear destruction itself to prevent the use of nuclear weapons—the abolition agreement would represent an extension of the doctrine of deterrence: an extension in which the most terrifying features of the doctrine would be greatly mitigated, although not finally removed.

The agreed-upon preparations would be based on the knowledge. In all likelihood, they would consist both of inspectable controls on nuclear reactors and on other facilities producing weapons-grade materials and of rules regarding the construction of delivery vehicles. One question that the policymakers would put to the scientists would be what precise level of technical arrangements would permit some particular, defined level of armament to be achieved in a fixed lead time to nuclear rearmament —say, six weeks. Possible lead times would be defined in such terms as the following: an eight-week lead time to the production of two hundred warheads mounted on cruise missiles, or a six-week lead time to a hundred warheads mounted in military aircraft. The lead time would have to be short enough so that the would-be aggressor, seeking to make use of the interval as a head start, would not be able to establish a decisive lead. "Decisive" in this, or any, nuclear context refers to the ability to destroy the victim's retaliatory capacity in a preemptive first strike. Preemption is the spectre that haunts the deterrence strategists, for if one side can destroy the retaliatory capacity of the other side in a preemptive strike, then deterrence dissolves. This is the point at which victory looms up again as a possibility, and force stops being self-cancelling. (At least, it does in the short run. It's much more difficult to see how a nuclear aggressor could escape retaliation over a longer run.) So it is today, and so it would be in a world of zero nuclear weapons.

The task for strategy in a nuclear-weapon-free world would be to design a capacity for nuclear rearmament which could not be destroyed in a first strike by a nation that took the lead in rearmament by abrogating the abolition agreement, secretly or openly. Retaliatory capacity would have to be able to keep pace with aggressive capacity—to the extent that a disarming first strike would be excluded. If that requirement was satisfied, possession in a nuclear-weapon-free world of the capacity for rebuilding nuclear weapons would deter nations from rebuilding them and then using them, just as in our present, nuclear-armed world possession of the weapons themselves deters nations from using them. Today, missile deters missile, bomber deters bomber, submarine deters submarine. Under what we might call weaponless deterrence, factory would deter factory, blueprint would deter blueprint, equation would deter equation. In today's world, when the strategists assess one another's arsenals they see that every possible escalation in attack can be matched by an escalation on the other side, until the arsenals of both sides are depleted and both nations are annihilated. So the two sides are deterred from attacking one another. With weaponless deterrence in effect, the strategists

119

would see that any possible escalation in rearmament by one side could be matched by an escalation on the other side, until both were again fully armed and ready to embark on mutual assured destruction. So they would be deterred from rearming.

It has often been said that the impossibility of uninventing nuclear weapons makes their abolition impossible. But under the agreement described here the opposite would be the case. The knowledge of how to rebuild the weapons is just the thing that would make abolition *possible*, because it would keep deterrence in force. Indeed, the everlastingness of the knowledge is the key to the abolition of nuclear arms within the framework of deterrence. Once we accept the fact that the acquisition of the knowledge was the essential preparation for nuclear armament, and that it can never be reversed, we can see that every state of disarmament is also a state of armament. And, being a state of armament, it has deterrent value. In pointing out the deterrent value of preparations for nuclear rearmament, and even of the mere knowledge of how to rebuild the weapons, we make the reply to the present opponents of abolition which Bernard Brodie made to Robert Oppenheimer. Oppenheimer, rightly observing that nuclear weapons could not be defended against, called them inherently "aggressive" weapons and predicted that they would inevitably be used in lightning-swift aggressive war. In such a world, of course, there would have been no stability whatever. But to this Brodie responded that the would-be aggressor would not be the only one possessing nuclear weapons, and that when the aggressor saw that its foe possessed them—and was ready to retaliate with them—its aggressive fever would be cooled down. Now we are told that aggressors will take advantage of the abolition of nuclear weapons to rebuild and use nuclear weapons, and to this the answer again is that the intended victims will have the same capacities, and these will act as a deterrent, saving the world's stability.

The notion that abolition is impossible because uninvention is impossible appears to stem from a failure to distinguish clearly between these two things. The confusion is exemplified in *Living with Nuclear Weapons*, in which, in support of their conclusion that a world without nuclear weapons is "a fictional utopia," the Harvard authors write, "The discovery of nuclear weapons, like the discovery of fire itself, lies behind us on the trajectory of history: it cannot be undone. Even if all nuclear arsenals were destroyed, the knowledge of how to reinvent them would remain and could be put to use in any of a dozen or more nations. The atomic fire cannot be extinguished." The authors fear that "the knowledge of how to reinvent" the weapons will upset any abolition agreement. But if one has "the knowledge," there is no need to "reinvent" anything, because one can go ahead and rebuild the weapons right away by using that knowledge. If, on the other hand, reinvention is really required, then one must have somehow lost the knowledge, but this is impossible. Of course, if one speaks of the knowledge of how to rebuild the weapons rather than "the knowledge of how to reinvent" them, the inconsistency disappears; but then one is speaking of rearming after abolition rather than after uninvention. By inadvertently blurring the distinction between the two, the Harvard authors, like many other proponents of deterrence, make abolition appear to be, like uninvention, impossible, and confer upon the world's nuclear arsenals a durability and irremovability that in fact only the knowledge of how to make them possesses. Though uninvention is impossible, abolition is not. Or if it were true that both were impossible it would have to be for completely different reasons—in the case of uninvention because we don't know how to rid the world of basic scientific knowledge, and in the case of abolition because we lack the necessary political will. If the distinction is kept clear, then the hope opens up that the impossibility of uninvention, which is the fundamental fact of life in the nuclear world, makes abolition, which is just one of the conceivable ways of organizing that world, possible. For it was the invention, not the buildup, of nuclear arms that irreversibly placed mankind within reach of its own self-slaughtering hand, ruined war as the final arbiter in global affairs, and set mankind adrift in a new and unfamiliar political world.

The stages of nuclear escalation are often pictured as a ladder reaching from a peaceful but nuclear-armed world up through various levels of nuclear attack and retaliation to the end of the world. Deterrence calls for the ability of each potential adversary to match the others at each rung of the ladder. The levels of nuclear armament, from zero up to a full-scale doomsday machine, can be pictured as lower rungs on that same ladder, and the levels of technical and industrial preparation for the production of nuclear arms as still lower rungs. On this extended ladder, the bottom rung is not zero nuclear weapons but the bare knowledge of how to make them, unaccompanied by any preparations to rebuild them. In actuality, however, this lowest rung can never be reached, because every general level of technical proficiency, whether geared to weapons production or not, is a state of readiness for nuclear armament at one level or another. That is why there can be no such thing as a return to the pre-nuclear world but only increases in the lead time to nuclear armament and from there to a holocaust. At present, the lead time is virtually the shortest possible: we might say that it is seven minutes—approximately the time that it would take for forward-based strategic missiles on each side to reach targets in the opposing country. If world government, or some equivalent political solution, were in place, the lead time might arguably be centuries, but there would still *be* a lead time, because the knowledge of how to build nuclear weapons would remain in the world. Under the abolition agreement described here, our modest but invaluable achievement would be in increasing this lead time from its present seven minutes to weeks or months.

The technical choice available to us, then, is not whether to possess or to eradicate nuclear weapons but what should be the state of readiness—or, if you want to look at it that way, of unreadiness—for nuclear hostilities in which, by international agreement, we would hold the world. The either-or character of the choice between deterrence with full-scale nuclear arsenals and world government without them no longer has to paralyze the world, for we find that within deterrence itself there are endless gradations, leading all the way down to zero and beyond, as the state of readiness is reduced and diplomatic and political arrangements are improved. Deterrence has more extensive possibilities than we have yet acknowledged. It is our curse—a kind of second fall from grace—that the knowledge of how to extinguish ourselves as a species will never leave us. And it is perhaps only modest compensation that that same knowledge, by ruining war—a lesser but more ancient curse under which our species has labored—has laid the foundations for a world at peace. Nevertheless, to throw this advantage away would be a monumental mistake, since it is one of the few elements that work in our favor as we seek to avoid extinction. The durability of the invention and the collapse of war which has come with it provide a strong foundation on which to begin to build our safety. But on this strong foundation we have so far built only a rickety, improvised shelter. We suffer the danger that flows from the fact that the fateful knowledge is inexpungible from our world, but we have so far turned down the advantages that flow from that fact. We arrange to terrorize one another with annihilation, but we have so far failed to achieve the full measure of safety obtainable from the terror. It is a paradox fully worthy of this elaborate doctrine that if we were to permit ourselves to recognize clearly the breadth and depth of the peril—to assure ourselves once and for all of its boundlessness and durability—we might thereby clear a path to our salvation.

Deterrence depends on foreknowledge. Without that, we have no barrier between ourselves and our doom. It is a system in which government leaders who might be inclined toward aggression look at the end of the story they would be setting in motion, see their own and everyone else's doom written there, and therefore decide not to take even the first step. Deterrence under an abolition agreement would work in precisely the same way, except that the story at the end of which doom was written would be somewhat longer and the foreknowledge a little farther-sighted. It would now take in all the rungs on the ladder, from the construction of the first nuclear weapon up to the end of the world. The changeover from today's system would be less drastic than it might at first appear. Even under the present doctrine, the weapons are only "psychological" arsenals, meant to create terrifying "appearances." Their targets are not people's bodies but their minds, and, theoretically, the weapons' physical destiny is to rust into powder in their silos, or to pass into honored retirement, as a new and still more fearsome "generation" is groomed to take their place. Indeed, because they are wholly devoted to creating the right menacing appearances and inducing the right states of mind, no one has ever been able to suggest any sensible or sane mission for them "if deterrence fails" and the moment for their supposed actual use arrives. The manifest failure of the nuclear-war-fighters to fill the gap only underscores the point. Furthermore, the weapons have been pulled back to a purely responsive —if not exactly a "defensive"—role. Everyone says that he will use them only if he is attacked. So, theoretically, if everyone behaves well, and no one attacks, no one will use them. (Unfortunately, though, if someone does attack we are committed to using them.) In military history (if we can call such unalloyed posturing "military"), these arsenals are unique in that they can fail simply by being employed in action. They have become semi-real, shadow things, designed to play a merely supporting role in a public-relations game. This role could be filled just as well by a sham, papier-mâché arsenal, if only we could be sure that the fraud would not be discovered. Abolition would carry the present quasi-retirement of the weapons one more step. Instead of literal-mindedly requiring that we keep the actual physical things under our noses to frighten ourselves with, we would make do with the capacity for rebuilding them, which should be frightening enough.

In chess, when skilled players reach a certain point in the play they are able to see that, no matter what further moves are made, the outcome is determined, and they end the game without going through the motions. This is also our situation in the nuclear world —with the difference that the predetermined outcome is not the victory of one side or the other but the destruction of both. The difference between our present world and a nuclear-weapon-free world would be only that people had all learned to see a few steps farther ahead than they do now—as though the chess players, having gained in experience, were to call off their game four moves before checkmate rather than two. Every statesman would see, just as he does today, that aggression leads inevitably to annihilation, and would feel no need to test the proposition in action. This does not seem too much for people to have learned after thirty-nine years of staring oblivion in the face.

The great advantage of our present situation is that by actually having built a doomsday machine we have played all the moves in this game except the last, and so know from experience, as people in the first years of the nuclear age could not, where the moves lead. We've played the game this far, and the result of the final moves is before our eyes—not the victory of one side over the other but doom. If mankind were ever to lift the nuclear peril, one saying that people might employ to keep themselves from backsliding would be "Remember 1984." (But if we use 1984 to turn the nuclear-arms race around we might give this year, prospectively slated for infamy by George Orwell, a place of honor.) It seems likely that, to an extent that we today can hardly begin to imagine, future generations, if there are any, will look back on our recent history with unutterable horror. They will recall incredulously a generation that, bowing down abjectly to a technical device of its own invention, set up the machinery for the destruction of humanity. They are likely to look back with particular incredulity, it seems to me, on us in the West. The world must count on us in the West to take the lead in resolving the nuclear predicament, because we enjoy freedom here, including the freedom to examine the nuclear predicament in a creative and unfettered way. But of what avail will our freedom have been to us and to the world if by making use of it we arrive only at fatalism? Perhaps it will be concluded in defense of our generation as a whole that it was *necessary* to build the doomsday machine, so that, like a child that makes a mask to frighten itself with, we could make the nuclear peril real to ourselves—real enough so that we would finally do something about it. If that is so, we could regard the nuclear-arms race of the last several decades as a gigantic educational device—a sort of classroom aid designed to teach us all about nuclear weapons and the doom they portend. (Such a role would be consistent with the "psychological" role which we now assign to the weapons in strategic doctrine.) The result offered by this perilous exercise, at any rate, is the advantage that we have over people who faced the question in 1945. But if we fail to avail ourselves of the advantage—if we fail to learn the lesson that our indirect experience offers—then there will be little to be said in our favor, and perhaps no one to say it.

Before we examine in greater detail how an abolition agreement might work, a cautionary word seems in order concerning hypothetical constructions of future events—or "scenarios," as they are called—and, in particular, scenarios involving deterrence. We want to arrive at a judgment about the general workability of an abolition agreement under which an ability to rebuild nuclear weapons would serve as a deterrent. The key word is "judgment." It is emphatically not "prediction." Judgment never claims certainty; it never pretends to *know* what the future holds. It is not a science, and in a world dominated by the relative certainties of science and the pseudocertainties of pseudoscience its admittedly fallible claims often fail to command respect. Judgment does not rely on reason alone; it also summons into play intuition, emotion, experience, temperament—in a sense, our whole being. But in the nuclear field judgment has a competitor—strategic "theory," which tries, like science, to proceed by reasoning. Strategic theory, however, lacks an element that is crucial to science: empirical verification. There is always the danger with theory that it will come to supplant reality in the minds of the theorists; and in nuclear-strategic theorizing the danger is especially acute, because, fortunately, mankind has had no direct experience of "nuclear war"—of two-sided nuclear combat—against which to measure its hypotheses. Strategic theory is in that respect like a physics without the benefit of experimentation, or a social science without the benefit of a society to observe. Never, perhaps, has pure deduction, uncorrected by empirical knowledge, been given freer rein or assigned a more important role in the regulation of human affairs.

When experience is replaced by theory, the possibility always exists that the theory's assumptions will be generally accepted as conclusions. One particularly harmful assumption of this kind in the theory of deterrence is that only the balance of terror counts in the decision-making of statesmen, so that if your adversary gets the slightest opening to do his worst to you he will do it. The effect of making this assumption is to introduce into policy an extreme reductionism, in which moral and psychological, and even diplomatic and political, influences on governmental conduct are ruled out of consideration. And since deterrence is not merely a theory but a policy there is a further danger that this reductionist assumption can take on the quality of a self-fulfilling prophecy. Two nations, starting by assuming unmitigated enmity between them, and proceeding on both sides to build their military forces accordingly, can soon find that the unmitigated enmity has become real. It has become a fact that each side menaces the other with annihilation, and this fact has emotional and psychological consequences of its own, independent of any prior, underlying enmity. At this point, the assumption, which may at the beginning have masked a more complex and subtly shaded reality, has become "true." The British historian E. P. Thompson has pointed out, in his recent book *Beyond the Cold War*, "By conditioning military and political élites, on both sides, to act in accord with the first premise of adversary posture —to seek ceaselessly for advantage and to expect annihilating attack upon the first sign of weakness—[strategic doctrine] could tempt one side (if a manifest advantage should arise) to behave as theory prescribes, and to seize the opportunity for a preemptive strike. And what would the war, then, have been *about*? It would have been about fulfilling a theorem in deterrence theory." It's a striking historical fact, and one that should make us reflect, that the severest crisis of the nuclear age, the Cuban missile crisis, was *about* the weapons themselves.

In truth, there is much evidence that contradicts the pessimistic chief assumption of deterrence. Three historical episodes, among many that could be mentioned, can serve as illustration. The first is the behavior of the United States between 1945 and 1949, when it possessed a monopoly of nuclear weapons. The United States not only did not immediately annihilate the Soviet Union but did not even seek any drastic change in Soviet policy —by, for example, using nuclear blackmail to force the Soviet Union out of Eastern Europe. The second episode is the behavior of the Soviet Union between roughly the mid-1950s and the present, during which time it has had complete nuclear superiority over China and has also been in a state of hostility toward China as least as intense as its hostility toward the United States. According to purely theoretical considerations, the Soviet Union has had every reason to launch a preemptive strike against China, for in all likelihood it could destroy China's nuclear forces entirely. Yet it has not launched a preemptive strike. This restraint is all the more telling because it involves a totalitarian country, which is relatively immune to public opinion. The third episode is the behavior of Britain in its recent successful war to regain the Falkland Islands from Argentina. Argentina, which is not a nuclear power (although it is now able to become one), seized territory that was claimed by a nuclear-armed Britain. According to present theory, Britain should at that point have used its absolute nuclear superiority to force Argentine withdrawal. Britain could, for example, have begun with threats; then backed these up by stationing a nuclear-armed submarine within range of Argentina; then set off a demonstration nuclear explosion, perhaps over the sea, or over an unpopulated part of Argentina; then destroyed an Argentine military base with a "small" (Hiroshima-sized) bomb; then destroyed a small city or two; and, finally, blown Argentina off the map (a feat well within the capacity of Britain's nuclear forces, comparatively small though they are). But, as far as I'm aware, the

British government did not breathe the merest suggestion that any of these things were remotely possible. What it did do was launch and win a conventional war, at a high cost in lives and in money. It is interesting to speculate on what Britain might have done if it had faced conventional defeat, but the complete lack of any mention of nuclear arms by government spokesmen, during the war or afterward, allows us to suppose that it would have suffered the defeat rather than resort to nuclear weapons. What was equally striking was the failure of outside observers of the war —columnists, diplomats of other countries, and the like—to mention Britain's nuclear arsenal. Somehow, its complete irrelevance to the situation was intuitively assumed by everybody.

These lessons of experience are of great value to the world— especially since they are hopeful. They prove to us, as we try to shape a safer future, that we have more—much, much more—to work with than terror. In our world, there is also courage, trust, prudence, imagination, decency. There is even love. Can it be "realistic" to exclude these proved good qualities of our species from our calculations? To do so would be to libel mankind and cripple our efforts. Indeed, the whole abolition agreement suggested here can be seen as a mere holding operation, giving us time in which these good qualities can be brought to bear on the vast political work that alone can lead to a true and fully satisfactory resolution of the nuclear predicament.

The theorists correctly justify their resort to pure theory on the ground that no experience of a nuclear holocaust is available; but this justification has been stretched too far, for while post-Nagasaki history does not show what starts nuclear hostilities it shows many examples of what does *not* start them. We should become careful students of negative history, inasmuch as the chief aim of our political efforts in the nuclear age must be to see to it that something does *not* happen—that we do *not* blow ourselves up. High-school students are required to study the "three causes," or the "four causes," of the First World War, or the Second World War, or whatever. We must study the causes of the lack of war— the causes of peace. Leaving the study of "nuclear war" to the theorists, we as historians can study its prevention. One of the first things our study shows us is that, while in theory even slight imbalances in nuclear forces lead to instability and war, in actuality they have not done so. Another thing it shows is that with a war in progress a power possessing a monopoly of nuclear weapons may choose not to use them, or even to remind the world that it possesses them. The statesmen of the nuclear age seem to act with a sobriety not credited to them by our theorists. Some of the assumptions of deterrence theory can never be tested in action (not if we hope to survive), but others can be and have been. Among them is the assumption that nuclear powers will seek out and exploit any nuclear imbalance to obtain political or military advantage. This assumption has now been put to the test of experience many times, and has proved each time to be false. Why did the United States not preemptively attack the Soviet Union in the 1940s? Why has the Soviet Union not preemptively attacked China? Why did Britain choose to expend the lives of its soldiers in the Falkland Islands rather than even rattle its nuclear sword at Argentina? We can only guess at answers. Perhaps in the back of the minds of the leaders of these nations was some notion that what you do to others will one day be done to you. Perhaps they felt that even to threaten a nuclear attack would shame them before the world and history. Perhaps they feared that a nuclear attack of any sort would engulf the world in a chaos in which their own nations would suffer. Or perhaps their consciences stayed their hands.

It would be self-defeating folly to deny the common sense of the central axiom of deterrence—that the fear of nuclear retaliation provides nations with an overwhelming incentive not to launch nuclear attacks—but it would also be folly if, granting that, we concluded that the fear of retaliation was the only sentiment at work in holding the world back from nuclear destruction. So it is not meaningless, after showing that no country could expect to profit by violating an abolition agreement, to point out that even if some statesman mistakenly concluded that his country could profit from aggression he might be restrained for any number of reasons, including the sense of shame and repugnance that almost every human being feels at the thought of murdering millions, and possibly billions, of innocent people in cold blood.

It is in the spirit of seeking to reach a broad judgment, not of trying to produce a whole new crop of scenarios, that I want to address the question of whether or not an abolition agreement would be workable. In the years ahead, a profusion of plans and ideas defining not just steps but whole stairways to nuclear disarmament will, in all likelihood, be put forward as people seek instruments for their newfound will to save the species. At the same time, people will be seeking to understand more profoundly what it means to live in a world in which we have the power to exterminate ourselves. And out of a deepening understanding will come still further thoughts about what we should be doing. For no single plan can guide us. And no single person can possess the wisdom to chart our course. It is in the very nature of things that the effort will be collective. The world is not to be approached, blueprint in hand, as if it were so much raw material waiting to be fashioned to someone's design. *We*—the people of the earth, each of us possessing an independent will—are that material, and it will be only out of the combined resolve of all of us that, probably at unexpected times and in unexpected ways, our will, the will of the world, will make itself known and felt. If the remarks in these pages are not predictions, neither are they would-be blueprints for the future. Rather, they, and the whole proposal for abolition described here, are an attempt to make a contribution to the broader discussion out of which, we must hope, will come the actual steps that lead us away from the abyss.

As the examples of nuclear restraint I have cited demonstrate, there are more motives acting in favor of military restraint in the nuclear age than a simple fear of nuclear retaliation. Strict deterrence theory recognizes only this fear, and disregards all other factors, and it is in that respect like an insurance policy—it deals with the worst case. It offers assurance that even if an aggressor were to disregard all other constraints and try his worst he could not hope for victory. It does not tell us that our adversary *will* try to burn our house down, or even that he necessarily wants to, but only that if this thought ever crosses his mind, and he is rational, he will have cause to dismiss it. Therefore, to whatever extent we fear that the adversary will do his worst, including his nuclear worst, and to whatever extent we are willing in return to do our worst, including our nuclear worst, the assurances offered by credible deterrence are important. To some people, they are all-important. But to someone who, like me, feels that he cannot find a justification for even threatening to use, to say nothing of using, nuclear weapons, in support of either armed or weaponless deterrence, any proposal that relies on a threat to use them, including the proposal for weaponless deterrence, raises an ethical question. I oppose any use of nuclear weapons, whether in a first strike or in a second strike or in any strike at all. But, as I have said, I believe that in dealing with the nuclear predicament we must support interim measures—measures such as the establishment of a Soviet-American control center for the exchange of information in a crisis; SALT or START agreements; a policy of no first use of nuclear weapons; the freeze; reductions in the nuclear arsenals; or the abolition of nuclear arms coupled with weaponless deterrence—that will help steer mankind away from its extinction, even though in the meantime we go on depending on morally obnoxious means. Today, mankind is like a person who lies bleeding to death on the street after an accident. Eventually, this person will require major surgery. But right now he needs to be rushed to the hospital in an ambulance, and given first aid on the way. It is pointless to say at this moment, "This person doesn't need an ambulance, he needs major surgery." The passage from our nuclear-armed world to a nuclear-weaponless world would be that ambulance ride. Once the life of mankind is out of immediate danger, we will have the time—we will have won it for ourselves—to address the radical and sweeping measures of global political renovation which alone can fully deliver us from the evil.

As we consider whether deterrence could remain in force under an abolition agreement, the work of present-day theorists of deterrence is helpful, because under the agreement the requirements of deterrence would be exactly what they are today. Deterrence would require stability, which would mean that under the system every statesman in his right mind would see that the almost certain result if he launched aggression would be the pointless destruction of all concerned, including, most definitely, his own country; that is, it would require that the hope of military victory vanish from his mind. It would require credibility, which would mean that the ability to visit devastation on an aggressor would have to be secure. It would therefore require a retaliatory nuclear capacity that would survive any first strike the adversary could mount. In connection with these requirements, the most important question to ask about a nuclear-weapon-free world is whether it could be arranged in such a way that no nation, by sudden or surreptitious rearmament, or by military action, could defeat an adversary or blackmail it into submission. (Obviously, the ability to defeat and the ability to blackmail are linked, since no country is going to allow itself to be blackmailed unless the prospect of defeat is virtually certain.) This question is far more complicated than is commonly acknowledged. Usually, it is disposed of in a few sentences that are prefatory to the author's getting down to his real interest, which, typically, is either to discuss the mechanics of armed deterrence or to set forth the provisions for world government. (The near-total lack of interest of each of these schools in the details of the other's thinking is remarkable.)

If the abolition of nuclear weapons were the same as their uninvention, a sudden violation of the agreement (by a nation that had somehow invented them again) would really constitute an insuperable advantage. The violator would then be in the position

133

that the United States was in vis-à-vis Japan in July of 1945. But since abolition is not uninvention, and the intended victim of nuclear blackmail would be able to retaliate in several weeks' time, the imbalance between the violator and his victim would be much less than it at first appears to be. In 1946, as I have mentioned, Brodie pointed out that if the aggressor "must fear retaliation," then "the fact that it destroys its opponent's cities some hours or even days before its own are destroyed may avail it little." A delay of a month or so would make equally little difference. The unimportance of delays is one more of the differences between deterrence and defense. In defense, the shield has to be raised at the moment the sword falls, not a few days later. But the avenging sword of nuclear retaliation is not dulled by a wait. There is, indeed, something awful—something "deterring"—about the prospect of delayed retaliation. It's interesting to ponder whether the United States would have used the atomic bomb against Japan if Japan had been known to be a few weeks away from having one itself (as in fact it was not). Would the United States have been ready to risk New York and Chicago for Hiroshima and Nagasaki? I doubt it. The point in the present context is that the imbalance between a country that has invented the bomb and one that hasn't is categorically greater than the imbalance that exists between two nations that have both developed the bomb but one of which has dismantled its arsenal.

As deterrence theory teaches us, to have a really decisive advantage in a first strike the violator would have to possess forces sufficient to erase the victim's capacity for retaliation. To be really worth anything, therefore, a first strike delivered out of secrecy under an abolition agreement would have to be utterly devastating to the victim's nuclear capacity and be followed up by the immediate and total occupation of the victim's country with conventional forces, in order to prevent its nuclear rearmament. It is perhaps imaginable that if the defenses of the capacity for retaliation were left to chance a determined aggressor could, with the use of concealed arsenals only, so thoroughly devastate and then so swiftly occupy its victim that the victim could not retaliate. However, the defenses of the retaliatory capacity would not be left to chance. Rather, under the abolition agreement not only would the readiness to rebuild nuclear weapons be in place but so would the anti-nuclear defenses and the defensively arrayed conventional forces. The violator's aggression would fail, because the abolition agreement would have been *designed* for it to fail. Under this agreement, whatever is necessary to defeat such aggression would be built in, probably redundantly, for the sake of everyone's peace of mind.

The question of the state of readiness for nuclear rearmament is complex. It would have to meet two basic requirements. First, it would have to permit a lead time long enough to be of real benefit to the world. (Yet any increase would be beneficial. For example, if the nuclear powers today did nothing more than remove the nuclear warheads from their missiles and store them nearby, so that it would take, say, six hours to put them in again, the gain would be great. It would increase the lead time by several thousand per cent.) Second, it would have to provide a smooth and assured path back to nuclear armament, in order to fulfill the need, as it is defined by deterrence theory, for the retaliatory force to be invulnerable. In all likelihood, the best way of providing such a path while at the same time lengthening the lead time would be to establish controls on fissionable materials. A more radical measure would be to ban nuclear reactors in general (probably with certain narrowly defined exceptions), or else to place them—as the Baruch Plan, proposed by the United States to the United Nations in 1946, did—under the control of an international body. Banning reactors would carry a higher economic cost, but it would provide a longer lead time, and it might be more easily verifiable, since nuclear reactors and the industry that builds and maintains them are a great deal more difficult to hide than bombs or delivery vehicles. Another set of provisions could cover delivery vehicles. Since any vehicle, whether it is a missile or the suitcase carried by a pedestrian, can be a delivery vehicle for nuclear weapons, removing delivery vehicles for nuclear weapons from the world forever is impossible, just as removing forever the ability to build the weapons themselves is impossible. The important, attainable goal would be to restrict national capacities for deploying delivery vehicles, much as nuclear-arms-control agreements attempt to do today.

Clearly, the complexity of the nuclear balance at the level of zero weapons would be great—though not, perhaps, as great as the complexity is today, with thousands of weapons and their varied delivery systems in existence. The decisions to be made would have to deal not only with the state of readiness to rearm but also with the extent of the technical means permitted, its deployment, and so on. For example, it would be an advantage to the agreement as a whole if the technical means were decentralized to begin with and, in addition, were further dispersible in the event of the agreement's breakdown. (In the agreement, a nation's right to rearm if an adversary had done so would, of course, be recognized.) Dispersibility, in particular, would be invaluable. It could suffice in itself to defeat nuclear blackmail by a violator of the agreement. Blackmail requires that a threat be openly made and that time be allowed for compliance with its demands. But that time could be used to disperse the technical means from their known and inspected places to secret places. Once dispersal had occurred, it would be impossible for the small, secretly assembled nuclear force of the violator to threaten the retaliatory capacity of the victim. The question of what to do if the abolition agreement should be violated would be analogous to the question today of what to do "if deterrence fails." But whereas today we cannot think of one single thing that it would make sense to do if deterrence fails, there would be many sensible things to do if the abolition agreement broke down, including beginning to rearm. To be sure, if the violations continued to grow, and the world began to return to full armament, the actions in response would start to make less and less sense. Yet, even as they continued, the world would have time—as it would not today "if deterrence fails"—to see where it was heading, to reflect, and to pull back.

The principal mission of the anti-nuclear defensive forces set forth in the agreement would be not to protect their nations—a task that in the long run they could perform no better than they can today—but to protect the retaliatory capacity as it was being mobilized for action. They would thus have the limited role of a hedge against cheating. For the defensive superiority that was arranged for in the abolition agreement would last only as long as that agreement did—or, rather, as long afterward as the defensive retained the upper hand. And this would not be indefinitely. It would be only long enough for the attacked nation to assemble its retaliatory force, at which point the balance of terror as we know it today would be restored. But, of course, just as today we keep our retaliatory force at the ready in the hope that its very existence will prevent the attack that would cause us to use it, so in a world of zero nuclear weapons we would preserve our well-defended readiness to rearm in the hope that it would prevent the rearmament that would lead us to rearm. Thus, although we would be relying provisionally on defense we would still be living in a deterred world. Defense would provide protection while the deterrent forces were assembled, but then deterrence would take over. The underlying facts of life in a nuclear-weapon-free world would be just what they are today—that defense is impossible and deterrence inescapable. And under deterrence, armed or unarmed, our hope is that deterrence itself would gradually become obsolete while the conditions for a real, full peace were being established. Our chief protection, then, which would operate before either defenses or deterrence was called into play, would be whatever political will we had mustered to institute, and then to uphold, the abolition agreement.

None of this is to say that defense of the population should be ruled out. The question of whether or not to deploy civil defense, as a further hedge against cheating, is debatable. It could be argued (as it is today by the advocates of deterrence) that civil defense, if it could be made to work (as it can't today, in the face of our giant nuclear arsenals), would be destabilizing, because it would erode the "effectiveness" of the foe's retaliatory capacity.

With an abolition agreement in force, however, the world would not be *counting* on cheating; it would be trying to discourage it, and in that effort protection of the population would be helpful, because it would reduce the effectiveness of blackmail. In general, defensive measures would constitute a sort of obstacle that would-be aggressors would know that they had to overcome before their aggression began to pay off. But since they would also know that before that moment came their intended victims would have armed themselves with nuclear weapons, in preparation for retaliation, the moment would actually never come, and they would abandon their aggressive plans.

A provision for a balance in conventional forces would be essential to the agreement as a whole, because it would prevent the nuclear-arms race from being replaced by a conventional-arms race. "Conventional" arms today are in fact anything but that. Though they are overshadowed by nuclear weapons, they have increased in destructive power to a point at which the doctrine of mutual assured destruction might be maintained by them alone—especially when biological and chemical weapons are taken into account. The principal strategic mission of these limited and balanced conventional forces would be to do their part in deterring a disarming first strike by a violator of the agreement. Since to be successful in preventing nuclear rearmament and retaliation such a strike would require full occupation of the attacked country, the conventional forces would be deployed to prevent invasion. But this would be so in two senses: they would be armed in such a way that they *could* repel an invasion by another country, yet they would be armed in such a way that they *could not* themselves invade another country. These armies would, for example, be loaded down with anti-tank weapons but low on tanks; well equipped with anti-aircraft weapons but ill equipped with aircraft. The present Swiss Army, which bristles with weapons to repel invaders but itself never invades anybody, might serve as a model. Equipping those armies would admittedly be a novel military task but not an impossible one, especially when

138

we remember that all the military planners would be on the same side: the side of defense. Their aim would be to equip every army with steel shields and rubber swords. It is only a little bit facetious to suggest that the two sides might establish a joint "defense department" (properly named, for once), devoted to the development of defensive weaponry. A new "arms race" would begin, between offensive and defensive arms, but, fortunately, all the nations of the world would be working together to support the defense.

The preservation on both sides of an ability to rebuild nuclear weapons, arrangements for inspection on whatever level was necessary to provide a safeguard against cheating, and the presence of limited and balanced conventional forces defensively arrayed would, it seems to me, be more than adequate to provide for the requirements of deterrence in a world without nuclear weapons. Each of these elements would exist in a balance with the others. For example, an estimate would be needed of how much cheating might be possible under a particular level of inspection. When the estimate was given, the deployment of the capacity for rearming would be adjusted to meet, or more than meet, that potential threat. As more inspection was made possible, the less ready the capacity for rearming would have to be, and the less extensive the defenses would have to be (although it seems that there would be little to be lost in making defenses redundant). Every advance in inspection, then, would permit a lengthening of the world's nuclear fuse, and an increase in the world's safety. For example—to pick arbitrary figures—if the estimated amount of conceivable cheating associated with a particular level of inspection was a hundred bombs on a hundred commercial airliners, then the level of readiness could be quite low and the needed defenses quite thin. If, however, the estimated amount of conceivable cheating was two hundred bombs on two hundred cruise missiles, then the readiness would have to be higher and the defenses stronger. Conversely, the better the defenses were, the less strict the inspection would have to be. And, of course, the precise technical form of the agreed-upon readiness to rearm would have a bearing on how effective the defense of it could be. The important point in the present context is that the levels of inspection, of readiness, and of defense are interdependent and adjustable, with considerable room for margins of safety to be built in when the abolition agreement is designed.

The difficulties facing a violator of an abolition agreement only multiply when one turns from purely technical considerations to strategic ones. Let us suppose that a violator of the agreement has assembled a clandestine nuclear arsenal. But an arsenal is not in itself a policy. How to gain a military or political advantage from it remains to be figured out. To begin with, the cheater has to take into account the possibility that its intended victim has cheated as well. The possibility of cheating cuts two ways: it permits violation of the agreement, but it also sows suspicion in the mind of the would-be cheater that the other side may have cheated, too. Those who cheat know from their own action that cheating is possible, and are likely to suppose that others have done it also. If that has happened, the cheater, when he pulls back the curtain of secrecy, reveals the hidden arsenal, and starts making demands, will find himself facing an opposing arsenal right away, and the exercise will be fruitless. In short, uncertainty about cheating can have a deterrent as well as a destabilizing effect. (Uncertainty, it seems, is in all circumstances the most steadfast ally of deterrence.)

A cheater might have either of two possible aims: to hedge against suspected cheating on the other side or to engage in aggression. If the aim was to secure a hedge, then the cheating, while dangerous and undesirable, would remain clandestine and without disastrous consequences. (This would be so even if it had occurred on both sides, because then, although nobody would know it, a nuclear balance would have been created, at very low levels of armament.) There is reason to believe, however, that nations would not find it in their interest to cheat even as a hedge. The protective benefit of the hedge would be offset by the extremely serious cost of being caught in a violation. When one considers that in order to act as a hedge a violation would have to continue indefinitely, and therefore discovery would be likely sooner or later, it is hard to imagine that a nation would find it worthwhile —especially if it knew that in the event of a violation by another nation its legitimate capacity to rearm was secure. If, on the other hand, the aim was aggression, then the violator would face all the defensive and retaliatory penalties that are built into the agreement to deter aggression. And yet, even without considering these, the government leader weighing the costs of cheating would have to reflect that his victim, or one of his victim's allies, might have cheated, and that in that case his plans would be aborted right there. In other words, the violator, after revealing himself to the world as an international outlaw of the most hateful and terrifying kind, might be thwarted immediately, without having a chance even to attempt some mischief in a brief moment of nuclear superiority.

In the event that a government overlooked all these obstacles and decided that it was ready to violate the agreement anyway, it would still need a strategy. It would have to have both an attainable political goal in mind and a plan for reaching it. Neither is easy to conceive of. Just as is true in our present world, the strategy for a first strike, whether only threatened or actually carried out, would have to be, in the jargon terms, either "counterforce" or "countervalue"; that is, the bombs would have to menace or destroy either the foe's military forces, in the hope of achieving a crippling first strike, or the foe's cities and population, in the hope of terrorizing him into submission. A successful counterforce strike would be impossible for all the reasons just mentioned; the entire abolition agreement would have been framed to preclude it. The idea, for example, that the Soviet Union, using a clandestine nuclear force, could destroy the ability of the United States to make nuclear weapons and then, in the space of a few weeks, conquer Europe, cross the Atlantic, and occupy the United States to prevent nuclear rearmament is patent fantasy. And if one adds that the first strike with the clandestine arsenal would be opposed by large-scale defenses, including swift dispersal of the nuclear-weapon-making capacity, and that the conventional forces of the Soviet Union had, under the agreement, been reduced from their present size and deprived of many of their offensive arms, then the idea of such an attack positively enters the realm of the surreal. That would leave the possibility of blackmail against cities or actual attacks on them—a possibility that is often pointed to as the decisive advantage of violating an abolition agreement. Such a threat or attack, however, would be even easier than the counterforce one to reply to. In the first place, the elaborate and technically advanced defenses of the victim might be adequate to actually defend in considerable measure against a threat made with the small, probably technically backward offensive forces of the aggressor. But even if the defenses were inadequate the victim's ability to retaliate with nuclear arms in a few weeks' time would erase the aggressor's advantage. The response of the threatened country would be exactly what it is today: it would threaten nuclear attack in return. Deterrence would be fully in force.

It is not, however, until one turns from the methods of a violator to his possible political goals that the ground for believing in the stability of a nuclear-weapon-free world stands fully revealed. The traditional nightmare of global politics is that some single nation or bloc will grow so strong that it will upset the balance of power and then move to dominate all other nations. The Romans once did it. In more recent times, Napoleon and Hitler came close. This larger possibility, standing in the background of smaller crises, can give even minor aggression, when it is launched by a great power, a momentous importance. It also provides the temptation that lures a statesman with grandiose longings onto the path of conquest. When nations are faced with such aggression, the question that their leaders always have to ask themselves is where it will be stopped if not in the instance at hand. This is the famed "lesson of Munich," learned from the experience of France and England in 1938, when, at a meeting with Hitler in Munich, they agreed,

142

essentially, that, rather than go to war with him, they would let him take over Czechoslovakia—only to find that they had to go to war with him anyway a short while later. It is the lesson, too, that is embodied in the so-called domino theory, of more recent times, which holds that aggression must be prevented at the earliest possible moment or it will run out of control and engulf everything. The wedding of this lesson to the doctrine of deterrence is what has led to the disproportion of means and ends in our current military strategy—forcing us to defend, say, the Persian Gulf by, in effect, risking the end of the world. The reason our statesmen are willing to risk the end of the world to protect the Persian Gulf is not that the Persian Gulf is so important (its oil *is* very important, of course, but not worth the extinction of mankind); it is that they are persuaded that if aggression is permitted there—or almost anywhere—it cannot be stopped later. The leader we fear—the one we build nuclear arsenals to deter—is not the one who wants to grab a disputed piece of territory from his neighbor but the one whose dreams are filled with triumphal visits to subjugated foreign capitals. (Hitler's early-morning visit to Paris in 1940, captured on film by his propagandists, comes to mind.) Our nation's leaders believe that Soviet leaders are determined to dominate the world and will actually do it if they are not stopped in an early stage. The Soviet leaders have reciprocal fears. It may be that in fact neither nation has these unlimited ambitions, but since each believes that the other has them both base their foreign policies on this conviction.

A precise way of posing the question of the stability of a nuclear-weapon-free world is to ask how such a would-be world conqueror might fare in it. I have argued that even the very first step, in which the aspiring Caesar of our time, having nursed his dream of world conquest behind a veil of feigned peacefulness, whipped back the curtain of secrecy, displayed his arsenal to the world, and demanded some political prize, on pain of nuclear devastation if it was denied, would meet with failure—and not for just one reason but for many, redundant reasons—and that, furthermore, he would know this before he started, and would not

143

start. But what is even surer is that if this first act of aggression somehow occurred and was successful it could have no sequel. For before it had been completed it would have set in motion all over the world the countermeasures that would prevent any repetition: not only the victimized nation but every other nuclear-capable nation in the world could rearm with nuclear weapons to confront the violator. And our budding Caesar would know all this, too: if he couldn't figure it out for himself, people would tell him. To an extent perhaps not yet fully appreciated, the development of nuclear arms has provided a surefire antidote to the world's ancient nightmare of military conquest by a single power. Such grandiose ambitions cannot be realized in our world, nor could they be in the world of an abolition agreement. The reason is not that nations are less ambitious or less ruthless than they were in the past; it is that the world has changed. And in this changed world it is not the physical existence of nuclear arsenals but the knowledge of how to build them that is fundamental.

It could be said that this knowledge, which is destined to spread over the whole globe, is like a quicksand in which the feet of the armies of the great powers are sunk. And the reason is deterrence, in the broadest sense of the word: no one wants to embark on an obviously self-defeating enterprise. In our strategic thinking, we seem to have become mesmerized by numbers, speaking easily of a thousand, ten thousand, fifty thousand nuclear weapons. But in reality just ten of them—which can carry the explosive force of *ten thousand* Hiroshimas—provide a level of destructive power outside all historical experience. What government leader in his right mind, knowing that these weapons are available to his enemies, can dream of the military conquest of the world? At best, the great powers can fight desultory, drawn-out, small wars—often unsuccessful—against non-nuclear-armed local peoples (the North Vietnamese, the Afghans). Never again can they sweep victoriously from nation to nation, as the armies of the great conquerors of the past did. They know what likely fate awaits them if they try: some justly infuriated enemy will let off the E in the m of a few kilograms of plutonium, multiplied by c^2,

A Deliberate Policy

and their armies will go up in a puff of vapor. You can't conquer the world with vapor armies. Regrettably, none of this means that nuclear weapons will not be used; it means only that they are unlikely to be used in the service of premeditated schemes of conquest or aggression. Their use, if it occurs, is likely to come by accident, or in the confusion and misunderstanding of a crisis, in which neither side is ready to back down. In a way, it is the very existence of the arsenals, rather than any intention to use them, that makes their use possible. As long as they exist, they can be used. And the moment we abolished them the chances of their use, although still present, would become comfortingly small.

Paradoxically, the anachronism of campaigns of world conquest in the nuclear age might emerge into view more clearly in a nuclear-weapon-free world than it does in our nuclear-armed world. Precisely because our present arsenals are so immense and no government leader can be assured that if he sets off one nuclear bomb they will not all go off, a shadow of doubt hangs over the threat of their use as a means of preventing aggression, and it seems conceivable (though very far from likely, once we think about it) that some power might get away with a serious act of aggression. In a nuclear-weapon-free world, however, with no preposterously overstocked arsenals ready to go off the moment a single bomb was used, the threatened nuclear retaliation for aggression would be less irrational and more "credible." To put it in terms of present strategy, "flexible response" would come into its own, for the self-paralysis that results from our natural reluctance to "defend" ourselves by taking steps that might start an unstoppable slide to the end of the world would no longer occur. Because in a nuclear-weapon-free world the path of aggression and rearmament would be broken into steps, we could see with greater clarity than we can today that every escalation of aggression—every crossing of a new national border—could be met with fully commensurate retaliation.

A further bar to world conquest deserves mention, though it is not nuclear in origin. Throughout our century, local people, inspired by an aroused national consciousness and by patriotic

145

feeling, have put up increasingly strong, and increasingly success-ful, resistance to foreign domination. Whatever other political principles people may subscribe to, they appear to be mightily determined to take charge of their countries. In our world, the "dominoes" have taken on a life of their own and are in rebellion against the players. The classical empires of the West have been effectively dissolved by this force, and so has the somewhat later Soviet aim of a Communist world revolution under Soviet leader-ship—today it is virtually a dead letter. Whatever atrocities people may suffer, it seems, they want to suffer at the hands of their own monsters and madmen. More and more, we live in a world in which local people rule in their own places. The single great ex-ception to this local takeover from great powers is in Eastern Europe, where the continued Soviet domination is ultimately maintained by occupying armies. But even there local resistance —especially in Poland—though it is not yet intense enough to expel the Soviets, makes one wonder how long this anachronistic form of political control can last. Today, even the greatest powers must think many times before embarking on a Vietnam or an Afghanistan. For this reason alone, quite apart from the influence of nuclear weapons, world domination by a single power has now become unthinkable. Thus, the ambitions of the great powers are doubly checked: while their nuclear forces are immobilized in the balance of nuclear terror, their conventional armies sink in the swamps of local resistance.

The abolition agreement might be accompanied by collective-security agreements, designed to make the fate of aggressors still clearer to any statesmen who were having trouble perceiving the realities of the world they lived in. Weaponless deterrence would not require collective-security agreements in order to work, but it would lend itself naturally to them and would be strengthened by them. The abolition of nuclear arms would be a militarily equal-izing measure. With a number of the technically competent nations standing at the same starting line (the agreed-upon readiness) in any race to rearm, their power would be more nearly equal—at least, in the short run—than it is today. This relative equality would give added importance to alliances. There would be safety in numbers, for even if the potential violator should think that he could escape retaliation by his immediate victim he would know that he could not escape it from a dozen or so nations to which the victim was allied in a collective-security agreement. In our nuclear-armed world, proliferation—of capacity, not of weapons—could be stabilizing. It would multiply the reasons for holding back from aggression. (It's interesting that at least one nation that is now nuclear-capable—India—has forgone actual construction of a nuclear arsenal. Its leaders may count it sufficient that their adversaries know that they *can* build the weapons if they want to.) Of all the developments occurring today, proliferation of nuclear weapons may well be the most dangerous. It raises the possibility that sooner or later a madman may have everyone's fate in his hands. An abolition agreement would not fully insure against this terrifying prospect, but it would give us incomparably more security against it than we have now.

Everyone agrees that nations want to survive, and we can be sure that, given the opportunity, they will take steps to assure their survival. Today, however, there are few steps that any but the two most powerful nations can take to protect themselves from the worst fate of all—annihilation in a general holocaust. All the others must simply wait and watch as their life or death is decided by a few men in Washington and Moscow. In a nuclear-weapon-free world, a field of action would open to them. In peacetime, they could work diplomatically and politically to strengthen the abolition agreement. A good way to begin would be with collective-security agreements. But even if nuclear aggression or nuclear blackmail should be attempted there would still be time to act. There would be an interval of some weeks between the original act of aggression and any nuclear response, and in that period pressures of all kinds—including the pressure of the threat of nuclear retaliation by any number of nations—could be exerted to resolve the crisis. These courses of action could be spelled out in advance, so that any would-be aggressor would be able to see clearly what was in store for him.

In judging a system of deterrence, one needs to concentrate on the train of thought that one believes would run through the mind of any national leader inclined toward aggression. In a nuclear-weapon-free world of the kind I have described, a would-be world conqueror contemplating the technical, strategic, and political consequences of aggression would see, I suggest, nothing but a vast field of insurmountable obstacles and, at the end of it—or even quite early—the same mutual assured destruction that we see today when we contemplate "nuclear war." The nuclear world is unconquerable. The peoples of the world refuse to be subjugated, and they have the means, including—in a world in which twentieth-century physics is an open book to all comers—the nuclear means, to prevent their subjugation. Where once a smooth plain stretched before the conqueror's eye, a would-be conqueror today looks out over a terrain that, like one of those glaciers high in the mountains which claim the lives of climbers, is crisscrossed with slippery crevasses, any one of which can prove fatal. Every step courts suicide. The tiny split atom yawns to swallow him up. One might just as well try to cross the desert in a sailing ship or cross the ocean in a tank as try to conquer the nuclear world with military force. And the abolition of nuclear arms would not change this outlook in any basic way. In the foreground of the nuclear-weapon-free world would be the victim's capacity for rearming, itself protected by powerful defensive forces. Beyond that would be the nuclear capacity of the victim's allies, and, beyond that, the nuclear and other retaliatory capacities of the whole world, enraged that it had been pushed back toward its doom by the violator, and possessing both the will and the means to resist further aggression. And, finally, there would be the ferocious local resistance of the peoples of the earth to subjugation: fifty, a hundred, two hundred Vietnams. The potential violator would see that even his first step was extremely unlikely to succeed, the second step impossible, the third pure fantasy. And, seeing all that, he would not take the first step. He would be deterred.

We fear cheating under an abolition agreement because we fear aggression; we fear aggression primarily because we fear that it will upset the balance of power; and we fear an upset of the balance of power because we fear that some single nation or bloc will gain irresistible military superiority and, with it, domination of the world. But in the nuclear world, whether armed or unarmed, these things cannot happen—not because cheating is impossible but because the entire military and political organization of the world in which cheating might have been the first step toward world domination has passed away. No balance of power can be upset, because there is no balance of power—only a balance of terror, which is something different. In a balance of power, each side faces the *power* of the other—power to achieve victory in war, to conquer and occupy other countries or the world—but in the balance of terror all *power* has evaporated, and the two sides are impotent in the face of the same oblivion: not anyone's victory or domination but unlimited and universal defeat; not a foe having its way with the world but the end of the world. All human powers are overmatched by the universal power that was unleashed in the world when the atom was split, and that universal power is what, in the final analysis, checks the would-be world conqueror at every step, including the step in which his maniacal dream might crystallize in his brain. When it turned out that E equals mc^2, his sort was doomed. The dreams of world conquest are dead dreams. They belong to a world that has vanished. Its ways and practices—the marching and retreating armies, the contests for "control of the seas" or "control of the air," the long strings of victories and defeats, spanning the continents, and all the rest of the moves and countermoves, the noise and the fire, of those great global pitched battles by which in the pre-nuclear world the political fortunes of mankind were settled—have, like the lances, armor, and escutcheons of feudalism, sunk under the waves of time forever. We cannot get that world back. Yet its loss can be our gain, for we can profit from it as we turn to face the real peril that has been put before us: the featureless, timeless nothingness of our doom.

In political affairs, it's a great advantage to be able to start with what is in place and improve on it, rather than to have to start over. An agreement freezing the world's boundaries in place and abolishing nuclear arms while keeping deterrence in force by retaining the ability to rebuild them offers this advantage. It would be a logical, evolutionary outgrowth of present-day deterrence. Deterrence is built on the foundation of the world's horror at the idea of either suffering a nuclear holocaust or, for that matter, perpetrating one. The abolition agreement would build a stronger and more effective policy on that same foundation. It would be a more reliable, more rational, and (within regrettably defined limits) more humane way of profiting from our horror. Under it, the rationale that the only sensible role for nuclear weapons is to guarantee that those same weapons are never used would not, it is true, be fully carried through to its logical conclusion, but it would be buttressed and strengthened. The latent agreement among adversaries on which deterrence depends would be made explicit and *acted upon*. Their de facto acceptance of the status quo would be institutionalized. Nations would still, in the last analysis, rely on their own nuclear capacities to preserve their independence. But the grotesque disproportion between the causes and the results of "war"—the threat to end the world so as to prevent every threat to the status quo—would be greatly reduced (although not yet removed).

The precise steps by which abolition might be reached would be the product of negotiations, but the most important stage in the great powers' negotiations would consist of an initial formal affirmation and definition, in technical, military, and political terms, of the goal. Agreement on the goal would have to come first because it is impossible to decide on precise steps until one knows where one is heading. At present, strangely, our procedure is the reverse. We concentrate all our energy on the steps (SALT, START, the freeze, and so on), and simply leave unanswered the question of where all this is going. (At the moment, it seems to be going nowhere.) Is our aim the stability of existing arsenals? Is it President Reagan's defensive world, protected from nuclear attack by weapons in space and elsewhere? Is it "reductions"? "Deep reductions"? If so, how deep? Down to "minimum deterrence"? What then? Or do we—as a number of Presidents, including President Carter and President Reagan, have hinted—seek abolition? If we do, what is the world going to look like then, and what are we going to do if trouble starts? Up to now, these questions have somehow been seen as unfit for government to answer. In this matter—the most important matter of all—government has been content to grope along a path that lacks a clearly defined destination. Even the peace movement has been shy about advocating full nuclear disarmament—showing a reluctance as crippling to its cause as hesitation to advocate the abolition of slavery would have been to that of the anti-slavery movement. The answer one gives to the question of the goal determines the character of the steps one takes. And the lack of an answer—of a destination for arms control—means that the steps falter, grow uncertain, cross back over each other, and finally stop. With no consensus in place on where we are going, policy shifts from Administration to Administration; and even within each Administration there is a lack of clarity about what would be desirable. The general public, for its part, is left in total confusion, unable to bring its will to bear, or even to form its will, on questions of specific policy. One Administration concentrates on delivery systems, another on throw-weight and numbers of warheads. Two Presidents say that they seek abolition, and Harvard and the *New York Times* say that abolition is impossible. One President sees anti-nuclear defenses as injurious to stability, and the next sees them as the key to stability. One school of expert thought says that the stabilization of forces, even at something like present levels, should be the goal of arms control, and another school thinks that reductions should be the goal. The point here is not so much to argue that any of these views is right or wrong per se as to suggest that without

151

agreement on a single, clear goal for arms control we have no standard by which to measure anyone's views.

A clear goal, once adopted, would serve as an organizing principle for both our steps and our ideas. If after study our government adopted abolition as its goal—not as a rhetorical flourish for the peroration of presidential speeches but as a practical, thought-out destination—many points currently under discussion would be clarified. The issue of anti-nuclear defenses is a case in point. As we have seen, such defenses are destabilizing *before* an abolition agreement (because they only spur increased offensive measures on the other side) but become stabilizing *after* an abolition agreement (as a hedge against cheating). Thus, until the great powers were well on their way to abolition we would rein in defenses, but once they were on their way we would encourage defenses. The issue of reductions would also be clarified. Reductions become unambiguously necessary. Because they would be the path leading to zero, they would lose the air of pointlessness that they necessarily have as long as it is believed that mutual assured destruction must be preserved, if only "minimally." (Reductions short of abolition, it should be said, might serve one invaluable purpose: they might—though when we consider the nuclear winter we can't be sure—bring the arsenals down to a level still adequate for mutual assured destruction but not sufficient to cause extinction.) The goal of stability, too, would gain a new context.

Once the goal had been studied, defined, and accepted, the steps, it seems to me, would not be hard to find. Without trying to go into detail, I shall mention a few principles by which they might be established. A basic principle governing the whole process would be that deterrence would remain in effect at every stage, including, of course, the final one—abolition itself. Most important, at every step, all the way down to zero, each side would retain a secure retaliatory capacity. The deterrence theory in use, however, would be "existential deterrence," rather than any of the more theoretically elaborate kinds. Instead of being guided by detailed scenarios of possible nuclear wars, we would rely on common sense and the lessons of history, which show that nations are even more reluctant to use nuclear weapons than deterrence theory suggests. Guided by this rough-and-ready version of deterrence, which, though it is less intellectually dazzling than some of the others, corresponds better to our actual, fallible human predictive powers, the negotiating partners would seek a balance at all stages of the reductions but would not get unduly alarmed if imbalances appeared in one area or another now and then.

As reductions continued, the capacity for retaliation would consist less and less of the possession of weapons and more and more of the capacity for rebuilding them, until, at the level of zero, that capacity would be all. Indeed, the more closely we look at the zero point the less of a watershed it seems to be. Examined in detail, it reveals a wide range of alternatives, in which the key issue is no longer the number of weapons in existence but the extent of the capacity and the level of readiness for building more. (At even quite high levels of warheads—say, the hundreds—the importance of capacity might eclipse the importance of stockpiles.) But there would also be the issue of control of delivery vehicles—an issue that at the zero level might well be even more important than the abolition of warheads. Since the man with a suitcase is a delivery vehicle, attaining "zero delivery systems" is in principle impossible. Instead, the task would be to set specifications for those which were allowed and those which were not. Defining the permissible states of readiness for building the bombs and for building delivery vehicles of various sorts would be the first task of negotiations.

One further strategic notion that would gain in depth and meaning in the context of negotiations to establish weaponless deterrence would be the principle of no first use. The value of this concept lies not only in the contribution it makes toward present stability but in its establishment of an almost purely deterrent role for nuclear weapons. (I say "almost" because of the unspoken reservation attached to no first use which specifies that it ceases to apply as soon as one side faces conventional defeat.) If two sides have declared a policy of no first use, then each side possesses its nuclear arsenals only to retaliate in the event that the other side uses them, and since neither side intends ever to strike first neither has any reason to keep its arsenals, and they can be abolished. All that remains is for each side to convince the other that it really *is* abolishing the weapons. When people are persuaded—as so many analysts have been since 1945—that a nuclear-weapon-free world is, in the absence of world government, inherently the least stable of worlds, the opportunity opened up by the two sides' willingness to forswear aggression is lost. But if, as I have argued here, a nuclear-weapon-free world can be stable, with deterrence remaining in effect, then the opportunity can be seized. The no-first-use principle coupled with the principle of achieving weaponless deterrence could provide the foundation for complete nuclear disarmament.

When a person or a society or, as in this case, a whole planet is embarked on a self-destructive and ultimately suicidal course, the first order of business is a decision to *reverse course*. To reverse course is not in itself to arrive at the safe shore, which may still be far in the distance, but it is at least to glimpse that shore and to turn one's craft in its direction. A discussion of what the ultimate aims of the United States' disarmament policy should be, culminating in the actual adoption of a goal, could be the means by which the needed course reversal would take place. The arena in which the debate over the ultimate goals of disarmament takes place should be government, but not government alone. Ideally, it should encompass all of society, but since it is in fact only in the West that free discussion can occur, the debate should begin here. One step in the direction of such a deliberation might be, for example, the appointment of a presidential commission to restudy the whole issue, from the ground up. Another might be for Congress to hold joint hearings on the question—hearings that would be televised in full before the nation. The press, the universities, and the other independent voices in the society could join in. But it may not be necessary for anyone to take any self-conscious steps to start this discussion. When the time is right, it will be unstoppable. Indeed, it may have already begun.

Just as the steps in arms control need to be placed in the context of the abolition of nuclear arms, so abolition needs to be placed in the context of a full resolution of the nuclear predicament. Abolition would not give us a world from which nuclear weapons had been eradicated forever, which is to say that it would not return us to the pre-nuclear world. Nothing can do that. Even in the realm of the possible, however, abolition would be only a halfway house—an interim solution. We sometimes say that we live on the brink of nuclear destruction. But, with no more than a mechanical or human mistake or two between us and the end of the world, it would be more accurate to say that we are hanging by one arm from a branch that sticks out over the brink. Abolition would get us up onto the brink. It would get us onto solid ground, where we would have the time and the peace of mind to look at the lay of the land and plan our next steps. Or, to change the metaphor, it would be like reaching a base camp, from which we could reconnoitre to plan the ascent of the mountain itself. To us now, who are unable to restrain ourselves from heaping up more and more nuclear weapons until we hardly know where to deploy them, abolition looks like the peak of Mount Everest. But when we got there we would find that we had climbed only a foothill, and that the real Everest—the political challenge of finding peaceful means for handling all disputes in the international sphere—still rose up before us.

It is tempting to suppose that a nuclear-weapon-free world of stalemated sovereign states could be long-lasting, or even permanent. To resort to one more metaphor, nations in the state of deterrence are like trains on the tracks of a roundhouse, all of which converge upon a central point, like the spokes of a wheel. Let us imagine that reaching the central point would give the engineer of any one train, if he rushed forward with his train and seized it, the means to control all the other trains ("world domination"). To prevent this, the engineers resolve that if they see any engineer rushing his train toward the center they will all do the same, destroying the first train and themselves in a single huge collision. But now let us suppose that these tracks extend outward indefinitely, that the trains have all retreated miles into the countryside, and that, furthermore, the engineers have voluntarily entered into a solemn agreement not to come within a defined distance of the center. This, it seems to me, is a fair representation of weaponless deterrence. In recognition of the futility of the resort to force in the nuclear age, nations would have pulled far back from the abyss. The agreement would be their first line of defense against threats both to their national sovereignty and to human survival. They would bend their efforts to preserve it. Yet ultimately they would still rely on the nuclear threat. The engineers are deep in the quiet of the countryside, but if, against all expectation and all reason, one of their number starts rushing toward the central point they are able and ready to do likewise. If we suppose, however, that they manage to stay in their pulled-back state long enough—say, centuries—then we can entertain the hope that something like permanence has been achieved. Theoretically, the trains are ready to rush suicidally to the central point, but actually they have, more and more, been conducting relations along branch lines that they have been building up. The whole business of crashing into each other at the central point has gradually become fantastic and unreal—a nightmare from a barbaric and insane past. The converging tracks fall into disuse and become overgrown. Then one day, perhaps, this paraphernalia of mass destruction can be carted off to village greens, to take its place alongside the naval cannons of the past, and to be played on by small children.

But life is movement and change. No stalemate can be eternal. Differences must arise. They will have to be resolved, and a means of resolving them will have to be found—a means other than violence. And then we are faced again with the revolution in our political affairs which some called for in the mid-1940s but which never happened. At issue in this revolution would be not just the outcome of one dispute or another—not even the outcome of the East-West struggle in its entirety—but how all nations were to conduct their political relations with one another from then on. Some observers have suggested that, given the limits of what we can hope to accomplish in the near future, it is meaningless to define the predicament in such broad terms. But it seems to me that even while we recognize these limits it is an essential element of honesty for us to measure our accomplishments not against what we have decided it is possible for us to do at a particular moment but against the objective magnitude of the task that, without our willing it or wanting it, has actually been imposed on us by nuclear weapons. This is the first requirement of realism in the nuclear age, and, I believe, it is in a spirit of realism that we should acknowledge that the abolition of nuclear weapons would be only a preliminary to getting down to the more substantial political work that lies ahead. The size of the predicament is not ours to choose; only the resolution is.

The resolution of the nuclear predicament as a whole, then, would fall into two broad stages. In the first (discussed here), the world would, by agreement, institutionalize the broad global stalemate that we are already in, and abolish nuclear weapons. Political changes would still occur, but no longer by military means. In this stage, the differences between nations would not be taken up and resolved but suppressed and postponed. The nuclear peril would still exist in our affairs, but passively. Nuclear weapons would not, by virtue of this arrangement, have become anachronistic, but to whatever extent we took advantage of the respite by finding diplomatic and political means for conducting the world's business peacefully we would *make* them anachronistic. And that process of invention and construction would constitute the second stage (not discussed here) of the resolution of the nuclear predicament. In it, the frozen world of deterrence would begin to melt and move—peacefully—as new, nonviolent means for decision-making were discovered and instituted. With the critical issue of national security provisionally taken care of, it would no longer be necessary for this political work to take the form of a desperate

157

and unwanted plunge into world government. Instead, the world could deal with its international business step by step—not out of panic that the world was about to end but out of a specific and positive desire to take care of the business at hand. Already the agenda of business calling for such attention is long. It comprises all those matters which come under the heading of "interdependence," including global ecological issues and global economic issues. In these and other areas of international life, "sovereignty" has already dissolved. There is no sovereign power over migratory birds, or over migratory capital, either. The current global debt crisis is a case in point. The world needs to institute a peaceful, orderly means of resolving it and other economic crises of its kind, in which the individual interests of nations can be served only to the extent that the common interest of all is attended to first. The resolution of the current debt crisis will not save the world from nuclear weapons. But if those weapons had been abolished, then the resolution of that crisis would be one of the limited steps along the path of global political changes ultimately necessary if we are to put nuclear weapons behind us once and for all.

Abolition backed up by weaponless deterrence would thus crack the link between nuclear disarmament and world government in not just one way but two: first, it would enable abolition to occur without our having to solve the underlying political problems; and, second, it would provide a foundation on which those political problems could be addressed piecemeal and gradually rather than all at once. In a word, it would resolve not the nuclear predicament—something that does require that we pursue the solution of the political question all the way to its revolutionary conclusion—but the problem of timing that was presented when, one July morning in 1945, our quick-thinking scientists handed our slow-moving politicians a device that simultaneously put our species in peril of self-extermination and made nonsense of the system of international relations with which, for better or worse, we had lived since the beginning of history. Abolition in this form would enable us to move swiftly to rescue our species from its desperate, moment-to-moment peril of self-destruction while allowing the political solution to proceed at the much slower pace that such vast work seems almost in the nature of things to require. When we first snap awake to the nearly unbelievable fact that our species is teetering on the edge of its doom, we are moved, like someone who sees a child wandering near the edge of a cliff, to spring forward immediately and save it. Yet as long as everyone —radicals and moderates alike—believed that we could not do this without first establishing world government our impulse was checked. If that requirement is waived, however, then, although the path ahead of us may still be difficult, we are free to obey our impulse and spring forward. In clearing away this obstacle, we would, for the first time since nuclear weapons were developed, stretch a frail bridge across the gap that opened at the onset of the nuclear age between the demands of the present global political system and the demands of survival. This would be the first major step toward bringing our policies back into some semblance of alignment with our scruples, and making our mortally imperilled, broken life well and safe and whole.

It might be objected that arranging to keep the world immobilized in national units unchallengeable from without would be a step away from, not toward, a world community—a step backward, in which such units, instead of passing from the world scene, would become more firmly entrenched than ever. And it is certainly true that this world of weaponless deterrence is the direct opposite of the "world without boundaries" of which so many have dreamed. In fact, in a world of weaponless deterrence boundaries, far from disappearing, would become virtually sacrosanct. The world would, in effect, be crystallized into units unchangeable from without—units in which peoples were sequestered, unable to conquer others but also safe from conquest by others. Yet, seen in another light, this organization of our global affairs, instead of impeding the eventual peaceful arbitration of international disputes, could set the stage for it nicely. If international institutions are ever to acquire real power—power to solve a world debt crisis, power to legislate a law of the sea, power to decide whom the Falkland Islands should belong to—then we want that power to be balanced and checked by local power. The great and growing patriotic feeling in the world today could be the source of that power. A world of intense patriotism would be the hardest sort of world in which to carry out either aggression or repression. It is sometimes said that patriotism is an obstacle to peace, and insofar as it has been used to feed and justify hatred of other peoples it has certainly been that. Yet patriotism, before it curdles into hatred, can be a generous, large-spirited sentiment, which lifts one out of one's private concerns and reinforces one's attachment and devotion to the community in which one lives. It might serve well as a staging ground for building the broader loyalties that we must develop if we are to survive.

A nuclear-weapon-free but conventionally armed and nuclear-capable world of sovereign and independent states linked together under an abolition agreement would remain an uneasy, dangerous world. Events in it could veer off in unexpected and unwanted directions. It would be subject to breakdowns of many kinds. One has many questions and doubts. Would some local crisis (and we can be sure there will continue to be many crises) draw the great powers into its vortex, and tempt one or more of them back down the path of rearmament, plunging the world into a mad scramble to get back to mutual assured destruction, or something worse? Would it all unravel—precipitately and catastrophically? Would some stern and resolute power, harboring an aggressive will behind smiles of friendship, suddenly burst forth and attack a peaceful and unsuspecting world? Would the West, breathing a vast sigh of relief at having abolished nuclear weapons, also push them out of mind, and grow complacent and soft, while the Soviet Union, still kept under a harsh discipline by totalitarian rule, remained militant and tough? Would the deterrent effect of mere preparations for nuclear armament be impressive enough to influence the actions of governments—to deter them? Would some power see nuclear disarmament as its opportunity to grab some advantage by launching conventional war? No one can say that these or any number of other disasters are impossible. And even if the system worked exactly as we wanted it to it would remain inherently flawed, because we would still be relying on nuclear weapons for our national defense. We would still be implicated in the intention—somewhere, someday, perhaps—of slaughtering millions of people. Instead of rejecting nuclear destruction categorically, we would still be relying on it. Our "no" to nuclear weapons would still be qualified. That this would be so is one more measure of how small a part of the distance to a full resolution of the nuclear predicament we would have travelled.

Our point of comparison, however, is not a world in which the disputes among nations have melted away or are being settled peacefully. It is today's world, in which in order to preserve a precarious "safety" we think we are obliged to threaten ourselves with doom. If we were to compare the world of an abolition agreement with the Garden of Eden, we would find it very unsatisfactory—very unstable. (But then the Garden of Eden turned out to be rather "unstable" itself.) But if we compare the world of weaponless deterrence with our present world, we find it to be immeasurably better: the impasse would be broken, and our long and difficult journey to a full resolution could begin. Nuclear weapons *would* be abolished. At first glance, a mere increase in the lead time to nuclear hostilities may seem a disappointingly modest gain to be won from the abolition of nuclear weapons. (It seems more impressive when one remembers that, given the everlastingness of the knowledge of how to build the weapons, an increase in the lead time of one length or another is technically the best we can do.) But in fact that modest increase in lead time—from about seven minutes to a month or six weeks—would mark a revolution in stability. The two most shocking features of our present system for organizing the world are the extreme precariousness of our balance on the nuclear tightrope—a precariousness defined by the short lead time—and the extreme price to be paid "if deterrence fails." In a world of weaponless deterrence, both these features would be removed. Strategic analysts largely agree that the two likeliest causes of a nuclear holocaust are, first, a preemptive strike launched out of fear that the other side would launch one and, second, miscalculation, confusion, panic, or accident (human or technological) in the midst of a crisis. Both perils arise from the presence of the arsenals themselves, and both would vanish with the abolition of the arsenals. Nuclear hostilities could begin only as the result of long premeditation and long preparation leading to cold-blooded aggression out of the blue—a course of action that present analysts regard as the unlikeliest of all causes of nuclear hostilities.

We are concerned with the stability of the nuclear world. The absence of the peril of a preemptive strike and the peril of the accidental or semi-accidental strike in a crisis would lend to a nuclear-weapon-free world a stability that we cannot even dream of in our present world of huge nuclear arsenals. For the same reason, the extremity of the penalty would have been reduced, too. Since there would be no huge arsenals, there would, of course, be no peril that the world would be blown up in an instant. Instead, in the event of a breakdown the number of nuclear weapons used—if any—would be small at first. In our present, abundantly armed world, the gruesome lessons of nuclear experience—of nuclear bombs killing people—could not be brought to bear to save us from the final abyss; once we went over the brink, there would be no hope that, horrified by what we had wrought, we would be able to turn back. But in a nuclear-weapon-free world, the lessons of experience would reinforce deterrence. It would be not only foreknowledge of the horror of nuclear destruction that would stop us from exterminating ourselves but, in the event of a breakdown, the actual spectacle of it. In short, diplomatic and political processes would not be suspended at the brink of nuclear hostilities, as they are likely to be today, but could be continued even after nuclear hostilities had begun. And while there is little hope that these processes could halt a holocaust involving tens of thousands of weapons and lasting a few hours, there is great hope that they could halt one involving hundreds of weapons and lasting weeks or months.

In a recent speech, George Kennan asked, "Can we not at

long last cast off our preoccupation with sheer destruction, a preoccupation that is costing us our prosperity and preempting the resources that should go to the solving of our great social problems?" He continued, "For this entire preoccupation with nuclear war is a form of illness. It is morbid in the extreme. There is no hope in it—only horror." Nuclear weapons are truly an evil obsession: they can somehow drag us down even as we try to fight them. They degrade us. They soil us. It is unfortunately true that in a world of unarmed deterrence we would still be relying for our defense on terror—relying for our safety on the threat of terrible crimes. Yet we would have succeeded in pushing the terror and the crimes into the background of our affairs. We would have withdrawn them from the center of the stage, thereby clearing a space into which the peaceful, constructive energies of humanity could flood. But even this retirement of the weapons would not be the most important thing that we had accomplished. It would be that we had made a decision as a species in favor of our survival and then had acted on it. We would have adopted a "deliberate policy"—an unfinished and imperfect one, but a deliberate policy nevertheless. It would not resolve the nuclear predicament, yet the day that the last nuclear weapon on earth was destroyed would be a great day. It would be a day for celebrations. We would have given substance to our choice to create the human future. We would have dispelled once and for all the fatalism and lack of faith in man which, like some dark shadow of extinction itself, have crept over us. And when the celebrations ended, we could turn with new hope and new strength to the unfinished business that lay before us.

INDEX

167

Falkland Islands, war over, 128–30
fallout, radioactive, 15
Fate of the Earth, The (Schell), 22, 86
fear, as motive to combat nuclear
    peril, 5
first strike, 134
    abolition agreement and strategy
      for, 141–2
    preemptive, 119, 128, 161–2
    see also no first use, policy of,
first-strike weapons, 59–60, 72
"Fiscal Year 1984–1988 Defense
    Guidance," 60–1
fissionable materials, controls on, 135
flexible response, policy of, 50–1, 145
Fox, William T. R., 39, 43
freeze, *see* nuclear freeze
future generations, nuclear
    predicament from perspective of,
    125

Goldberger, Marvin, 16
Great Britain, Falkland Islands war
    and, 128–30
greenhouse effect, 24–5
Gromyko, Andrei, 42–3
guilt, for intending to extinguish
    mankind, 5

Hamilton, Alexander, 38–9
Hitler, Adolf, 142–3
Hoffmann, Stanley, 7
holocaust, nuclear, *see* nuclear
    holocaust
Huntington, Samuel P., 7
hydrogen bomb, 46

inspection
    abolition agreement and, 139–40
    Acheson-Lilienthal report and, 40–1
    Soviet rejection of (1946), 42
    see also verification
international disputes
    deterred state and, 99–100, 102

suppression or postponement of,
    157–8
war "spoiled" as final arbiter of,
    25–7, 95, 97, 102–3
world government as means of
    settling, *see* world government
see also war

John Paul II, Pope, 3
Jones, T. K., 9

Kahn, Herman, 44, 83, 89
Kennan, George, 53, 162–3
Khrushchev, Nikita S., 6
Kissinger, Henry, 50, 52
knowledge of how to make nuclear
    weapons, 23–4, 82, 110, 118, 120–1,
    144

lead time to nuclear rearmament, 122,
    135, 161
Lehman, John, 58
Lilienthal, David E., 40
limited nuclear war, 51, 52, 54, 57, 58
    bishops' pastoral letter on, 70
Living with Nuclear Weapons, 7, 47,
    68, 83–4, 108, 120–1
*Long-Term Worldwide Effects of
    Multiple Nuclear-Weapons
    Detonations* (National Academy
    of Sciences), 15
love, as motive to combat nuclear
    peril, 5

Mandelbaum, Michael, 96–7, 103
Mariner 9, 17
Marks, Paul, 16
Mars, 17
McNamara, Robert, 50, 52
meaninglessness, extinction of
    mankind as threatening life with,
    4
Middle East, 54–5

170